JAFFREY PUBLIC LIBRARY
38 Main Street
Jaffrey, NH 03452
(603) 532-7301

INSIDERS' GUIDE® TO

GETTYSBURG

DATE DUE

JUN 1 1 2013		
GAYLORD		PRINTED IN U.S.A.

MAR - - 2010

HELP US KEEP THIS GUIDE UP TO DATE

Every effort has been made by the author and editors to make this guide as accurate and useful as possible. However, many changes can occur after a guide is published—establishments close, phone numbers change, facilities come under new management, etc.

We would love to hear from you concerning your experiences with this guide and how you feel it could be improved and be kept up to date. While we may not be able to respond to all comments and suggestions, we'll take them to heart, and we'll make certain to share them with the author. Please send your comments and suggestions to the following address:

The Globe Pequot Press
Reader Response/Editorial Department
P.O. Box 480
Guilford, CT 06437

Or you may e-mail us at: editorial@GlobePequot.com

Thanks for your input, and happy travels!

INSIDERS' GUIDE® TO

GETTYSBURG

SECOND EDITION

KATE HERTZOG

INSIDERS' GUIDE®

GUILFORD, CONNECTICUT
AN IMPRINT OF THE GLOBE PEQUOT PRESS

The prices and rates in this guidebook were confirmed at press time. We recommend, however, that you call establishments before traveling to obtain current information.

INSIDERS' GUIDE®

Text design by Sheryl Kober
Maps by XNR Productions, Inc. © Morris Book Publishing, LLC

ISSN 1930-3521
ISBN 978-0-7627-5031-3

Printed in the United States of America

10 9 8 7 6 5 4 3 2 1

To loved ones who no longer walk this earth.
I carry you with me every day . . . in my heart.

And to my husband, Tim, who's been there
through it all—thanks for walking the path of life
with me.

CONTENTS

Directory of Maps

Regional Overview

N

0   10   20 km
0   10   20 mi.

Gettysburg National Military Park

Gettysburg

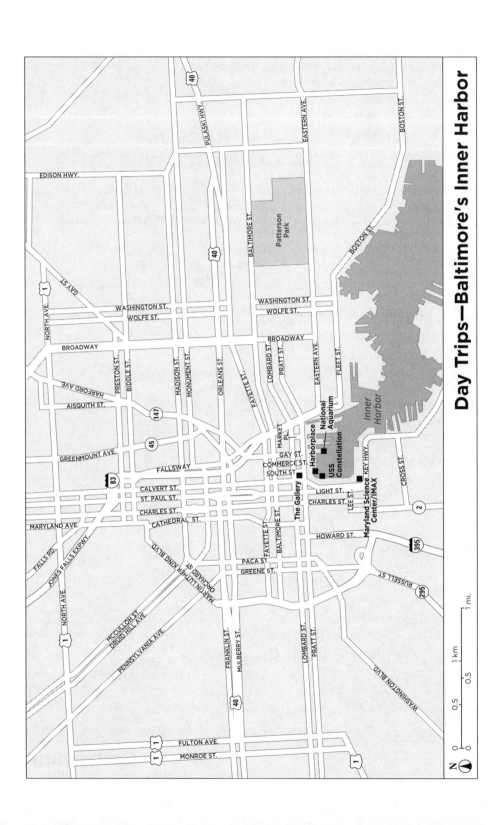

Day Trips—Baltimore's Inner Harbor

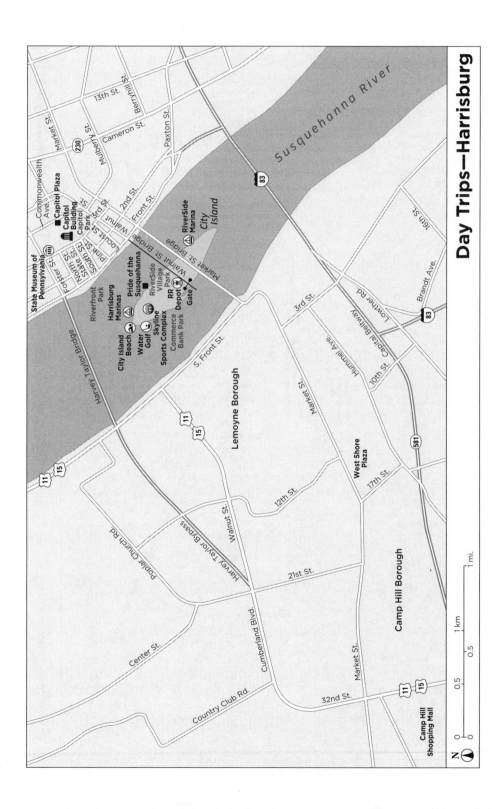

Day Trips—Harrisburg

Susquehanna River

State Museum of Pennsylvania

Capitol Plaza
Capitol Building
Capitol Park

Commonwealth Ave.
Market St.
13th St.
Berryhill St.
Cameron St.
Mulberry St.
Paxton St.
230

2nd St.
Front St.
3rd St.
North St.
State St.
South St.
Locust St.
Pine St.
Walnut

Foster St.

Riverfront Park

Harrisburg Marinas

Pride of the Susquehanna

RiverSide Village Park

RR Depot
Gate

City Island Beach
Water Golf
Skyline Sports Complex
Commerce Bank Park

Walnut St. Bridge
Market St. Bridge

RiverSide Marina

City Island

Harvey Taylor Bridge

83

16th St.
Brandt Ave.
Lowther Rd.

S. Front St.

Lemoyne Borough

Market St.
Hummel Ave.
3rd St.
10th St.
17th St.

West Shore Plaza

581

11
15

12th St.

Walnut St.

Poplar Church Rd.

Harvey Taylor Bypass

21st St.

Cumberland Blvd.

Center St.

Country Club Rd.

32nd St.

Market St.

Camp Hill Borough

11 15

Camp Hill Shopping Mall

N

0   0.5   1 km
0   0.5   1 mi.

11
15

Day Trips—Hersheypark

PREFACE

This second edition of *Insiders' Guide to Gettysburg* is chock-full of changes that have occurred since the first edition was published in 2006. Perhaps the biggest impact on the area has been the opening of a new visitor center at the Gettysburg National Military Park in September 2008, which has the whole town buzzing. Everyone has an opinion on it, as you would expect on any big change happening to a small town. And essentially, Gettysburg is a small town. It just comes with a huge history. That history is what prompts most first-time visitors to visit where the famous battle of the Civil War took place in July 1863. Some travel great distances and others drive in for the day. Many visitors come back time and again, and some become permanent residents in order to be closer to the history that emanates from the area. But there are also those who live in the area who visit the battlefield once, or maybe never at all. For some Gettysburg is considered a rural oasis, with bluegrass festivals, apple festivals, fairs, and recreational opportunities to enjoy throughout the year. Others consider it a cultural hub and attend concerts, art shows and festivals, and theater performances. And yet the diverse visitors, this cultural yet rural atmosphere, and all the area history mesh together very well.

As a rule, Gettysburg residents take a sincere interest in their town and the battlefield that surrounds it. Often there are conflicting opinions on the best way to preserve Gettysburg's past while ensuring Gettysburg's future, but everyone shares that universal goal. As with most tourist towns, Gettysburg is constantly evolving. New businesses seem to pop up every summer, along with a new hotel every so often, but there are also businesses that have been operating in town for decades. That's what makes Gettysburg such a fun place to write about—I'm always discovering new places while revisiting old haunts. I'm thrilled to be able to show you all that Gettysburg has to offer—on the battlefield and off. Besides the military history that permeates the area, you'll also be able to enjoy first-rate theater performances and cultural events, wonderful dining experiences, free concerts, and fun pubs, just to name a few of the ways you can spend your time while visiting the area. I hope this guide shows you what I find every time I look at the area through fresh eyes as I do the research that ensures everything is up to date for you—a fun, vibrant place to visit that has something to offer everyone.

Many people contributed to this update, and I'd like to take this opportunity to say thank you, especially to all the area residents who took time to converse with me. I heard some great stories and enjoyed hearing everyone's opinion on the new visitor center! And this guide would not be in your hands today without the dedicated staff of Globe Pequot Press; thanks to everyone who had a part in its formation, especially senior travel editor Amy Lyons.

HOW TO USE THIS BOOK

Gettysburg, Pennsylvania, appears in every book that covers the Civil War, and the events that occurred here in July 1863 are known to all who study history. Entire books have been written on the Battle of Gettysburg, and many past and present (and no doubt future) scholars have devoted entire lifetimes to studying the military strategies employed by the opposing forces engaged at the town of Gettysburg. This guide will not recount the battle, nor will it provide new insights on the conflicts involved in this battle, or the Civil War in general. Instead, it will give you a good idea of what you can expect to find in the town of Gettysburg today. Of course, the battlefield is a major attraction, and you'll find a lot of information on battlefield tours and sites in the Gettysburg National Military Park chapter. But you'll also get a thorough exploration of all the other great ways to spend your time here at Gettysburg.

After practical tips on getting here and a beefy history of the town, there are listings of the best places to eat and stay, followed by what's available in the way of shopping, sightseeing, and cultural events. Be warned—there's a lot to pick from. The Attractions chapter alone is divided into general, ghostly, and historical attractions! You'll also discover what recreational activities are available and some ideas on ways to spend your evenings. A separate chapter highlights area events and sites that are especially appealing to kids. Trips to the area's five state parks are included, as are day trips to the Inner Harbor at Baltimore, Maryland, Pennsylvania's capital city of Harrisburg, and the amusement-park rides of Hersheypark. Throughout the book you'll also find lots of Insiders' Tips, which are helpful hints or bits of trivia about the area.

Most of the sites people come here to see are within a few miles of Lincoln Square, which, just as it was during the Battle of Gettysburg, is the center of town. For that reason Lincoln Square will serve as the geographic center in chapters that contain a lot of information. The chapter introduction will tell you if information is arranged in a format other than alphabetically. Smaller chapters have their entries arranged alphabetically while larger ones may be arranged in a number of different ways. For instance, entries in the Hotels, Motels, and Resorts chapter are listed by direction from the square while entries in the Shopping chapter are listed by category, then by direction from the square. If you're at Culp's Hill and perusing the book to see where to eat lunch, you'll find the restaurant entries broken down by direction from the square and then listed in alphabetical order.

A town name (and state if in Maryland) is provided in the entry only if the address is not in Gettysburg. Most readers will find plenty to do right within the town limits, and that is the overall scope of Insiders' Guide to Gettysburg. However, no book on Gettysburg would be complete without mentioning some places outside of town, such as the Fairfield Inn, a bed-and-breakfast only 8 miles from Lincoln Square that houses one of the oldest taverns still operating in America (see the Bed-and-Breakfasts and Guesthouses chapter). And some places are such fun they're worth a short drive, which is certainly the case with Mr. Ed's Elephant Museum in Orrtanna (see the Attractions chapter).

Gettysburg hosts almost two million visitors each year, so some advance planning is in order. Use this guide to become familiar with what the town and the battlefield have to offer. The reenactment of the Battle of Gettysburg is July 1 through July 3, and this is when the town is busiest. But Gettysburg is a year-round destination, with many businesses using special offers during the winter months to draw visitors to town. You'll find First Friday sales each month at area merchants, many bed-and-breakfasts offer specially priced romantic getaways, and new events seem to pop up every year.

Since it is difficult to absorb all the history and fun of Gettysburg in one trip, use this guide to narrow your choices and plan what to see on your return trip. Once you've experienced Gettysburg's small-town charm and monumental history, you'll definitely want to come back for more.

Perhaps you've considered relocating to Gettysburg, so you can enjoy all it and the surrounding region have to offer at your leisure. If so, this book can help you get to know Gettysburg quickly and intimately. Use it to find out about local events held throughout the year, to check out the nightlife scene, and to discover the recreational opportunities in Gettysburg's backyard. If you decide to join the many others who have relocated to Gettysburg, the Relocation chapter will provide contact information to get your planning under way.

AREA OVERVIEW

Gettysburg is the county seat of Adams County, which consists of 21 townships and 13 boroughs. (See Adams County Vital Statistics later in this chapter.) The southern part of the county abuts the Mason-Dixon Line, and the borough of Gettysburg sits at the crossroads of two national highways—U.S. Route 30 and U.S. Route 15. The Gettysburg National Military Park, which commemorates the famous Civil War battle that was fought here in July 1863, surrounds the town on the south, west, and north sides.

This is a small town that fate took hold of and never let go. Generals Meade and Lee didn't plan a battle at Gettysburg, and President Lincoln was only asked to say a few words when he dedicated the cemetery that had been created to honor those who died fighting here. But the significance of those actions lives on, with almost two million people coming to Gettysburg annually to connect with the area's past.

Surrounded by other rural communities, Gettysburg retains its small-town ambience despite the influx of tourists every year. The *Gettysburg Times* newspaper regularly prints pictures of locals on their birthdays. Rich in cultural heritage, Gettysburg is home to Gettysburg College and the Lutheran Theological Seminary, both established in the early part of the nineteenth century. The college is in the northern part of town while the seminary is at the town's western edge.

Lincoln Square is the center of town, and most directions in this guide start from this spot. The Gettysburg National Military Park Visitor Center, where you should begin your tour of the battlefield, is to the south of the square. South of the square is also where you'll find the greatest concentration of restaurants, shopping, and sightseeing opportunities.

Visitors also come to see attractions other than the battlefield. The Eisenhower National Historic Site draws many who wish to see the farm where the 34th president resided with his wife, Mamie. Some come to seek out ghosts, others come to enjoy the rural landscape and nearby skiing, and still others come to attend the area festivals. And those of us lucky enough to live here don't have to travel far at all to take part in all the history and fun the Gettysburg area has to offer. Perhaps that's why you meet people who have traveled to Gettysburg year after year without fail. And maybe it's why you won't be in town long before you meet someone who decided to set up a permanent home in the area.

Of course, all the people enjoying themselves at Gettysburg can make for a crowded little town. The tourist season now extends from April through December, and during the summer the attractions, restaurants, and streets are packed. But the nice part about Gettysburg is that it's still a small town not only in size but also in heart. Stop and talk to the people who live here, who manage and work at the attractions, shops, and restaurants in town. Many are genuinely immersed in the history that surrounds them, and the stories they tell are really something to hear. Some have ancestors who lived here during the battle, and many know every detail of the history of the house in which they reside.

Although the residents of Gettysburg relish their history, don't be fooled into thinking they're stuck in the past. Community leaders and business people are constantly trying to strike a balance between retaining the rich history of the past while finding new ways for the town to thrive. Sometimes residents disagree on the best way to move forward, but everyone agrees that Gettysburg is looking to the future as well as the past.

Close-up

New in Gettysburg

It seems there's something new everywhere you look in Gettysburg these days, and I'm not talking about the new hotels or new places of business. After all this is a tourist town and those types of changes are always ongoing. No, I'm referring to the new ways the national park, concerned organizations, town leaders, and local business leaders have created for visitors to experience the history of Gettysburg.

The new Gettysburg Museum and Visitor Center off Baltimore Pike is probably the biggest change that visitors will experience. The old visitor center and cyclorama center along Taneytown Road have closed as part of an ongoing project by the National Park Service and an organization called the Gettysburg Foundation to return the battlefield to how it looked in 1863 so visitors and historians can better study the nuances of the conflict. The new visitor center features one of the largest collections of Civil War relics in the world, a 20-minute film about the Battle of Gettysburg, and the viewing of the restored cyclorama painting *Battle of Gettysburg*, which depicts Pickett's Charge.

At the eastern end of town near the intersection of US 15 and US 30 is Gateway Gettysburg, a pedestrian-friendly one-hundred-acre campus that contains two hotels, restaurants, and movie theaters. This is where the film *Fields of Freedom*, which sweeps the viewer into the conflict of Gettysburg by following the lives of two young men on opposite sides of the battle, is shown.

Two new attractions are downtown. The Lincoln Train Station, which dates from 1859, underwent a $3 million restoration project and reopened to the public in July 2007. This is where Lincoln arrived in Gettysburg to give his now-famous address, and it's also where, months earlier, more than 15,000 wounded soldiers passed through after the Battle of Gettysburg. The train station stopped passenger service in 1942, and at one time it was the home of the Gettysburg Convention and Visitors Bureau. Today it features museum displays about the historic significance of the station.

The David Wills House is the other new downtown attraction that opened in February 2009 honor of Lincoln's 200th birthday. After extensive renovation, six galleries have been created in this museum. The bedroom where Lincoln stayed the night before he gave the Gettysburg Address and the office where David Wills began planning the creation and dedication of a cemetery for the soldiers who died at Gettysburg have been restored to their 1863 appearance.

So be sure to check out all the new ways available to experience the historical significance of Gettysburg.

Adams County Vital Statistics

Area: 526 square miles

Average Maximum Temperature: 74.8 degrees Fahrenheit

Average Minimum Temperature: 32.2 degrees Fahrenheit

Average Snowfall: 32.2 inches

Average Rainfall: 41.0 inches

County Population: 100,779 (2007 Census Estimate)

Gettysburg Population: 8,065 (2007 Census Estimate)

"Pillow" Tax: 3 percent; this is a tax on lodging that is in addition to the 6 percent state sales tax.

Major Nongovernmental Area Employers: Knouse Foods Cooperative; Lincoln Intermediate Unit #12; Liberty Mountain Resort; Gettysburg Hospital; Gettysburg College

Emergency Sirens

Adams County's emergency-alert system uses sirens to alert fire and rescue personnel as well as the general public to emergencies. Four types of sirens are used; each siren is three minutes long but the siren modes differ. A standard wavering siren means fire personnel are to report to their stations, while an extralong wavering siren means rescue personnel should also report to their fire stations. A long and steady siren tells the public to tune to their radio (1320 AM) for essential emergency information, and a short wavering siren indicates that the public should go to the nearest shelter or take the best cover immediately available.

Numbers to Keep Handy

Fire, Police, Ambulance: 911

Gettysburg Police (nonemergency): (717) 334-1168

Pennsylvania State Police: (717) 334-8111

Gettysburg Hospital: (717) 334-2121

Gettysburg National Military Park: (717) 334-1124

Eisenhower National Historic Site: (717) 338-9114

Gettysburg–Adams County Area Chamber of Commerce: (717) 334-8151

Gettysburg Convention and Visitors Bureau: (717) 334-6274

GETTING HERE, GETTING AROUND

The town of Gettysburg is located in the south central part of Pennsylvania, and it's surrounded by rural countryside and other small towns. It sits at the crossroads of numerous highways, just as it did when it witnessed one of the most famous battles of the Civil War. Although getting to town if you don't have your own car can be a problem, navigating the area once you're here is a breeze.

GETTING HERE

Most visitors to Gettysburg arrive by car, probably because no forms of mass transit stop here. The train gets you only as close as Harrisburg, Pennsylvania, or Baltimore, Maryland. (For Amtrak information, call (800) 872-7245 or visit www.amtrak.com.) The nearest bus stop is in Hagerstown, Maryland, and it's a secondary stop without amenities.

If you do decide to travel by train, neither of the stations has rental-car kiosks. At Harrisburg you can make arrangements for Enterprise (717-238-7541, 800-736-8222) to drop off a car for you. The station in Baltimore has a phone on which you can call Hertz, or you can take a shuttle to Baltimore-Washington Airport and pick from the many rental-car companies located there. Those traveling from a distance will probably end up flying into one of the area's international airports and renting a car from there.

There is one other option—and it's a good one. If you make arrangements in advance, Gettysburg Tours (778 Baltimore Street; 717-334-6296) will pick you up at the Baltimore-Washington, Dulles, or Harrisburg airports or at the train stations.

If you're doing the driving, you will want to eventually use one of two major highways to get to Gettysburg. U.S. Route 30 is the major east-west road, and U.S. Route 15 is the major north-south route. US 30 takes you directly to the heart of downtown at Lincoln Square, and US 15 has six Gettysburg exits. (Consult "Which Exit Do I Take from U.S. Route 15?" in this chapter to see which exit will best serve you.)

Airports

BALTIMORE-WASHINGTON INTERNATIONAL AIRPORT (BWI) BALTIMORE, MARYLAND (410) 859-7111, (800) 435-9294 www.bwiairport.com

BWI is a large airport with 5 concourses, 69 Jetways, and 9 commuter gates that are serviced by 31 commercial airlines. Some of the better-known airlines that fly here are American Airlines, British Airways, Continental, Delta Airlines, Northwest Airlines, Southwest Airlines, United Airlines, and US Airways. (See the Airline Information box for airline phone numbers and Web sites.)

There are numerous amenities at the airport, including restaurants, food concessions, gift shops, an outdoor walking/jogging trail, and an observation gallery that offers a virtual tour of airport operations and the chance to listen to real-time communications between the tower, ground control, and aircraft. High-speed wireless Internet access is available at all the food courts and at the US Airways Club.

A rental-car facility offers a free shuttle service to transport passengers between the facility and the airport. The ride takes approximately 10 minutes. The following companies currently run rental-car kiosks.

Alamo: (410) 859-8092, (888) 826-6893; www.alamo.com

Avis: (410) 859-1680, (800) 331-1212; www.avis.com

Budget: (410) 859-0850, (800) 527-0700; www.budget.com

Dollar: (800) 800-4000; www.dollar.com

Enterprise Rent-A-Car: (410) 684-3295, (800) 736-8222; www.enterprise.com

Hertz: (410) 684-7900, (800) 654-3131; www.hertz.com

National Car Rental: (410) 859-8092, (888) 826-6890; www.nationalcar.com

Thrifty Car Rental: (800) 367-2277; www.thrifty.com

To travel to Gettysburg after picking up your rental car, take Interstate 195 to Interstate 95 North. Travel I-95 for only a couple of miles and turn left onto Interstate 695 and follow I-695 to Interstate 795. At the Reisterstown exit, take Maryland Route 140 North to Westminster, Maryland, where you will pick up Pennsylvania Route 97 North, which will take you directly into Gettysburg.

WASHINGTON DULLES INTERNATIONAL AIRPORT (IAD) DULLES, VIRGINIA
(703) 572-2700
www.mwaa.com

There are four concourses at this gigantic airport, which has more than 30 major airlines serving it. Most travelers arrive at either Concourse A or B, which have 78 gates between them. Just about every major airline flies into here, including Air Canada, Air France, Alitalia, American Airlines, British Airways, Continental, Delta, KLM, Lufthansa, Northwest Airlines, SAS, United Airlines, and US Airways. (See the Airline Information box for airline phone numbers and Web sites.)

Dulles has all the amenities you would expect, with myriad shopping and eating options to please everyone in your party. Wireless high-speed Internet access is available throughout the airport.

For rental cars, information screens and courtesy telephones are located in the main terminal's

Airline Information

Aer Lingus: (800) 474-7424;
www.aerlingus.com

Air Canada: (888) 247-2262;
www.aircanada.com

Air France: (800) 321-4538;
www.airfrance.com

AirTran: (800) 247-8726;
www.airtran.com

Alitalia: (800) 223-5730;
www.alitaliausa.com

American Airlines: (800) 433-7300;
www.aa.com

American Eagle: (800) 433-7300;
www.aa.com

British Airways: (800) 247-9297;
www.ba.com

Continental: (800) 525-0280;
www.continental.com

Delta Airlines: (800) 221-1212;
www.delta.com

KLM Royal Dutch Airlines:
(800) 225-2525; www.nwa.com

Lufthansa: (800) 645-3880;
www.lufthansa.com

Midwest Airlines: (800) 452-2022;
www.midwestairlines.com

Northwest Airlines: (800) 225-2525;
www.nwa.com

Southwest Airlines: (800) 435–9792
www.southwest.com

United Airlines: (800) 241-6522;
www.ual.com

US Airways: (800) 428-4322;
www.usairways.com

Which Exit Do I Take from U.S. Route 15?

There are six Gettysburg exits off US 15, and many travelers just take the first one they come to. This can result in a lot of frustration, especially if you take an exit that leads you to the southern part of town and you have to fight tons of traffic to arrive at your hotel at the north end of town. So be a smart traveler—get off at the exit that takes you closest to your destination. The exits are listed in the order you come to them while traveling to Gettysburg from the north.

Routes 394 (Hunterstown) and **U.S. Business Route 15**—This exit takes you directly to Gettysburg College, located in the northern end of town.

York Street (US 30)—This east-west road takes you to Lincoln Square.

Hanover Street (Route 116)—This east-west road merges with US 30 and takes you to Lincoln Square. US 30 can get awfully busy, so this is sometimes a more relaxing alternative.

Baltimore Street (Route 97)—This exit brings you into the southern end of town and to Baltimore Street. This is also the exit for the visitor center at the Gettysburg National Military Park.

Taneytown Road (Route 134)—This is the best exit to take if you're going straight to the battlefield.

Steinwehr Avenue (US Business 15/Emmitsburg Road)—This exit takes you into the southern end of town and to Steinwehr Avenue. This is also the exit for Boyds Bear Country. (See the Attractions chapter.)

lower level at the Ground Transportation Centers. Those renting cars are transported to the agencies by shuttle bus. To catch a bus, go down any ramp from the Baggage Claim Level and proceed outside to the second curbside. The following companies currently operate out of Dulles.

Alamo: (888) 826-6893; www.alamo.com
Avis: (800) 331-1212; www.avis.com
Budget: (800) 527-0700; www.budget.com
Dollar: (800) 800-4000; www.dollar.com
Enterprise Rent-A-Car: (800) 736-8222; www.enterprise.com
Hertz: (800) 654-3131; www.hertz.com
National Car Rental: (888) 826-6890; www.nationalcar.com
Thrifty Car Rental: (800) 367-2277; www.thrifty.com

To drive to Gettysburg from the airport, take Virginia Route 267 (Dulles Expressway) west to Leesburg, where you pick up US 15 North. (Consult the Which Exit Do I Take from U.S. Route 15? box to determine which exit you want to take to enter Gettysburg.)

i President Eisenhower selected the site for Washington Dulles International Airport in 1958, and he attended the dedication ceremony that was held in November 1962. The airport was named for John Foster Dulles, who served as Ike's secretary of state from 1953 to 1959.

HARRISBURG INTERNATIONAL AIRPORT (HIA) MIDDLETOWN
(717) 948-3900, (888) 235-9442
www.flyhia.com
Although not as large as the other more well-known airports in the area, Harrisburg International Airport unveiled a new state-of-the-art terminal and multimodal transportation facility in 2004. The Y-shaped terminal has 12 departure gates, and the first floor of the transportation facility, which is connected to the terminal via a climate-controlled sky bridge, houses the rental-car ready/return lot.

Seven airlines service HIA: Air Canada, AirTran, Continental, Delta, Northwest, United, and US Airways. (See the sidebar for airline phone numbers and Web sites.) Airport amenities include food concessions, a restaurant that serves drinks and classic American fare, and a gift shop. The entire terminal is wired for free wireless Internet access, and there's an observation deck on the third floor for watching planes arrive and depart.

The following companies provide rental cars for HIA travelers, and their kiosks can be found on the first floor of the transportation facility.

Avis: (717) 948-3721, (800) 331-1212; www.avis.com

Budget: (717) 944-4019, (800) 527-0700; www.budget.com

Enterprise: (717) 948-5910, (800) 736-8222; www.enterprise.com

Hertz: (717) 944-4081, (800) 654-3131; www.hertz.com

National Car Rental: (717) 948-0390, (888) 826-6890; www.nationalcar.com

Thrifty Car Rental: (717) 944–9024, (800) 367–2277; www.thrifty.com

When you leave the airport in your rental car, follow the signs to the Pennsylvania Turnpike (Interstate 76) and head west toward Pittsburgh. From the turnpike exit onto US 15 South, and travel about 25 miles to the Gettysburg exits.

i **U.S. Route 30 was the first cross-country road built in the United States. Completed in 1913, it stretches from New York City to San Francisco. A large mural on the exterior wall of the Dollar General store facing Springs Avenue, just off US 30, is one of 11 Pennsylvania murals that commemorate the history of the road.**

GETTING AROUND

Downtown Gettysburg is pretty easy to navigate. Lincoln Square is the center of town, and the town's four main streets lead out from the square. These streets are named for the towns you reach when you travel them. North of the square is Carlisle Street, south is Baltimore Street, east is York Street, and west is Chambersburg Street. Confusion begins to seep in only once you leave the downtown area, where all the roads change names and all eventually split into different roads.

Carlisle Street heads north and splits into US Business 15 and Route 34. US Business 15 heads northeast and back to US 15, and Route 34 heads north to Biglerville and Carlisle. Baltimore Street travels south to a light at a Y intersection. If you go straight (left) at the light, Baltimore Street becomes Baltimore Pike (Route 97), which leads to US 15. If you turn right at the light, you're now on Steinwehr Avenue and will come to another light. At this light Steinwehr Avenue continues straight and leads to US 15. If you turn left you'll be on Taneytown Road (Route 134), which also takes you to US 15. York Street heads east and splits into US 30 (York Road) and Route 116 (Hanover Road). Both roads eventually lead to US 15. Chambersburg Street travels west and is called Buford Avenue for a bit before again being called Chambersburg Road. Route 116 can also be taken westward, but you must go south of the square and pick up Middle Street, which becomes Route 116 and is called Fairfield Road as it heads west.

The traffic circle of Lincoln Square isn't as confusing as it may seem at first. Just remember that drivers in the circle have the right-of-way. If the thought of navigating around the circle sets your teeth on edge, avoid it by taking Washington Street for north-south travels and Middle Street for your east-west trips.

Most visitors choose to walk to the major attractions, which are mostly along the major routes I've described. Battlefield tour buses pick up at most of the hotels, and they also take you to other major attractions. There's also a trolley that operates from mid-April to mid-October. A map of the trolley route is available at the Gettysburg Tour Center (778 Baltimore Street; 717-334-6296). The trolley stops at the square, at the southern end of Baltimore Street, along Steinwehr Avenue, and at the visitor center.

The closer you are to Lincoln Square, the more you pay to park. Meters around the square give you 15 minutes of time when you feed them a quarter, with a two-hour limit. That same quarter at a meter at the southern end of Baltimore Street will buy you an hour of parking with a 12-hour limit.

There's free parking at the Gettysburg National Park Visitor Center, but most parking downtown consists of metered street parking, small lots on side streets that also have meters, and a parking garage on Race Horse Alley, which runs behind the Gettysburg Hotel. To reach the garage, take York Street from the square and make a left onto Stratton Street. Make another left onto Race Horse Alley and the garage is on your right. Parking in the garage is 75 cents per hour with no time limit.

HISTORY

The early history of Gettysburg mimics that of many towns located along the East Coast of the United States. Early settlement by Europeans eventually displaced the indigenous Native American tribes of the area, and a town grew up at the crossroads of the travel routes of the day. But the Battle of Gettysburg altered Gettysburg's projected fate as a typical small Pennsylvanian town, and that event, as well as the event's historic preservation for future generations, continues to affect the very essence of the town right up to present day.

NATIVE AMERICAN HISTORY

The area of Gettysburg was originally the land of the Susquehannock Indians, who occupied the area along the Susquehanna River and its branches from southern New York State to the north end of Chesapeake Bay. It's believed Susquehannock was an Algonquin name meaning "people of the muddy river." The tribe probably had a population of 5,000 to 7,000 members in 1600, but not a great deal of information about them exists because Europeans rarely visited their inland villages during early exploration. In 1608 Capt. John Smith was the first European to meet the Susquehannock, and he described them as giants. They must have been very tall because the Swedes who met the Susquehannock 30 years later also commented on their height.

Besides being farmers, hunters, and fishermen, the Susquehannock were fierce warriors who were feared by many of the tribes around them. They were enemies of the Iroquois and trading partners with the Erie and Huron tribes of Ontario. The French were the next Europeans to make contact with the tribe, and in battle the Susquehannock sided with the French and the Huron against the Iroquois. Despite this the Susquehannock were able to maintain trading relationships with all the European nations that were then exploring the area. This allowed them to obtain armaments from their European trading partners, which helped them maintain a strong position during the Beaver Wars, a time

of intertribal warfare from 1630 to 1700 to determine which tribes would dominate the lucrative European fur trade.

But all this warfare, combined with epidemics brought on by contact with the settlers, began to take its toll. In the 1650s the Susquehannock ceded their lands in the lower Susquehanna Valley to the English, and in 1676 the last 300 Susquehannock surrendered to the Iroquois. In 1706 the Iroquois allowed them to set up a village in the Susquehanna Valley, where they became known to Pennsylvania colonists as the Conestoga, from the name of their last village in Pennsylvania. Quaker missionaries arrived, some tribe members left, and the Conestoga village was converted to a Christian community. By the end of the French and Indian War in 1763, there were only 20 of the Susquehannock left, and they were a peaceful community. Unfortunately, tensions between colonists and Indians were very high at this time, and the last Susquehannock were massacred in Lancaster County by a mob of colonists named the Paxton Boys. Although the tribe was no longer, Susquehannock descendants are found among the Iroquois, Delaware, and Tuscarora people.

WHITE SETTLEMENT

In 1736 the land west of the Susquehanna River was purchased from the Indians as part of Chester County, one of the original three counties of Pennsylvania. Chester County was eventually divided, and out of that division, Lancaster County came into being; subsequently, Lancaster County itself was divided, and York County came into being. In 1800 York County was divided, and Adams County was established. Eventually, Gettysburg was named as the county seat of Adams County.

The first white settlers came to the area we know as Gettysburg in 1734. They began the Marsh Creek Settlement, which was developed from 1736 to 1760 by pioneers of German, Scotch, and Irish descent. In the 1760s Samuel Gettys purchased from John Penn (grandson of William Penn) a land grant of more than 300 acres that surrounded a crossroads where the Philadelphia-Pittsburg (east-west) and Baltimore-Shippensburg (north-south) roads met. Realizing the potential of the crossroads during this time of settlement expansion, Gettys built a tavern there in 1772, where he sold supplies and refreshments and a bed for the night to settlers who were moving to the west and to the north from Maryland. Continental troops were mustered at the Gettys' Inn and Tavern during the Revolutionary War.

Samuel Gettys died in 1783, and some of his land was auctioned off to satisfy his debts. His son James bought 116 acres of the land, which included the tavern, in 1785, and by 1790 he had laid out a town of 210 lots, which was named Gettystown in his honor. Because of its location at a crossroads, the town grew steadily, and as Gettysburg, it was named the county seat of the newly formed Adams County in 1800. The first session of the new county's court was held in the Gettys' Tavern in 1802, the first courthouse was erected in the square in 1804, and Gettysburg was incorporated as a borough in 1806.

The first half of the nineteenth century brought the establishment of Gettysburg as an agricultural transportation corridor and the founding of two educational facilities within the town, the Gettysburg Lutheran Theological Seminary in 1826 and Pennsylvania College, now called Gettysburg College, in 1832. The years between 1830 and 1860 saw the town develop the industry of carriage and wagon making, and in 1858 the Gettysburg Railroad was extended into town, connecting Gettysburg with other markets. By 1860 Gettysburg had 2,400 residents and 10 roads leading into town. It was said at the time that all roads led to Gettysburg, a fact that propelled the town to its fate in July 1863.

THE BATTLE OF GETTYSBURG

General Robert E. Lee's Confederate army of 75,000 men and Gen. George G. Meade's Union army of 97,000 men met by accident at Gettysburg in July 1863 when a Confederate brigade sent to Gettysburg for supplies observed a forward column of the Union cavalry. This chance encounter led to the Battle of Gettysburg, what many believe to be the turning point of the Civil War. The battle went on for three days, culminating in Pickett's Charge, where Maj. Gen. George E. Pickett ordered a massed infantry of some 12,000 Confederate troops across an open field and toward the Union center on Cemetery Ridge. Pickett's men reached the Union line, but they failed to break it. Confederate casualties from the charge totaled 6,800 in 50 minutes, and the Battle of Gettysburg was at an end. The casualty count was 51,000, making Gettysburg the bloodiest battle in American history. More men fought and more men died than in any other battle on North American soil. Although the Civil War continued for almost two years after Gettysburg, the Confederacy never recovered from its losses there, and General Lee never attempted another offensive operation of such proportions.

The Battle of Gettysburg raged in the town itself, and many citizens had their houses overtaken by soldiers from both sides of the conflict. Although the three days of the battle were hard on the townsfolk, only one citizen, Jennie Wade, was killed during the action. The harder part came after the warfare, when the citizens' homes

i Casualty counts include not only soldiers killed but also those wounded, captured, or missing at the end of a battle. At Gettysburg about 7,100 of the 51,000 total casualties were actually killed in the three days of the battle.

Close-up

Lincoln's Gettysburg Address

Gettysburg is lucky to have its very own Abraham Lincoln living right in town. His name is James Getty, and his resemblance to Lincoln is uncanny. Mr. Getty has been portraying Abraham Lincoln since 1978 at town events such as Remembrance Day, which commemorates when Lincoln traveled to town to say a few words during the dedication of the National Cemetery on November 19, 1863. Those few words have lived on in history, and most of us learn the words to the address as schoolchildren. For those whose memories may not reach back that far, here is Abraham Lincoln's famous speech:

"Four score and seven years ago our fathers brought forth, upon this continent, a new nation, conceived in Liberty, and dedicated to the proposition that all men are created equal.

"Now we are engaged in a great civil war, testing whether that nation, or any nation so conceived, and so dedicated, can long endure. We are met here on a great battlefield of that war. We have come to dedicate a portion of it as a final resting place for those who here gave their lives that that nation might live. It is altogether fitting and proper that we should do this.

"But in a larger sense we can not dedicate—we can not consecrate—we can not hallow this ground. The brave men, living and dead, who struggled, here, have consecrated it far above our poor power to add or detract. The world will little note, nor long remember, what we say here, but can never forget what they did here. It is for us, the living, rather to be dedicated here to the unfinished work which they have, thus far, so nobly carried on. It is rather for us to be here dedicated to the great task remaining before us—that from these honored dead we take increased devotion to that cause for which they here gave the last full measure of devotion— that we here highly resolve that these dead shall not have died in vain; that this nation shall have a new birth of freedom; and that this government of the people, by the people, for the people, shall not perish from the earth."

—President Abraham Lincoln

were turned into hospitals, and the townspeople had to deal with the ugly aftermath of war.

LINCOLN'S GETTYSBURG ADDRESS

The National Cemetery at Gettysburg is the first cemetery that was dedicated exclusively to the burial of soldiers. A few days after the battle, then-governor A. G. Curtin appointed David Wills, a prominent attorney, to establish a cemetery for the Union soldiers who had died in the fighting. Wills invited President Abraham Lincoln to make a speech at the dedication, which was held November 19, 1863. Lincoln traveled by train from Washington, D.C., the night before the dedication and stayed in David Wills's house on Lincoln Square. The morning of the ceremony, he traveled from Lincoln Square south on Baltimore Street to Evergreen Cemetery, earning the route its name—The Historic Pathway. Although Lincoln's speech was only two minutes in length, it is probably one of the most quoted speeches in American history. (See the Close-up for the memorable words of Lincoln's Gettysburg Address.)

To create the National Cemetery, 17 acres were purchased on Cemetery Hill at the apex of what had been the triangular battle line of the Union army. Exhumation of the bodies began on October 27, 1863, and this work wasn't completed until March 18, 1864. Lots in the cemetery were given to each state with dead on the field. Graves were arranged in a semicircular plan with the land allotted to each state, converging on a central point. A space of 2 feet wide was allotted for each body, and the bodies were laid with their heads toward the center. The headstones are uniform in size and contain the name, regiment, and company, if obtainable, of each soldier. Because the cemetery is part of the battlefield, it contains monuments that were erected in honor of Union regiments that fought on the soil. Union cannons that were part of the fighting are also found in the cemetery.

The cemetery was completed in 1872, and by the battle's 25th anniversary in 1888, many had traveled to Gettysburg to view the battlefields and the cemetery. A massive reunion of the Blue and Gray was held in Gettysburg on the 50th anniversary in 1913. The townspeople of Gettysburg have played willing hosts to visitors and have taken great care to preserve the town's history.

DWIGHT D. EISENHOWER

During WWI, then-captain Eisenhower fell in love with the area around Gettysburg when he was the commanding officer at Camp Colt in 1918. Camp Colt was a tank-training camp that at one time housed 8,000 soldiers. During training, weapons were mounted on flatbed trucks that sped around camp as trainees took aim at Little Round Top, the famous hill that figured so prominently in the Battle of Gettysburg.

Eisenhower loved the rural area, and in the 1950s he purchased a farm just west of where the Confederates were positioned on Seminary Ridge. The home served as a weekend retreat for the president, and it was here that he hosted

> **i** Volunteers were plentiful at the beginning of the Civil War, but volunteer numbers eventually dropped off. This led both sides to begin drafting men, with the South beginning its conscription in 1862 and the North following suit in 1863.

many world leaders, including Nikita Khrushchev, Winston Churchill, and Charles de Gaulle. After the presidency Eisenhower and his wife, Mamie, retired here.

Today the home has been preserved and is open to the public as part of the Eisenhower National Historic Site.

GETTYSBURG TODAY

The town of Gettysburg takes its role in history very seriously, and preserving that history is very important to its residents.

But the town is not just a preserved showplace. It's a thriving tourist town that also hosts diverse interests—rural countryside to play in, festivals to attend, and art and culture to absorb. The town has recently seen the completion of many improvement projects, including the restoration of the Lincoln Train Station off Carlisle Street and the renovation of the Wills House on Lincoln Square, where Lincoln stayed before giving his famous address. The Gateway Gettysburg complex has brought new hotels, restaurants, and a movie theater to the eastern end of town. A new theater complex also opened beside the Outlet Shoppes at the southern end of town. Within town the historic Majestic Theater on Carlisle Street reopened in 2005 as a performing-arts venue and has been packing in first-rate acts ever since. Other changes in town include a new hotel being built as well as the ongoing opening and closing of business ventures that are part of any tourist town.

But the most significant change to Gettysburg has to be the new visitor center at the Gettysburg National Military Park that opened in September 2008. Located farther from town than the old visitor center, some business owners worry that the center will take tourists away from town. Only time will prove whether this is a valid concern, and many believe the town and the national military park will work together to enhance the visitors' experience both on the battlefield and in the borough of Gettysburg.

As always Gettysburg's future is deeply connected to its past.

HOTELS, MOTELS, AND RESORTS

Gettysburg offers a wide range of accommodations with so many choices that I've included a separate chapter on bed-and-breakfasts and guesthouses and one on campgrounds and RV parks. This chapter will focus on the hotels and motels in the area, from which there are many to choose. I've also included two resorts, one with skiing and one with golfing, which are located next to each other about 10 miles west of town.

Competition to attract business compels most area hotels and motels to offer a wide range of services as standard fare. Although motels don't have as many amenities as hotels, many people prefer the ease of parking right at their front door. Expect most motels in the area to offer phones and cable or satellite TV in the rooms, free coffee and free newspapers, and microwaves and refrigerators available for a fee. Most hotels include these motel amenities as well as offering in-room hair dryers, irons and ironing boards, coffeemakers, a pool, free local calls, and pickups for battlefield tours. Almost all offer smoking rooms; I'll tell you if an establishment offers only smoking or smoke-free rooms. All the businesses in this chapter accept credit cards and, if you're eligible, make sure to ask about AAA or AARP discounts when making reservations. The hotels listed here are wheelchair accessible, but although most of the motels have ground-level rooms, the rooms are not really equipped for wheelchair access. You should assume that pets are not welcome unless specifically mentioned.

Since there are a good number of hotels and motels available in Gettysburg, I've first broken them down by geographic location from Lincoln Square and then listed them alphabetically. I realize that many travelers decide what sites they want to be close to and then pick a hotel or motel based on its location in relation to those sites. Although there is nothing wrong with this method, remember that walking in Gettysburg can be an experience in itself, and the trolley is also available to zip you around town.

PRICE CODE

Prices quoted are for one night's lodging in a basic room with one or two people in the room during the season, which is April through December. State and local taxes are not included. Pennsylvania has a 6 percent sales tax, and Adams County has an additional 3 percent "pillow tax."

$.................	Less than $70
$$	$71 to $99
$$$	$100 to $135
$$$$	$136 and higher

LINCOLN SQUARE

**BEST WESTERN HISTORIC
GETTYSBURG HOTEL**   **$$$$**
1 Lincoln Square
(717) 337-2000, (866) EST-1797 (reservations)
www.hotelgettysburg.com
Established in 1797, this is the premier hotel in town. When you enter the lobby, the rich woods and deep pile carpets give you a good feel for the hotel's quiet elegance. Sitting on the square, its six floors contain 119 guest rooms and suites that are outfitted with Civil War–period furnishings,

and the hotel staff dressed in period costume completes your transformation to the days of the past. The name of the hotel's restaurant—Centuries on the Square—says it all. Here you can enjoy casual fine dining daily (see the Restaurants chapter). There's also a historic English pub on-site—McClellan's Tavern, which has a turn-of-the-century mahogany Van Tromp Bar imported from Brick Lane in England. The Gettysburg Hotel is featured on the Historic Gettysburg Walking Tour (see the Attractions chapter), and it's also listed on the National Register of Historic Places and on the Historic Hotels of America for the National Trust for Historic Preservation.

All the amenities you would expect to find are here. In addition, there's room service from 7:00 a.m. to 9:00 p.m., babysitting and dry-cleaning services and in-room movies are available, and local calls are free if they're less than 30 minutes long. You'll also have free high-speed Internet access, free transportation to the battlefield bus tour, complimentary afternoon tea, and turndown service. Two-room family units are available, children younger than age 17 stay free in the room with a paying adult, and fireplaces and Jacuzzi baths grace the hotel's suites.

NORTH OF LINCOLN SQUARE

BLUE SKY MOTEL $
2585 Biglerville Road
(717) 677-7736, (800) 745-8194
www.blueskymotel.com
This motel has 17 rooms to choose from, ranging from a room with a double bed and a shower stall to suites with two double beds, a sleeper sofa, and a living room. In between, you'll find family rooms outfitted with a fridge and efficiencies outfitted with kitchens. The Blue Sky is nothing more than it appears to be—a small motel that offers clean, affordable lodging. It's not fancy, but it is run by friendly people who want your stay in Gettysburg to be a happy experience. You won't have a paper delivered or have a free continental breakfast here, but there is a wake-up service and a late-check-in service, local calls and

morning coffee are free, and battlefield tours pick up at the motel. Located a little less than 5 miles north of the square and practically next to the National Apple Harvest Festival held in Arendtsville (see the Annual Events and Festivals chapter), Blue Sky Motel, which was built in 1950, had its rooms completely gutted and renovated in 2000. You'll find rooms with modern heating and air-conditioning and random-width hardwood panels that have caused more than one guest to say it felt like he was staying in a cabin. Technically, you won't find any nonsmoking rooms here. If you request it at the time of your reservation, the staff will do an intense cleaning of your room, including wiping down the walls and cleaning the carpets. In the summertime you'll find a playground, a picnic area where you can barbecue, and a pool. Since the motel sits on four acres, there's also plenty of room for horseshoes, croquet, badminton, and volleyball. With notice the motel will also pick up discount tickets to Hersheypark (see the Day Trips chapter) for you.

SOUTH OF LINCOLN SQUARE

AMERICA'S BEST VALUE INN $$$
301 Steinwehr Avenue
(717) 334-1188,
(888) 315-2378 (reservations)
www.abvigettysburg.com
America's Best Value Inn certainly has one of the best locations in town. It sits between the American Civil War Museum and the Lincoln Train Museum on Steinwehr Avenue, right across from the Gettysburg National Military Park. This two-story hotel was built in the 1960s and offers 76 rooms, which are routinely renovated on a rotating basis. Most of the rooms have double beds, but some are equipped with king-size beds. If you want a smoking room, call early; all but two rooms are nonsmoking. And call early if you want the one room that comes equipped with a small efficiency kitchen. A free deluxe continental breakfast is available to guests, and you can get free coffee in the office 24/7. When you're done touring, you can relax by the outdoor pool, enjoy

a soak in the hot tub, or utilize the high-speed Internet access in your room. Children younger than age 18 stay for free with a parent.

BUDGET HOST—THREE CROWNS
MOTOR LODGE $–$$
205 Steinwehr Avenue
(717) 334-3168,
(800) 729-6564 (reservations)
The Budget Host and the Colton Motel (see subsequent listing) have been owned by the same people since 1996. This franchise motel, which is painted red, white, and blue, has 29 rooms with either one king-size bed or two double beds. It also has a fabulous location—you're only about a block from the military park and 6 blocks south of Lincoln Square. Built during the 1940s and 1950s, the motel rooms have undergone constant upkeep, and they receive a renovation every year. Besides comfortable rooms you'll also have access to the outdoor pool, data ports, and free local calls, and children younger than age 18 stay free with a paying guest. The Budget Host offers a free continental breakfast for guests, and a free copy of the *Gettysburg Times* newspaper is available in the lobby.

COLTON MOTEL $$
232 Steinwehr Avenue
(717) 334-5514,
(800) 262-0317 (reservations)
The Colton has the dubious distinction of being the last independently owned motel in the borough of Gettysburg. But there's nothing dubious about the distinction of sleeping on hallowed ground on Cemetery Ridge, with the National Cemetery as the motel's backdrop. This is where soldiers from the Ohio 73rd Company D Infantry unit held the Union line at the burr of the fishhook before it started to bend around Culp's Hill. The exterior of the Colton, which was built in 1953, is painted blue and gray, and the rooms have been kept up well. The motel has the benefit of an ideal location to walk to restaurants and attractions.

The Colton has 25 rooms, including two family rooms, and all rooms but the family suite are on the ground level. The second-story family suite has three bedrooms with four double beds, and the other family room has three queen-size beds. The motel has an outdoor pool, and Internet access is available. You can also make free local calls, and the office has complimentary coffee and a copy of the *Gettysburg Times* and the *Hanover Evening Sun* newspapers available.

COUNTRY INN & SUITES BY CARLSON $$$
1857 Gettysburg Village Drive
(717) 337-9518,
(888) 201-1746 (reservations)
www.countryinns.com/gettysburgpa
Just about anyone from Gettysburg can tell you where this hotel is—it sits across from the Gettysburg Village Factory Stores (see the Shopping chapter). Located only 2.9 miles from Lincoln Square, Country Inn & Suites is also close to Boyds Bear Country (see the Attractions chapter) and the battlefield. The three-story hotel was built in May 2001 and is entirely nonsmoking. It has 83 rooms and offers the choice between a standard room or a suite. All but two of the standard rooms come with two queen-size beds; the other two are wheelchair accessible and come with a king-size bed. There are six types of suites to pick from, all with refrigerator and microwave, and some are equipped with two-person Jacuzzis. An indoor pool and fitness center round out your exercise options, and rooms have dataports and high-speed Internet access. Or perhaps you'd rather relax with a good book—feel free to borrow one from the hotel's lending library and return it on your next visit to a Country Inn & Suites. A donation is made to a literacy organization for every book returned. Having complimentary beverages and cookies available 24/7 is one of many ways this chain hotel makes you feel at home. They also feed you a deluxe complimentary continental breakfast and welcome guests younger than age 18 traveling with a parent for free. Hungry travelers will find restaurants in the food court in the nearby outlet mall and a TGI Friday's restaurant beside the hotel. The hotel accepts AAA discounts, and pets are allowed for a fee of $20 per night.

Close-up

Drawn to Gettysburg

You'll meet many residents of Gettysburg who will tell you they were drawn here. Some have traveled to the battlefield since their youth and eventually felt the need to relocate to the area. Andrew Manley, former manager at the Colton Inn, is one such person. His first visit to the battlefield was in 1968 as an eight-year-old on vacation with his family. Manley returned often and walked the battlefield many times, feeling compelled to visit the area but never really knowing why. On a battlefield visit in the late 1990s, he stumbled across the grave of one Timothy Manly (as the spelling appeared on the headstone), and he wondered . . . could this be a family relative? He decided to do some research, which eventually turned into a lot of research, and he discovered that Timothy Manley (the headstone has the spelling wrong) was, indeed, a relative—a great-great-cousin.

Timothy Manley was a private in the 63rd Irish Brigade who was mortally wounded in the battle for the Rose Wheatfield on July 2, 1863. He was taken to the Camp Letterman Field Hospital (a marker for the hospital is near the Giant grocery store on York Road), where he died of his wounds in early September. His body was buried on the hospital grounds but was later exhumed and interred in the National Cemetery just days before Lincoln arrived in November to say a few words in honor of the fallen Union soldiers. Lincoln well might have gazed upon Timothy's grave as he delivered what would be his most famous speech—the Gettysburg Address.

After living in many parts of the country, Andrew Manley decided after 9/11 that he wanted to live in Gettysburg. He picked up and moved from Las Vegas to Gettysburg with only the promise of a job interview, which never materialized once he hit town. But Manley felt he was destined to stay here; in fact, he says, he felt the spirit of Timothy Manley calling him to Gettysburg. After a lot of hardship, Manley was offered a job at the Colton Motel as its manager, which he readily accepted. As he often did, Andrew Manley visited the battlefield and placed a flag upon his great-great-cousin's grave. Only when he was back in the office of the Colton did he realize he could easily view the flag he had placed there. The great pull he had felt all his life was finally realized, and he was at peace, knowing he had found where his home was meant to be. Manley feels that his great-great-cousin is also finally at peace and that his spirit was able to move on to its eternal resting place.

"Old soldiers never die, they just stand sentry" is Manley's take on the line from an army ballad that Gen. Douglas MacArthur made famous. He believes his great-great-cousin was standing sentry, waiting for Andrew to come to Gettysburg and discover his grave. Many visitors to Gettysburg are drawn here but cannot exactly say why. If you are one of them, perhaps you have a sentry waiting for you as well.

COZY COUNTRY INN　　　　　**$–$$**
103 Frederick Road, Thurmont, MD
(301) 271-4301
www.cozyvillage.com

History buffs won't mind the 18-mile drive south from Gettysburg on U.S. Route 15 that's required to reach the Cozy, which is on the list of America's Historic Inns. To them, staying in one of the inn's 21 historic, quaint, and unique rooms and cot-

tages, which are decorated in the style of presidents and dignitaries who have visited Camp David and/or the Cozy Country Inn, will be worth the drive. In April 2005 the Camp David Museum opened, and now you can view pictures, many never before seen by the public, of past presidents visiting Camp David. The also-famous Cozy Restaurant, which seats 150 and is the oldest restaurant in Maryland still operated by descendants of its founding family, offers both lavish buffets and an a la carte menu. The Cozy has a pub where you can get a tall, cool drink. Or, if you prefer, order from room service, which is offered from 11:00 a.m. to 9:30 p.m. Your free continental breakfast, which is served in the lobby during the week, is served in the restaurant on the weekend. The inn and restaurant are part of Historic Cozy Village, which offers some unique shops for you to browse.

EISENHOWER INN & CONFERENCE CENTER $$$
2634 Emmitsburg Road
(717) 334-8121,
(800) 776-8349 (reservations)
www.eisenhower.com

With 308 rooms available, this is one of the largest hotels in the area. Located only 4.5 miles south of Gettysburg on U.S. Business Route 15, the Eisenhower Inn is next door to and associated with the All-Star Events Complex (see the Attractions and Kidstuff chapters), which has tons of recreational choices for you and the kids, such as go-karts, minigolf, fishing, and tennis, just to name a few. The Eisenhower actually consists of two connected buildings. The Eisenhower I is the original facility, and the Eisenhower II is the addition. All rooms in the Eisenhower II are nonsmoking, and all but five rooms in the Eisenhower I are also nonsmoking. The standard rooms offer double beds, and there are some rooms with one king-size bed. Queen leisure rooms are all located in the Eisenhower II and include two queen-size beds and a sleeper sofa; executive rooms are also equipped with microwave and minifridge, as are the presidential suites, which also have a living room and bedroom. More than 100 rooms come with a microwave and minifridge for your convenience.

In addition to the expected amenities, such as in-room coffeemakers, hair dryers, and irons and ironing boards, you'll also enjoy an indoor/outdoor pool with a Jacuzzi, a guest laundry, dry saunas, an exercise room, and Internet access. The pool area, with its open sky dome and cabana seating area, is an especially inviting place

for relaxation. When hunger hits, choose from the on-site deli, called the Marketplace, or Richard's Restaurant and Lounge, which has a French Country motif and seats 120. Or enjoy the luxury of calling room service, which operates from morning to early afternoon and in the evening.

GETTYSBURG TRAVELODGE $$$
613 Baltimore Street
(717) 334-9281,
(800) 578-7878 (reservations)
www.travelodge.com

Located opposite the Gettysburg Tour Center (see the GNMP chapter), this chain hotel has 47 rooms that are equipped with two double beds or one king-size bed. The hotel actually consists of two buildings—one that was constructed in May 2000 and a second, renovated building that used to be the Heritage Motor Lodge. Suites with a king-size bed, a queen-size pullout bed, a microwave, a refrigerator, and a whirlpool tub are available, as is Sleepy Bear Den, a suite geared toward folks traveling with kids. Although the hotel does charge for local calls, a high-speed wireless Internet connection is available, and children younger than age 18 stay free with an adult. A select number of rooms have balconies, and you can park directly in front of some of the ground-floor rooms. Parking is free. Walking to major attractions is a breeze from here; you're only 7 blocks south of Lincoln Square and 3 blocks from the Gettysburg National Military Park. To round out your travel stay, you'll receive a free continental breakfast and daily newspaper. And feel free to bring your pet—they're welcome at the Travelodge.

HOLIDAY INN BATTLEFIELD $$$
516 Baltimore Street
(717) 334-6211, (888) HOLIDAY
www.ichotels.com

This Holiday Inn was completely renovated in 2003. Most of its 111 rooms have two double beds, but there are a few rooms that have king-size beds, microwaves, refrigerators, and whirlpools in the bathroom. The Brigades Food Wine & Spirits Restaurant & Lounge (see the Restaurants chapter) is located in the hotel, which is adjacent to the Gettysburg Tour Center. You'll also find a fitness center, outdoor pool, and guest laundry, and pets are welcome in most rooms. Although this hotel is very conveniently located, some guests note that it can be quite noisy and that you can hear your neighbor easily, so if you're a light sleeper, you might want to make a different lodging choice.

QUALITY INN GETTYSBURG
MOTOR LODGE $$$–$$$$
380 Steinwehr Avenue
(717) 334-1103,
(800) 228-5151 (reservations)
www.gettysburgqualityinn.com

All of the 109 rooms in this two-story motel are nonsmoking, and most have either one king-size bed or two double beds. There are some rooms with three double beds, and eight spa rooms have a whirlpool in the bathroom. One efficiency suite with a kitchen is also available. All rooms are renovated on a rotating basis. Owned by Choice Hotels, the Quality Inn offers high-speed Internet access and allows children younger than age 18 to stay free with a parent. In the morning enjoy a free expanded continental breakfast in the Victorian breakfast cottage, which dates from the 1880s, and then walk to the battlefield and attractions nearby. Depending upon the season you can relax in the outdoor or indoor (heated) pool, or perhaps in the whirlpool in the pool area. There's also a fitness room with a sauna, and a putting green is available in summer. Be sure to check out the inn's unique underground cocktail lounge, which is called the Reliance Mine Saloon (see the Nightlife chapter).

EAST OF LINCOLN SQUARE

COMFORT INN $$$
871 York Road
(717) 337-2400, (800) 4CHOICE
www.choicehotels.com

This eight-room hotel located 1 mile east of Lincoln Square was built in 1990, and its indoor heated pool was redone in 2003. There's a Jacuzzi in the pool area, and Jacuzzi suites, which come with a minifridge, are also available. As with other Choice Hotels, children younger than age 18 stay free in a parent's room, and rooms have high-speed Internet access. Most rooms have queen-size beds, but some are outfitted with king-size beds. Although only two stories, the hotel is equipped with an elevator, and it's adjacent to the Gettysburg Family Fun Center (see the Kidstuff chapter). The hotel offers a free continental breakfast and 24-hour free coffee and tea, and there's also a Perkins Family Restaurant adjacent for more substantial fare. Pets are allowed at $10 per night, per pet.

i Don't attempt to walk to the downtown area from hotels east of the square, with the exception of the President Inn & Suites. York Road (U.S. Route 30) is a busy highway, and walking along it is not a safe practice.

DAYS INN GETTYSBURG $$$
865 York Road
(717) 334-0030,
(800) DAYS INN (reservations)
www.dhotelgroup.com/days_inn.htm

Located a mile east of Lincoln Square on York Road, the Days Inn has 112 rooms with king- and queen-size beds. You can choose a room with two queen-size beds; a Work Zone Room, with a king-size bed, comfy recliner, and two-line dataport phone; or a Jacuzzi Room, outfitted with a king-size bed, sofa, and Jacuzzi for two. To round out your stay, there's a heated outdoor pool open from May through September, a fitness center that's open 6:00 a.m. to 11:00 p.m. daily, a complimentary deluxe continental breakfast, complimentary hot beverages 24 hours per day, and guest laundry facilities. If you choose a room that doesn't have a refrigerator or microwave, they are available for rent. The Perkins Family Restaurant is adjacent to the hotel.

ECONOLODGE $$$
983 York Road
(717) 334-4208, (866) 334-6479
www.econolodge.com

The EconoLodge is located where the Country Hearth Inn used to be. Under new management this 30-room motel offers free wireless high-speed Internet access, a free continental breakfast, and smoking as well as nonsmoking rooms. Each room is equipped with cable/satellite TV, hair dryer, in-room coffeemaker, individual climate control, and iron and ironing board as well as a microwave and refrigerator. Wake-up service is available.

HAMPTON INN $$$$
1280 York Road
(717) 338-9121,
(800) HAMPTON (reservations)
www.hampton.com

This chain hotel was built in 1996, and since 2000 it's already had its rooms and lobby renovated—this place is kept up to date. And it keeps up on its technology, also. The Hampton Inn has high-speed wireless Internet throughout the hotel. You can cruise the Web in your room and while enjoying the free continental breakfast that's included in your stay! And although there's no room service available, the Ruby Tuesday restaurant next door delivers.

With 79 rooms within four stories, the Hampton has two elevators for guests' convenience. Most rooms have two double beds, but there are also two-bedroom family rooms that sleep six, and King suites, which are outfitted with a fireplace, Jacuzzi, kitchenette, and sofa bed, are available. Active guests have access to an indoor pool, a spa, and a fitness room, and all but five of the rooms are nonsmoking. A free continental breakfast that has some hot entrees is served, and guests younger than age 18 stay for free with a paying guest. As with all Hampton Inns, your satisfaction is 100 percent guaranteed—if not, your money is returned.

HILTON GARDEN INN $$$$
1061 York Road
(717) 334-2040
www.gettysburg.stayhgi.com

The 88 guest rooms in this chain hotel that opened in July 2004 come with either two queen-size beds or one king-size bed, and all rooms have microwaves, refrigerators, and coffeemakers. If you like to stay connected with the world while you travel, you'll have access to private voice mail, complimentary high-speed Internet, and data-ports. The hotel offers room service, and breakfast and dinner are served in the Great American Grill restaurant. If hunger strikes between those meals, you can order food from the Ruby Tuesday next door, which delivers. Or you can find food as well as sundries at the 24-hour Pavilion Pantry. The Hilton Garden Inn does have a breakfast-only restaurant, which is open to the public. You can work off any unwanted calories by using the cardio equipment in the fitness center or doing laps in the indoor pool. There's also a Jacuzzi available for relaxing at the end of a long day of sightseeing.

HOLIDAY INN EXPRESS $$$
869 York Road
(717) 337-1400, (888) HOLIDAY
www.hiexpress.com/gettysburgpa

Renovated in January 2003, the two-story Holiday Inn Express has 51 rooms and two suites. Double beds outfit 46 of the rooms, and the remaining five rooms have king-size beds. One of the suites has a king-size bed and a queen-size pullout couch while the other has one queen-size bed and a full kitchen. All but five of the rooms and both the suites are nonsmoking. If you don't like climbing steps, book a first-floor room—there's no elevator. There is a large indoor pool and a whirlpool. As at all Holiday Inn Express locations, you can partake in the complimentary deluxe continental Express Start™ Breakfast, and there is 24-hour coffee service also. Phones are equipped with voice mail, data ports are available, and there's high-speed Internet access. Small pets are allowed to stay with you for a fee of $10 per night.

21

MARRIOTT COURTYARD GETTYSBURG $$$$
115 Presidential Circle
(717) 334-5600, (800) 321-2211
www.marriott.com/hargt

New in 2006, Courtyard Gettysburg is part of the Gateway Gettysburg complex at the junction of US 15 and US 30. (See the Close-up in the Area Overview chapter for more on Gateway Gettysburg). This five-story completely nonsmoking hotel has 152 guest rooms, including four suites. Seven of the rooms and one of the suites is wheelchair accessible. The accommodations are meant to combine comfort and functionality, and rooms are spacious and feature a well-lit work desk with an executive chair as well as a desk-level electrical outlet and phone voice mail. Rooms are wired for high-speed Internet access, and you can get wireless access in public areas. Other room amenities include remote-control TV with cable, alarm clock, coffeemaker/tea service, individual climate control, hair dryer, iron and ironing board, luxury bedding, and a pullout sofa bed.

Hotel amenities feature an indoor pool, a whirlpool, and an exercise room, and a complimentary *USA Today* newspaper is delivered to each room on weekdays. Breakfast is available on-site at the Courtyard Café, and drinks in the evening can be enjoyed at the lobby bar. Also within the complex are Garibaldi's Ristorante, which serves Italian cuisine and brick-oven pizza and is open for dinner, and the Old Eagle Grill, which serves classic American cuisine and is open for lunch and dinner.

i If you're interested in the Days Inn's Jacuzzi rooms, book early—there are only three.

PRESIDENT INN & SUITES $$$
606 York Street
(717) 334-4274

Originally opened as a Super 8 in spring 2000, its 52 guest rooms are large enough to accommodate two queen-size beds. King deluxe suites, complete with whirlpool tub, sofa bed, microwave, and refrigerator, are also available. Located

1 mile east of Lincoln Square, this three-story motel has a large lobby, interior corridors, and an elevator. You'll be treated to a free continental breakfast, and the motel also has an indoor pool and a spa. Although there are data ports in the rooms, the lobby is the only place where free wireless high-speed Internet access is available.

i By the time you are reading this, the President Inn & Suites may have changed names again. Although under the same management throughout, the place was a Super 8 before it was a President Inn, and plans are for it to become a Motel 6 by summer 2009. Contact information for the Motel 6 will be (800) 466-8356; www .motel6.com.

SLEEP INN & SUITES $$$
1650 York Road
(717) 334-3866, (877) 424-6423
www.sleepinn.com

Opened in 2007, Sleep Inn & Suites is operated by Choice Hotels, an owner of many hotels in town, and it is totally smokefree. The 39 guest rooms offer high-speed Internet access, cable/satellite TV, flat-screen/plasma TV, microwave, refrigerator, multiple phone lines, and free local calls. All the usual amenities are also available, including coffeemaker, individual climate control, hair dryer, iron and ironing board, and wake-up service. There's a desk in every room if you need to get some work done, and an exercise room and indoor pool are available when you want to relax. For ultimate relaxation, inquire about staying in a room equipped with an in-bath whirlpool. A free continental breakfast is available in the morning to get your day started right.

WYNDHAM GETTYSBURG $$$
95 Presidential Circle
(717) 339-0020, (877) 999-3223
www.wyndham.com/hotels/MDTGE

This six-story Federal-style property boasts old-world charm at its location within the Gateway Gettysburg complex at the junction of US 15 and

US 30. (See the Close-up in the Area Overview chapter for more on Gateway Gettysburg.) Built in 2006, the premises are entirely smoke-free, and of the 248 total rooms, 13 are equipped for handicap accessibility and 11 are suites. Accommodations feature a 27-inch LCD flat-screen television, high-speed Internet access, cordless speakerphone, an ergonomic desk chair, and an in-room safe that's large enough to fit a laptop. Bathrobes are provided so you can lounge in luxury. Other room amenities include luxury bedding, alarm clock, coffeemaker/tea service, a stereo, individual climate control, a spare electrical outlet at desk level, hair dryer, iron and ironing board, and a pullout sofa bed. A newspaper is delivered to your room each weekday, and an indoor pool, a whirlpool, and an exercise room are at your disposal.

On-site dining for breakfast, lunch, and dinner is available at the stately 1863 Restaurant. If you prefer more casual surroundings, the lobby bar adjacent to the restaurant also serves lunch and dinner. And if you don't wish to leave your room, room service is available 24/7. Pets are permitted to stay with you at the Wyndham provided they weigh 50 pounds or less. The nonrefundable pet fee is $20 per day per pet.

WEST OF LINCOLN SQUARE

CARROLL VALLEY RESORT $$$
121 Sanders Road, Fairfield
(717) 642-8211,
(800) 548-8504 (reservations)
www.carrollvalley.com

This is the Gettysburg area's golf resort, although many people also stay here when swooshing down the slopes of Ski Liberty, which is but steps away. The stone mountain lodge you'll drive up to is where you register, and the actual accommodations are located in the two-story building just behind the lodge. The resort's restaurants, fitness and billiards rooms, and banquet and conference facilities are also within the lodge. For your accommodation choices you can pick between a room with a view of the Catoctin Mountains south of Gettysburg or a view of the golf course. The resort has 58 rooms, of which 46 are standard rooms equipped with two double beds. The other 12 are parlor rooms. Eight of the parlor rooms have two double beds and a Jacuzzi tub, and four of them have a king-size bed, a sofa, and a Jacuzzi tub. You can enjoy fireside dining at the Inn at Carroll Valley, and casual dining for breakfast or lunch is available downstairs in the Tavern at Carroll Valley. For golfers, the resort has a driving range and two eighteen-hole Ault & Clark championship golf courses (see the Golf chapter). You'll have a choice of a lot of different golf packages, with lodging, spa treatments, and dining included.

LIBERTY MOUNTAIN RESORT AND
CONFERENCE CENTER $$$
78 Country Club Trail, Carroll Valley
(717) 642-8282
www.libertymountainresort.com

Liberty Mountain Resort is nestled at the bottom of the 16 ski slopes of Ski Liberty (see the Recreation chapter). It's open year-round right beside the Carroll Valley Resort (see the previous listing). The Liberty Mountain Hotel sits on a hill above the ski lodge, which also contains McKee's Tavern. Wireless Internet is available throughout the hotel and the ski lodge. If you book a mountainside room, you'll have a balcony to relax on and take in the views. All 41 rooms are individually decorated with a country motif and include cable, voice mail, and computer ports. The luxury suite has a bedroom with a king-size bed and a balcony, a separate living room that also has a balcony, a fully equipped kitchenette, a bathroom with a two-person whirlpool tub and an oversize shower with glass block walls, and a stackable washer/dryer. Ski and Stay packages are available in winter, and in summer guests enjoy the outdoor swimming pool or a round of golf at the Carroll Valley Resort.

i Gen. George Patton and President Dwight D. Eisenhower are two famous military leaders who have stayed at the Quality Inn Larson's at General Lee's Headquarters.

QUALITY INN LARSON'S AT
GENERAL LEE'S HEADQUARTERS $$$
401 Buford Avenue
(717) 334-3141
www.gettysburgusa.com,
www.thegettysburgaddress.com

With many of its rooms overlooking the battlefield at historic Seminary Ridge, this Quality Inn is adjacent to the small stone house that was owned by Thaddeus Stevens and that served as the headquarters of Gen. Robert E. Lee during the Battle of Gettysburg. In fact, General Lee's Headquarters Museum (see the Attractions chapter) is on-site and free to guests of the inn. The Lutheran Theological Seminary (see the Education chapter) is adjacent to the inn. The inn is also a pickup site on the battlefield tour, and the jumping-off point for the Ghosts of Gettysburg Candlelight Walking Tours of Seminary Ridge (see the Attractions chapter).

Owned by Choice Hotels, the inn has 41 rooms and seven suites. The rooms come in a variety of bed choices, and each suite is unique. One suite might have a Jacuzzi while another will have a fireplace. Four of the suites are in Civil War–era buildings, and they have full-size kitchens. All the rooms are ground level while two of the suites are two stories. In addition to free coffee in the lobby, you also receive a free continental breakfast. The fitness center and outdoor pool lure active sports-oriented guests, while the hotel's gift shop satisfies guests who prefer to exercise their credit cards. You can also pamper yourself by using the inn's valet laundry service. And you won't go hungry (or thirsty) while staying here—the Appalachian Brewing Co. brewpub (see the Restaurants chapter) is located beside the inn.

BED-AND-BREAKFASTS AND GUESTHOUSES

Bed-and-breakfasts and country inns abound in the Gettysburg area. At last count, there were more than 40 within 20 to 25 miles of Gettysburg. For the purposes of this book, an establishment will be considered a country inn if it offers breakfast to nonguests as well as guests. The accommodations included here are either within or very close to Gettysburg proper. They include in-town homes and homes surrounded by acres in the country. At the end of the chapter, guesthouses that are available for rent are also included. These are not bed-and-breakfasts; you rent the entire house and you take care of your own meals.

Many of the bed-and-breakfasts included here were built in the 1700s, and some retain parts of the original homes, such as wide plank flooring. Some of the homes have bullet holes and bloodstained floors to attest to the role they played during the Battle of Gettysburg. Others are Victorian charmers, with period antiques gracing the rooms. Still others are rural nirvanas, with a lot of open space and outdoor activities to keep you busy. Each bed-and-breakfast has unique qualities, with history and location playing only one part. Some innkeepers run small, intimate abodes, with guests receiving individual attention, while others are bigger establishments, with group activities offered.

Once you've narrowed your choices, you might want to employ the services of one of the bed-and-breakfast associations available to you. These organizations allow you to find out about vacancies, special offers, and the nuances of their member inns. See the Gettysburg Bed-and-Breakfast Associations box within this chapter for contact information.

Web sites are given for all the bed-and-breakfasts; if possible, take the time to visit these sites. Most have views of the rooms available to guests as well as pictures of the house and common rooms. This allows you to get a good idea of where you're going to feel the most comfortable during your stay.

This chapter is arranged geographically, with the inns categorized by their direction from Lincoln Square. You can count on all the bed-and-breakfasts to have a two-night minimum stay during the season (April through December) and to impose an additional charge for more than two people in a room. Most offer customized packages and special-event deals, as well as off-season savings, so be sure to ask!

Unless otherwise noted, assume that smoking and pets are not allowed. Also assume that an accommodation isn't wheelchair accessible unless that fact is specifically noted. If credit cards aren't accepted, that will be mentioned in the establishment's entry. (Be aware that some inns require a personal check rather than a credit card to hold your reservation.) For those readers who sneeze when they are around a dog or cat, I'll let you know if a home has a resident pet.

The degree to which a bed-and-breakfast welcomes children varies widely. Some have set age limits, and just about all request that children be "well behaved." Since this term is subjective, it's probably best to talk directly to the innkeeper as to whether you and your child will find the accommodations suitable.

Here's one bit of advice you need to remember: Check on cancellation policies before you book. These vary considerably, depending on your time and length of stay.

Gettysburg Bed-and-Breakfast Associations

Bed and Breakfasts INNside Gettysburg
www.bbonline.com/pa/innsidegettysburg
This site consists of six bed-and-breakfasts with a physical Gettysburg address that organized to promote their businesses during the off-season and midweek times. The inns cooperate to provide winter weekend packages for guests. The following inns belong to this association: the Baladerry Inn, the Battlefield Bed & Breakfast Inn, the Brafferton Inn, the Gaslight Inn, the James Gettys Hotel, and the Lightner Farmhouse Bed & Breakfast.

Country Bed & Breakfasts of Gettysburg
www.gettysburgbnbs.com
Six owner-owned and -operated country inns banded together to promote their attentive and personalized service by forming this association. The participating inns are the Baladerry Inn, the Brierfield II, the Cornerstone Farm Bed & Breakfast, the Gettysburg Pond View Farm, the Red Bud Inn, and the Slocum House Inn.

Inns of the Gettysburg Area
(717) 624-1300, (800) 587-2216
www.bbonline.com/pa/gettysburg
This bed-and-breakfast association consists of 17 historic inns in and around Gettysburg. When you call, an innkeeper will be able to tell you which members have available lodging. Participating inns that are included in this chapter are the Battlefield Bed & Breakfast Inn, the Brafferton Inn, The Brickhouse Inn, the Cashtown Inn, The Doubleday Inn, the Farnsworth House Inn, Gettystown Inn, the Herr Tavern & Publick House, the James Gettys Hotel, and the Keystone Inn Bed & Breakfast.

PRICE CODE

$................. Less than $95
$$ .... $96 to $120
$$$ .... $121 to $160
$$$$ .... $161 and higher

Prices quoted are for one night's lodging with one or two people in the room during the season, which is April through December. State and local taxes are not included. Pennsylvania has a 6 percent sales tax, and Adams County has an additional 3 percent "pillow tax."

NORTH OF LINCOLN SQUARE

**BRIERFIELD II COUNTRY GUEST
COTTAGES** $
1060 Belmont Road
(717) 334-8725
www.gettysburgcottages.com
Owner and innkeeper Nancy Rice opened the first Brierfield Bed and Breakfast in town in 1988, but she closed it in 1998 and opened the Brierfield II out in the country so she could give greater attention to fewer guests. The Brierfield II consists of two country guest cottages that sit at the end of a gravel path that winds from the

main house along a beautiful pastoral setting. Each cottage comes equipped with a private bath, guest-controlled heat and air-conditioning, a kitchen, and a TV. The Pool House features a private porch for taking in all the beauty around you. A queen-size cherry canopy bed graces the Salt Box Cottage, and the Pool House Cottage has a king-size bed that can be converted to twin beds. A phone for guests' use is located in the main brick ranch house.

The one-story cottages are surrounded by 16 acres in the country, four of which are wooded, making them especially perfect for couples wanting to enjoy the bed-and-breakfast experience while still having privacy. But Nancy also caters to business and government workers, who enjoy corporate and government per diem rates while relaxing in the peaceful surroundings. Nancy loves being able to cater to her guests, and she certainly does this at breakfast time. Guests are asked not only what they'd like for breakfast but also when they'd like it served. Breakfast is laid out in the sunroom at the back of the main house, where picture windows allow you to start your day off right with a beautiful view of nature. Nancy loves the bed-and-breakfast business, and it shows. Ninety percent of her business comes from repeat guests or referrals from past guests.

CORNERSTONE FARM BED AND BREAKFAST $$$–$$$$
305 Crooked Creek Road
(717) 334-8205
www.cornerstonefarmbandb.com

The Cornerstone Farm was built in the 1880s and is surrounded by more than 100 acres of private farmland where you'll find quarter horses, cattle, and lots of wildlife. Birders will delight in the large variety of eastern species and warblers found in the area. You can arrange a guided horseback ride among the Texas longhorn cattle on the farm, which is near the site of the first shot of the Battle of Gettysburg and adjacent to what was a Confederate Civil War hospital. Or if you prefer, you can ride in the large outdoor ring. The Cornerstone can also arrange an escorted horseback

tour of the battlefield. Cross-country skiing is available on the grounds in winter.

Quiet patios and private dining tables make the Cornerstone an oasis for relaxation. The living room features French doors that open to the patio and the swimming pool and cabana, which are surrounded by gardens. Each of the five guest rooms comes with a cozy fireplace and private bath, and there's central air-conditioning throughout the house. The Sunrise, Lincoln, and Log Cabin Rooms have king-size beds, with the Log Cabin's being a four-poster bed. The Charleston Room has a black cherry queen-size canopy bed, while the Blue Room is outfitted with twin beds. One room, the Sunrise Room, is wheelchair accessible, and the Lincoln Room, with its private balcony that looks out across miles of country land, is requested the most often. To complete your perfect stay, gourmet breakfasts of fresh fruits, home-baked breads and pies, a hot entree, and a side dish are served daily. Your scrumptious breakfast is served in a large dining room that has floor-to-ceiling windows, and tables are outfitted with fine linen, flowers, and candlelight.

The Cornerstone welcomes children age eight and older. There are strict regulations on smokers, with specific designated outdoor smoking areas.

THE DOUBLEDAY INN $$–$$$
104 Doubleday Avenue
(717) 334-9119
www.doubledayinn.com

Splendid views of Gettysburg and the battlefield await you at the Doubleday Inn. Nestled on Oak Ridge and adjoined by the battlefield on three sides, the Peace Light Memorial, Confederate artillery on Oak Hill, and the Railroad Cut are all within walking distance. The inn is named for Gen. Abner Doubleday, who assumed command of the first corps at what is now the site of the inn upon the death of General Reynolds. General Doubleday held off Confederate forces that greatly outnumbered his own for seven hours, allowing the Union forces to regroup that evening and enabling them to place themselves ℹ️ General Doubleday, for whom the Doubleday Inn is named, was a captain stationed at Fort Sumter when Confederate troops attacked the fort and the Civil War began. Captain Doubleday gave the command for the first Union shot to be fired in response. It was thought for a long time that Doubleday also invented the game of baseball, but this isn't true. He did, however, refine the sport by organizing the game and modifying some of the basic rules.

in a strategically advantageous position for the second day of the battle.

Today the centrally air-conditioned Doubleday Inn offers nine guest rooms decorated in English country fashion with Civil War accents, and each room has a private bath. Eight of the rooms are for double occupancy, and one is for single occupancy. Two large patios offer a panoramic view of 8 to 10 miles, and there are also great views from the second-floor deck, named "The Porch on Oak Ridge." Within the house you'll find some artwork by Dale Gallon, a premier Civil War artist whose studio is in Gettysburg. Christine and Todd Thomas, your delightful hosts, treat their guests to afternoon tea or refreshments and a full candlelight country breakfast daily. On selected nights they also host a battlefield historian who leads a discussion on the Battle of Gettysburg. Christine and Todd welcome well-behaved children age 13 and older, and there are designated outside smoking areas. Although guests are not allowed to bring pets, the Thomas's golden retriever, Molly, is available for guests to love.

The Doubleday has been featured in *Washingtonian Magazine*, *New York Magazine*, and *Potomac Magazine*, as well as being included in the books *Secrets of Entertaining from America's Best Innkeepers* (Globe Pequot Press) and *Teatime at the Inn* (Rutledge Hill Press).

RAPHAEL INN BED & BREAKFAST $$$
32 East Lincoln Avenue
(717) 398-8580
www.raphaelinn.com

Opened on Veteran's Day 2004, Raphael Inn is located just three doors from Gettysburg College. The beautiful three-story brick house was built by the Wolf family in 1922 and operated as a tourist home for more than 30 years before being sold for use as a private residence. Current owners and innkeepers George and Alexandra Escalera bought the place in 2003 and began its rebirth as an oasis for tourists. Refinements are constantly being made, and the inn always seems to be a little different when guests make a return visit. The Escaleras' dog, Heidi, is on the premises, and she loves to be petted by guests.

Two guest rooms and a suite are available. The Evangeline Room is filled with shades of purple and is a peaceful place to rest after a day on the town. It features a queen-size bed, private bathtub and shower, air conditioner, cable TV, and a view of the backyard gardens. The Abraham Lincoln Room has all those amenities plus a writing desk, a sofa, and an adjacent coach room, a quaint sitting room which provides a view of the backyard gardens. The California-Rose Suite is the largest room, and it's filled with a king-size bed, a private large shower complete with a seat, a large couch, and a small table with chairs. The room also has air-conditioning and cable TV.

Guests enjoy a country-style breakfast in the Paris Cafe Dining Room or outside on the screened-in front porch the Escaleras call the Blue Moon. Guests are welcome to sit and socialize or enjoy a book or a board game in the in the parlor. Or they may choose to get closer to nature by taking a walk in the backyard and enjoying Jenny's Pond. The backyard gardens are also where guests may enjoy a smoke if they wish. Another amenity offered here is free off-street parking, a precious commodity this close to a college campus.

SLOCUM HOUSE INN $

200 Blue Berry Road, Gardners
(717) 528-7390
www.slocumhouseinn.com

Sitting on 25 acres just north of Gettysburg and named for Union general Warner Slocum, this restored circa-1759 home enfolds you in country experiences. Here you can walk along country lanes, wander through the gardens, relax by the pond, and swim in the outdoor pool, all just minutes from the heart of Gettysburg. Originally built as a settler's log cabin, the home has been expanded with stone additions but still maintains its original character. Owner and innkeeper Carol Shafer has decorated the inn in Williamsburg style with period antiques and reproductions throughout. While relaxing in comfy seating and enjoying the common room's fireplace, guests are invited to partake of satellite TV, VCR tapes, the well-stocked bookshelves, and complimentary beverages.

Slocum House Inn has three guest rooms, and a fourth room can be combined with one of the guest rooms to create a two-room suite. General Slocum and his division generals provide the rooms' names. The Greene Room is in the guest cottage and provides plenty of privacy. This romantic room is outfitted with a queen-size canopy bed, gas log fireplace, private bath, cherry-wood furniture, and colonial wall stencils. Also located in the guest cottage is the Geary Room. Here you'll find a four-poster queen-size bed, private bath, a Queen Anne wing chair perfect for reading beside the gas log fireplace, and colonial decorating. The Williams Room is upstairs in the section of the main house that was built in the 1750s. It boasts wide pine floors and low ceilings, and it has a private bath, a queen-size bed with a handmade quilt, and stenciled walls. This is the guest room that can be combined with the Slocum Room, also upstairs in the main house and also with a queen-size bed, to form a two-bedroom suite with a shared bath.

Carol serves a full breakfast in the dining room, and she fills you up with coffee, juice, fruit, fresh-baked goods, and gourmet dishes that are prepared fresh daily.

The Slocum House Inn does not accept credit cards, so you will have to use cash or a personal check to pay for all this country living. Children age 14 and older are welcome at the inn.

SOUTH OF LINCOLN SQUARE

A SENTIMENTAL JOURNEY BED & BREAKFAST $$

433 Baltimore Street
(717) 337-0779 (10:00 a.m. to 5:00 p.m.),
(717) 642-5188 (5:00 to 10:00 p.m.),
(888) 337–0779
www.asentimentaljourneybb.com

Owners and innkeepers Barbara and Steve Shultz were raised in Gettysburg, and at one time Steve was the chef at the historic Farnsworth House (see the listing within this chapter). A Sentimental Journey, their latest venture, houses the B&B as well as their first business, the art- and picture-framing studio and gallery of aviation art the couple began in 1992. (See The Arts chapter for more on Aces High Gallery.)

Built in 1928 of burgundy bricks, this three-story home has five romantic guest rooms, each decorated in an early 1900s time period. One room has a turn-of-the-nineteenth-century motif, complete with an iron queen-size bed and claw-foot tub, and another is decorated in WWI memorabilia, including a turn-of-the-twentieth-century phone and a doughboy uniform. A third room is decked out in art deco style, and two rooms honor the WWII era, one depicting the home front and one honoring the men who fought in the CBI (China, Burma, India) theater. All the rooms have cable TV and air-conditioning, and all except the CBI room have queen-size beds and private baths. The CBI room has a full-size bed and is half price when rented in conjunction with the art deco room. (The rooms also share a bath.) A continental breakfast is laid out in the 1950s kitchen for you to enjoy, and off-street parking is available to guests. If you and your sweetheart want to journey back to the romantic days of yesteryear, let A Sentimental Journey's 1940s porch glider transport you to a gentler, slower time. Located in the historic district, this bed-and-breakfast is close to all the Gettysburg attractions.

BALADERRY INN AT GETTYSBURG $$$–$$$$
40 Hospital Road
(717) 337-1342, (800) 220-0025
www.baladerryinn.com

The Baladerry Inn consists of three homes that are surrounded by four acres at the edge of the battlefield near Little Round Top. At the end of a winding driveway, you'll spy the Carriage House on the right and the Main House and the brick Federal-style 1812 House on the left. Looking at the homes against their backdrop of huge trees, you know you're about to experience country graciousness at its best. These homes give new meaning to the word spacious. Staying at the Baladerry also allows you to experience a bit of history—the 1812 House served as an Army of the Potomac field hospital during the Battle of Gettysburg. Today guests gather around the massive brick fireplace in the 1812 House's two-story great room, which is also where breakfast is served. For guests who enjoy the great outdoors, the sprawling grounds offer a brick terrace off the 1812 House that serves as a gathering spot and a garden gazebo for more private rendezvous. There is also a tennis court, so be sure to pack your racket.

Accommodations are spread out among the houses—two rooms are in the Main House, three rooms are in the 1812 House, and four rooms and a suite are in the Carriage House. All are named for flowers. The two-room Cottage Rose Suite is outfitted with a sunroom with a full-size sofa bed, a large bedroom with king-size bed, a private patio, a fireplace, and a private entrance adjacent to the tennis court. All the rooms but one have queen-size beds, and the Primrose Room, in the 1812 House, has twin beds that can be converted to a king-size bed. The Primrose Room's private bath is across the hall; the rest of the rooms have a private bath within the room.

All the accommodations have in-room phones and air-conditioning. In the Carriage House, the Rose and Daisy Rooms have private patios while the Marigold and Shamrock Rooms have a fireplace and sitting area. The Windflower Room, in the 1812 House, has a whirlpool tub. While the Garden and Tulip Rooms in the Main House may not have a patio or fireplace, they do enjoy the luxury of being close to the common areas.

A full country breakfast is served in the two-story great room. You might feast on sausage and stuffed French toast with apricot sauce or "crepes Suzinn" with bacon garnish or one of the many other delicious choices. The inn wants you to have the perfect vacation, and they'll arrange for deliveries of flowers, chocolates, and wine. They'll also work with you to create your ideal personalized evening. Children age 12 and older are welcome.

BATTLEFIELD BED & BREAKFAST INN $$$$
2264 Emmitsburg Road
(717) 334-8804, (888) 766-3897
www.gettysburgbattlefield.com

History abounds at the Battlefield Bed & Breakfast Inn, an 1809 stone farmhouse that sits on 30 acres of the South Cavalry Battlefield. The eight guest rooms within the inn are named for and decorated with Civil War art related to the units that fought on the property during the Battle of Gettysburg. Four are standard rooms with queen-size beds, and the other four either are specialty rooms with fireplaces and more than one bed or are suites. All of the rooms have a private bath and air-conditioning. Your stay also includes a full two-course breakfast served by staff costumed in Civil War attire. Along with orange juice, coffee, and tea, the first course might be poached pears and raisin rum muffins or apple cobbler with whipped cream, followed by a second-course selection of heart-shaped pancakes with bacon, fried eggs, and farm potatoes or raspberry-cream crepes with ham and farm potatoes. (If you haven't guessed, the Battlefield is famous for their farm potatoes.) Breakfast is served at 9:00 a.m. in the great room overlooking the pond. Or, if you prefer, you can arrange to have a private breakfast in the Lincoln Room. If you like to get an earlier start on your day, just let innkeeper Florence Tarbox know when you check in, and breakfast will be fixed at a time chosen by you.

The inn conducts Civil War history presentations with hands-on demonstrations at 8:00 a.m. in the gathering room. The programs change daily, allowing guests to attend a different program each day of their stay. A Wednesday afternoon program that focuses on Civil War weapons, including teaching the participants how to fire a musket, began in 2004. The history programs are available to inn guests only and are free, but you have to make reserve a place when you check in. Ghost stories, theme weekends, and special packages are also offered by the inn. If you're planning on riding your own horse on the battlefield, inquire about boarding your horse here. Dogs are accepted on a case-by-case basis.

THE BRICKHOUSE INN BED & BREAKFAST $$$
452 Baltimore Street
(717) 338-9337, (800) 864-3464
www.brickhouseinn.com

A stay at the Brickhouse Inn transports you back to the Victorian era. Located in the heart of the historic district, the imposing 1898 three-story brick Victorian home and adjacent circa-1830 residence are decorated with selected antiques reminiscent of the turn of the twentieth century. Although the feel is Victorian, complete with some original wood floors and chestnut woodwork, the amenities are modern, and off-street parking directly behind the inn allows you to forget about driving while you walk to area sites.

Each of the 10 guest rooms, nine of which are named for states represented in the Battle of Gettysburg, comes with a private bath, individually controlled air-conditioning and ceiling fans, a telephone, and cable TV. The beds are covered with cozy comforters and are queen-size except for the Virginia Room, which has a full-size bed. Located on the third floor in the rear of the house, this slightly smaller room is decorated

in summer colors and white lacy curtains. The most popular room of returning guests is the Delaware Room, which boasts a gas stove in the original fireplace, 1868 pine floors, an original claw-foot tub, and a private first-floor entrance. The other rooms have their own charms. There are bay windows in the Maryland, South Carolina, Tennessee, and New York Rooms, a private porch in the North Carolina Suite, and claw-foot tubs in the New England and North Carolina Suites and the Georgia Room. The Ohio Room has an Amish feel and is decorated with a matching antique oak dresser and washstand.

Breakfast is served out on the garden patio during warmer weather, and it always includes the inn's signature dish, Pennsylvania Dutch shoofly pie, made from a secret family recipe. You'll also be served a hot entree, fruit, juice, coffee, and bread or muffins. Later in the day, guests are invited to gather on the wraparound porch for afternoon lemonade and homemade cookies. All in all, the Brickhouse Inn promises genteel accommodations with all the conveniences of the modern world and the added attraction of an in-town location.

FARNSWORTH HOUSE INN $$$–$$$$
401 Baltimore Street
(717) 334-8838
www.farnsworthhouseinn.com

The Farnsworth House is considered one of the most haunted inns in America. The tradition of ghost telling in Gettysburg began here, and you can partake in the inn's candlelight ghost walks and visit the Civil War Mourning Theatre downstairs. (See the Attractions chapter for more on these and other places in Gettysburg where you can hear eerie stories and possibly see a ghost or two.) If you want to take every opportunity to try to contact the otherworld, why not stay in one of the inn's haunted guest rooms—five of the 11 guest rooms are supposedly haunted, and spirits have been known to walk the halls. It's not surprising that Civil War spirits roam the house—the house was in the midst of some heavy fighting during the Battle of Gettysburg. (For more on the house's history and role in the battle, see the Close-up in this chapter.)

Located in the historic district, this Victorian beauty on the Register of Historic Places is decorated throughout with nineteenth-century antiques. Each of the guest rooms is air-conditioned and has a private bath, and many of the baths have claw-foot tub/shower combinations. Two of the rooms, both with four-poster queen-size beds, are rented only to adults. The Lincoln Room has a mirrored two-person Jacuzzi, and the Belle Boyd Room, named for a notorious Confederate spy, has a large oil painting of a reclining nude and a two-person Jacuzzi with a stained-glass window. The significance of some of the guest-room names may elude you unless you know the home's history. The McFarland Room, the only room with twin beds rather than a queen-size bed, is named for John McFarland, who built the house. The Catherine Sweney Room, which has stained-glass windows, is named for one of the Sweney family members who lived in the house during the Battle of Gettysburg, and the Sara Black Room, with its queen-size canopy bed, is named for a previous owner. Featuring unique Bradbury & Bradbury ceiling and hallway panels and a cherry four-poster bed, the Shultz Room is named for the current owners. The remaining rooms are named for historic figures, and their names are familiar to everyone. Longstreet is the newest room, and you'll also find the Custer, Jennie Wade, and Eisenhower Rooms. (By the way, the Eisenhower Room is named for Mamie, not Ike.)

Open to the public, the Farnsworth House serves breakfast to guests in the authentically restored dining rooms, which are accented by oil paintings of Generals Lee and Meade. The main dining room features candlelight and period-dressed waitstaff, and here you will find Civil War–era fare served for lunch and dinner, such as game pie, peanut soup, sweet potato pudding, and the like. If the weather is nice, you may want to dine in the patio garden beside the spring-fed stream. For more casual fare the Killer Angel Tavern fits the bill. Also on the grounds are the Farnsworth House Military Impressions bookshop (see the

Shopping chapter) and the Gettysburg Quartermaster (see the GNMP chapter), both great places for Civil War buffs to spend some time.

GASLIGHT INN $$$–$$$$
33 East Middle Street
(717) 337-9100, (800) 914-5698
www.thegaslightinn.com

This in-town 1872 three-story Italianate-style yellow-brick house exudes elegance, with its windows veiled in lace and a wrought-iron gate that opens to a brick path that takes you past a beautiful gaslight to the old-fashioned covered front porch. As you enter the house, where you might be greeted by the resident dogs, there are two parlors separated by pocket doors and a dining room decked out with a chandelier and oriental carpet.

The Garden Room, which is customized to accommodate disabled guests, is on the first floor and opens onto a large brick patio that's beside a pond. There are eight more guest rooms on the second and third floors. The second floor also has the sitting room, with a television, video library, full bookshelves, and an entrance to the covered deck that overlooks the garden. A deck overlooking the gatehouse weather vane is accessible from the third floor. All guest rooms have a private bath, central air-conditioning, and in-room cable TV and phones. There are three levels of rooms at the inn, with three rooms in each level. Standard rooms have a queen-size bed, and their private baths have stall showers. Superior rooms have a queen-size bed, a fireplace, and a private bath with a spa, which is a 5-foot-wide shower that has two molded seats and converts to a steam bath at the touch of a button. You're given a choice between the Deluxe rooms—either a queen-size bed and a fireplace in the bedroom and the bathroom, which has a double-wide Jacuzzi, or a king-size bed, a fireplace, two convertible love seats in a sitting area, sliding doors onto a deck that overlooks the gardens, and a spa in the private bath.

A full gourmet breakfast, served on the brick patio in nice weather, is included with your stay, and guests often gather on the front porch in the

Close-up

The Farnsworth House

The Farnsworth House is the central part of a complex that sprawls along Baltimore Street and contains a tavern, a bookshop, and a sutlery in addition to the bed-and-breakfast and its outside dining area. The oldest part of the house was built in 1810, followed by the brick structure in 1833, and the original walls, flooring, and rafters remain intact. The Sweney family lived in the Farnsworth House during the Battle of Gettysburg, and they sheltered Confederate sharpshooters. One hundred bullet holes can be seen in the south side of the house, where it was ravaged by Union soldiers. It's believed one of the Confederate sharpshooters in the house accidentally shot Jennie Wade, the only civilian to perish in the three days of fighting. (See the Attractions chapter for information on the tour of the Jennie Wade House.) Bullet holes are also visible in the door that's in the back room of the dining area on the home's first floor. In the early 1900s the house was opened as a lodging home by the George E. Black family. The Loring H. Shultz family purchased the home in 1972 and started restoring it to its 1863 appearance. The house is named for Elon John Farnsworth, who was promoted to brigadier general on the eve of the battle. Soon after the failure of Pickett's Charge on the third of July, Farnsworth's regiments were ordered to charge the right flank of Longstreet's position on Cemetery Ridge. In this ill-fated charge, Farnsworth and 65 of his men perished.

If you enjoy talking about the Civil War, the Farnsworth House is full of opportunities to do so. The owner is very knowledgeable on the subject, and he knows the history of the house in detail. Movie fans will also want to visit the Killer Angel Tavern on the grounds, which has a great assortment of clothing and props from the movie *Gettysburg* displayed.

afternoon for snacks and refreshments. Ample parking is located behind the inn. Innkeepers Becky and Mike Hanson set themselves apart by their hospitality and attention to details. Every guest receives an orientation to the area, and Becky and Mike will provide personalized itineraries, arrange private tours, chill your wine, whatever they can do to make your stay with them perfect. They also welcome well-behaved children older than age ten.

GETTYSTOWN INN $$$
89 Steinwehr Avenue
(717) 334-2100
www.dobbinhouse.com
You can truly gaze upon where history has been made when you stay at the Gettystown Inn—three of its suites overlook the National Cemetery. And the inn is adjacent to the Historic 1776 Dobbin House Tavern, Gettysburg's oldest

house. Centrally located within walking distance of the battlefield, Gettystown Inn has a wide variety of room choices, beginning with which of its three Civil War–era houses you want to stay in. Accommodations in all three houses feature air-conditioning, antique-filled rooms, and private baths. The Victorian House has the Lincoln Suite, a three-room suite that comes with a king-size canopy bed, a private sitting room with a cherry daybed, a full kitchen with a table that seats six, a private porch, and two cable TVs.

The Remembrance House has two suites that overlook where Lincoln gave his Gettysburg Address. The sitting-room windows of the first-floor Gettysburg Address Overlook Suite I provide a view of the spot, while the bedroom windows of the second-floor Gettysburg Address Overlook Suite II' overlook the historic location. Overlook Suite I is equipped with a queen-size bed, a refrigerator, a microwave, two cable TVs, and a sleeper sofa and a game table in the sitting room. Overlook Suite II's two-room suite has a queen-size carved cherry four-poster bed, a private sitting area, a small refrigerator, and two cable TVs. Aunt Holly's Garden Suite is also in the Remembrance House, and it's named for the abundance of rhododendron planted around the suite's porch, which were transplanted from the innkeeper's aunt's garden. This is a two-story, two-room suite, with a first-floor sitting room complete with a sleeper sofa, a second-floor bedroom with a queen-size black-iron bed, a private bath, a private back porch, and two cable TVs.

The Leister House has one two-room suite and four other guest rooms, each named for a Civil War commander and each outfitted with a queen-size bed and a small refrigerator. The Steinwehr, Stuart, and Reynolds Rooms are on the second floor, and the Meade Room is a large first-floor room that has a private entrance and a private porch for you to enjoy. The Lee Suite features an eighteenth-century clothes closet and a porch off its sitting room. It also has cable TV.

Your included country breakfast is served at the Dobbin House, which is also open to the public. (For more on the Dobbin House, see the Restaurants chapter.) Breakfast includes fresh-baked breads, fresh fruits, cereals, juice, and eggs or a hot entree. The Gettystown Inn also has plenty of free parking available to its guests. To complete your experience at this historic site, there's also a tavern and a gift shop on the grounds.

LIGHTNER FARMHOUSE BED AND BREAKFAST $$–$$$
2350 Baltimore Pike
(717) 337-9508, (866) 337-9508
www.lightnerfarmhouse.com
Dennis and Eileen Hoover bought the Lightner Farmhouse Bed and Breakfast in March 2004, and until 2006 they owned both it and the Cashtown Inn (see subsequent write-up in this chapter). Dennis handles the maintenance and upkeep of the inn and also cooks for the guests. Eileen handles the front desk and also writes and

produces Murder Mystery weekends during the winter season.

The Federal-style brick building was constructed circa 1862 by Isaac Lightner, an Adams County sheriff and farmer. The First Corp of the Union Army used the house as a hospital in July 1863, and the property was used as a hospital area for five weeks following the Battle of Gettysburg. It sits on 19 acres of countryside only 3 miles from the center of Gettysburg, and it's truly amazing how such beautiful countryside can be only a five-minute drive from town. The house's original character is expressed through the wide molding, random-plank floors, and four fireplaces that have been preserved, and it has a Victorian parlor full of books and magazines. Guests gather to enjoy all sorts of videos and games as well as cable TV in the common room, where free refreshments are provided.

Although this bed-and-breakfast preserves the spirit of nineteenth-century rural life, it has also embraced the modern world: Wireless Internet is available in every room. The farmhouse has central air-conditioning, and each of the guest rooms, which are named after Pennsylvania's native trees, has a queen-size or king-size bed, private bath with shower, hair dryer, and small watercooler. Four guest rooms, the two-room Pine Tree Suite, and the two-floor Walnut Cottage are available. The cottage is ideal for romantic getaways. Guests are served a private breakfast in the breezeway, and they can also relax on their private wraparound deck. Another attraction of the cottage is its beehive oven, where bread was baked for Union soldiers in 1863.

Between 8:00 and 9:00 a.m., guests gather in the dining room for a breakfast that consists of several courses. Along with coffee, tea, and juice, you'll be offered warm sweet bread or muffins followed by a fruit dish. The main entrees alternate daily between sweet fare and egg dishes, often served with sausage or bacon on the side. In the afternoon guests relax in rocking chairs on the porch while afternoon tea is served.

i The walking trails on the grounds of the Lightner Farmhouse Bed and Breakfast are available for guest exploration. Be sure to take along the *Lightner Farmhouse History and Natural Trail Guide* on your walk; it was specially designed to help guests understand the farmhouse and surrounding countryside's historical and environmental significance.

MARY-PENN BED AND BREAKFAST $$$
716 Mason Dixon Road
(717) 334-5055
www.mary-pennbb.com

A couple who stays here can sleep in the same bed but stay in two different states! The Mary-Penn is actually located on the dividing line between Pennsylvania and Maryland, and the bed in one of the house's rooms is situated so it straddles the line. The house was built in 1743, 20 years before the survey team of Mason and Dixon established the border to settle a land dispute between the proprietors of the two colonies, the Penns of Pennsylvania and the Calverts of Maryland. In fact, the notes kept by Mason and Dixon mention them passing by the house. After the survey was complete, two-thirds of the house ending up residing in Pennsylvania and the other third in Maryland.

The home changed hands many times, and it was in a dilapidated state when David Waybright and his father, Paul, took over ownership when they bought 246 acres of area farmland in 1979. The men planned on tearing the house down until David's mom, Mary, did some research on the home and decided its history justified its restoration. The family began a decade-plus renovation of the home, where Mary and Paul lived out the remaining years of their lives. David and his wife, Bea, decided to open the house as a bed-and-breakfast in 2008 to fulfill Mary's wish that the history of the house continue to be shared after her death.

Today the Mary-Penn has three guest rooms on the Maryland side of the house and a suite on the Pennsylvania side. In the walkout basement, you'll find a large, stone fireplace, a sitting room, and a game room. One of the Maryland rooms is on the first floor while the rest are located on the second level of the house. Named for the person who built the first story of the house in 1743, the John Mckinley Room is on the first floor, and it's outfitted with an 1800s-style double bed and a private bathroom. Also on the first floor are a parlor, a large breakfast room, a full kitchen, and a large family room that was added in 1990 and overlooks Marsh Creek. On the second floor the Wm. J. Stewart Room is named for the person who added the house's second story in 1793, and it boasts a double canopy bedroom suite. The other room upstairs on the Maryland side is the Mary B. Room, named for David's mother and outfitted with a pineapple-post queen-size bed and a fireplace. The Pennsylvania side of the second floor is occupied by the William Penn Room, a large suite with an 1800s-style queen-size bed and access to a smaller room outfitted with a single bed. A newly remodeled bathroom that includes a whirlpool tub with shower is also located on the second floor.

The house sits on the back 200 acres of the 900-acre Waybright family farm, and you're surrounded by countryside as you meander up the 1-mile lane that leads to the house. Be sure to take some time to explore Marsh Creek and to enjoy the nature that surrounds the home. But most of all, enjoy the novelty of visiting two states at the same time!

PASSAGES INN $$$
267 Baltimore Street
(717) 334-7010
www.passagesinngettysburg.com

Passages Inn brings a unique spin to the Gettysburg B&B experience. The renovated house on Baltimore Street predates the Civil War, but it's not decked out in period decor. Instead, the home sparkles with international flair provided by well-traveled owners Paulette Lee and Gary Froseth. Paulette, who speaks French, has lived and worked in Rwanda and Ethiopia, and husband Gary is a broadcast journalist. Both love to share stories of their travel adventures, and Gary is also an avid aviation and rail transportation buff. International artifacts can be found throughout the home, and the three guest rooms on the second floor are decorated with objects from the areas of the world they represent.

The European Suite contains a small art gallery with photographs and prints from many European countries, the Australasia Room has objects that represent Australia and Asia, and the Africa Room has photos and artifacts from North, East, and South Africa. Each accommodation has reading materials from its part of the world to go along with the appropriate antiques as well as a queen-size bed, private bathroom, cable TV, air-conditioning, wing chairs, and rockers. The European Suite is the quietest of the three rooms since it is in the back of the house, and it has a sunroom and beautiful hardwood floors. The other two rooms overlook historic Baltimore Street, with the Australasia Room featuring Victorian mahogany and marble furniture and the Africa Room boasting an ornamental fireplace. The suite and the Australasia Room have en suite bathrooms while the Africa Room has a large private bath down the hall. To complete your relaxation during your stay, there's also a small game room that features a handmade needlepoint chessboard with hand-carved pieces from England and a parlor where guests gather to socialize amid artifacts from around the world.

A first-floor guest service area has a refrigerator loaded with juices, soda, and water, and coffee and tea is available there for early risers. A full gourmet breakfast is served in the dining room between 8:30 and 9:30 each morning, and it is a true feast. You might be offered mushroom broccoli quiche, grilled tomatoes and sausage, apricot-walnut bread, berry puff pancakes, or a plethora of other mouthwatering temptations.

The Passages Inn has many specials throughout the year, including pairing the B&B experience with area wine and historical tours and winter family getaways, where the whole guest area is yours at a discount. Although located right downtown, the inn does offer off-street parking.

TILLIE PIERCE HOUSE $$$
303 Baltimore Street
(866) 585-1863
www.tilliepiercehouse.com

The name of this bed-and-breakfast pays homage to the 15-year-old girl who lived here with her family when the Battle of Gettysburg occurred. Tillie was an eyewitness to the history made during those days, and her writings of her experiences led to her becoming known as the voice of the civilian side of the conflict. The Confederate line was almost directly in front of the house on Baltimore Street as fighting spread into the town on the first day of the battle, and both Union and Confederate soldiers used the Pierce house as a makeshift hospital. To keep Tillie out of harm's way, she was sent with her neighbor Hettie Schriver to the Weikert farm on Taneytown Road. But Tillie had actually been sent right into an area that would see some of the heaviest fighting in the next two days—the farm was within a few hundred yards of Little Round Top. Tillie became a volunteer nurse at the farm, and when she returned home, she cared for five wounded men within her family's home. She published a book about her experiences titled *At Gettysburg . . . or What a Girl Saw and Heard of the Battle in 1888*. It was an immediate best seller, and many historians consider it to be the best account of the civilian experience of the battle.

Although the house witnessed history in 1863, it was actually built in 1829, and it's one of the oldest and most historic buildings on Baltimore Street. It was in pretty bad shape when Keith and Leslie Grandstaff purchased the home in 2005, but their loving two-year restoration project returned the home to its original splendor. The house opened as a bed-and-breakfast in November 2007 and all the hard work the Grandstaffs did on the renovation earned them the prestigious 2008 Historic Preservation Award from the Historic Gettysburg–Adams County organization. The plaque is prominently displayed on the right front façade of the building, right along with the home's Historic Civil War Building plaque.

The house's nineteenth-century furnishings and period artwork complete your immersion into the past, and the Grandstaffs' meticulous attention to detail means that even the interior paint colors are historically correct. But you'll be able to enjoy every modern amenity while living in the past. The house is fully climate controlled, and it's equipped with new plumbing and wiring, backup lighting, sprinklers, and more. Accommodations include four rooms and a suite, and all are outfitted with private bathrooms supported by state-of-the-art tankless hot-water heaters, so there is no fear of a cold shower here. You can stay in the room where Tillie slept, appropriately titled the Tillie Pierce Room, which is decorated with period antiques and features original wooden floors in its large bathroom. The other three rooms are also outfitted with antiques, and two of them face onto Baltimore Street. The Elizabeth Thorn Suite is situated at the back of the house, and it's named for the heroic woman who buried numerous men after the Battle of Gettysburg while serving as caretaker of Evergreen Cemetery—and while she was six months pregnant. A large sitting area where guest can relax, read, or socialize and a gorgeous dining room complete the house. The breakfasts that Leslie makes here are so delicious and so many guests requested the recipes that the Grandstaffs decided to publish the most popular recipes in a book, the *Tillie Pierce House Cookbook*. Besides feeding you scrumptious food, the Grandstaffs also have a selection of hospitality baskets they will make up for you, and you can't help but become infected by their genuine love of history while staying in this truly historic home.

EAST OF LINCOLN SQUARE

BRAFFERTON INN $$$
44 York Street
(717) 337-3423, (866) 337-3423
www.brafferton.com
Built in 1786, this stone home is the oldest continuous residence in historic downtown. The inn also includes the carriage house, which was added to the stone house in the 1850s, the Olde Shop annex at 42 York Street, circa 1850–1900, and the Lane Studio building. Listed on the National Register of Historic Places, the house is known to many locals as the Codori House, after the family that lived here for 124 years. (See the Close-up on the Codori House in this chapter for more on the house's history.) The home was bought in 1984 and converted into a bed-and-breakfast in 1986. Innkeepers Joan, Brian, and AmyBeth Hodges purchased the inn in spring 2005.

You'll find antiques, stenciling, and colonial murals throughout the inn, and artist Keith Rocco has turned the parlor into a minigallery of his works. There are twelve rooms and six suites spread out between the three houses. With its original exposed stone walls, open-rafter cathedral ceiling, and wide pine floorboards, the third floor of the stone house brings the house's history to life. Here you'll find the Loft Suite, which is one large room that takes up about ⅔ of the entire floor. The suite includes a queen-size bed, attached tub and shower bathroom, comfy chairs, a small fridge, a wet sink, and another room with a daybed, TV, and desk. A wall-unit air conditioner allows you to control the room's temperature. The second floor of the stone house has three guest rooms or a suite to pick from. The Deck Suite has a private balcony that overlooks the inn's gardens and deck, a queen-size bed and antique maple bureau, a cable TV, an attached double-stall shower bathroom, and a window-unit air conditioner. If you want to stay in an original bedroom, the Olde Master Bedroom fits the bill. This large room boasts a stately hand-carved queen-size cherry rice poster bed, a walnut Victorian dresser, wingback chairs, a nonworking fireplace, and a window-unit air conditioner. The stall shower bathroom is across the hall but it isn't shared with any other guests. Robes are provided for trips back and forth. The Battle Room is also a good choice for the history buff; this is the room that has the minié ball lodged in its fireplace's mantel. The room also has a queen-size cherry sleigh bed, an Edwardian armoire with mirrors, a sitting chair and slipper bench, an attached bathroom with a stall shower, and a window-unit air conditioner. The third room on the second floor is the Michael Hoke Room, a romantic little corner with an iron queen-size bed and a cherry bureau. The room has an attached full tub and shower bath and a window-unit air conditioner.

The Carriage House contains the bulk of the guest accommodations, with one suite and six guest rooms under its roof. Both the Lincoln and the Chamberlain Rooms in the North Wing have antique beds—one double and one twin each—antique dressers, a skylight, comfy chairs for reading in, and window-unit air conditioners. The Brass Room's bathroom, with its stall shower, is located off the floor's hallway, and the full tub and shower bathroom for the Chamberlain Room is also located off the hallway. Although these bathrooms are not attached to the rooms, each is private to its room and not shared with other guests. The South Wing contains the Codori Suite and the Gettys Room, which is a smaller room with a skylight, a queen-size colonial pediment bed, a butter-print Victorian dresser, reading chairs, an attached double-stall shower bathroom, and a window-unit air conditioner. The spacious Codori Suite has a sitting room that contains a queen-size sofa bed, comfy chairs, cable TV, and a master bedroom that has a king-size iron bed. The suite, which also has a skylight, has an attached full tub and shower bath and central air. Both Tillie's Room and the Garden Room are near the house's flower gardens and deck. These quiet rooms have queen-size beds, antique bureaus, comfy chairs, and attached full tub and shower bathrooms. Tillie's Room has a fireplace and central air, and the Garden Room has a window-unit air conditioner. Completing the carriage house lodgings is the Nook, a cozy economy room for a single traveler with an antique double bed, one-person shower stall bathroom, and window-unit air conditioner.

The Olde Shop is the home of the North and South Suites, both on the second floor. As you enter the South Suite through its private entrance, you'll discover a sitting room with a queen-size sofa bed, comfy chairs, and cable TV. The master bedroom reveals a hand-painted queen-size bed and a marble-top bureau, and the attached full tub and shower Jacuzzi bathroom is another door down within the suite. You'll also find window-unit air conditioners throughout the suite. The North Suite has an inviting sitting room with a queen-size sofa bed, comfy chairs, and cable TV as well, but it also boasts a gas fireplace. Its bedroom has a queen-size cherry colonial pediment bed and a matching bureau. The full tub and shower Jacuzzi bathroom is down the hallway within the suite, and there are window-unit air conditioners throughout.

The two rooms and two suites within the Lane Studio building are decorated in Victorian style. The two-room Brafferton Suite on the second floor boasts a king-size four-poster bed, a double sofa bed, comfy chairs, a TV, a see-through fireplace that is useable from both rooms, and central air-conditioning. The suite has an outdoor balcony and a large bathroom with a two-person Jacuzzi with separate shower. The other suite is named after President Eisenhower, who was photographed at the Lane Studio by famed photographer Walter Lane. Within the third-floor Eisenhower Suite, you'll find central air-conditioning, a queen-size four-poster bed, a sitting area with a gas fireplace, a TV, minifridge, and microwave, and a private bath with full shower and tub.

Completing the second floor is Dorothy's Hideaway, named after Dorothy Lane, a photographer in her own right and Walter Lane's wife. This room has a queen-size bed, an armoire, and an overstuffed chair and comes equipped with a TV, microwave, refrigerator, and wall-unit air conditioners. It also has an outdoor balcony and a private bathroom with a Jacuzzi tub for two. On the third floor is the cozy Robert E. Lee Room, which has a queen-size bed, full tub with shower, a gas fireplace, a TV, and wall-unit air conditioners.

Your stay includes a full breakfast served in the 1815 dining room, where the four walls are covered by a folk mural by artist Virginia Jacobs McLaughlin that depicts the area's history. As you admire this unique piece of art, you'll enjoy treats such as stuffed French toast and homemade pas-

Close-up

The Codori House

The Brafferton Inn got its name from Jim and Mary Agard, who opened the home as a bed-and-breakfast in 1986. They named it after Brafferton Hall at the College of William and Mary in Williamsburg, Virginia. But many locals will always think of this place as the Codori House, after the family that made it their home for more than a century.

The home dates from 1786, making this the oldest deeded house in Gettysburg. Michael Hoke was a tanner who worked with the Gettys family, and he purchased the lot the house sits on for "3 pounds, 15 shillings of real gold." In 1796 he transferred ownership of the house to his brother Henry, and since neither Hoke brother had sons who could inherit the property, it was eventually sold out of the family. Nicholas Codori purchased the home in 1843 for $1,600. Codori was a local butcher who had 11 children, thereby needing a large house, so he also bought the property on either side of the house. Behind the house, he built a carriage house and also set up his meat market. Nicholas was a good businessman, and at the beginning of the Civil War, he purchased a farm on Emmitsburg Road that he used to raise livestock and as a slaughterhouse. This farm would become famous during the Battle of Gettysburg; it sits in the middle of the area known as Pickett's Charge.

The Codoris were at their house, not the farm, during the battle. They hid in the basement as bullets whizzed through the floors above them. One of the rooms of the house still has a minie ball embedded in its fireplace mantel. After the battle the home was used as the Catholic chapel since the church was occupied with wounded soldiers.

The Codoris resumed their peaceful existence after the battle, and the house was passed down through generation after generation of Codoris, until it was eventually sold out of the family. The house is still often referred to as either the Hoke-Codori House or just the Codori House. The farm retains the name Codori, and it's a stop on the battlefield tour.

tries. Some of the rooms of the inn can accommodate children age eight and older. Parking is located behind the inn at the parking garage.

KEYSTONE INN BED & BREAKFAST $$
231 Hanover Street
(717) 337-3888
www.keystoneinnbb.com

Flowers are in their full glory at the Keystone Inn Bed & Breakfast. You'll find them outside in the garden, and inside they can be found throughout the house. The inn was built in 1913 by Clayton S. Reaser, a local furniture maker, and the first thing you notice as you approach this late-Victorian three-story brick house is its leaded-glass front door and high-columned wraparound front porch.

Once inside, be sure to take note of the original chestnut and oak gleaming throughout the house—there's an oak and chestnut staircase, chestnut in the high-ceilinged rooms of the first floor, and natural oak in the rest of the house. Each of the five guest rooms and two suites has a private bath, individually controlled air-conditioning, and a reading nook. The Clayton Reaser's Room features the impressive antique bedroom set the Reasers used while living here, including a queen-size solid cherry bed with a 6-foot-high headboard. Completing the room are two rocker recliners, a refrigerator, and a TV, and the private bath has an oversize shower. General Reynold's Room also has a queen-size bed, two rockers (in white wicker), a refrigerator, and a TV, and the added fun of an electric fireplace. Its private bath has a tub and shower. The Michael Bowers Room is pet friendly and features a private veranda with a view of Culp's Hill. It's equipped with a king-size feather bed, a TV, microwave, and refrigerator, and an electric fireplace. General Ewell's Room celebrates the glory of the outside landscaping with its floral decor, and it is outfitted with a king-size bed, stuffed rockers, a TV, and a refrigerator. The General Johnson's Room is billed as an economy room because it doesn't offer a TV and its private bath is across the hall, but it has hidden charms. Its queen-size Reaser Furniture bedroom suite, which was made in Gettysburg, features reading lights in the headboard and a cedar closet in the footboard.

Both of the Keystone Inn's suites can accommodate a family of four or five and come with TV, microwave, and refrigerator. General Greene's Suite has a king-size bed and Lane recliners in the bedroom and a double-size sleeper sofa in the sitting room, while General Early's suite has a king-size bed and a queen-size sleeper sofa in the sitting room. General Early's Suite also has a Jacuzzi tub, a table with two chairs, a coffeemaker, and an outside entrance.

A full country breakfast is served to guests in the dining room. You might choose from fruits, muffins, juices, coffee, tea, Denver French toast, waffles made from scratch, pancakes, scrambled eggs, oatmeal, and a variety of meats. The inn has off-street parking, wireless Internet, and a courtesy phone available to guests.

RED BUD INN AT THE HISTORIC
ISAAC MILLER FARM $$
240 Cavalry Field Road
(717) 334-1909
www.red-budinn.com
The Red Bud Inn sits on 13 acres only minutes east of Gettysburg. The grounds border the East Cavalry Field battlefield, and during the Battle of Gettysburg, this small farm was turned into a Confederate hospital for Stuart's cavalry. Be sure to enjoy a leisurely stroll around the tranquil grounds and visit the barn, where there are six horse stalls for overnight horse stabling.

The addition to the farm was added in 1989. You'll find two guest rooms, each with a queen-size bed, private bath, and walk-in closet. A three-bedroom suite is in the original house. There's also a common room, where you can read or watch TV. Innkeepers Peggy and Dennis Bear welcome children age 14 and older. For breakfast, which is included in the daily rate, guests receive a gift certificate for a buffet breakfast at a local family restaurant.

WEST OF LINCOLN SQUARE

CASHTOWN INN $$$
1325 Old Route 30, Cashtown
(717) 334-9722, (800) 367-1797
www.cashtowninn.com
The Cashtown Inn was built around 1797 as the first stagecoach stop west of Gettysburg. It's located 8 miles west of town on Old Route 30, and in 1863 the inn was used by Gen. A. P. Hill as his Confederate headquarters while the 22,000 men of his Third Corp camped throughout town. If you think the inn looks familiar, it very well might. It has appeared in the movie *Gettysburg* and in the Mark Nesbit book and video *Ghosts of Gettysburg*. It's also been featured on the cover of *Blue and Gray* magazine, in the video *Haunted Gettysburg*, and in the book *Haunts of the Cashtown Inn*. Civil War artist Dale Gallon also depicts the inn in his limited-edition print *Serious Work Ahead*, which shows Confederate generals Lee and Hill meeting on July 1, 1863. This is the same scene created by artist Mort Künstler in his 1998 painting *Distant Thunder*.

The inn, along with its fine-dining restaurant and tavern, is decorated with Civil War art and antiques, and the guest rooms are original to the 1797 house. The most famous guest room is the Heth Room, with its antique double bed. The other three rooms have queen-size beds, and you can choose between an iron bed in the Pettigrew Room, a four-poster bed and a view of South Mountain in the Imboden Room, or a lace canopy and a view of the village of Cashtown in the A. P. Hill Room. The inn has three two-room suites in addition to its four guest rooms. All accommodations come with private bath, clock radio, and air-conditioning. The General Lee Suite is located under the eaves on the inn's third floor. Outfitted with a TV, VCR, refrigerator, and couch in the living room, this suite has a king-size bed, and it's where Sam Elliott stayed while filming the movie *Gettysburg*. The Pender and Anderson Suites are identical and next door to each other at the rear of the inn. You'll be very comfortable in either suite, with a private entrance and porch, a queen-size four-poster bed in the bedroom, and a couch in the living room. Groups of four to eight can rent both suites for a private retreat. Children age 12 and older are welcome in the rooms, but those younger are welcome only in the Pender and Anderson Suites.

Breakfast is included with your stay, and it's a fully served meal on the weekends and a continental breakfast on weekdays. For dining choices during the day, lighter fare and a more casual ambience are served up in the tavern, while the formal dining room is the perfect spot for an elegant evening. For a full description of the inn's culinary delights, see the Restaurants chapter. Guests are welcome to walk off their meals in the inn's gardens, where the chefs pick the fresh herbs used in the restaurant's dishes. Many a guest has found relaxation by sitting and swinging on the front porch while admiring the beautiful vistas around the inn. For guests who wish to have a weekend of activity, the inn offers many packages and theme weekends, such as murder-mystery weekends and ghost-hunters weekends.

THE FAIRFIELD INN 1757 $$$
15 West Main Street, Fairfield
(717) 334-8868, (717) 642-5410
www.thefairfieldinn.com

The Fairfield Inn was built in 1757 to serve as the Mansion House of Squire Miller, an original founder of the town of Fairfield. It was believed that the Mansion House first began welcoming guests when it became an inn and stagecoach stop in 1823. But in November 2004, a colonial-era tavern license for the inn dated 1786 was discovered, making this one of the oldest taverns still operating in America. The inn has welcomed such famous Americans as Patrick Henry, Thaddeus Stevens, Gen. Robert E. Lee, Gen. J. E. B. Stuart, and Ike and Mamie Eisenhower.

When the fighting at Gettysburg ended, the Confederate army retreated west through Fairfield, and many homes, including the Mansion House, were used as field hospitals. The Fairfield Inn was operating as an inn, so General Lee and other Confederates stopped here for food. And the house was also a stop on the Underground Railroad. With all this history it's no wonder that the Fairfield Inn is on the National Register of Historic Places.

Innkeepers Joan and Sal Chandon, who previously owned the Doubleday Inn (see the Doubleday Inn entry earlier in this chapter), began an extensive renovation to the inn in February 2003. Five years later, Joan and Sal are thrilled with the results—five of the six guest rooms are completed and hosting guests. All of the inn's suites have private baths, air-conditioning, and cable TV. And there are plenty of places to warm up—the inn has eight fireplaces. Wireless high-speed Internet service is available throughout the inn.

Although the amenities at the Fairfield are totally modern, the accommodations are steeped in history. One room is named for Patrick Henry, famous for the quote "Give me liberty or give me death." He often stayed in this very second-floor room while visiting his aunt, who once owned the home. Filled with antiques, the Patrick Henry Room has a full-size iron bed and a claw-foot tub as well as a separate shower. Another guest room is named after J. E. B. Stuart, who stayed in the room in 1862 while on a Confederate mission, and who revisited the inn on July 4, 1863, as part of the Confederate retreat from Gettysburg. This room has a queen-size bed, a seating area with a foldout full-size sofa, and a whirlpool tub. The Major Starr Guest Room is named after Sam Starr, a dragoon who fought in the Battle of Fairfield, which unfolded directly behind the inn's property on July 3, 1863. This battle secured the Hagerstown Road for the Confederates, which helped facilitate their retreat from Gettysburg. In this room you'll find a full-size Lincoln suite antique bed and a whirlpool tub. The Grumble

Jones Room is named for the Confederate general who led his troops to victory during the Battle of Fairfield, and it features a lace-topped, full-size four-poster bed and a whirlpool tub.

The Three Colonels Guest Suite is named for three Confederate colonels who were treated at the inn when it served as a field hospital during the Battle of Gettysburg. Situated on the third floor, the suite has a private balcony that overlooks Fairfield's main street, which is lined with historic homes. It contains a parlor that boasts a trundle bed, a sitting area, a separate bedroom with a queen-size bed, and a claw-foot tub with separate shower.

Breakfast is served in the restaurant in the original Mansion House. The inn's two chefs and their staffs present mouthwatering meals that can be enjoyed beside a blazing fire in the winter months or on the patio garden off the restaurant in warmer weather. To satisfy your culinary needs throughout the day, lunch and dinner are available at the Squire Miller Tavern and the Mansion House Restaurant. (See the Restaurants chapter for more on the Mansion House Restaurant.) The tavern is on the first floor of the Mansion House, and it has seating for about 25 people. The inn also offers dinner theater, where you can hear ghost stories and see a re-creation of a Civil War séance (see the Gettysburg Civil War Era Dinner Theatre entry in The Arts chapter).

GETTYSBURG POND VIEW FARM
BED & BREAKFAST $
530 Carr Hill Road
(717) 642-9493, (877) 888-1957
www.bbonline.com/pa/pondview

Innkeepers Peter and Karen Samuels welcome you to their Civil War–era brick farmhouse. This cozy bed-and-breakfast has central air-conditioning and three guest rooms. Each has a queen-size bed, with the Brass Room having a brass bed and the Canopy Room having—you guessed it—a canopy bed. Both rooms come with a private bath. The Corner Room has a very large private bath that is down the hall from the room.

Because the bed-and-breakfast is small, Peter and Karen can give guests special attention.

One wonderful way they do this is by serving a fabulous breakfast of lox and bagels, muffins, or omelets on their wraparound, glassed-in porch.

Also due to the size of the farmhouse, Peter and Karen do not allow guests younger than age eight. This farm 15 minutes from Gettysburg is surrounded by countryside. Take time to walk the grounds and enjoy the serenity of the pond. And be sure to admire the horses, the sheep, and Coco, the goat. If you're bringing your horse, overnight horse boarding in open pasture may be available.

GRANITE HILL BED & BREAKFAST $$
Granite Hill Camping Resort
3340 Fairfield Road
(717) 642-8749, (800) 642-TENT
www.granitehillcampingresort.com

One of the best perks of staying at this bed-and-breakfast is that you also get access to all the amenities the camping resort has to offer, including minigolf, fishing, boating, tennis, volleyball, and more. (See the Campgrounds and RV Parks chapter for info on the camping resort.) Here you experience personal attention while enjoying resort-hotel amenities, and you do it all while staying in a beautifully restored brick farmhouse that dates from the 1860s. The original owner of the farm was Felix Drais, who was wounded in the Wheatfield during the second day of the Battle of Gettysburg. If you ask for a tour of the attic, you can see his signature etched in the wood.

Four guest rooms are available in this historic home, each with a ceiling fan. Guests share a powder room and one full bath, which is equipped with a shower and tub, sink, and commode. A kitchen is also available, and guests partake of their breakfasts in the dining nook. Relaxing and socializing is done in the great room and library, as well as outdoors on the porch.

HERR TAVERN & PUBLICK HOUSE $$$–$$$$
900 Chambersburg Road
(717) 334-4332, (800) 362-9849
www.herrtavern.com

Thomas Sweeney built a tavern and publick house on this site in 1815. In 1828 the establishment was sold to Frederick Herr, and the business was run by the Herr family for almost 40 years, and sometime during this time, the house was a stop on the Underground Railroad. The ridge the house stands on came to be known as Herr's Ridge, and the Battle of Gettysburg began in the fields around the tavern buildings. The publick house was used as the first Confederate hospital during the battle, and much of the house was converted into operating rooms. After the war it became a boardinghouse for the many visitors to the battlefields. After that it became an operating farm, and then rental property, which is what it was when current owner Steven Wolf bought it in 1977. Steven researched the history of the house and restored it to its original purpose, opening for business in May 1978. Everything went well until June 1987, when the original house was nearly leveled by a windstorm that hit Gettysburg. Today the house, which is on the Register of Historic Places, has been faithfully restored to its nineteenth-century appearance.

But Steven didn't stop at restoration. In 1997 he added a banquet room and seven more guest rooms, and in 2001 he purchased an adjacent property and added an annex. The annex is home to four unique guest suites, and this sprawling bed-and-breakfast has a total of 16 luxurious guest rooms. Suites 1 through 5 are in the original historic building, Suites 6 through 12 are in the wing built in 1997 off the original building, and Suites 14 through 18 are in the adjacent annex. If you're wondering how 16 rooms are numbered one through 18, there isn't a number 13 suite and Suite 12 is the massage room, where you can be pampered by the in-house masseuse. Each suite is decorated with period pieces and has a private bath, fireplace, cable TV, air-conditioning, and telephone with answering machine, and most have a queen-size bed, double Jacuzzi tub with shower, and sitting area. The romantic Garden Room has an oversize round bed. Room 14 has a ground-level entrance and is wheelchair accessible.

But some of the rooms here boast more than fine furniture and accoutrements. Some of the rooms are haunted. It's no wonder when you realize what hospitals were like in the days of the Civil War. It was reported that amputated limbs were thrown out a window into a waiting wagon for burial. Sterilization techniques didn't exist, and there were few painkillers. Who knows how many spent their last days or hours during the wretched heat of July 1863 at this spot. There are numerous stories of ghost sightings here by Steven, by the staff, and by the guests. Ask around and you'll hear many firsthand ghostly encounters, such as things moving, voices heard when there's no one there, and lights turning on and off, just to give a few examples. Be prepared if you stay in Rooms 1, 2, 3, or 4—they seem to have the most ghostly activities.

Your included breakfast is served at the posted time, and continental breakfast is available at other times as needed. The inn does not accommodate children younger than age 12, and there is a strict no-smoking rule—you'll be charged a $75 service fee if you smoke in the rooms. The Herr Tavern & Publick House offers gourmet dining in one of five dining areas in the main house, and each room accommodates 20 to 35 diners. There is an extensive wine cellar, and guests of the inn may arrange to dine privately amongst the 3,000-bottle collection. (For more on the Herr Tavern restaurant, see the Restaurants chapter.) The Livery is a casual-atmosphere tavern where you can get food inside or outside on the deck (see the Nightlife chapter).

i The lobby of the James Gettys Hotel is one of the few places in town where you'll find a brochure for Gettysburg's self-guided walking tour.

JAMES GETTYS HOTEL $$$
27 Chambersburg Street
(717) 337-1334, (888) 900-5275
www.jamesgettyshotel.com
With red awnings covering each window, the James Gettys Hotel looks as it did in the 1920s. As you enter this fully renovated circa-1804 four-story historic hotel, you're gazing upon its original chestnut staircase, which has been impeccably restored. Ring the bell at the desk if you don't see

anyone around—one of the owners is also co-owner of Lord Nelson's Gallery, an art gallery next door. (For more on Lord Nelson's Gallery, see The Arts chapter.) A chair and a table with selected brochures on it complete the lobby.

A climb up the magnificent chestnut staircase will lead you to 11 suites, each with a sitting area, a kitchenette with a full-size refrigerator, stove, and microwave, a bedroom with a queen-size or full-size bed, and a private bath. Each suite is named for a business that existed in or near the building in the past 200 years. Guest-room amenities are sure to please even the most discriminating traveler. They include complimentary fresh-ground coffees and imported British teas, fine toilet soaps, fresh-cut seasonal flowers, additional pillows, and Egyptian-cotton bath towels. Guests also receive evening turndown service, and morning begins with continental breakfast served in your suite. The hotel staff will also make your travel and tour arrangements, and same-day laundry and dry-cleaning services are available upon request. And here's a real benefit to readers who will be traveling with children—there's no charge for children younger than age 12 who are sharing a room with parents. There is, however, a maximum of four persons per suite, depending on the suite you choose. The hotel also offers extended-stay vacation packages.

This building is on the National Register of Historic Places, and it does indeed have a full and varied history. It was originally known as the Union Hotel, and it served as a hospital for the wounded during the Battle of Gettysburg. By April 1888 Gettysburg had become a popular tourist spot, and the City Hotel, as it was then named, readied for the influx of visitors for the battle's 25th anniversary by expanding to accommodate 250 guests. Sometime after this the hotel was renamed the James Gettys Hotel, and it enjoyed a thriving business until the 1960s, when motels gained in popularity and the hotel closed its doors. The building functioned as an apartment house until the 1980s and then served as a youth hostel for 10 years. The current innkeepers bought it in 1995, revived the name, and began the hotel's transformation back to its 1920s look. Besides Lord Nelson's Gallery, the Blue Parrot Bistro (see the Restaurants chapter for more information) is also located within this historic building.

QUITE THE STIR BED AND BREAKFAST $$$
500 West Middle Street
(717) 798-1788, (866) 550-0894
www.quitethestir.com

This cozy bungalow with two rooms for rent re-creates the era of the 1940s, and authentic clothing from both the WWII and Civil War eras is available for you to wear out on the town if you wish (and if it fits!). If you enjoy immersing yourself in the WWII era, be sure to use the "built-in-the-wall" fold-down ironing board and iron. Although the innkeepers have you feeling like it's the 1940s, modern amenities abound throughout the bungalow, including air-conditioning, high-speed Internet access, and HDTV.

A continental breakfast, which is in reality a brunch and high tea combined, is served in the elegant dining room. You have the choice of dining by candlelight or chandelier as you enjoy fruit, yogurt, scones, quiches, pastries, and more on fine china with silver service. Be sure to wander into the kitchen to admire its original woodwork and steel porcelain sink. There's also a parlor and study for you to explore, and the bathroom is totally retro. It features a Swarovski chandelier, a pedestal sink, and black-and-white tile flooring. The feel of the forties is carried outside the bungalow onto its front and rear porches, which are screened in and complete with ceiling fans for those warm summer months. To complete your experience, be sure to stroll through the small yard to see the innkeepers' 1940s Victory Garden.

Although there are two rooms available, the bungalow is rented to only one party at a time so guests' privacy is ensured. Special packages are available, as are extended stays at reduced rates. Accommodations for children are limited, and pets and smoking are both not allowed.

GUESTHOUSES

CANTER BERRY TAILS APPLE RANCH
989 Center Mills Road, Aspers
(717) 677-8900
www.farmstay.us

This fully furnished, 10-room, 4-bedroom, 1½-bath 1822 center-hall colonial farmhouse, which is owned by Ted and Sandy Abahazy, can be rented for $550 for two nights on a weekend to $1,200 for a full-week stay. Once you check in, the run of the house is yours; no one enters the house until you check out. Sitting on an apple orchard surrounded by 35 acres and located only 8 miles north of Gettysburg, the house is often rented by Gettysburg College alumni for reunion weekends.

The house is beautifully furnished with antiques in a country colonial motif, and each of the four bedrooms has a theme. The North Room, with stenciling throughout, has a four-poster queen-size bed, and the South Room has a canopy queen-size bed. Both the North and South Rooms have mannequins outfitted in ladies' dresses from the Civil War era. The Garden Room has a full bed and is filled with all things related to gardening. A three-quarter bed (a little shorter than a full-size bed) is in the Hunting and Fishing Room, which is often used as a child's room. In addition to the modern kitchen and baths, you'll also find a living room, dining room, laundry room, and game room, which has chess, many board games, and a record player that actually plays 45s and 33s (records are supplied also—you can give the kids a history lesson while you're being nostalgic). Don't worry about doing laundry— towels left in the laundry basket on the front porch are replaced by fresh ones daily, and one extra set of sheets is also available. You don't need to bring any essentials except food, and Ted and Sandy will be glad to direct you to the local grocery. The house comes with a TV with basic cable and a phone for local calls only. It also has central air-conditioning with separate controls for the upstairs and downstairs levels of the home.

If you're feeling adventurous, be sure to ask to see the alpacas that are raised on the neighboring farm by Ted and Sandy's daughter. Or visit the henhouse and retrieve a few eggs for your morning meal. Guests may also pick their own apples, with the first bushel being free of charge. Corn and pumpkins are also available for harvesting.

THE COTTAGE AT GETTYSBURG
770 Goldenville Road
(570) 622-2460
www.thecottageatgettysburg.com

Located halfway between Gettysburg and Biglerville to the north, the Cottage accommodates eight guests with a master bedroom on the first floor and two bedrooms upstairs. The upper-level bedrooms are named the Masculine Upstairs and Feminine Upstairs rooms. The Masculine Room is set up dorm style, with three twin beds and a built-in closet, and it's decorated in contemporary style with hardwood floors. Floral designs on the bedding of the double and twin beds in the Feminine Room earn this cheery room its name. It also has hardwood floors, a built-in closet, and an antique makeup table with bench and mirror. Both rooms have two windows, one of which is in a cozy alcove, that provide a lot of light and opportunities to witness nature in the countryside around you. The master bedroom has a four-poster double bed and a walk-in closet as well as a rocking chair and side table.

A living room, kitchen, and bathroom are also located on the first floor, and there's a relaxing porch where you can sit and admire the expansive views. The owners of the cottage live in Pottsville, Pennsylvania (about 100 miles from Gettysburg), and they ask that you call the above number between 9:00 a.m. and 9:00 p.m. to make arrangements for your stay. The rate is $150 per night.

CRICKET HOUSE AT GETTYSBURG
162 East Middle Street
(717) 337-0941
www.crickethouseatgettysburg.com

Located near the Culp's Hill area of the battlefield, Cricket House is an oasis of Victorian splendor. The house restoration completed by owners John and Debi Pedersen won the Historic Gettysburg–

Adams County 2006 Historic Restoration Award, and when you view the home, it's easy to see why. The first thing you notice is the home's ornamental cedar and copper roofs, and the inside is filled with antiques and tile and wood accents of the Victorian era. Modern amenities are far from lacking among this old-time charm. The first floor has a full modern kitchen with a cozy sitting nook, a comfortable living room, and a bath that contains a steam room. Upstairs you'll find a luxurious master suite with a separate sitting area and a bath with a whirlpool tub. Three cable TVs can be found throughout the house, as well as wireless Internet access. Guests can take advantage of this house's location in the heart of the historic district to walk to many historic sites. When you want to relax after returning from your outings, the backyard features a privacy fence that allows you to fully enjoy the enclosed spa and garden. Cricket House can accommodate up to six people, and it can be rented on a daily or weekly basis. Daily rates start at $175, and the weekly rental fee is $975.

LITTLE ROUND TOP FARM
991 Taneytown Road
(717) 334-2100
www.dobbinhouse.com/lrtf01.htm
This five-bedroom farmhouse is located near Little Round Top, and a walking trail on the property leads you to where Gen. Joshua Chamberlain led his men in the downhill charge that kept the Confederates from gaining access to the rear flank of the Union line during the Battle of Gettysburg. Built in 1858, the farmhouse predates the Civil War, and the home was occupied by the Weikert family during the time of the battle.

Today the farmhouse is part of the Dobbin House complex, and the Dobbin House Restaurant about 2 miles away on Steinwehr Avenue is where your included breakfast is served. (See the Restaurants chapter for more on the restaurant, and see the Gettystown Inn B&B write-up earlier in this chapter if you prefer to stay at the Steinwehr Avenue location.) A weeklong Sunday-to-Sunday stay is required to rent the farmhouse, which has a living room, dining room, full kitchen, laundry room, and 1½ baths. Able to sleep 10, three of its five bedrooms have queen-size beds while one has a double bed and the other has two twin beds. Amenities include a working gas fireplace and a cable-equipped TV in the living room, and the kitchen is fully outfitted. Bed and bath linens are provided, and the laundry room includes a washer and dryer. The home sits on 12 acres that offer a large pond to explore, granite boulders to climb, and the walking trail mentioned above to meander. Weekly rentals run $1650.

QUAKER VALLEY ORCHARDS & GUEST HOUSE
315 Quaker Valley Road, Biglerville
(717) 677-7351
www.quakervalleyorchards.com
This fully furnished guesthouse is attached to the owners' 1882 brick home that sits on a 230-acre fruit farm 10 miles north of Gettysburg. The owners are Winn and Winifred Schulteis, and the farm has been in the Schulteis family since 1963. The guesthouse sleeps 6 to 10 people, and the rate is $90 per night with a two-night minimum, or it can be rented for $575 per week. To reach the guesthouse, head north from Lincoln Square on Route 34 (Biglerville Road). At the traffic light in Biglerville at York and Main Streets, continue straight 2 miles north and turn left onto Quaker Valley Road. Quaker Valley is the first farm on the right.

The air-conditioned guesthouse was added on to the original home in the 1980s. It has its own private entrance, and inside you'll discover a large living room with a queen-size sleeper sofa and a spacious bedroom with two double beds. There's also a bath and kitchen, and the house's TV has an outdoor antenna and a VCR. Besides linens the Schulteises provide you with an iron and ironing board, a hair dryer, a clock radio, and coffee and teas. All guests need to bring is food, and you're invited to pick some of the farm's fresh fruit and vegetables. The farm has three ponds, and one is a fishing pond. There's also a phone that guests can use for local calls. Smoking and pets are prohibited, and credit cards are not accepted.

CAMPGROUNDS AND RV PARKS

Camping around the Gettysburg area offers you the chance to sleep under the same starlit skies that Civil War soldiers gazed upon so many years ago. Here you can imagine yourself among those men, waiting for dawn so the day's battle could begin. This is especially easy during June, when the campfires of Civil War reenactors illuminate the grounds.

Along with this chance to reconnect with history, Gettysburg campgrounds and RV parks offer affordable lodging with all the modern amenities. You'll find full-facility restrooms, including hot showers, and laundry facilities, and each campground and park offers a pool, a game room, and a playground in addition to myriad recreational activities. Camp stores are there in case you forgot anything, with gift shops to round out your shopping expedition. Bus tours to the Gettysburg battlefield and to Washington, D.C., are offered, and there are planned activities every weekend in season. But don't think that the campgrounds are interchangeable—each is unique, and each has something special to offer.

None of the campgrounds is more than 6 miles from Lincoln Square, with Artillery Ridge and Round Top to the south, Gettysburg, KOA, and Granite Hill to the west, and Drummer Boy to the east. Pets are welcome at the campgrounds but not in the rental units.

The rates listed are for the 2008 season. You'll pay more if visiting during some special weekends, such as around the reenactment. Expect to be required to stay a minimum of two nights during the summer season, and sometimes a three- or four-night minimum might be in effect.

ARTILLERY RIDGE CAMPGROUND & NATIONAL RIDING STABLES
610 Taneytown Road
(717) 334-1288, (877) 335-5596,
(866) 932–2674
www.artilleryridge.com

Artillery Ridge, which is open April through November and located about a mile south of town on Route 134 (Taneytown Road), is the home of both the National Riding Stables (see the Gettysburg National Military Park chapter) and the Gettysburg Miniature Battlefield Diorama (see the Attractions chapter).

Here you'll find 135 hookup sites, 45 non-hookup sites, and 3 cabins to rent. If you have access to the Internet, the Web site has a great map of the campground. Rates are for two people at one camping site. A site without hookups is $31 a night or $186 a week. If you want a site with water and electric, the cost is $39 a night or $234 a week. If you also want sewer hookup, the price is $42 a night or $252 a week. There are large open tenting grounds with some secluded sites, and every tent site has a picnic table and a fire ring. Internet access is available. The log cabins sleep either four or six persons and include a ceiling fan, air-conditioning, electricity, an outside water tap, a porch and chairs, a picnic table and fire ring, and a driveway. The four-person cabin has a double bed and a set of twin bunk beds while the six-person cabin has a queen-size bed and two sets of bunk beds. Cooking and pets are prohibited within the cabins. The four-person cabin rents for $57.00 a night, and the six-person cabin runs $79.50 per night.

Since this is also the site of the National Riding Stables, you can bring your own horse or rent one. The campground offers a two-hour battlefield tour on horseback that covers the history of the three-day battle (see the Attractions chapter for details).

Recreational activities here include fishing (no license required) or paddleboating on the property's pond and playing horseshoes, basketball, or volleyball. There are also pony rides for the little ones and church services on Sunday. You might find bingo being played at the pavilion or maybe you'd rather catch that night's movie. And be sure to check out the planned activities if you're staying over the weekend—maybe you'll take a hayride, attend an ice-cream social, or lose yourself in a Western- or 1950s-themed weekend.

DRUMMER BOY CAMPING RESORT
1300 Hanover Road
(717) 334-3277, (800) 293-2808
www.drummerboycamping.com
Drummer Boy is the largest campground in the area: It has more than 400 sites. But you won't feel crowded here—the tent sites, deluxe full-service cottages, and camping cabins sit on 95 acres of woodlands. The place is so big that you can rent a golf cart in order to zip around the campground during your stay. And there's a daily shuttle to downtown Gettysburg when you're ready to visit town.

Open the first Friday in April until the last Sunday in October, Drummer Boy also added a swimming-pool complex with waterslide in 2005, and high-speed wireless Internet can be accessed from your site. Good old-fashioned fun is also at your fingertips, with volleyball, horseshoes, basketball, minigolf, and a walking trail available. There are nightly movies in the minitheater from June through September, and fishing (no license required) at the pond. There's also a snack bar, and church services are held on Sunday. The Web site has a great map of the campground and also offers virtual tours, so check it out if you get a chance.

A site without hookups is $47 a night or $257 a week; one with water and electric is $56 a night or $297 a week, one with water, electric, and cable is $58 a night or $311 a week, and a site with water, electric, sewer, and cable is $60 a night or $325 a week. Rates are for two people at one camping site. For $85 a night or $500 a week, you can rent a one-room camping cabin, with a double bed and one set of twin bunk beds, electricity, a dorm-size refrigerator, and heating and air-conditioning. A two-room camping cabin costs $100 a night or $605 a week and comes with a double bed and two sets of twin bunk beds, electricity, a dorm-size refrigerator, and heating and air-conditioning. There are six one-room and six two-room cabins, none of which have cooking facilities. Outside each cabin is a charcoal grill, picnic table, and water faucet.

Drummer Boy also has three levels of cottages available, all of which come outfitted with dishes, pots, pans, and utensils. Log cottages sleep six and rent for $175 a night or $1,005 a week. The main room has a queen-size bed, a dining table, and seating, and a separate bedroom has two sets of twin bunk beds. There's also a bathroom, kitchenette, heat, air-conditioning, and cable TV. A kitchenette is equipped with a dorm-size fridge, two-burner stove top, microwave, and coffeemaker.

Log cottages with a loft area sleep eight and rent for $195 a night or $1,095 a week. They include a queen-size bed in the downstairs bedroom, a full bed in the loft bedroom, a queen-size sofa sleeper in the living room, a second loft area, and a spacious furnished deck. The loft cottages include electricity, water, heat, air-conditioning, a full bathroom with flushing toilet, tub, and shower, color TV, DVD player, linens, a full-size stove, refrigerator, microwave, coffeemaker, and toaster. Outside you'll find a picnic table and a fire ring.

The three-bedroom deluxe cottages can accommodate up to eight people, and they come with a large main area equipped with a futon, an LCD TV, and a dining table with seating. The main bedroom has a queen-size bed, while the second bedroom has a full-size bed, and the third bedroom has one bunk bed. Deluxe cottages include a bathroom with shower, a kitchenette, heat, air-conditioning, and cable TV. Inside cooking facilities include a full-size refrigerator, a four-burner stove top, a microwave oven, and a coffeemaker. The deluxe cottages rent for $250 a night or $1,680 per week.

Depending upon when you're camping at Drummer Boy, your weekend planned activities might be a treasure hunt, a NASCAR race, or a beach luau.

GETTYSBURG CAMPGROUND
2030 Fairfield Road
(717) 334-3304, (888) 879-2241
www.gettysburgcampground.com
Gettysburg Campground is located on Marsh Creek, the western boundary during the Battle of Gettysburg. It's also located adjacent to the Black Horse Tavern, a historic landmark that was used as an inn and hospital during the Civil War years. In June you can be transported back to those days as you observe Civil War reenactors camping on the grounds.

Open April through November, the campground has 260 sites and offers RV repairs on-site. While staying here, you're a mere 10 miles from the South Mountain Fairgrounds, home of the South Mountain Fair and the National Apple Harvest Festival (see the Annual Events and Festivals chapter). There's also a daily shuttle bus to downtown Gettysburg during the summer.

When you want to relax at the campground, you can enjoy the ice-cream parlor or take in a movie. For those who want more activity, there's a ball field, shuffleboard, minigolf, creek stocked with fish (no license required), volleyball, and horseshoes available. Planned weekend activities such as a sock hop, a night of ghost stories, a fishing contest, or a crab feast are sure to round out your stay.

All sites have a picnic table and a fire ring. A site without hookups is $32 a night or $192 a week; a site with water and electric is $37 a night or $222 a week. Having a site with water, electric, and sewer will run you $39 a night or $234 a week, and if you want 50-amp electric, there's a $4 fee per day. Rates are for four people at one camping site.

There are also two cabins and two cottages available for rent. Outside of each is a picnic table and a fire ring for cooking, and you supply your own linens. The cabins are $67 per night and they have one full-size bed and one set of bunk beds

in one room, a small refrigerator, a small table with two stools, and heat.

The cottages rent for $135 per night. One cottage has a full-size bed and the other has a queen-size bed. Both cottages have heat, air-conditioning, two sets of bunk beds in a separate room, full private bathroom with shower, a table and chairs, refrigerator, stove top, microwave, coffeemaker, toaster, dishes, pots and pans, and utensils.

GETTYSBURG KOA KAMPGROUND
20 Knox Road
(717) 642-5713, (800) 562-1869
www.koa.com
Open April through October, the Gettysburg KOA Kampground has 100 private wooded sites as well as air-conditioned cottages and cabins. Be sure to check out the Kamper Kitchen, which is located at the pavilion and outfitted with a stove, sink, and counter space. You might also want to head to the pavilion to take advantage of the inexpensive all-you-can-eat pancake breakfast that's held every summer weekend. Campers will also find minigolf, horseshoes, bike rentals, shuffleboard, and nature trails to fill up their days. A history film is shown nightly, and a shuttle to and from town is available twice a day for a fee. Weekly planned activities include a Civil War–era fashion show, candlelit ghost walks through the campground, and the chance to experience living history by observing Civil War encampments.

A campsite without any hookups is around $45 a night, and a pull-through site with all amenities will cost you around $60 a night. Rates are for two adults and two children younger than age 13 at one camping site.

The campground's 16 one-room and two-room Kamping Kabins, which rent for $50 to $85 per night, are equipped with air-conditioning, heat, a porch swing, a picnic table, a fire ring with grill top, and a charcoal grill. Pets are allowed in the cabins for a $10 fee. There are also four Kamping Kottages. The basic camping cottages have all the amenities the cabins have plus a bathroom, and they rent for $70 to $97 per night. The Deluxe Kamping Kottages also have a bathroom with shower; a propane fireplace; a kitchenette with refrigerator, stove top, coffeemaker, toaster, microwave, pots and pans, dishes, cooking and eating utensils, and dish towels; and a dining area with a log table and chairs. The deluxe cottage is $100 to $149 per night. No pets are allowed in the cottages, and there's a two-night minimum stay.

There are also two Kamping Lodges available for rent. Each has a complete bathroom with shower; a kitchenette with refrigerator, stove top, coffeemaker, toaster, microwave, pots and pans, dishes, cooking and eating utensils, and dish towels; a dining area with log table and chairs; wood-frame beds; air-conditioning and ceiling fans; heat; a porch swing and a picnic table; and a fire ring with a grill top. Renting a lodge will cost you $120 to $160 per night. No pets are allowed, and there's a two-night minimum stay.

GRANITE HILL CAMPING RESORT
3340 Fairfield Road
(717) 642-8749, (800) 642-TENT
www.granitehillcampingresort.com
Granite Hill sits on a farm that was granted from Penn's Charter in the late eighteenth century and was called the Drais Farm. The owner at the time of the Battle of Gettysburg was Felix Drais, who was wounded while fighting in the Wheatfield on July 2. The bank barn that sits on the property was used to shelter wounded soldiers during the battle, and General Lee's retreat on July 4 passed directly by Granite Hill on what is now Route 116. The Drais Farm became the property of the Cornett family in 1972 and is the only Gettysburg Civil War farm to become an RV park. In 2008 the farmhouse was converted into a four-bedroom bed-and-breakfast (see the Bed-and-Breakfasts and Guesthouses chapter).

Open April through October, the campground has 300 sites on 150 acres of woodlands, meadows, and rolling hills, where you can camp in your own RV or tent or stay in one of their rustic cabins. This is the site of the Gettysburg Bluegrass Festivals, which are held in May and August (see the Annual Events and Festivals chapter). Adventure Golf is an 18-hole state-of-the-art minigolf course sculpted from a stone mountain overlooking the campground's Bass Lake (for more on the Adventure Golf, see the Kidstuff chapter). The golf is challenging, fun for kids and adults, and open to the public. Kayaks and paddleboats are also available for rent at Bass Lake, and there's a trout pond for fishing (no license required). Shuffleboard, tennis, softball, horseshoes, volleyball, and basketball add to your recreational choices, and there's also a snack bar available for when you need to refuel. Wireless Internet service is available, and planned weekend activities run the gamut from hayrides to a trout derby to ice-cream socials and hoedowns to pig roasts.

A site without any hookups is $29 a night or $143 a week, and one with water and electric runs $34 a night or $175 a week. A site with water, electric, and sewer costs $37 a night or $192 a week. Rates are for two people at one camping site. There is also a two-room cabin available that rents for $71 a night or $400 a week. It has one double bed and two sets of bunk beds and comes equipped with a heater, fan, picnic table, and outdoor grill.

ROUND TOP CAMPGROUND
180 Knight Road
(717) 334-9565
www.roundtopcamp.com
This is the only Gettysburg campground that is open year-round. When you camp here, you're on the battlefield at the south end of Big Round Top. The campground has 260 sites as well as cabins and cottages. Permanent sites are also available. The rentals have heat and air-conditioning, and the lodge has a lounge for you to relax in. For your convenience liquid propane gas is sold here. When you want to relax, you can play basketball, shuffleboard, tennis, or minigolf on the one-acre 18-hole course. You'll also find a snack bar and pavilions, and church services are held on Sunday during the season.

Campsites without hookups go for $22 a night or $132 a week; one with water will cost $35 a night or $210 a week. Sites with water, electric, and sewer are $38 a night or $228 a week. There are also sites with water, electric, sewer, and cable, which are $42 a night or $252 a week. Water, electric, sewer, cable, and a 50-amp hookup at your site will run you $45 a night or $270 a week. Rates are for two adults at one camping site. Cabins that sleep four persons are available for $57 a night. Downstairs are a double bed and a small table and chairs while the crawl-in loft upstairs has twin beds. The cabins have heat and air-conditioning, and outside there's a water hookup, a fire ring, and a picnic table.

Three sizes of cottages are available for rent. All provide fully equipped kitchens, a full bathroom, separate dining, living, and sleeping areas, a TV, heat, air-conditioning, a porch, a fire ring, and a picnic table. Four-person cottages rent for $110 a night, while six- and eight-person cottages rent for $135 per night.

RESTAURANTS

One thing's for sure about dining in Gettysburg—there are lots of choices. You can get dressed up and head out for a five-course meal one night and the next night grab something at whatever casual place is nearby when hunger strikes. Dressy casual is the most dressed up you need to be in any of the restaurants, and all the finer restaurants except the Cashtown Inn also have a tavern or more casual dining area on the premises. But that's not to say you can't put on your best outfit if you're so inclined, especially if you plan on dining at Herr's Publick House or Centuries on the Square. At most restaurants you'll find a varied menu that aims to please many different tastes. Pasta, chicken, seafood, and beef dishes, as well as sandwiches and lighter fare, appear on most menus. If you like to try ethnic fare, you can sample Italian, Greek, Asian, and Irish cuisines.

Some of the dining establishments are housed in historic landmarks, making dining there about much more than enjoying excellent food. For instance, the Farnsworth House housed Confederate sharpshooters during the Battle of Gettysburg, and the Dobbin House and Herr's Tavern were stops on the Underground Railroad. You really shouldn't miss these places, and you might want to try their dishes that are representative of the Civil War period.

The southern end of town contains the most concentrated area of restaurants, probably because many tourist sights are also in this part of town. Gettysburg doesn't have many chain restaurants—a McDonald's, a Friendly's, and a Kentucky Fried Chicken are in the southern end of town, and a Ruby Tuesday, an Arby's, a Perkins Family Restaurant, a Hoss's, and another McDonald's are along York Street east of the square.

Most of the restaurants described in this chapter are within the borough limits.

Although this makes them conveniently located by attractions and shopping, it also sometimes leads to congestion. If you can, leave your car behind and walk. I'll mention if a place has a lot of parking available; otherwise, assume there's either no customer parking or very little parking available, often behind the restaurant. If you're driving, be prepared to have to find a spot on the street and feed the meters. There's also a parking garage on Race Horse Alley behind the Gettysburg Hotel on the square. As of September 2008, restaurants in Pennsylvania are smoke-free.

When asked, most establishments claim to be wheelchair accessible, but this often means coming in a back door or the staff putting down a ramp for easier access. My best advice to those needing special assistance is for you to call ahead and speak about the facilities directly with someone from the restaurant.

Gettysburg is a tourist town, so most places accept credit cards. But there are a few exceptions, which I'll note in those restaurants' write-ups. Reservations are often accepted only at the fine-dining establishments, and waiting for a table is a common experience. Many tourists seem to break for lunch late, about 1:00 to 1:30 p.m., so don't think you'll outsmart everyone by delaying lunch—you'll just be hungrier while you wait.

Entries in this chapter are arranged geographically from the focal point of Lincoln Square and then listed alphabetically.

PRICE CODE

Prices represent the average cost for two dinner entrees, excluding appetizers, desserts, refreshments, tax, and tip. If you have a large party, check whether a gratuity is automatically added to your bill. And check the rate of the gratuity—it might range from 15 to 20 percent.

$....................... Up to $15
$$ .... $16 to $25
$$$ .... $26 to $40
$$$$$............$41 and higher

LINCOLN SQUARE

CENTURIES ON THE SQUARE
MCCLELLAN'S TAVERN $$$$
Best Western Historic Gettysburg Hotel
1 Lincoln Square
(717) 337-2000
www.hotelgettysburg.com

The Gettysburg Hotel, then known as Scott's Tavern, was established in 1797. The hotel basks in this history, as evidenced by the name of its restaurants, Centuries on the Square and McClellan's Tavern. (William McClellan, a local sheriff, bought the tavern in 1809.) Open for breakfast and dinner, Centuries on the Square offers you fine dining as you enjoy its colonial decor. For dinner you'll find elegant beef, chicken, and seafood dishes. Prime rib of beef is available on Friday and Saturday evenings; the salmon is filleted in-house to ensure its fresh quality. A children's menu is available, and your server will be attired in period dress.

McClellan's Tavern is open for lunch and lighter fare during the evening. As you enter the pub, you're sure to notice the gleaming mahogany bar before you. This turn-of-the-twentieth-century Van Tromp bar was imported from Brick Lane in England, and it's a beauty. The bar stools are mahogany and soft, soft leather that you can't help but caress. Cozy tables sit around the bar area, and there's a separate dining area to the right that features a large fireplace.

Gourmet sandwiches dominate the menu, which also has a good selection of appetizers.

ℹ **Some establishments have separate entrances for the dining area and the bar area, often within a few feet of each other.**

THE PLAZA RESTAURANT AND LOUNGE $$$
2–8 Baltimore Street
(717) 334-1999

Open seven days a week for lunch and dinner, The Plaza has gyros, kebobs, souvlaki, and other Greek dishes as well as more traditional dishes featuring fresh-cut steaks, seafood, chicken, chops, and barbecued spareribs. Grilled deli sandwiches, such as the grilled reuben, are featured at lunchtime, which also finds many customers ordering the homemade soups. Favorite Greek dinner dishes are the gyro platter and the chicken kebob platter, which are served on pita bread with tzatziki (Greek sauce made from garlic, cucumbers, and yogurt) and accompanied by a small Greek salad and fries or a potato. The barbecued spareribs, crab cakes, and lamb chops also are frequent dinner choices. The menu includes kids' meals reasonably priced for children age 12 and younger.

The Plaza has two entrances, one that opens onto the bar area and one that takes you directly into the dining room. The entrance to the bar is on the square while the restaurant entrance is a few steps down Baltimore Street. The bar area serves as the Plaza's smoking area, and the dining room has booths along its perimeter and tables in the middle. You'll find a casual atmosphere here, with good views of the square from the bar area.

THE PUB & RESTAURANT $$$
20–22 Lincoln Square
(717) 334-7100
www.the-pub.com

This upscale restaurant and pub offers a full-service menu with something for everyone. You'll find appetizers, salads, soups, wraps, nachos, burgers, sandwiches, pasta, steaks, seafood, and desserts. The Pub is known for its generous portions and for its burgers and chicken sandwiches. The restaurant is on one side and the pub is on the other. The dark wood booths and tables on the restaurant side add to the old-world ambience, as does the abundance of dark wood on the pub side. And the view of the square can't be beat. The pub side has tables as well as the bar seats, and there are a few arcade games to keep the kids busy as you wait for your meals. There's also a kids' menu available for children age 10 and younger, with prices in the $4 to $7 range. You'll find a wide range of cocktails, wines, and beers here. There are 12 drafts on tap, one of which is always Guinness.

The Pub is open for lunch and dinner daily, and it serves dinner until at least 10:00 p.m. during the week and until 9:00 p.m. on Sunday. The place closes during the first week of January and for certain holidays but is open the rest of the year. If you're visiting the Pub for a drink, it serves until 1:00 a.m. Monday through Saturday and until 11:00 p.m. on Sunday.

The Pub gets really crowded sometimes, so be aware . . . there are two sets of restrooms, one downstairs on the pub side and one upstairs. The upstairs ladies' room also has a changing table.

NORTH OF LINCOLN SQUARE

DELISO PIZZA, PASTA AND SUBS $$
829 Biglerville Road
(717) 337-9500
Located on Route 34 (Biglerville Road) and just a bit more than a mile from the square, Deliso's has been around since 1995. Since the parking lot encircles the building, parking isn't a problem here. Open seven days a week, Deliso's has a wide variety of menu selections. Besides such Italian fare as pizza, subs, strombolis, calzones, and Italian dinners, the menu also offers burgers and a few fish choices. Or you can order a gyro or honey-dipped chicken. Beer and wine are available to accompany your meal, and Deliso's also sells six-packs of beer for carryout.

Deliso's decor is similar to many pizzerias, with booths and a few tables available for those who wish to eat inside the restaurant. Deliso's is closed on Monday.

DISTELFINK DRIVE-IN $
2710 Old Harrisburg Road
(717) 337-3665, (717) 337-9636
Distelfink Drive-in has been in operation since 1952, but it's no longer a true drive-in. Instead, you can either eat inside or order at a walk-up window. Open daily for breakfast, lunch, and dinner, Distelfink is located 4 miles north of town along U.S. Business Route 15 (Old Harrisburg Road). Besides soups, salads, sandwiches, pizza, and subs, you can also find 50 flavors of soft-serve ice cream and milk shakes as well as soft pretzels. While you're at Distelfink, you can also pick up some fresh produce, flowers, and crafts.

LINCOLN DINER $
32 Carlisle Street
(717) 334-3900
The Lincoln Diner is open 24 hours a day, seven days a week. It's a block off the square, across the street from the Lincoln Train Station museum. The Lincoln is also beside the Flying Bull Saloon, and some patrons of the saloon stop at the Lincoln on their way home.

When you enter the Lincoln, you'll first be struck by just how like a diner it is. Booths line one side and the other side has a long, long lunch counter. Beyond this room is another room that serves as the dining room. Here you'll find mostly tables and a few more booths. The menu at the Lincoln covers the spectrum. Depending on your hunger level, you can choose from homemade soups, sandwiches, burgers, salads, seafood, steaks, chops, chicken, and pasta. There's also an inexpensive kids' menu for children age 10 and younger. The diner's on-site bakery creates delicious desserts, and the Lincoln is especially known for its cheesecake.

The Lincoln Diner does not take credit cards or personal checks. Cash is the name of the game here, although they will take a traveler's check.

SOUTH OF LINCOLN SQUARE

THE AVENUE RESTAURANT $$
21 Steinwehr Avenue
(717) 334-3235
www.avenuerestaurant.net
This casual restaurant has been locally owned and operated since 1958, and the couple who bought the place in 2005 are only the fourth owners. The Avenue offers home-style cooking daily for breakfast, lunch, and dinner, and its location puts it right in the heart of everything. The inside of the restaurant is set up like a diner, with a counter to the left and plenty of booths throughout the large dining area. Everyone in your group will find something that appeals here, from sandwiches to chicken to beef to seafood. Be sure to try their old-fashioned milk shakes.

BRIGADES FOOD, WINE & SPIRITS
RESTAURANT & LOUNGE $$$
Holiday Inn Battlefield
516 Baltimore Street
(717) 334-6211
Located within the Holiday Inn Battlefield, Brigades serves breakfast Monday through Sunday and dinner Monday through Saturday. The lounge is also open Monday through Saturday evenings. When you enter the Holiday Inn, Brigades is to your left, and the focal point of the large dining area is the huge brick fireplace at the back of the restaurant. White linen tablecloths with burgundy overlays and cloth napkins outfit the tables, but casual is the attire of choice here. There is plenty of off-street parking for patrons at the side of the hotel, and the menu is extensive and varied. Brigades is popular with locals from the area as well as hotel guests.

CAFÉ SAINT-AMAND $
48 Baltimore Street
(717) 334-2700
www.cafesaintamand.com
This French bistro serves breakfast and lunch Tuesday through Sunday (closed Monday) at its corner location along Baltimore Street. Opened in late 2008, the restaurant features homemade soups and salads, hot and cold sandwiches, and an extensive assortments of coffee, latte, cappuccino, and tea. Tables are arranged a nice distance from each other in this spacious dining room, and a few tables are raised and placed at the restaurant's large windows, just at the right height for watching the crowds passing by on Baltimore Street.

DINO'S PIZZA, PASTA & SUBS $$
226 Steinwehr Avenue
(717) 337-3453
Dino's serves piles of pasta, which are accompanied by garlic bread and a salad, and if you don't want the salad, they'll take a dollar off your bill. They also offer a kid's spaghetti that is served without the salad at an even more reduced rate. You'll find Greek touches throughout the menu, such as the *tzatziki* sauce (Greek sauce with cucumbers, garlic, and yogurt) and the Zorba the Greek Pizza, which has tomatoes and steamed spinach leaves and feta cheese crumbs in an olive oil garlic sauce atop a blend of mozzarella and cheddar cheese. Dino's tops their fresh pizza dough with their family-recipe tomato sauce and a blend of mozzarella and cheddar cheese, and their hot subs are served toasted on freshly baked Italian rolls. Their Italian meatballs are homemade, and besides having them with pasta or in a sub, you can get them as a side order.

This BYOB restaurant is open daily, and they also offer carryout and delivery.

DOBBIN HOUSE TAVERN $$$–$$$$
89 Steinwehr Avenue
(717) 334-2100
www.dobbinhouse.com
Built in 1776, the Dobbin House is the oldest building in Gettysburg and is listed on the Register of Historic Places. Just across the street from the National Cemetery, the home served as a hospital for the wounded after the Battle of Gettysburg. The house's native stone walls, seven fireplaces, and hand-carved woodwork have been restored to their original eighteenth-century beauty and decorated with period antiques. (For more on the

rich history of the Dobbin House, see the Close-up in this chapter.)

Here you can enjoy colonial and continental cuisine, either in the casual Springhouse Tavern or in the more formal Alexander Dobbin Dining Rooms, and in both you'll be served by waitstaff whose period clothing is completely authentic. The tavern is in the lower level of the house, and you are transported back in time the minute you enter. The room is dimly lit with a colonial candle on each table and hanging colonial lanterns, and the deep wood of the exposed wood beams and tall wooden booths gleams against the stone walls and brick floor. The trickling of the underground spring mingles with the Irish and colonial music that plays in the background. But atmosphere is not the only thing in abundance here. Good, hearty fare also awaits you. You'll find a variety of salads, burgers, and sandwiches, and there's also spit-roasted chicken, a grilled catch of the day, and char-grilled steak for those looking for a more filling meal. The tavern is open daily for lunch and dinner, and reservations are not accepted.

There are actually six separate dining rooms on the main level of the house, and each is decorated in a different colonial motif. My favorite is the cozy Library, complete with bookshelves and a fireplace. But perhaps you'd rather dine in the Dining Room, Parlour, Study, Spinning Room, or Bedroom. Yes, you read that right—you can actually dine in bed. The food here is exquisite—Dobbin House recipes have been published in *Bon Appétit* and *Cuisine* magazines. You'll find plentiful choices, with beef, chicken, pork, and seafood dishes available. The restaurant makes its own breads, soups, and desserts; people rave about the onion soup. As you dine, the china and flatware you'll be using exactly match fragments that were uncovered during the reexcavation of the cellar. The dining rooms are open for dinner only, and reservations are a must.

After you've eaten your fill, be sure to check out the secret slave hideout behind the pantry shelf (see the Close-up in this chapter). The premises also house the Country Curiosity Store, a great gift shop; the Gettystown Inn (see the Bed-and-Breakfasts and Guesthouses chapter); and the Abigail Adams Ballroom. With all that's going on here, it's a good thing the Dobbin House has a large parking area.

FARNSWORTH HOUSE $$$–$$$$
401 Baltimore Street
(717) 334-8838
www.farnsworthhouseinn.com
The Farnsworth House, which was built in 1810, has three locations for dining: the main dining room, where you can dine by candlelight and be served by period-dressed waitstaff; the open-air garden, where you choose from the same fine-dining menu as you relax beside a spring-fed stream that served as a water source for both the Confederate and Union armies; or the Killer Angel Tavern, which serves light fare with a touch of Pennsylvania Dutch cooking thrown in. The tavern also houses South Street Pizza (717-334-4419), which has sandwiches, hoagies, and, of course, pizza. (For more on the tavern, see the Nightlife chapter.) The Civil War is the topic of conversation at all the dining locations, which isn't surprising given the house's history during the Battle of Gettysburg. The house sheltered Confederate sharpshooters during the battle, and one of them is believed to have fired the wayward shot that killed Jennie Wade, the only civilian to perish in the three-day battle. More than 100 bullet holes can still be seen in the south wall of the building.

The Farnsworth House has been owned by the Loring Schultz family since 1972, and they are responsible for restoring the house to its 1863 appearance, complete with its original walls, flooring, and rafters. The house serves as a bed-and-breakfast, and many news stories have been written about the ghosts that supposedly reside here. (See the Bed-and-Breakfasts and Guesthouses chapter for more on the eerier side of the Farnsworth House.) The main dining room is smoke-free, as is the tavern, which houses a unique display of *Gettysburg* movie props and uniforms.

Lunch and dinner are served here, and Civil War–period fare figures prominently on the

Close-up

The Underground Railroad in Gettysburg

The Civil War comes to mind when you think of Gettysburg, not the Underground Railroad. But the network that helped slaves escape to freedom had a stop at the Dobbin House on Steinwehr Avenue. Now a restaurant, the Dobbin House was built in 1776 by Alexander Dobbin, an Irish minister who had come to the area in 1773 with his wife, Isabella. After the forming of Gettysburg, Alexander was a community leader, and he opened the first classical school west of the Susquehanna River in his home. He and Isabella had 10 children before her death in 1800, and before his death in 1809, Alexander married Mary Agnew, who had nine children of her own. Although town records show that Alexander owned slaves, the house would help many slaves obtain freedom.

You can view where slaves hid in the Dobbin House while journeying north to freedom. The hideout is along a staircase that leads from the main floor to the second floor, and a pane of glass has been installed so visitors can peer into the tiny and cramped space. Look closely to the left; the first time I looked I didn't see the slave hiding in the corner.

If you're dining in the main dining rooms, the staircase leading to the hideout is to the left of where the hostess will greet you as you arrive for dinner. If you're eating at the tavern, you can get to the hideout by going through the door to the left of the colonial bar, which was built in 1818 by the current owner's great-great-great-grandfather for his tavern near Dillsburg, Pennsylvania. As you step through the door, be sure to stop and admire the underground spring that you can see right ahead of you. (The spring is also visible in the tavern's dining area.) The original three springs, which have been diverted into one area to help preserve the house, were used as a well (especially important during Indian attacks) and a refrigerator. After looking at the spring, go up the staircase and to the left there will be another door leading to another staircase. As you head up this staircase, the hideout is to your left. After viewing the hideout, continue up the steps and you'll enter into a room that has pictures of the Dobbin House in times past, and you can view some of the original stone of the house. This room also contains artifacts from colonial times. As you head back down the staircase, watch your step. The staircase is windy and the steps are narrow.

menu. You'll be able to try game pie, peanut soup, spoon bread, and pumpkin fritters. For those with less adventuresome palates, steaks, chicken, and fish are also available. A good selection of beer, wine, and cocktails accent your dining pleasure. The food at the Farnsworth House has many admirers—*Bon Appétit* magazine has described it as "History never tasted so good." A children's menu, with entrees for less than $10, is available, and reservations are required for the main dining room.

Plenty of parking is available behind the Farnsworth House, and Civil War buffs will definitely want to check out the Farnsworth House Military Impressions bookshop and the Get-tysburg Quartermaster (see the Shopping and the Gettysburg National Military Park chapters), which are also on the grounds. During the summer there's entertainment here on Friday and Saturday nights.

i Be careful as you leave the Farnsworth House and cross the street that runs behind it to get to the parking lot. As you leave the trellised walkway, it's easy to forget that this alley is traveled by many cars. Stop at the end of the sidewalk on the side of the Farnsworth House and look both ways before stepping into the alley.

GENERAL PICKETT'S BUFFETS $$

571 Steinwehr Avenue
(717) 334-7580
www.generalpickettsbuffets.com

If your group has big appetites, these all-you-can-eat-buffets will satisfy everyone in your party. And those with smaller appetites will appreciate being able to order just the soup and salad bar for a reduced price. Although groups make up a large part of the business here, individuals are also welcome. It's open every day during the season but closed in January and open reduced hours in December and February. The lunch buffet begins at 11:00 a.m. Monday through Saturday, and the dinner buffet is served Monday through Sunday at 4:30 p.m. and Sunday at 11:00 a.m. With room for 225 people and the bountiful buffet offered, it's easy to see why this place is so popular with tour groups. Visitors who plan on returning should check out the Regulars' Club Card, which offers price reductions on meals as well as free meals.

The buffets feature down-home cooking in a family atmosphere. The soups, rolls, and desserts are homemade, and the dinner buffet features hand-breaded deep-fried catfish. Lunch features a selection of daily specials, such as baked chicken, meat loaf, and Salisbury steak. If you like, you can order an alcoholic beverage with your dinner. General Pickett's location across from the Gettysburg National Military Park is ideal, and their large lot makes parking a breeze. Although General Pickett's and the Gettysburg Battle Theatre (see the Attractions chapter) are located in the same building, they are not associated.

THE GINGERBREAD MAN $$$

217 Steinwehr Avenue
(717) 334-1100
www.thegingerbreadman.net

Known to locals as the G-Man, you'll find lots of casual ambience and lots of food and drink choices here. From the outside it looks like someone's house, but when you enter the restaurant, you realize it's much larger than it looks. The front part of the main level has many tables, and the bar area is in the back, where you'll find more tables available. Upstairs is another room that can be used for private parties or overflow business.

All the food served here except for the potato salad and coleslaw is homemade. For lighter fare, you can choose from soup, salads, burgers, sandwiches, and fajitas. Dinners, which are served beginning at noon, include beef, seafood, chicken, pork, and pasta selections. And don't overlook the Snacks, Treats, and Eats part of the menu—most of these are ample enough to serve as a meal. My husband is always stuffed after eating the supreme nachos from this part of the menu, and my cousin Teresa always orders the potato skins for lunch when she's in town visiting. My favorite selection for lunch or dinner is the English-style roast-beef sandwich, which is served with au jus for dipping.

The G-Man also offers an extensive kids' menu, ranging from a peanut butter and jelly sandwich to battered shrimp and fries, with prices in the reasonable $4 to $5 range.

HUNT'S CAFÉ $–$$

61 Steinwehr Avenue
(717) 334-4787

Hunt's Café and Battlefield Fries was formerly known as Hunt's Battlefield Fries, but the name has been changed to reflect that there's a lot more than just fries here. Breakfast is available, and for lunch or dinner you can pick from cheesesteaks, hamburgers, wings, salads, and hot and cold sandwiches. There's also old-fashioned bottled soda, hand-dipped ice cream, fresh lemonade, milk shakes, and desserts, including whole pies.

You'll want to add the fries to anything you order—they're fresh cut, and owner Scott Hunt lets you jazz them up with numerous topping selections. Scott's proud of his fries and of his cheesesteaks—he has patrons that have driven from Philadelphia, home of the cheesesteak, just to get one!

Hunt's has been serving up great food since 2002, and the place opens at 8:00 a.m. every day during the season. (Hunt's is closed on Wednesday from November through April.) You can relax at an inside table or enjoy watching the world go by from your outside table. But remember to bring cash—Hunt's doesn't accept credit cards.

MAY FLOWERS ASIAN BUFFET & RESTAURANT $$
533 Steinwehr Avenue
(717) 337-3377, (717) 337-9998
www.themayflowers.com

May Flowers is set among chain restaurants, and its building actually looks like it used to be a fast-food restaurant. But inside, the BYOB restaurant is spacious and beautifully decorated with tables with high-backed chairs and a near forest of plants. Featuring dishes of southern Chinese, Japanese, and American cuisine, all items on their extensive menu are available for takeout. You'll find everything from shrimp egg rolls to filet mignon to lobster to Peking duck. If you can't manage to limit your choice to one item on the menu, you can always try the lunch or dinner buffet. May Flowers has special dishes for dieters, and they will gladly steam most items on the menu if you're watching your calorie intake.

Open seven days a week for lunch and dinner, May Flowers has ample parking. It also has a drive-through for take-out orders. Be sure to check out their lunch specials, which are served Monday through Saturday up to 3:00 p.m.—they're great bargains.

MOM'S COFFEEPOT $
65 West Middle Street
(717) 337-9034

This has been the location of a coffeehouse for years, with current owners Brian and Mary Eastman taking over the operation in October 2004. They spruced the place up quite a bit but didn't change its relaxed, living-room atmosphere. Artwork from local artists adorns the walls, and artists stop by and paint as the mood strikes them. Two tables and a wraparound couch are the only seating you'll find in this small space. But you will find many ways to tempt your taste buds. This eatery offers breakfast sandwiches, bagels, baked goods, sandwiches, soups, and salads in

addition to what many consider the best coffee in town. The place opens at 6:00 a.m. Monday through Friday and serves breakfast and lunch. And on Saturday mornings you can find Mom's Coffeepot at the farmers' market that's held on Lincoln Square.

OLIVIA'S MEDITERRANEAN GRILLE $$$
3015 Baltimore Street
(717) 359-9357
www.olivias.biz

Although Olivia's is 4.5 miles south of Lincoln Square, the short drive is well worth it. When you pull into the parking lot, the place looks small and not overly impressive, but the inside is quite a different story. The large dining room has clusters of booths and tables, and some tables sit in a private alcove. An abundance of plants and accents contribute to the Mediterranean-cafe feel of the place. Olivia's is named after the daughter of owner Harry Tassou. And this is definitely a locally owned and run restaurant—Harry lives across the street, and the last time I stopped by he was preparing chocolate-covered strawberries for Valentine's Day dining.

The dinner menu is a mix of fresh seafood, hand-cut steaks, and Greek and Italian cuisine. Olivia's also serves lunch, and kids have their choice of seven meals priced at $5.99. Food is served here every day but Monday. Bottled domestic and imported beer, wine, and spirits are available to complement your dinner, and there's entertainment on the weekends (see the Nightlife chapter for more information). If you like beef, you may especially enjoy the Jack Daniel's steak. Olivia's has been recommended by the *Washington Post,* and although the atmosphere is casual, reservations are suggested.

O'RORKE'S FAMILY EATERY AND SPIRITS $$$
44 Steinwehr Avenue
(717) 334-2333

This is a lively place, and you'll often see reenactors in full garb enjoying good food, beer, and conversation here. The finer casual cuisine includes soups, salads, burgers, seafood, steaks, and a few Irish entrees. I especially like the Guinness beef stew, a rich combination of beef, potatoes, carrots, and a hint of Guinness served in a bread bowl.

O'Rorke's, which opened in March 2003, is named for Patrick O'Rorke, an Irish-born American soldier who was killed on the western slope of Little Round Top during the Battle of Gettysburg. A monument to the colonel stands on the spot where he died. O'Rorke's is open daily for lunch and dinner, and they host entertainment on Friday and Saturday nights. There are six beers on tap, including Guinness and Harp, wine by the glass, and cocktails, including a variety of martinis. You can dine outside on the patio in season, but be sure to take a trip inside to admire the two walk-in fireplaces you'll find there.

THE PIKE RESTAURANT & LOUNGE $$$
985 Baltimore Pike
(717) 334-9227
www.thepikerestaurant.com

Located just up the road from the new visitor center, the Pike Restaurant is open for lunch and dinner daily and for breakfast on Sunday. You have three choices for dining ambience here. The dining room has a family atmosphere, the large deck out front is great for kicking back and relaxing, and the sports lounge features a big-screen TV and is open until 2:00 a.m. (For more on the lounge, see the Nightlife chapter.) Casual dining at all three locations includes homemade soups, sandwiches, wraps, quesadillas, Angus burgers and steaks, and pasta dishes. Lunch and dinner specials are offered daily, and the kids' menu offers those age 10 and younger meals for less than $6.

There's plenty of parking available at the Pike, and it's better to drive here rather than walk from town. Although it's located at the edge of town, the sidewalk stops at the Evergreen Cemetery, and I don't advise walking along the berm of this busy road.

PING'S CAFÉ $$
34 Baltimore Street
(717) 334-2234

Ping's Café serves Japanese and Chinese cuisine, and it's the only restaurant in town where you'll find a sushi bar, let alone one with a professional sushi chef. As you enter Ping's, the sushi bar is in the back, and booths round out the rest of the area. To the left is a large room that has numerous tables available. Ping's has more than 30 varieties of rolls, but these aren't the type you slather butter on. You might want to try their spicy tuna roll or the dream roll, which has smoked salmon, eel, caviar, cucumber, and seaweed salad. Lunch specials are combinations of rolls, and they're served until 3:00 p.m. There's also Japanese ice cream for dessert. Ping's is open for lunch and dinner Tuesday through Sunday (closed Monday).

i Don't assume that the cheesesteak you order in Gettysburg will be made the same way it is in your hometown. It might be made with beef, onions, provolone cheese, and tomato sauce, or with beef, onions, provolone cheese, lettuce, tomato, and mayo, or with just beef and Cheese Whiz, or . . . well, you get the idea. So clarify what a cheesesteak is to you before you order; most likely, the place can make it just the way you like it.

SPIRITFIELDS PUB & FARE AND POE'S PATIO $$
619 Baltimore Street
(717) 334-9449
www.spiritfield.com

Spiritfields opened its doors in May 2005, and it serves daily year-round from 11:00 a.m. to 11:00 p.m. Everything on the menu is made on the premises according to owners Tami and Ed Reese, including the hand-pattied burgers. Among the specialties are Maryland seafood dishes prepared according to secret family recipes, ale-soaked and seasoned briskets of beef served up in sandwiches, and the daily "chef's whimsy." A full bar, specialty drinks, and wine and beer are available to complement your meal. The full menu is also available on the outside deck, Poe's Patio, which features evening entertainment on occasion.

TOMMY'S PIZZA $$
105 Steinwehr Avenue
(717) 334-4721, (717) 334-8966
www.tommyspizzainc.com

Tommy's has been family owned and operated and serving pizza to the community since 1973. Its location is convenient to all the sites on Steinwehr Avenue and Baltimore Street, and there is parking available on-site. Tommy's gives you the choice of pizza, stromboli, hoagies, salads, and wings seven days a week, but you won't find full pasta dinners here. The dining area can seat quite a few people, with both booths and tables. Delivery service is available, and there's also a drive-through pick-up window for customers who call their order in for carryout. If you like a beer with your pizza, Tommy's can accommodate you. They also have six-packs of beer available for takeout only.

EAST OF LINCOLN SQUARE

APPLE BLOSSOM TEA ROOM AND GIFTS $$
39 York Street
(717) 334-0904
www.appleblossom-tearoom.com

Area resident Brandi Bolger bought the tearoom that used to operate here under the name Civil-La-Tea in December 2006 and made the place her own both in decor and in the menus she personally creates. Tea and light sandwiches and salads are served Tuesday through Saturday from late morning to late afternoon in the vintage tearoom and, during nice weather, on the veranda of this Civil War house. Enjoying tea on the veranda is particularly lovely because you sit back from the street, allowing you to observe the crowds passing by without being a part of them.

When you enter the house from the veranda, you first step into a beautiful gift shop filled with bagged and loose teas, jewelry, stationery, tea books and magazines, and more. The tearoom is located in the two rooms beyond the gift shop. Brandi feels tearooms are a place where woman can connect, and she has made the atmosphere within the tearoom very, very feminine. Tables are draped in pink satin and tulle or delicately colored patchwork quilts, and the walls are adorned with inspirational hand-penned quotes.

Brandi's details can be noted everywhere, such as the lavender petals nestled in the sugar bowls and the mint sprigs in the water pitchers. Offerings range from a pot of tea with scones to a full afternoon tea that includes tea, soup, a salad, a gourmet scone with all the trimmings, tea sandwiches, and tea sweets to finish the feast. Theme teas and children's tea parties are also available, and reservations are requested.

EASTSIDE LOUNGE AND RESTAURANT $$
1063 York Road
(717) 337-0118

The Eastside sits along U.S. Route 30 in front of the Hilton Garden Inn. Here you'll find a varied menu available for breakfast, lunch, and dinner seven days a week. But don't come here for an early breakfast—they open at 10:00 a.m., and breakfast is served until noon. For lunch you can choose from homemade soup, hot and cold sandwiches and subs, fish, chicken, and hamburgers. If you're really hungry, try the Eastside Nightmare—ham, roast beef, turkey, American and Swiss cheeses, lettuce, tomato, onion, and ranch dressing served on a roll and big enough for two to share. Crab cakes are the house specialty, and the prime rib, broasted chicken, and barbecue spareribs are also favorites. Other dinner selections include steaks, pasta dishes, ham, and seafood.

There's a large parking area beside the Eastside, and there are separate entrances for the lounge and restaurant. The restaurant entrance opens onto a casual dining room decorated with green chairs and matching plastic tablecloths. The lights above the tables are illuminated candles placed inside upside-down bushel baskets, a tribute to the area's orchards. The lounge, which you can also enter through the dining area, has a large bar, a few tables, and a game room with three pool tables.

GARIBALDI'S RISTORANTE $$–$$$
70 Presidential Circle
(717) 338-9400

Head to Garibaldi's if you crave wood-fired pizza. The oven is prominently featured in the center of the restaurant so you can watch the master-pieces being made and cooked. This ristorante also serves old-world Italian cuisine at its loca-tion on the Gateway Gettysburg campus, at the junction of U.S. Routes 15 and 30. (For more on Gateway Gettysburg, see the Close-up in the Area Overview chapter.) Garibaldi's is open for dinner only, and its specialties include lasagna and baked ziti in addition to the pizzas. There's an extensive wine list available as well as a full bar, and reservations are suggested. Garibaldi's shares its kitchen (and executive chef) with the other restaurant in the complex, Old Eagle Grill (see the write-up later in this chapter), although the two are separate establishments.

The ristorante is named after the Garibaldi Guard, which was the nickname of the 39th New York Infantry, a Civil War regiment of Ital-ian Americans recruited mostly from New York City. Giuseppe Garibaldi, a militant hero back home, was their inspiration, and the regiment wore a distinctively styled red shirt as part of their uniform to show their connection to their countryman, whose partisans had worn such a shirt in Italy.

The 39th Infantry Regiment Monument stands near the "Angle" on cemetery ridge at Gettysburg National Military Park.

GETTYSBREW RESTAURANT &
BREWERY $$$
248 Hunterstown Road
(717) 337-1001
www.gettysbrew.com

Gettysbrew offers casual fine dining in a restored brick-end barn on the historic Monfort Farm, which was used as one of the largest Confederate field hospitals following the Battle of Gettysburg. Wounded soldiers were left at the farm when the Confederates retreated, and 47 men were buried here. Their bodies were later disinterred and moved to Hollywood Cemetery in Richmond, Virginia. Gettysbrew opened in 1997 as the area's largest brewery, and all beer, root beer, and ginger ale are crafted on-site. The beverages are also available for takeout in half-gallon glass jugs called growlers. If you bring your growler back for a refill, you get it at a reduced price. Wine is also available to complement your meal.

To get to Gettysbrew from Lincoln Square, take York Street about a mile and then bear left onto Hunterstown Road. Gettysbrew is on the left in about half a mile. Closed in January and February, Gettysbrew is open seven days a week the rest of the year, opening at noon on the weekends and at 4:00 p.m. during the week. Lighter fare includes piegga sandwiches, which are served hot and open faced on piegga bread, which is folded focaccia bread with a hint of honey. Entrees feature seafood and steaks, and a children's menu is available for those age 12 and younger.

GETTYSBURG FAMILY RESTAURANT $$
1275 York Road, Peebles Plaza
(717) 337-2700

Family owned and operated, Gettysburg Family Restaurant is located in Peebles Plaza along York Road. It's open seven days a week for breakfast, lunch, and dinner. Early risers can grab a bite beginning at 7:00 a.m. on Sunday and at 6:00 a.m. the rest of the week. And seniors receive discounts on dinner entrees after 2:00 p.m. If you like, you can also order an alcoholic beverage to go with your dinner.

Reminiscent of a large diner, the restaurant has a counter in the back and plenty of booths and tables. There are also plenty of choices on the menu, with homemade soups, sandwiches, broasted chicken, pasta dishes, meat loaf, ham, steaks, and seafood being among them. Children age 12 and younger can order from the children's specials, which are all priced less than $5, and some are less than $3. All items on the menu are available for takeout, and you can even order up to 25 pieces of broasted chicken, which is the house specialty.

LA BELLA ITALIA $$
402 York Street
(717) 334-1978

La Bella Italia is conveniently located downtown at Fourth and York Streets, and its new building, completed in late 2005, seats about 100. The restaurant is divided into small alcoves and decorated like an Italian villa, with rounded archways, exposed bricks and beams, trellises, and bottles filled with assorted foods showcased in many wall inserts and ledges.

Finding something on the menu to please each person in your group is a snap at this family-owned and -operated business, which is open daily. You can choose from New York–style pizza, stromboli, calzone, subs, and salads to full dinners featuring pasta, chicken, veal, seafood, and steak. Low-calorie dinners are available, as is a kids' menu, which offers a wide variety of dinner choices that are priced in the $4 to $6 range. Bottled beer is available to accompany your meal, and you can also pick up six-packs of beer to go here. Everything on the menu is available for takeout, and La Bella also makes 4-foot subs and party trays for takeout.

NEW GARDEN CHINESE RESTAURANT $$
20–44 Natural Springs Road
(717) 337-9995

The New Garden is tucked into the strip mall in Gettysburg Marketplace, which also houses a Giant grocery store among its tenants. Although New Garden appears miniscule from the outside, once you're inside, its size seems just right. There are plentiful tables for four and a buffet area tucked away in the back. If the New Garden is your first foray into sampling Chinese food, you'll appreciate the descriptions of the dishes given on the extensive menu and that hot and spicy dishes are clearly labeled. If you're adventurous but a little timid, you can also ask for a hot and spicy dish to come mild. Dishes that represent Szechuan, Hunan, and Cantonese cuisine are available.

New Garden has steamed dishes for dieters and a children's menu with items priced at less than $3 on it. If your children don't want Chinese, fried chicken nuggets and fried scallops are available. Lunch specials, always a great bargain, are available until 4:00 p.m., and the restaurant is open for lunch and dinner seven days a week.

OLD EAGLE GRILL $$–$$$
70 Presidential Circle
(717) 338-9200

This casual restaurant serving American comfort food with a twist opened in April 2007 as part of the Gateway Gettysburg complex at the junction of US 15 and US 30. (For more on Gateway Gettysburg, see the Close-up in the Area Overview chapter.) The decor consists of tables and overstuffed booths in cozy sections decked out in modern style, and the walls are adorned with paintings of works of the local land conservancy. A focal point is the full-size wood-burning fireplace in the center of the room, which completes the comfy atmosphere.

Old Eagle Grill is owned by local entrepreneur Robert Monahan Jr., a driving force behind the creation of the complex. The restaurant, which is open seven days a week for lunch and dinner, is named after the Old Eagle Hotel that resided on Chambersburg Street until it was destroyed by fire in the 1960s. Specialties include fried calamari salad, grilled meat loaf, chicken potpie, and Old Eagle chili, made with roasted andouille sausage and black beans. Pizza is available at lunchtime, along with pasta, sandwiches, and complete meals. The dinner menu also offers pasta and sandwiches and expands the variety of complete meals offered. Wine by the glass and beer, including a nice selection of drafts, microbrews, and craft beers, are available to accompany your meal. Reservations are suggested, and takeout is available. The Old Eagle Grill shares its kitchen with the other restaurant in the complex, Garibaldi's Ristorante (see the write-up earlier in this chapter), although the two are separate establishments.

WEST OF LINCOLN SQUARE

APPALACHIAN BREWING CO. (ABC) $$$
401 Buford Avenue
(717) 334-2200
www.abcbrew.com
This restaurant and brewery serves lunch and dinner daily, and it's an extension of the brew-pub's original location in Harrisburg, Pennsylvania's capital.

You'll find plenty of parking at this restaurant, which sits at the crest of Seminary Ridge beside General Lee's Headquarters Museum (see the Attractions chapter) and the Quality Inn Larson's (see the Hotel, Motels, and Resorts chapter). The menu includes sandwiches, brick-oven pizza, strombolis, burgers, steaks, fish, and pasta dishes. You'll find traditional fare, such as crab cakes and Delmonico steak, and not-so-traditional fare, such as the Chesapeake chicken cake sandwich, which is similar to a crab cake but made with diced chicken breast that's tossed with their signature chipotle wing sauce and other secret ingredients. Wine, cocktails, and, of course, beer are available to accompany your meal, and fresh-brewed beer is available for takeout in six-packs, 12-packs, or "growlers." Growlers are 64-ounce jugs filled with beer that you can bring back for discounted refills. ABC also brews gourmet soda products, including root beer and ginger beer. Call-ahead seating is available on Friday and Saturday nights. Call at least an hour before you plan to arrive.

BLUE PARROT BISTRO $$$
35 Chambersburg Street
(717) 337-3739
This is another restaurant that isn't nearly as small as it seems to be from the outside. If you peek in the window, you see only the lounge, which consists of an impressive wooden bar and a few tables. The lounge and dining room each has a separate entrance, with the dining room's entrance a few steps farther westward down the street. The dining room is actually behind and to the left of the lounge, and a pool table occupies the space between the lounge and dining room. The intimate booths in the bistro are veiled from

the lounge area by plants and adorned with cloth tablecloths and napkins. But you don't have to get dressed up to enjoy the food here; blue jeans and black-tie attire are accepted equally.

The bistro fare is varied, with beef, veal, pork, chicken, seafood, pasta, and vegetarian dishes available. Some of the dishes are adventuresome, such as the filet mignon topped with Brie cheese and a mushroom demi-glace, while others are deliciously familiar, such as the angel-hair pasta topped with marinara sauce and Parmesan cheese or the beef lasagna. The artwork by local artists that you'll find on the walls is for sale, and the selection is always changing. Closed on Monday, the Blue Parrot Bistro has been serving lunch and dinner since 1988. It shares space with Lord Nelson's Gallery and the James Gettys Hotel in a circa-1804 building that's on the National Register of Historic Places.

CASHTOWN INN $$$$
1325 Old Route 30, Cashtown
(717) 334-9722, (800) 367-1797
www.cashtowninn.com
Located 8 miles west of town on Old Route 30, the restaurant at the Cashtown Inn is closed on Sunday and Monday and serves lunch and dinner the rest of the week. Here you'll find elegant fine dining in a historic building that was used as a Confederate headquarters during the Battle of Gettysburg. The inn was featured in the movie *Gettysburg*, and it has also graced the cover of *Blue and Gray* magazine.

Reservations for dinner are strongly recommended, and you'll find a full range of meals featuring beef and seafood in inventive dishes, as well as some chicken, veal, and pasta dishes. Local produce and herbs are featured in many dishes. Although you'll dine at a table dressed with a cloth tablecloth and cloth napkins, your dress may be casual if you choose.

DUNLAP'S RESTAURANT & BAKERY $$
90 Buford Avenue
(717) 334-4816
www.dunlapsrestaurant.com
Dunlap's is locally owned by Barry and Ruth

Dunlap, and their son is often the host who greets and seats you. Open seven days a week for casual family dining for breakfast, lunch, and dinner, Dunlap's sits across from the post office and has a large parking lot for your convenience. The restaurant is much larger than it appears from the street, with leather booths, a counter, and tables for seating. Be sure to check out their daily dinner specials, which are very reasonably priced. And definitely feast your eyes on the desserts in the case beside the register—they're all homemade. You'll want to either save room for these delights or order a slice to go.

Besides the dinner specials you'll also find a salad and soup bar, sandwiches, burgers, and wraps for lighter fare. Entrees include beef, pork, poultry, vegetarian, pasta, and seafood selections. Their crab melt sandwich is a house specialty, as is their filet mignon, veal parmigiana, seafood platter, and crab cake dinner. On the weekends Dunlap's has a breakfast buffet, and kids can always order from their own menu.

EL COSTEÑO $–$$
51 West Street
(717) 339-0029

This delightful Mexican restaurant opened in April 2005 within the small shopping center beside the Dollar General store. The refurbished space has a fiesta theme, complete with waitstaff dressed in traditional Mexican attire. The dining area is not large, but tables are spaced well enough apart that somehow the area doesn't seem as small as it is. Owner Arturo Gyento often adds to the restaurant's festive mood by visiting the seating area and interacting with the costumers.

The menu is extensive, with selections ranging from salads, burritos, enchiladas, fajitas, and tacos to lunch specials, full meals, kids' meals, and desserts. Descriptions are given for all items, and the menu notes when a particular dish is especially spicy, so you can be sure of what you're ordering. The prices are right, too, with six lunch platters that are each less than $5.50. El Costeño is open daily for lunch and dinner, and you're welcome to bring your own beer to accompany your meal.

ERNIE'S TEXAS LUNCH $
58 Chambersburg Street
(717) 334-1970

Ernie's has been a fixture on Chambersburg Street since 1921, when the original Ernie opened a sandwich shop across the street from the restaurant's current location. Ernie moved his business to its present site in 1934, and Ernie's grandson, also named Ernie, now runs the place.

This 1930s-style diner serves breakfast, lunch, and dinner Monday through Saturday. Ernie's has only eight booths, one of which is family-size, and a lunch counter, so seating is often at a premium here. But the tables turn over quickly; the service is fast and efficient, just as you would expect in a diner. Ernie's is famous for its Texas hot weiner, the same sandwich the first Ernie opened his shop with. It's a hot dog in its natural casing that's topped with mustard, chopped onion, and chili sauce. Other hot dog concoctions are available, as well as hamburgers, hot and cold sandwiches, deep-fried chicken and fish, homemade soups, and salads. Bring cash when you eat here—Ernie's doesn't accept credit cards or checks.

> **i** Ernie's Texas Lunch really is reminiscent of a 1930s diner—its grill is in the restaurant's front window.

THE FAIRFIELD INN 1757 MANSION
HOUSE RESTAURANT $$$$
15 West Main Street, Fairfield
(717) 642-5410, (717) 334-8868
www.thefairfieldinn.com

When you enter the Mansion House Restaurant at the Fairfield Inn, you step back in time. The inn dates from 1757, when it was the home of the founder of the town of Fairfield, Squire John Miller, and you can actually dine in the room that served as the home's downstairs. The Fairfield Inn is also a bed-and-breakfast (see the Bed-and-Breakfasts and Guesthouses chapter), and its Squire Miller Tavern is one of the oldest taverns still operating in America, with a license that's dated 1786.

Besides providing lodging for many famous Americans, the Fairfield also served General Lee chicken and biscuits as the Confederates stopped throughout the town of Fairfield on their retreat from Gettysburg. You can order this dish just as General Lee did almost 150 years ago; the restaurant serves more than two tons of it annually. Other menu selections include grilled and roasted game, pasta, seafood, and steaks. Your meal will be served in one of several dining areas, with tables throughout dressed in linen tablecloths and napkins. (The ambience is elegant, but casual dress is perfectly okay.) If you're interested in knowing the historic significance of the room you're dining in, the inn has a great brochure that takes you on a history tour of the inn. The tour also shows the hidden attic room that served as a stop on the Underground Railroad.

The Mansion House Restaurant serves lunch on Friday and Saturday, dinner Tuesday through Sunday, and a colonial brunch on Sunday. Fireplaces are featured throughout the house, and a patio garden filled with flowers and privacy hedges makes for perfect outdoor dining in nice weather. In 2008 the Fairfield Inn was voted the Best Romantic Restaurant in *Celebrate Gettysburg* magazine's annual readers' poll.

GARRYOWEN IRISH PUB $$
126 Chambersburg Street
(717) 337-2719

Garryowen Irish Pub opened in summer 2007, taking the place of the former Hamilton Tavern that resided here for years. Owner Kevin McCready, an Ireland native, has brought his Irish love of music, talk, and fun to the pub, where you can relax either at the long bar or at a table and enjoy some traditional Irish fare. The menu offers homemade Guinness beef stew, Dublin fish and chips, homemade shepherd's pie, bangers and mash, and more. American fare, such as Angus burgers, chicken sandwiches, and mozzarella sticks, is also available. Nighttime usually brings the chance to listen to some Celtic music and converse with fellow patrons in a friendly, relaxed atmosphere (see the Nightlife chapter).

HERR TAVERN & PUBLICK HOUSE $$$$
900 Chambersburg Road
(717) 334-4332, (800) 362-9849
www.herrtavern.com

Established in 1815, the Herr Tavern & Publick House offers gourmet dining in five dining areas that each seat 20 to 35 guests, and reservations are a must on the weekends. Located about 1.5 miles from Lincoln Square, the restaurant is in the same building as the bed-and-breakfast located here, and diners are invited to walk throughout the house to enjoy the decor. (See the Bed-and-Breakfasts and Guesthouses chapter for more on the lodging.)

Herr's is open Monday through Saturday for lunch and dinner and Sunday for dinner. Eating here is an elegant affair, with fine-dining ambience. Lunchtime fare includes sandwiches, burgers, and light entrees, such as the seared salmon. Dinner selections are highlighted by the chef's weekly specials, which feature local produce and products.

If linen tablecloths and candles are beyond your dining plans, the Livery tavern across the parking lot is available for lighter fare and casual dining. The Livery opens at 3:30 p.m. during the week and at noon on the weekends. The menu consists of sandwiches, burgers, steaks, chicken, and seafood. For your entertainment the Livery has dartboards, foosball, touch-screen video games, and a black-light poolroom.

HONG KONG $$
28 Springs Avenue
(717) 338-9954, (717) 338-0948

Hong Kong entered the Gettysburg restaurant scene in 2005. It's located in the Gettysburg Shopping Center, which is 3 blocks up Chambersburg Street from Lincoln Square. The dining room is not large, but it is nicely decorated with tables and high-back chairs. Serving Szechuan, Hunan, and Cantonese cuisine, Hong Kong is open seven days a week for lunch and dinner, and lunch specials are available until 3:00 p.m. The menu has dishes especially for dieters and a wide selection of lunch specials and combo platters. Don't forget to order your fortune cookie!

MAMMA VENTURA'S RESTAURANT $$$
13 Chambersburg Street
(717) 334-5548
www.mammaventuras.com

This Italian restaurant has been owned and operated by the same family for almost three decades, and the experience shows. The menu is filled with a wide range of pasta dishes served in imaginative and traditional ways, as well as dishes featuring beef, poultry, veal, and seafood. There are also pizzas, calzones, and stromboli, and children age 10 and younger can choose from one of five dishes especially sized for a child's appetite. The front part of Mamma's has booths and tables, and there's a cozy bar at the back of the room. To the left of the bar are many more seats that travel down a long hallway, so don't assume that there aren't any seats if the front part of the restaurant is full. Mamma's serves lunch and dinner Monday through Saturday and is closed on Sunday.

MONTEZUMA MEXICAN RESTAURANT $$
225 Buford Avenue
(717) 334-7750

This place looks *really* small from the outside but doesn't feel cramped at all once you enter. Decorated as a Mexican cantina and open daily for lunch and dinner, Montezuma is outfitted with a good number of roomy booths, and there is nothing small about the menu here. Choices range from a side order of rice to full meals, with seemingly everything in between. Side orders include four kinds of tacos, six kinds of enchiladas and burritos, and seven kinds of quesadillas, and filling options include bean, beef, shredded beef, chicken, cheese, mushroom and cheese, spinach and cheese, and chorizo Mexican sausage. There are seven types of salads, eight vegetarian dishes, lunch and dinner platters featuring beef, beans, chicken, steak, shrimp, chorizo, and pork, combination dinners, and dinners for two. Even dessert presents a whirlwind of choices, including fried ice cream, flan (caramel custard), sopapillas (fried pieces of flour tortillas with honey, butter, and cinnamon), and fried apples in a pastry shell and covered with sugar and cinnamon). There's a children's menu available for those patrons age 12 and younger, with seven meals to choose from, all priced less than $4. And don't worry if you're the only one in the group who isn't a fan of Mexican cuisine—Montezuma's also serves traditional American food such as the steak Americano, a T-bone topped with fried onions and served with vegetables, french fries, and salad.

RAGGED EDGE COFFEEHOUSE & JASPER'S JUICE WORKS $
110 Chambersburg Street
(717) 334-4464
www.raggededgecoffeehs.com

The apartment building next door to Ragged Edge had a fire in January 2003, and the coffee shop sustained smoke, water, and fire damage. The decision was made to completely renovate, and the Ragged Edge reopened in December 2004 with a new layout, new lighting, and new floors. The second floor now has a stage, which is used for live performances. Open seven days a week from morning to late evening, Ragged Edge offers breakfast, sandwiches, and salads in addition to Jasper's juices, smoothies, and supplement drinks. You'll also find hot and cold Ragged Edge specialty drinks, such as Italian or French sodas and mochas, and the smell of delicious baked goods fills the air.

You'll find room to spread out here. Besides the counter where you order, the downstairs has two large rooms, and the room in the back has a computer available for your convenience. Up the stairs you'll find a nice-size room with a stage and seating, and another room has groups of tables comfortably arranged. When the weather is warm, seating is also available outside in the back of the coffeehouse.

ROMAN INN PIZZA & SUB SHOPPE $
102 Chambersburg Street
(717) 334-3310

Finally there is a pizza shop just a block off the square! Opened in summer 2007, the Roman Inn offers handmade pizza by the slice and by the pie and 26 varieties of hot and cold subs. Stombolis, pepperoni poppers, roman candles, and homemade soup round out the selections. The cozy space has a few tables if you want to eat your food there, and there's a comfy sofa and chair for you to relax in if you're waiting for your take-out order. Roman Inn also delivers with a minimum order of $10. Bring cash if you want to eat here or plan on ordering a good amount of food—Visa and MasterCard are accepted only with a $10 minimum order.

SEASONS BAKERY AND CAFÉ $$
100 Chambersburg Street
(717) 334-0377
This no-frills space consists of a few small tables with chairs, a counter, and two display cases, but what else does a bakery/cafe really need? Open for breakfast and lunch, Seasons lets you eat with your eyes first by filling one of the display cases with assorted pastries, including croissants, sticky buns, muffins, Danish, scones, cannolis, cookies, éclairs, cupcakes, and seasonal pies and cakes. Be sure to get here early for the best selection because items are not always replenished throughout the day. The other display case is filled with lunch fare such as meats used to make panini sandwiches and salads. Sandwiches include both hot and cold selections, and soup served with house-made bread is also available by the cup or bowl. While you're waiting for your food, be sure to check out the work of local artists that fills the walls and that is for sale. Seasons opens at 7:00 a.m. Tuesday through Saturday and 8:00 a.m. on Sunday, and it is closed on Monday.

GETTYSBURG NATIONAL MILITARY PARK

Gettysburg National Military Park (GNMP) measures 6 miles by 7 miles, and its 1,400 monuments and markers and 400 artillery pieces along 35 miles of scenic avenues pay homage to the 51,000 men who became casualties upon this battlefield in July 1863.

The opening of the new museum and visitor center at 1195 Baltimore Pike (717-334-1124) in summer 2008 was a major achievement in an immense project managed by the nonprofit Gettysburg National Battlefield Museum Foundation to restore the battlefield to its 1863 appearance. The $103 million facility replaces the old visitor center and cyclorama that are located on the actual battlefield, and the plan is to demolish their buildings and continue to wipe out landscape changes that have occurred between the time of the battle and now. Controversy swirls around the benefit of this project, but no one can deny the effectiveness with which the new center tells the story of the Battle of Gettysburg within the larger context of the causes and results of the Civil War.

Designed as a Civil War–era Pennsylvania farmstead and sitting on land that saw no major fighting in the battle, the 139,000-square-foot center includes 24,000 square feet of exhibit space, a cyclorama painting, two film theaters, a book and museum store, a computer and resource room, and a 250-seat period-themed snack bar. The new Cyclorama Gallery displays *Battle of Gettysburg,* a cyclorama painted in 1884 whose skyline, canopy, and three-dimensional diorama, which had been missing for more than four decades, have been restored. Twelve galleries make up the museum, and 11 of them are based on phrases from Lincoln's Gettysburg Address. In fact, the entire 272-word speech is etched in a 5-foot-by-7-foot, 260-pound piece of glass that is displayed in one of the artifact rooms. The Civil War collection housed here is one of the largest in the world, consisting of more than 300,000 objects and artifacts and 700,000 archival materials. Interactive stations are situated throughout the museum so visitors can personalize their experience. Five of the galleries include short video presentations and the theaters feature readings from battle participants, while the twelfth gallery showcases temporary and traveling exhibits.

To get the most out of your visitor experience, you'll want to view the 20-minute film *A New Birth of Freedom,* which is shown every 30 minutes throughout the day and features the voices of Sam Waterston and Morgan Freeman. After the film visitors are shown to the cyclorama auditorium to view the restored *Battle of Gettysburg* painting. Visiting Gettysburg National Military Park is still free of charge but an entrance fee (another controversial decision) is now being charged at the visitor center to explore the museum and view the film and the cyclorama painting. Admission to the exhibits, film, and cyclorama is $7.50 for adults, $6.50 for senior citizens and those in the military, and $5.50 for those ages 6 through 18, while children younger than age 6 are admitted for free.

Tickets to Eisenhower National Historic Site are sold at the center, which is also where the tours depart from. The museum and visitor center open at 8:00 a.m. daily. They close at 6:00

p.m. in April, May, September, and October; at 7:00 p.m. June through August; and at 5:00 p.m. in November through March. Gettysburg National Military Park is open 6:00 a.m. to 10:00 p.m. April through October and to 7:00 p.m. November through March. You can visit the battlefield on foot, on bicycle, on horseback, in your car, by bus, or by Segway. It's up to you whether you want to explore on your own or you'd like someone to help interpret the events of July 1863.

The short films *Fields of Freedom* and *A New Birth of Freedom* put the Battle of Gettysburg and the Civil War in perspective, and they serve as excellent introductions to your battlefield explorations. *Fields of Freedom* is shown at Gateway Gettysburg, and *A New Birth of Freedom* plays at the GNMP visitor center.

i With 1,400 monuments and markers, the Gettysburg National Military Park has the largest collection of outdoor sculptures in the country. Monuments and cannons, which number 400, were placed to mark positions of regiments and to honor the sacrifices made by the men who fought here. The park requests that you not sit, stand, climb, or hang on any sculptures.

GETTYSBURG FOUNDATION
1195 Baltimore Pike
(866) 889-1243
www.gettysburgfoundation.org
This nonprofit educational organization works with Gettysburg National Military Park to restore, preserve, and enhance the consecrated ground of the Gettysburg battlefield. The foundation, along with park officials, is the driving force behind the current changes being made to the battlefield, including the relocation of the visitor center and the cyclorama painting.

i Historic preservation of the Gettysburg battlefield took a giant leap forward when the Gettysburg Foundation purchased the George Spangler Farm in 2008, ensuring the integrity of its historic location for the benefit of future historians. The 80-acre farm sits at what was the logistical center of the Union battle line during the Battle of Gettysburg.

TOURING GETTYSBURG NATIONAL MILITARY PARK

Auto Tours

AUTO TOUR USING GNMP OFFICIAL MAP AND GUIDE BROCHURE
GNMP Visitor Center
97 Taneytown Road
(717) 334-1124
www.nps.gov/gett
This free brochure is available at the information desks within the visitor center. It follows the three days of the battle in chronological order on an 18-mile tour that has 16 stops. A map guides you along the way, and brief descriptions of the action that occurred at each stop are included.

AUTO TOUR USING AUDIO CASSETTES OR CDS
GNMP Visitor Center Bookstore
97 Taneytown Road
(717) 334-1124
www.nps.gov/gett
The bookstore in the visitor center sells audiotapes that you use in your own car to tour the battlefield. Tours vary from two to four hours in length, and some include maps and photos. Some are very detail oriented, and some are dramatized with sound effects. The top-selling audio tour is the *Gettysburg Field Guide,* narrated by Wayne Motts. Wayne is a historian at the Adams County Historical Society who served as a licensed battlefield guide. His field guide has historic photos and detailed battle maps along with

the audio tour. Wayne also offers the *Gettysburg Expedition Guide,* which has all that the field guide offers and a CD-ROM for home use.

AUTO TOUR WITH A LICENSED BATTLEFIELD GUIDE

GNMP Visitor Center
97 Taneytown Road
(717) 334-1124
www.nps.gov/gett

Battlefield guides are tested and licensed by the National Park Service, and they must meet park service standards for accurately interpreting the Battle of Gettysburg and the American Civil War. They will accompany you in your car for personalized two-hour tours on a first-come, first-serve basis beginning at 8:00 a.m. at the visitor center. Operating since 1915, this is the nation's oldest professional guide service. Tours are customized to your need and level of knowledge; cost is $40 for up to six people per vehicle.

Bike Tours

GETTYSBIKE TOURS

241 Steinwehr Avenue
(717) 752-7752
www.gettysbike.com

This outfit began operations in the summer of 2005, and it can team you up with a licensed battlefield guide who specializes in bike tours of the park. You'll travel on two wheels to see Little Round Top, Devil's Den, the Peach Orchard, the Angle, and the High Water Mark. GettysBike arranges everything for you, including, of course, the bikes. The tours last approximately 2.5 hours and cover 8 miles of the park. If you want, you can rent the bikes for additional time after the tour for reduced rates and explore the park on your own. All rentals include a helmet, and all bikes are equipped with bottle racks to carry a drink. Escorted trips to the highlights of the battlefield that are led by one of the GettysBike employees are also available. Or you can simply rent a bike from them and explore on your own. Children

4¹/₂ feet or taller who are competent on a bike may ride on their own, and toddlers and small children may accompany a parent or guardian on a trailer carrier or trailer tandem (child trailers that attach to an adult bike). GettysBike is open Wednesday through Sunday beginning at 8:00 a.m. and on Monday and Tuesday by reservation only. The cost to rent a mountain bike is $8 per hour or $40 per day for an adult and $5 an hour or $25 a day for a child. A tour with a licensed battlefield guide is $61 for an adult and $26 for a child, and reservations are requested.

> **i** The bookstore at the GNMP visitor center has a wide variety of audiocassettes and CDs for sale that you use to tour the battlefield in your own car. Many stores throughout town also carry these same audio tours—but usually at a higher price than the visitor center.

GETTYSBURG BICYCLE & FITNESS

307 York Street
(717) 334-7791
www.gettysburgbicycle.com

At Gettysburg Bicycle & Fitness, you can rent a bike and explore the battlefield on your own. The outfit has been in business since 1990, and with advance notice they can arrange a tour of the battlefield with a licensed guide on a case-by-case basis. Cost to rent two wheels is $7 per hour or $25 for the entire day. All rentals include helmets, locks, rear racks, and bungee cords. On busy weekends and holidays, every bike in their large inventory is usually rented, so you should reserve your bike in advance if possible. Serious cyclists gather at this location every Wednesday at 6:00 p.m. for a two-hour ride, and Gettysburg Bicycle & Fitness also sponsors bike races around the area. The shop is open every day but Sunday, and parking is available at the rear of the building.

Bus Tours

GETTYSBURG TOURS
Gettysburg Tour Center
778 Baltimore Street
(717) 334-6296
www.gettysburgbattlefieldtours.com

Gettysburg Tours offers a two-hour battlefield bus tour, with your choice of either a dramatized stereo tour aboard a double-decker bus for $22.95 per adult and $12.95 per child or a tour led by a licensed battlefield guide aboard an air-conditioned motor coach for $25.95 per adult and $15.50 per child. The main office for Gettysburg Tours is listed above, but you'll find satellite offices throughout town. The business has been operating year-round since the 1960s, and tours take place throughout the day. If you plan on visiting other attractions in addition to the battlefield, the package plans offered here are a great bargain. You get unlimited use of the Gettysburg Town Trolley and, depending on which plan you choose, admission to five or all of the following six attractions: the Hall of Presidents, the Soldier's National Museum, the Jennie Wade House Museum, the Lincoln Train Museum, the Gettysburg Battle Theatre, and the American Civil War Museum.

HISTORIC TOURS
Historic Tour Company
55 Steinwehr Avenue
(717) 334-8000
www.historictourcompany.com

If you want to tour the battlefield in a bit of history, Historic Tours is the place for you. Tours are given in a 1933 modified school bus and two modernized 12-passenger 1936 and 1937 Yellowstone buses. The Model 706 Yellowstone buses were developed specifically for sightseeing within the western national parks, and the Yellowstone buses were used in Yellowstone National Park from 1936 to the mid-1960s.

As you tour in style, an audio CD tells the story of the entire three days of the battle as you travel the battlefield. The driver has the ability to stop the CD and start it again, and both of the drivers/tour guides are extremely knowledgeable about the battle. The 2.5-hour tour runs twice a day Monday through Saturday and once on Sunday. Advance reservations are encouraged but not required. Cost is $19.95 for adults and $12.00 for children age 7 to 11; children age six and younger ride for free with a paying adult.

Horseback Tours

HICKORY HOLLOW FARMS
219 Crooked Creek Road
(717) 334-0349
www.hickoryhollowfarm.com

Hickory Hollow Farms offers one-hour scenic rides on the battlefield for $40 an hour, two- to four-hour scenic rides on the battlefield for $35 an hour, or a two- to six-hour historic ride on the battlefield with a licensed battlefield guide for $50 an hour. The scenic rides are just that—scenic; they're led by wranglers, not battlefield guides, and they don't provide a history of the battle. Tours are kept to small groups of six to seven riders, and children must be eight years old to ride. Riders have a 250-pound weight limit, and helmets must be worn by children younger than age 16. When calling, ask for Pam or Jackie. Riding lessons are also available, and you can board your own horse if you'd like (see the Recreation chapter). Hickory Hollow Farms is open seven days a week.

NATIONAL RIDING STABLES ARTILLERY RIDGE CAMPGROUND
610 Taneytown Road
(717) 334-1288, (877) 335-5596
www.artilleryridge.com

On the "Ride into History" tour offered here, you can relive the Gettysburg battle while on horseback. A two-hour ride reviews the entire three-day battle, and you ride across the sites involved on the second and third days. A CD by a licensed battlefield guide pipes the history in through headsets. You can either rent one of their horses or bring your own; Artillery Ridge Campground offers box stalls and corrals. The cost to rent a horse and enjoy the tour is $65 per

Close-up

History vs. History

The National Park Service and the Gettysburg Foundation made much progress toward their goal of returning the battlefield to its 1863 appearance with the opening of the new visitor center in April 2008. The *Battle of Gettysburg* painting that was housed in the cyclorama building has been restored and is on display in the new visitor center, and the next step in the overall plan will be the removal of the old visitor center and cyclorama building from their location along Taneytown Road. Controversy swirls around the benefit of this project even as it moves along, especially concerning tearing down the cyclorama building, which many consider to be of historic significance.

The distinctive round building that housed the cyclorama since 1962 was closed in November 2005 to complete the removal and restoration of the painting. The *Battle of Gettysburg* is a 360-degree circular oil-on-canvas painting that depicts Pickett's Charge, the famous offensive maneuver of 12,000 Confederates who were attempting to overtake the Union troops on Cemetery Ridge on the final day of the battle. At the beginning of the restoration, the *Battle of Gettysburg* measured 356 feet by 26 feet and weighed an estimated three tons. Hanging at the new center, the restored painting once again measures 377 feet at its widest points and is 42 feet high. With its new backing and hanging system, the painting now weighs 12.5 tons.

No one disagrees that the 1884 painting is displayed more effectively in a safer environment for the canvas in the new center. The disagreement arises over whether the old cyclorama building deserves to stay based on its own historic significance. The building was built by architect Richard Neutra in 1961, and it has been said that this was Neutra's greatest public commission and the finest example of his work east of the Mississippi. In September 1998 the Cyclorama Center was determined to be eligible for the National Register of Historic Places, and in December 1999 the Association of Architectural Historians nominated the building as a National Historic Landmark—the highest honor a building can receive. A lawsuit is currently under way to stop the destruction of the cyclorama. Only time will tell which history will win out as the more significant.

---

person, and some restrictions apply. Riders must be at least eight years old, no more than one rider is allowed on the horse, and a weight limit of 240 pounds applies to riders. Also, riders age 15 and younger must be accompanied by an adult, and riders younger than age 18 must have a parent or guardian sign a waiver in order to ride. Tours are offered several times a day seven days a week. Reservations are required, and they usually need to be made well in advance if you want a weekend ride on this popular tour.

Segway Tours

Imagine seeing the battlefield on foot but never being tired from walking. If this sounds like heaven, a tour using a Segway personal transporter may be for you. A Segway is a two-wheel self-balancing electric vehicle that is guided by your body movements. Its top speed is around 12 miles per hour, and two companies in town train you on how to ride the vehicle and offer various tour options. Both provide helmets for your safety.

SEGS IN THE CITY
Taneytown and Wheatfield Roads
(410) 276-7347, (800) 734-7393
www.segsinthecity.com
Three tours, which are called safaris, are offered. The three-hour Battlefield Explorer safari is an

in-depth look at the battlefield while the two-hour Great Circle safari follows the events of the second day of the battle. A Segway guide, who is knowledgeable on the history of the battle, leads the tours, or you can have Segs in the City arrange for a licensed battlefield guide to lead your safari. The Battlefield at Sunset tour lasts two hours and is led by a licensed battlefield guide. Cost for the Battlefield Explorer, which is a morning tour, is $80. The afternoon Great Circle safari is $70 per person, while the sunset tour costs $80. Reservations are required 24 hours in advance, and riders must be 14 years of age and weigh less than 260 pounds. Safaris are limited to six riders, but larger groups may be accommodated on a case-by-case basis.

SEGTOURS

380 Steinwehr Avenue (rear parking lot of the Reliance Mine Saloon)
(717) 253-7987
www.segtours.com
Two tours of the battlefield are available, and both are escorted by staff members of SegTours, who consider themselves historians who are utilizing a new technology to immerse themselves and visitors deeper into the study of the Battle of Gettysburg. The Western Battlefield tour takes about 2.5 hours, covers the three days of the battle by following the Confederate and then the Union battle lines, and visits all the battlefield's most famous sites. It costs $65 per person. The Eastern Battlefield tour is shorter, at about 1.5 hours, and it covers the lesser known but many pivotal engagements that occurred on this side of the battlefield. Its cost is $45 per person. On both tours you can either listen to an audiotape that was designed and narrated by a licensed battlefield guide or opt to have a licensed battlefield guide accompany you on your tour for an extra fee of $15. Reservations are encouraged for all tours and required if you wish to be accompanied by a licensed battlefield guide. Riders must be at least 16 years old.

Walking Tours

PARK RANGERS GNMP VISITOR CENTER

97 Taneytown Road
(717) 334-1124
www.nps.gov/gett
Park rangers offer many free guided walks and tours of the battlefield during the summer. Programs range from about half an hour to three hours. You can get a guided tour of the National Cemetery, explore the importance of Little Round Top in the battle, accompany a ranger on a hike of the battlefield, or enjoy a myriad of other activities. For a full schedule of all the free programs offered, check at the information desk at the visitor center or visit the Web site. There are also programs specifically tailored for children; see the Kidstuff chapter for details.

MILITARY MEMORABILIA SHOPS

South of Lincoln Square

ARSENAL OF THE ALLEGHENYS

141 Steinwehr Avenue
(717) 334-1122
www.arsenalofthealleghenys.com
Arsenal of the Alleghenys owners Jay and Melody Thomas travel to more than 20 Civil War and antiques shows each year to find unique artifacts to sell out of their store. Jay focuses on artifacts from the Civil War and the Indian War period while Melody specializes in Victorian-era items. All items they offer are guaranteed to be authentic relics that are considered investment-grade quality. Military memorabilia might include weapons, clothing, journals, corps badges, and medical items, and you can usually also find some Indian-related memorabilia and antique silver, glassware, and porcelain from the Victorian era. On show is Victorian jewelry, as well as accessories such as shawls, gloves, and hankies. The shop is open every day but Monday, and it's located at the southern end of Steinwehr Avenue.

DIRTY BILLY'S HATS
20 Baltimore Street
(717) 334-3200
www.dirtybillyshats.com

Dirty Billy's motto is "Historical Artwork You Can Wear," and this shop is full of hats, hats, and more hats. You'll find hats representing the ranks of the North and South as well as ladies' bonnets, straw hats, and tall top hats such as Lincoln wore. The hats are precise replicas that Billy creates from examining pictures and artifacts. Billy's attention to authentic details has resulted in his hats being worn by Martin Sheen and Sam Elliott in *Gettysburg,* Patrick Swayze in *North and South,* and Tom Berenger in *Rough Riders.* Dirty Billy's is open on Friday, Saturday, and Sunday and by appointment the rest of the week.

GETTYSBURG GIFT CENTER
297 Steinwehr Avenue
(717) 334-6245, (800) 887-7775
www.gettysburgmuseum.com

Although it's located in the lobby of the American Civil War Museum (see the Attractions chapter), this store, with more than 3,000 square feet of space, is anything but tiny. It has a complete selection of gifts and souvenirs, including books, hats, flags, shirts, and limited-edition art. On display are miniature statues by Chilmark and George Fund, reproductions of handpainted photographs of Civil War generals, White House china, numerous Mort Künstler items, and many more interesting collectibles. The back of the store is where you'll find souvenir-type items, the middle of the store has military memorabilia, and a section at the front of the gift center has a nice selection of Americana gifts. On my last visit I was especially intrigued by the earrings that were made from hair—and you could have a set made out of your own hair if you'd like! The Gettysburg Gift Center is open daily.

GETTYSBURG MINIATURE SOLDIERS
200 Steinwehr Avenue
(717) 338-1800

This store doesn't just appear small from the outside—it is small. But how big does a store that carries historical miniatures and toy soldiers need to be? This one-room store manages to stock thousands of metal and plastic soldiers, and that's all you'll find here. Open daily, this tiny gem shares a building with the Gettysburg Tour Center; the entrance is around the corner on the right when you're facing the building.

GETTYSBURG QUARTERMASTER
419 Baltimore Street
(717) 334-8838
www.farnsworthhouseinn.com/quartermaster.html

Located on the Farnsworth House complex, the Gettysburg Quartermaster has thousands of items for the Civil War collector. Here you'll find fine original military relics from the Revolutionary War to the war in Vietnam, with an emphasis on Civil War and WWII items. Cases of museum-style shelves are filled with rare artifacts, photographs, and military correspondence, and collectors come here to buy, sell, trade, and broker consignments. Browsers who wish to peruse the goods will also find much to interest them. Among the many great finds here are a McClellan saddle and military memorabilia posters. You'll also be surrounded by rack upon rack of WWII fatigues, helmets, and uniform badges and buttons, as well as bayonets and a variety of guns on display. The Gettysburg Quartermaster has been in business since 1972, and it's open on Monday, Thursday, and Saturday afternoons.

HORSE SOLDIER
Old Gettysburg Village
777 Baltimore Street
(717) 334-0347
www.horsesoldier.com

If you love admiring military goods but dislike the cramped spaces that often accompany such excursions, plan a visit to the Horse Soldier. Since the Small family opened their business in 1971, it has grown and grown and grown . . . and grown. It now fills eight spacious rooms within its location in Old Gettysburg Village. This is the largest store featuring military antiques and memorabilia in Gettysburg, and you can find items dating from the Revolutionary War to WWI, with an emphasis on Civil War items. Artillery, currency, bottles, guns, swords, soldiers' letters, documents, autographs, prints, musical instruments, medical instruments, 19th-century civilian and military photographs, and a myriad of other intriguing items are housed here. Military-related books (old and new), music, and videos are also available.

Be sure not to miss the two cases filled with Gettysburg-related items. The Horse Soldier displays items from the John Plank Geiselman Museum Collection, the last major grouping of Gettysburg artifacts assembled and documented by a local resident. In many instances Geiselman noted not only the source of the Gettysburg relic and the date of its recovery but also the part of the battlefield it came from. All items at the Horse Soldier are guaranteed to be authentic, and the staff also conducts appraisal and soldier research services. The store is open daily except on Wednesday. Adjacent to the Horse Soldier on the Baltimore Street entrance is Hallowed Ground, also owned by the Small family, where you can get Gettysburg T-shirts and Horse Soldier hats.

THE REGIMENTAL QUARTERMASTER
49 Steinwehr Avenue
(717) 338-1864, (800) 929-1863
www.regtqm.com

The Regimental Quartermaster makes the most of its limited space. In the front of the store, you'll find Civil War reproductions, muskets, swords, leather goods, equipment, accessories, books, and manuals. Toward the rear of the store are period civilian wear and military uniforms, including one of the largest collections of shoes from the era. The Jeweler's Daughter (see the Shopping chapter) is located in the middle of the store. Reenactors can find everything they need in this one spot to completely outfit themselves appropriately.

STONEHAM'S ARMORY
5 Steinwehr Avenue
(717) 337-2347
www.tbhabitat.com

Stoneham's fills the ground floor of its early 20th-century Prairie-style brick building with a wide assortment of historically authentic reproduction swords, revolvers, muskets, and memorabilia from the Civil War through the WWII time frame. Pewterware, copperware, tinware, books, CDs and DVDs, flags, and Civil War chess sets complete the upscale ambience. Up the stairs are five more rooms where you'll find Irish gifts, sculptures, clocks, and more. Stoneham's and the two shops beside it, Battlefields Souvenirs and Habitat, as well as the American History Store around the corner, are owned by the same couple, and their good taste is evident throughout the four shops.

TARBOX TOY SOLDIERS
Arbor House
45 Steinwehr Avenue
(717) 338-1865

This miniature "wax museum" of historical figures includes Civil War military figures and dioramas, and owner Charlie Tarbox purchases some of the collectibles from Russian miniature dealer Sergei Ilyashenko, of the company Lead Army. Charlie is as much a reason to visit as his beautiful pieces of art. He's known as Gettysburg's resident historian, and his knowledge of the Civil War and Gettysburg is truly remarkable. Charlie is a published military author and noted lecturer who has great stories to tell as well as beautiful historical art to offer.

THE UNION DRUMMER BOY
13 Baltimore Street
(717) 334-2350
www.uniondb.com

The Union Drummer Boy shows off its collection of authentic Civil War artifacts in glass cases within this spacious shop. Every item within the place is guaranteed to be authentic, and the owners attend more than 20 Civil War and military shows yearly throughout the country, where they buy and sell Civil War artifacts. Among the treasures are muskets, revolvers, carbines, uniforms, canteens, photos, leather goods, letters, artillery shells, documents, flags, autographs, swords, and relics. You can also have your Civil War goods appraised here. The Union Drummer Boy is open daily.

East of Lincoln Square

FIELDS OF GLORY
55 York Street
(717) 337-2837
www.fieldsofglory.com

Fields of Glory is filled to the brim with Civil War relics. As you enter, it's hard to decide whether to start at the original Civil War muskets and swords hanging along the left wall or at the glass cases full of memorabilia that line the wall on the right. There's also a room to the left and a room in the back, both filled with authentic Civil War–era items. You'll find tintype photographs, buttons, medical supplies, soldier accessories, uniforms, drums . . . the list never seems to end. Fields of Glory is open seven days a week.

GETTYSBURG ANNIVERSARY CIVIL WAR BATTLE REENACTMENT

Held on the weekend closest to the Fourth of July, this annual three-day event features battle reenactments, sutlers, entertainment, special guests, living-history events, and educational demonstrations. The reenactment takes place in conjunction with Gettysburg Heritage Days, more than a week of events happening throughout town. (For more on Heritage Days, see the Annual Events and Festivals chapter.) This is definitely the event of the year for area tourism and those who want to commemorate the Battle of Gettysburg. Reenactments that take place on five-year anniversaries of the battle usually draw 15,000 to 20,000 reenactors, while the in-between years usually draw 3,000 reenactors and 25,000 to 30,000 visitors. In 2008 the reenactment to commemorate the 145th anniversary of the battle was made into the DVD docudrama *Gettysburg: Darkest Days and Finest Hours.* Call (717) 338-1525 or visit www.gettysburgreenactment .com to purchase the DVD or for updates about the current year's reenactment.

The first thing you need to know about the reenactment is that it's not held on the hallowed ground of Gettysburg National Military Park,

where the actual Battle of Gettysburg unfolded. Instead, it's held at a site near the town, usually at an area farm. Every yearly event is unique, but you can expect to see battle reenactments and mortar fire competitions each day, and every reenactment culminates in the battle of Pickett's Charge. Throughout the three days there are also living-history demonstrations, and visitors are welcome to tour the military camps and meet the reenactors. Sutlers showcase their military goods to the reenactors, just as they did when they followed the soldiers during the war, and visitors can find food, beverage, and souvenir stands.

Two types of tickets are available to visitors. A general admission ticket gets you into the reenactment site and includes all activities and demonstrations. You may bring lawn chairs or blankets and view the reenactments from the grounds, with spaces on a first-come, first-serve basis. A grandstand ticket, which is bought in addition to the general admission ticket, includes admission to grandstand seating on bleachers that are located to give the best view of field events and demonstrations. Grandstand seating is limited, and your ticket guarantees you *a seat* in the grandstand, not *a particular seat.*

Tickets may be purchased for one, two, or all three days of the event, and you can buy them in advance or at the gate on the day you wish to attend. Tickets are nonrefundable and cost less if you purchase them in advance. Tickets are sold by phone, via the Web site, and at many area stores. The reenactment is subject to weather conditions, and although it's rare for the event to be rescheduled, it has happened—in 2003 it was moved to August because the farmland was too wet from a particularly soggy spring. Grandstand seating usually sells out prior to the event, and grandstand seats cannot be ordered without also purchasing general admission tickets. In 2009 advance ticket prices were $24 for one day, $40 for two days, and $54 for three days for those age 13 and older, and $12 for one day, $20 for two days, and $25 for three days for those age 6 through 12. Children younger than age six are admitted to the event free of charge, but a grandstand seating ticket must be purchased if they're going to sit in the grandstand. At the 2009 event grandstand seating was $10 per day for all ages. Most people don't realize that the reenactors also have to pay to partake in the event. They pay a registration fee rather than having to buy a ticket. The registration fees for the 2009 event were $8 for reenactors who registered before December 31, 2008, $12 for those who registered before March 15, $15 for those who registered before June 1, and $25 for reenactors who registered later than June 1.

Attending a battle reenactment is an exciting way to see history come to life. All the descriptions in the world don't compare to actually witnessing the smoke from the guns or hearing the Rebel Cry as Pickett's Charge begins. It's also enlightening to talk to the reenactors, who often are walking historians about their units.

i Each weekend from April through October, reenactors camp within Gettysburg National Military Park at Spangler's Spring, Pitzer Woods, and the Pennsylvania Monument. Anyone is welcome to stop by and see what camp life was like for soldiers at Gettysburg. For more information contact Gettysburg National Military Park at (717) 334-1124, ext. 446.

REENACTORS

Contributing a large part to the Gettysburg experience are the reenactors you see around town, who bring the Civil War and the Battle of Gettysburg to life through their hobby. Most casual observers don't see much beyond someone dressed in military or period-style clothing, but reenactor dress varies from beginners who may not realize their uniform was made in Pakistan to those who are wearing an outfit that is authentic down to the number of threads used and the thread's country of origin. Although the level of authenticity varies, most reenactors agree that all you really need to enjoy the hobby is a love of

the Civil War era. But becoming a reenactor is not quite as simple as that.

Reenactors usually do a great deal of research to ensure they make the most realistic impression they can. Civilians don't just put on a period-style dress; they also research the correct hairstyle, accoutrements, and jewelry being worn at the time. Most military reenactor groups are set up to parallel military life, with new recruits entering as privates and working their way up the ranks, with promotions based on how authentic their portrayals are. Looking the part doesn't come cheap—a basic Union soldier outfit with rifle, tent, clothes, belt, and ammo pouch can easily run $1,200 to $1,500.

Groups dedicated to Civil War reenacting have members throughout the states and even in some foreign countries. Often the love of reenacting is passed down from generation to generation, and many hobbyists love that reenacting is something the entire family can enjoy together.

Civil War Clothing and Accessories

ABRAHAM'S LADY
25 Steinwehr Avenue
(717) 338-1798
www.abrahamslady.com
Owner Donna Abraham has been making Civil War–era clothing and accessories for ladies since 1991, and she's especially known for making beautiful Garibaldi red shirts. Everything Donna makes is authentic to the Civil War period. You'll find skirts and dresses, underclothes, jewelry, accessories, and shoes—everything needed to outfit you completely for your trip back in time. A healthy selection of period-authentic patterns for women, men, and children is also available for those who prefer to make their own clothes.

i If you're a fresh fish (new recruit) and you don't want to commit a farby—a Civil War–reenactment term for anything not typical of the period—visit www.cwreenactors.com for excellent information on how to get started in the hobby.

A CIVIL AFFAIR
100 Baltimore Street
(717) 338-1565
www.acivilaffair.com

From ball gowns to camp clothing and clothes for every occasion in between, A Civil Affair has what you need to be an authentically dressed Civil War–era lady. Their garments are produced on the premises, or you can choose from their patterns and make your own clothes. And you can complete your outfit with all the appropriate accessories, including period wigs and hairpieces, hats and hat pins, period jewelry, Victorian fans, and lots more. While you're picking out your outfit, you can shop for Victorian goods at Battlefield Baskets & Gifts, also at the same location (see the Fine Gifts and Home Accents section of the Shopping chapter). A Civil Affair is closed on Monday and Tuesday.

CIVIL WAR CENTER
17 on the Square
17 Lincoln Square
(717) 339-0017
www.17onthesquare.com

The Civil War Center is located within 17 on the Square, a group of businesses that share a historic building (see the Shopping chapter for more on the other shops). Here you can find handmade clothing for military and civilian reenactors, as well as the appropriate accessories and accoutrements. The Civil War Center will also display and sell on consignment Civil War items you no longer want.

CORNER CLOTHIERS
2215B Fairfield Road
(717) 334-4429
www.cornerclothiers.com

This small shop is located on the left side of the building that houses Needle & Thread Fabrics (see separate entry within this chapter), and it's dedicated to mid-19th-century men's fashions. You can choose your clothing off the rack or arrange for a custom-made outfit to be created. Co-owners Brian Merrick and Kara Bartels reproduce authentic fashions of the time based on original clothing they have in their collection and/or meticulous research they conduct. Clothing offered includes many different types of coats, trousers, shirts, vests, and suspenders. For instance, you can order a frock coat, a sack coat, an overcoat, or a *paletot*, an extremely versatile quilted wool coat worn for nearly any occasion from the 1840s to 1890s. Besides the clothing on display at the store, you can also find some exquisite neckties and cravats. Other accessories available include starched collars, wallets, and tobacco bags, which are lined with leather to keep your tobacco fresh. Corner Clothiers is open on Friday, Saturday, and Sunday, and by chance on Thursday. To reach the shop, travel Route 116 West (Fairfield Road) for about 3.5 miles from the square and turn in at the parking lot for Needle & Thread Fabrics.

i Don't walk into the mirror within Corner Clothiers! It's along the back wall of the shop, and at first you think you're looking into another room, but it's just a trick of the eye—one that also makes the shop seem twice as big as it is!

GETTYSBURG SUTLER
1180 Hanover Road
(717) 337-9669

The Gettysburg Sutler has appropriate Civil War–period clothing for civilian as well as military reenactors, male and female, adult and child. A room in the front of the shop is filled with ladies' clothing and accessories, including jewelry, bonnets, and patterns for those who like to make their own clothes. The main room contains uniforms for officers and enlisted men, as well as clothing for civilian men and boys. You'll also find equipment and accessories, including weapons, canteens, medical supplies, and much more. The Gettysburg Sutler is located just west of the Hanover Road interchange with U.S. Route 15, and the store is open daily.

HIGHLAND ROSE CIVIL WAR SUTLERY
Old Gettysburg Village
777 Baltimore Street
(717) 339-0660

Open mainly on the weekends, this compact store offers attire for those who want to dress as one did during the Civil War. You'll find garments on the rack to choose from, which can be altered, or you can have an outfit custom designed. Liz, the owner, also does beautiful work on period wedding gowns, with extensive hand beading being her forte. The shop is located in the courtyard of Old Gettysburg Village.

Sutlers, civilians licensed by the government to follow the armies in wagons and sell luxury goods to the soldiers, were more prevalent among Union than Confederate troops. Today many stores within Gettysburg still call themselves sutlers; unlike their historical ancestors they carry goods for reenactors from both sides of the war.

HOME FRONT GENERAL STORE
312 Baltimore Street
(717) 338-1776
www.homefrontgeneralstore.com

Owners Kirk Davis and Diana Thomas opened this Civil War and WWII outlet in the beginning of 2008, and the store offers a nice selection of uniforms as well as clothing for civilians. All kinds of accessories are also available, from swords and haversacks to housewives (sewing kits). You'll also find period jewelry as well as artwork and books on all things military. Upstairs is the Ladies Parlor, where you can browse a nice selection of day dresses, parasols, shawls, purses, and hats. There are also candles, quilts, Victorian soaps and powders, and mourning jewelry you can choose to complete your immersion into the past. But the coolest part of the store has to be the Wall of Honor, pictures of servicepersons that hang along the entire wall of the staircase. Anyone can send in a picture (copies only please—Kirk and Diana don't want the only copy of your precious memory) and have their loved one honored for his or her service to our country. There's also a corner of the store dedicated to the platoon the Thomases have adopted through the federal AdoptaPlatoon program. Visitors can write letters, make cash donations, and drop off packages, all based on the specific needs of the adopted platoon, and Diane and Kirk then forward the items to the troops.

LA BELLE FEMME
1015 Baltimore Street
(717) 337-9200

Owner Maggie Abbott has more than 20 years of historical-costuming experience, and she has owned various Civil War clothing stores in town over the years. She opened a shop at this location in late 2008, and the small but comfy space here suits Maggie's personality, allowing her to interact with her customers on a personal level. The shop focuses on custom-made historical clothing from the mid-1800s, especially wedding and formal attire, as well as rentals of both military and civilian Civil War clothing. Wigs, hats, jewelry, and numerous other accoutrements are available to complete your outfit. Maggie also carries the largest selection of period perfumes available in the eastern United States. La Belle Femme is open Thursday through Sunday.

NEEDLE & THREAD FABRICS
2215 Fairfield Road
(717) 334-4011
www.needleandthread.biz

Sewers and quilters will be in heaven at this shop, which fills its large building with bolt after bolt of Civil War–style patterns and fabrics. Everything you need to complete your outfit also can be found here, as well as notions, quilting and sewing supplies, smocking supplies, foam rubber, cross-stitch, and much, much more. Needle & Thread also stocks everything needed to make curtains, quilts, tablecloths, place mats, and more. With all that's within this store, your only limit is your own imagination. Needle & Thread is about 3.5 miles west of the square right along Route 116; the shop is closed on Tuesday and Sunday.

Close-up

Zouave Units in the Civil War

The Zouave uniform, which consists of baggy trousers, a braided jacket, and a tasseled fez, is modeled on the uniform worn by French colonial troops. Elmer Ellsworth organized the first American Zouave unit, the Chicago Zouaves, and he drilled them in tactics adopted from French manuals. Ellsworth and 50 of his best Chicago Zouaves toured the country in 1860 on a 6-week, 20-city tour to challenge other state militias in a drill competition. The unit's precise drills not only won them the competition hands down but also awed thousands of spectators. Before long dozens of new Zouave companies were formed throughout the country.

The fighting skills, precise maneuvers, and colorful Zouave uniforms of the Fifth New York Volunteer Infantry, known as Duryee's Zouaves, made them one of the most renowned regiments of the Civil War. Gen. George Sykes was quoted as saying, "I doubt whether it had an equal, and certainly no superior among all the regiments of the Army of the Potomac."

In the 1970s several Civil War reenactors decided to organize a living-history unit that would pay homage to the Zouave units of the Civil War. Company A, Fifth New York Volunteer Infantry, is currently active in living-history programs, encampments, and battle reenactments. Members dress in full Zouave regalia and pride themselves on their military skills.

S&S SUTLER
331 Buford Avenue
(717) 338-1990
www.ss-sutler.com

This delightful shop is owned by Tim and Debbie Sheads, both originally from Gettysburg and both a wealth of information on the life and mind-set of reenacting. After working for the state and raising a family in nearby Bendersville, Tim and Debbie decided to move back to Gettysburg and open a sutlery. Their first shop was on Steinwehr Avenue, but they moved to their current location across from the Lutheran Theological Seminary when the home of an ancestor of Tim's became available. The Carrie Sheads House was built in March 1862, and it certainly saw fighting on the first day of battle. A projectile is embedded in its front wall, and three soldiers etched their names in one of the house's windows. The Carrie Sheads House is listed on the National Register of Historic Places, and the sutlery is located in a converted garage at the rear of the house.

Tim put on his first reenactment uniform when he was four years old. As an adult he's been a reenactor since 1969, and today he is an active member of the Fifth New York Duryee Zouaves (see the Close-up on the Zouaves above). Debbie is also an avid reenactor, and both Tim and Debbie strive to offer the most historically correct garments and equipment at the best prices. Here you will find only authentic goods that are of good quality and value, and many are handcrafted. They stock uniforms, military goods, and civilian accessories. The sutlery is open Friday through Monday and other days and evenings by appointment.

SOMEWEAR IN TIME HISTORICAL CLOTHING
76 Steinwehr Avenue
(717) 337-2143

This shop opened in 2005 up the street from its current location. The address may have changed, but the quality of clothing offered here has not. At Somewear in Time, the emphasis is on hand-made historical clothes—primarily clothing of the Civil War era. You can also find various accoutrements, including underclothing and handmade and reproduction jewelry. Somewear in Time is open Monday through Saturday.

ATTRACTIONS

Of course, the number one attraction in Gettysburg is the Gettysburg National Military Park (GNMP), and this site of the three-day battle in July 1863 that many feel was the turning point of the Civil War is usually what brings travelers to Gettysburg. Many people feel one trip to the battlefield isn't enough; in fact, some visit time and again, and others move here to be nearer. Gettysburg and the battle are so intertwined that an entire chapter of this book is devoted to the Gettysburg National Military Park and the role of reenactors in the Gettysburg experience.

This chapter covers the other attractions that Gettysburg has to offer, and it's split into three categories—historical, general, and ghostly. Since most visitors here are interested in history, the chapter begins with that category. Around town there are many attractions that help one interpret the battle and the entire Civil War. Since President Lincoln made his famous address here, you'll also find attractions dedicated to Lincoln. And another president, Dwight D. Eisenhower, who made a farm near Gettysburg his home, also shares the historical attractions spotlight.

If you need to take a break from all this historical knowledge, check out the general attractions Gettysburg has to offer. You can visit a winery, take a scenic train ride, or visit some of the fruit orchards in the area. After all, Adams County is the leading fruit-producing and -processing county in the state of Pennsylvania. Tours are also available that take you on walks in town, drives through the countryside, and romantic jaunts around town and the countryside in horse-drawn carriages.

I doubt many visitors leave Gettysburg without taking a ghost tour. At times it seems the ghosts are as big an attraction as the history that was made here. There are numerous tours to pick from that will satisfy your curiosity about the spirit world.

PRICE CODE

Prices represent the cost for one adult admission. Most places reduce the price for children and senior citizens, but each establishment sets its age ranges differently, so be sure to ask about prices for specific ages. Many attractions allow children younger than a certain age to be admitted for free, and I'll mention this when it applies.

$	$2.00 to $5.50
$$	$5.51 to $7.50
$$$	$7.51 to $15.00
$$$$	More than $15

HISTORICAL ATTRACTIONS

Gettysburg Tours offers package plans that combine a bus tour of the Gettysburg National Military Park with attractions in town. See the Bus Tours section of the Gettysburg National Military Park chapter for details.

Lincoln Square

THE DAVID WILLS HOUSE $$
8 Lincoln Square
(717) 334-1124
www.nps.gov/gett,
www.mainstreetgettysburg.org
After extensive remodeling inside and out, the David Wills reopened on the 200th anniversary

of Lincoln's birthday (February 12, 2009). This is where President Lincoln stayed the night before he gave his famous Gettysburg Address. David Wills was a local attorney who owned the house from 1859 to about 1895, and after the Battle of Gettysburg, the house was the center of much of the cleanup activities. All this history is no doubt why the site of the Wills home has been run as a museum since 1938.

In 2004 the Borough of Gettysburg sold the house to Gettysburg National Military Park, which spent more than $6 million turning the house, which is on the Register of Historic Places, into a downtown museum and orientation center for visitors. The exterior of the house has been restored to its 1863 appearance, and visitors come in from the York Street entrance, just as the Wills family did almost a century and a half ago. A reception area with an information desk serves as the orientation center, and seven galleries are featured inside the museum. The orientation center is free, but a fee is charged to enter the museum. Two rooms inside have been restored to their 1863 appearance. One is the bedroom Lincoln stayed in and the other is Wills's office, where he coordinated many efforts after the battle. A bookstore featuring all things Lincoln rounds out the experience. The David Wills House is open daily, and children age five and younger are admitted for free.

North of Lincoln Square

LINCOLN TRAIN STATION
35 Carlisle Street
(717) 337-8233
After undergoing a $3 million restoration project, the station where Lincoln arrived in November 1863 the day before delivering a few remarks at the opening of the country's first national cemetery now features museum displays about its historic significance. The station first began operation in 1859, with its large brass bell in the cupola announcing the arrival and departure of passenger trains. Four years later it would serve as a makeshift hospital during the Battle of Gettysburg, and more than 15,000 wounded soldiers

would pass through it after the battle on their journey to established hospitals.

The train station supported passenger service until 1942, and for a while it served as the home of the Gettysburg Convention and Visitors Bureau. But by 1998 the building was in poor condition and in desperate need of preservation. Several Gettysburg citizens wanted to restore the building to its former glory, and their cause was made possible when the children of the deceased owner of the building donated it to the borough in 1998 with the condition that it be made into a museum. The current railroad owner, CSX, donated the station to the Borough of Gettysburg, some federal funding was secured, and the restoration began. The project itself was fascinating, often unearthing artifacts such as railroad tracks way below the surface of the current station. After an almost decade-long endeavor, the station is now open daily and you can tour the museum for free.

South of Lincoln Square

AMERICAN CIVIL WAR MUSEUM $
297 Steinwehr Avenue
(717) 334-6245
www.gettysburgmuseum.com
Many return visitors may know this museum as the National Civil War Wax Museum, which was its name for about 40 years until 2003, when the name was changed to better represent the museum. Whatever you call it, this is the number one private attraction in Gettysburg. Dioramas of life-size wax figures tell the story of the Civil War from its beginnings through to its conclusion. After visiting the dioramas, you can view a digitally enhanced audiovisual presentation that includes more than 200 life-size figures highlighting Pickett's Charge and a finale that has an animated President Lincoln delivering the Gettysburg Address. There's always something going on in front of the museum, too. Reenactors are camped outside as part of the living-history programs that are held on weekends April through November, and there are special activities for children most Saturdays from June

through August (see the Kidstuff chapter for details). This is also the home of the Gettysburg Gift Center (see the GNMP chapter). The museum is open daily from 9:00 a.m. to 6:15 p.m., with the gift shop open until 7:00 p.m. Children younger than age six are admitted for free.

BATTLEFIELD MILITARY MUSEUM $$
900 Baltimore Pike
(717) 334-6568

George Marinos spent more than 60 years collecting military artifacts, all of which are on display at the Battlefield Military Museum, a large building at the south end of town that usually has a major piece of military equipment sitting out front. George and the rest of the Marinos family have been operating the museum at this location since the 1960s, and they claim to have the largest collection of authentic military artifacts in Gettysburg, with 10,000 items. More than 7,000 of the war relics are from the Civil War, and they include uniforms, weapons, photos, flags, medical kits, and more. Many pieces of the Civil War collection are from the Gettysburg struggle, including the medical kit of Gettysburg's only doctor at the time, Dr. Tate. The main floor is dedicated to the Civil War, while items downstairs are mainly from WWI and WWII, with a few displays of items from the Korean and Vietnam Wars. Here you can see gas masks from WWI, the WWII uniforms of actor Jimmy Stewart and Gen. Hap Arnold, and a letter an American soldier wrote home on Hitler's personal stationery. All displays are behind glass, and the museum is open daily. An inviting gift shop greets you as you enter the building, where some relics, Gettysburg memorabilia, and other

i **A new cell phone audio tour is available at the Eisenhower National Historic Site. Call (717) 253-9256 to hear stories about the Eisenhowers and the features around their home and farm. The rose gardens and the guesthouse are just two of the 17 stops along the tour. The tour is free but cell phone minutes apply.**

cool stuff can be purchased. Children younger than age six are admitted to the Battlefield Military Museum for free.

EISENHOWER NATIONAL HISTORIC SITE $$
250 Eisenhower Farm Drive
(717) 338-9114
www.nps.gov/eise/

This was the home and farm of Gen. Dwight D. Eisenhower, 34th president of the United States, and his wife, Mamie. The Eisenhowers bought it in 1950 at the end of Ike's 30-year military career, and the site is preserved as it was during their time here. Once Ike was elected president in 1952, he used the farm as a weekend retreat and "temporary White House," and he and Mamie retired to the home in 1961.

Access is gained by taking a shuttle bus from the visitor center at the Gettysburg National Military Park to the site; arrangements may be made on a first-come, first-serve basis at the center. You begin your adventure into the past with a 15-minute orientation tour of the farm and grounds. The reception center traces Eisenhower's life through exhibits and a video, and you can tour the first floor of the house, which features some of the Eisenhowers' original furnishings. There are also three self-guided walks that cover the grounds, the farm, and the skeet range. You can also attend 20-minute ranger-conducted walks and talks that focus on facets of Eisenhower's life, such as his military career, his presidency, his hobbies, his relationships with other world leaders, and more.

Much of Ike's presidency is defined by the Cold War, and there's a program where kids can become Junior Secret Service Agents (see the Kidstuff chapter). There are also special events held throughout the year, such as the '50s and the World War II Weekends (see the Annual Events and Festivals chapter) and the decking out of the house for Christmas as the Eisenhowers had it, including some original decorations and Christmas cards. The site is open daily except for New Year's Day, Thanksgiving, and Christmas, and admission is free for children younger than age six.

Winston Churchill, Charles de Gaulle, and Nikita Khrushchev are just three of many world leaders who were guests of President Eisenhower and his wife, Mamie, at their farm outside of Gettysburg.

EVERGREEN CEMETERY
799 Baltimore Street
(717) 334-4121
www.evergreencemetery.org
Evergreen Cemetery was established in 1854, and its grounds hold the graves of some of the most famous names in Gettysburg history. Encompassing 30 acres, this is the final resting place of Jennie Wade, the only civilian killed during the Battle of Gettysburg, and John Burns, a 69-year-old Gettysburg citizen who took up arms against the invading Confederates. Elizabeth Thorn is also buried here. Elizabeth was acting caretaker during the Battle of Gettysburg, and she personally dug the graves for 91 casualties of the fighting while six months pregnant. The Gettysburg Civil War Women's Memorial, which sits about 50 feet southwest of the gatehouse, is a 7-foot bronze statue of a six-month-pregnant Elizabeth leaning on a shovel as she takes a rest from her burial duties. The memorial was created by famous Civil War sculptor Ron Tunison in 2002, and it honors all the women who served in various capacities before, during, and following the Battle of Gettysburg. Another of many famous people buried here is the founder of Evergreen Cemetery, David McConaughy. You can visit the McConaughy History Room inside the gatehouse to learn more about this historic figure.

If you'd like to visit the graves of these and many other famous Gettysburg natives, your best bet is to buy the book *Beyond the Gatehouse: Gettysburg's Evergreen Cemetery,* which contains summaries of the lives of many of the notable people buried in Evergreen and an overview of the history of the cemetery. The book includes a map so visitors can easily find grave sites. It's written by Brian Kennell, the eighth and current superintendent of Evergreen Cemetery, who is a native of Gettysburg and who has lived at the cemetery gatehouse since 1976. The book is available at many bookstores in town, including the one at Gettysburg National Military Park Visitor Center.

All visitors to the cemetery are asked to remember where they are and to act accordingly. This is the final resting place for many, and respect should be paid to all who lie here and all who visit loved ones here. Evergreen is still an active cemetery—please visit with silence and respect.

GETTYSBURG BATTLE THEATRE $$
571 Steinwehr Avenue
(717) 334-6100
www.gettysburgbattlefieldtours.com
Located next to the field that was the site of Pickett's Charge and adjacent to the battlefield, the Gettysburg Battle Theatre puts on a multimedia presentation of the three days of the battle and the events leading up to it. The theater is open daily, and the presentation runs every 45 minutes from 9:00 a.m. to the last showing at 8:15 p.m. There's also a gift shop filled with Gettysburg gifts and collectibles on-site. And if you decide it's time to satisfy your stomach as well as your brain, General Pickett's Buffets (see the Restaurants chapter) is located downstairs. (The restaurant and theater share a building, but they're not affiliated.) Children younger than age four are admitted for free.

GETTYSBURG MINIATURE BATTLEFIELD
DIORAMA $
Artillery Ridge Campground
610 Taneytown Road
(717) 334-6408
www.artilleryridge.com
Consisting of about 20,000 handpainted soldiers, cannons, horses, and buildings, the Gettysburg Miniature Battlefield Diorama is one of the largest military dioramas in the United States. It allows you to visualize the entire three days of the Battle of Gettysburg at once, leaving a lasting impression of the magnitude of the conflict. The diorama is accompanied by a light and sound

show, adding to the realism. You'll also see the entire battlefield as it appeared in 1863, before nature and time changed some of the vistas. Gettysburg Miniature Battlefield Diorama is located at Artillery Ridge Campground, about 1 mile south of town, and it's open every day. Children age five and younger may view the diorama for free. (See the Campgrounds and RV Parks chapter for more on Artillery Ridge Campground.)

GETTYSBURG NATIONAL CEMETERY
(717) 334-1124

This is the burial site of 3,512 Union soldiers killed in the 'Battle of Gettysburg, and its dedication was the reason Lincoln came to Gettysburg and delivered his Gettysburg Address on November 19, 1863. The cemetery consists of 17 acres on Cemetery Hill, part of the battleground near the center of the Union line. It was designed by landscape architect William Saunders, founder of the National Grange. Saunders placed the Soldiers National Monument at the center of his design, and the Union graves were arranged in a series of semicircles around the monument. A space 2 feet wide was allocated for each body, and the bodies were laid with their heads toward the center. The headstones are uniform in size and contain the name, regiment, and company, if obtainable, of each soldier. Graves are grouped by state, with one section for unknowns.

The cemetery was completed in March of 1864 when the last of 3,512 Union dead were reburied. It became a National Cemetery on May 1, 1872, when control was transferred to the U.S. War Department. Today it is administered by the National Park Service and contains the remains of more than 6,000 individuals who served in a number of American wars. The cemetery also contains other monuments in addition to the Soldiers National Monument, including the New York Monument, the first statue to Maj. Gen. John F. Reynolds, and the monument to Lincoln's Gettysburg Address.

You might wonder what happened to the Confederate dead who were buried in makeshift graves on the battlefield. The removal of these bodies was only undertaken seven years after the battle. From 1870 to 1873, 3,320 bodies of Confederate soldiers were disinterred and sent to cemeteries in southern cities for reburial.

Gettysburg National Cemetery is open daily from 6:00 a.m. to 10:00 p.m., and there is no entrance fee.

HALL OF PRESIDENTS $$
789 Baltimore Street
(717) 334-5717
www.gettysburgbattlefieldtours.com

Wax figures tell the story of America at the Hall of Presidents, which sits beside the main entrance of the National Cemetery. Each president tells his own story, often in his own voice. A Smithsonian collection of First Ladies' Inaugural Gowns is authentically reproduced in the Hall of First Ladies, and the "Eisenhowers at Gettysburg" exhibit highlights the years Ike and Mamie spent at their farm in Gettysburg. Books on the presidents as well as on the Civil War along with souvenirs related to the Civil War and Gettysburg can be found in the gift shop. Children younger than age five are admitted for free. A tour takes about an hour, and the tours run daily. Tours begin every 15 minutes from 9:00 a.m. to the last tour, which begins at 7:45 p.m. Although informative, this attraction could use a bit of updating—President Bush doesn't even mention 9/11.

JENNIE WADE HOUSE MUSEUM $$
528 Baltimore Street
(717) 334-4100
www.gettysburgbattlefieldtours.com

Jennie Wade was the only civilian killed during the Battle of Gettysburg, and this is where she died while visiting her sister, who had just given birth. Only minor changes and repairs have been made to the house since the battle, and the house is authentically furnished from cellar to attic. Jennie was struck by a stray bullet while baking bread, and the actual bread tray that she was using is on display.

The house opens daily at 9:00 a.m., and tours begin about every 20 minutes, with the last tour starting at 7:00 p.m. The average time people spend on the tour is about half an hour, and children younger than age five are admitted for free. A docent begins the tour by giving you a short overview of Jennie's story, and then you tour the house on your own. Your self-guided tour begins in the kitchen, where an animated soldier describes the fighting and Jennie's death and its aftermath. After his story is done, you walk through the upstairs of the house, through a wall to the other side of this double home, and down to the home's cellar, where evidence of ghostly happenings at the house is displayed. When you're done in the cellar, you must exit the tour through the Jennie Wade Gift Shop, which features lots of Jennie Wade–related souvenirs. You'll also find Gettysburg souvenirs, Amish goods, and a nice selection of Civil War–related books on display. Tickets for the Ghostly Images of Gettysburg ghost tours are sold at the counter (see this chapter's Ghostly Attractions section).

LINCOLN TRAIN MUSEUM $$
425 Steinwehr Avenue
(717) 334-5678
www.gettysburgbattlefieldtours.com

This museum is home to the Lincoln Train Ride, where you accompany President Lincoln aboard the Presidential Train as he travels from Washington, D.C., to Gettysburg to dedicate the National Cemetery in November 1863. It's also the home of the Lincoln Toy Train collection, a truly impressive array of more than 1,000 pieces that consists of toy trains from the 1800s to present day, with some of the trains displayed within operating layouts. One layout goes around the top of the museum and the adjoining train shop, chugging along on tracks above your head. You'll find trains of all gauges, HO to Z, and you can have fun running some of the trains and admiring the railroad memorabilia found here, such as the train menu from 1911 and some collectibles from the 1830s. There are also dioramas illustrating the role of the railroad during the Civil War, and the Stations Masters Gift Shop has an extensive selection of railroad memorabilia and Gettysburg souvenirs. The Lincoln Train Museum is open daily 9:00 a.m. to 9:00 p.m., and children younger than age five are admitted for free.

NATIONAL SHRINE GROTTO OF LOURDES
Mount St. Mary's University
Emmitsburg, MD
(301) 447-5318
www.msmary.edu

The National Shrine Grotto of Lourdes is one of the oldest American replicas of the revered French shrine, dating from about two decades after the apparitions at Lourdes (1874). Sitting on a mountainside overlooking Mount St. Mary's campus, the grotto, which draws more than 55,000 visitors a year, is about 10 miles south of Gettysburg off U.S. Route 15. The grotto turnoff is on the right just beyond Mount St. Mary's College and Seminary, and there are plenty of signs to follow.

The grotto marks the site of a church built on the hill in 1805 by Father John DuBois, who was the founder of Mount St. Mary's College and Seminary. Today it overlooks the Shrine of Saint Elizabeth Ann Seton, who often prayed at the grotto. Mother Seton founded the Sisters of Charity in the United States, and she was canonized on September 14, 1975, becoming America's first native-born saint.

This is a peaceful place for prayer and reflection, and attending Mass here is a special event. The area is full of rugged beauty, with rocks and streams and plenty of wildflowers, and retreats and pilgrimages are held here throughout the year. If you want to take home a remembrance of the grotto, limited-edition prints of Frederick, Maryland, artist Harry Richardson's painting of the grotto are available only at Mount St. Mary's College and Seminary.

RONN PALM'S MUSEUM OF CIVIL WAR IMAGES $
229 Baltimore Street
(717) 337-1867

Civil War photographs are what this museum is all about, and Ronn Palm has amassed a collection of about 2,000 images. They're displayed within the second-oldest house in town, and Ronn has papers showing the owners of the house from 1802 onward. Ronn's passion is collecting and identifying photos of Civil War soldiers, and his photos have been used in numerous books and films. Most of the photos at the museum are of Pennsylvania soldiers, and the layout is arranged by regiments. The display cases in the front room have photos that are for sale, while the museum is in the back. If you had a relative who served in a Pennsylvania unit, you have a good chance of finding a picture of him in the museum. The Museum of Civil War Images is open only on Friday night, Saturday, and Sunday.

RUPP HOUSE HISTORY CENTER
451 Baltimore Street
(717) 338-1243
www.friendsofgettysburg.org
The Rupp House opened in 2003 as a project of the Friends of the National Parks at Gettysburg (FNPG), a group dedicated to preserving and providing education on the battlefield and the Eisenhower National Historic Site. Interactive exhibits and hands-on displays relay the battle as seen through the eyes of John and Caroline Rupp, who lived at this address at the time. (The Rupps's original house was heavily damaged during the fight for Cemetery Hill; the current structure was built in 1868.) Both the military and civilian experiences during the battle are highlighted, and visitors can imagine what it was like for both soldiers and townspeople during the battle through sight, sound, touch, and even smell. You tour the house, which is divided into parlors dedicated to each day of the battle and its aftermath, at your own pace. The Rupp House is open March through December, and there's no entrance fee, although there are donation jars throughout the

i The stench of death from the Battle of Gettysburg could be smelled as far away as Harrisburg from July until the first frost. Locals put peppermint oil under their noses to cover the odor. A period peppermint oil pump is just one of the many interactive displays at the Rupp House History Center that takes you back to those times.

center if you choose to contribute to the work of the FNPG. A walking tour that highlights the events that happened on Baltimore Street during the Battle of Gettysburg is sponsored by the Rupp House every Saturday. It departs from the center at 8:00 a.m.

SCHRIVER HOUSE MUSEUM $$
309 Baltimore Street
(717) 337-2800
www.schriverhouse.com
The Schriver House tour relays the experiences of one family during the Battle of Gettysburg. You are escorted on an informative half-hour tour that tells the story of George and Hettie Schriver and their two daughters, occupants of the house during the battle. George had already enlisted in the Union army, and Hettie gathered the children and went to her family's farm for safety once fighting broke out along Baltimore Street. Hettie made it to her family farm, the Weikert farm at Little Round Top, which turned out to be the site of some of the bloodiest fighting of the battle. Wounded soldiers streamed in almost from the moment they arrived at the farm. Meanwhile, Confederate soldiers moved into the house on Baltimore Street and set up a sharpshooter's position in the garret for two days. Several bullet holes can still be seen in the walls of the garret and along the house's outside wall. When the current owners, Del and Nancie Gudmestad, bought the place and started renovations in 1996, they found live Civil War bullets and medical supplies in the floorboards of the garret. Also found throughout the house were a pair of eyeglasses that date from the late 1800s, a child's shoe (putting a shoe in the floorboards was considered good luck back then), and a 1960s-era *Mad* magazine. These items and more can be seen at the Schriver House Museum Shop, located next door. Nancie has also written a book about the Schrivers—*The Shriver's Story - Eyewitnesses to the Battle of Gettysburg*; it is available at the shop or online. The Schriver House is open daily, and the last tour is given at 4:30 p.m.

> ℹ️ Fifteen-year-old Tillie Pierce accompanied Hettie Schriver to the Weikert farm on Little Round Top and kept a diary of her experience there. *At Gettysburg . . . or What a Girl Saw and Heard of the Battle* is considered one of the best personal accounts of the time. The book is still in print, and it's available at the Schriver House gift shop.

SOLDIER'S NATIONAL MUSEUM $$
777 Baltimore Street
(717) 334-4890
www.gettysburgbattlefieldtours.com

When you tour this museum, keep in mind that the building you're in has historical significance. It was used by General Howard as his headquarters during the Battle of Gettysburg, and from 1866 to 1877 it served as the Soldiers National Orphanage, where children orphaned as a result of the war resided. Here you'll find a large collection of artifacts and memorabilia that tells the story of the wars that have been waged throughout time. After you peruse this history lesson, you continue through the museum by passing through a life-size narrated Confederate encampment and then viewing miniature dioramas of 10 major conflicts of the Civil War. At the end of the tour, you enter the gift shop; go up the steps and view the Charlie Weaver Museum of the Civil War, which tells the story of those orphaned by the war. The basement, which many believe to be haunted by the souls of the unfortunate children who were often mistreated here, is a stop on the Ghostly Images of Gettysburg ghost tour (see the entry within the Ghostly Attractions section of this chapter). The Soldier's National Museum is open daily 9:00 a.m. to 9:00 p.m., with the last tour beginning at 8:30 p.m. Children age five and younger may tour for free.

U.S. CHRISTIAN COMMISSION CIVIL WAR MUSEUM $
242 Baltimore Street
(717) 339-0339
www.usccgettysburg.org

The U.S. Christian Commission (USCC) was formed in 1861 by the YMCA, and it consisted of 5,000 Christian volunteers who served the spiritual and temporal needs of Civil War soldiers on both sides of the battle lines. The site of the museum is the house where Jennie Wade, the only civilian to be killed during the Battle of Gettysburg, was born and grew up. Although most visitors to Gettysburg know Jennie Wade's story, this tour highlights the contributions the Wade family made to the commission's efforts. A period-attired living historian leads you through the historic and period-furnished home on this 30- to 45-minute tour, and along the way you'll learn the story of the commission through artifacts and historical documentation. A gift shop features USCC-reproduced items, numerous books about the role faith played for so many in the Civil War, and Civil War items, with proceeds supporting the nonprofit USCC. The museum is open Thursday, Friday, and Saturday only, and children age five and younger are admitted for free.

East of Lincoln Square

FIELDS OF FREEDOM
Gateway Theaters
Gateway Gettysburg
(717) 334-5576
www.gatewaygettysburg.com

The film *Fields of Freedom* is shown exclusively at Gateway Theaters, and it was produced by Gateway Gettysburg maverick Robert J. Monahan Jr. and Greystone Films. (For more on Gateway Gettysburg, see the Close-up in the Area Overview chapter.) The 30-minute film runs on a three-story-tall screen, and many visitors feel they have a greater understanding of the impact of the Battle of Gettysburg after viewing it. Based on the discovered diaries of soldiers from both sides of the conflict, the riveting film follows the lives of two young men—one a Confederate and one a Yankee. You'll be drawn into their lives as each prepares for the battle, and you'll feel their fear and courage during the famous charge and their anguish while dealing with the bloody conflict's aftermath.

West of Lincoln Square

ADAMS COUNTY HISTORICAL SOCIETY $
111 Seminary Ridge
(717) 334-4723, ext. 201
www.achs-pa.org

The Adams County Historical Society resides in Schmucker Hall on the campus of the Lutheran Theological Seminary. It contains primary and secondary resource material for researching county history, and it has about 8,000 feet of display space. Nearly 3,000 feet are occupied by museum galleries on three floors, and about 4,200 cubic feet are occupied by manuscripts. Guided tours of the museum are available by appointment. Among the collections are a Civil War Gallery, fossilized dinosaur footprints, and 1823 wooden water pipes. Free parking is available across the street from Schmucker Hall, which is accessed by stairs and therefore not wheelchair accessible. The society is open during the day Wednesday through Saturday and on Thursday evenings.

GENERAL LEE'S HEADQUARTERS
MUSEUM $
401 Buford Avenue
(717) 334-3141
www.civilwarheadquarters.com

General Lee occupied the eastern side of this stone house at the top of Seminary Ridge and used it as his personal headquarters during the three-day battle at Gettysburg. Built in 1834 and owned by famous abolitionist Thaddeus Stevens, the house was probably a duplex at the time of the battle, and Mrs. Mary ("Widow") Thompson lived there with her daughter-in-law. While visiting the museum, you can stand in the very room where Lee met with his generals during the Gettysburg campaign. The museum also contains artifacts from the house, Civil War–related items, and photographs from the time. Opened to the public as the Lee Museum in 1922, the museum has been in continuous operation ever since, making it one of the oldest museums in Gettysburg. The stone house has a nice gift shop on one side and the museum on the other, and you get your ticket for the museum at the gift shop. The

gift shop is filled with lots of Lee memorabilia, as well as Civil War–related books, gifts, artifacts, and memorabilia. General Lee's Headquarters is open daily, and it's part of the Quality Inn complex along Chambersburg Road. Guests of the inn, children younger than age 16, and Adams County residents can tour the museum for free.

GENERAL ATTRACTIONS

ADAMS COUNTY WINERY
251 Peachtree Road, Orrtanna
(717) 334-4631
www.adamscountywinery.com

This is Gettysburg's oldest winery and its grapes cover about 10 acres of land 9 miles west of Gettysburg off U.S. Route 30. Signs direct you from US 30 down country lanes for the 3 miles you travel off the main road to reach the winery. Once you arrive, you enter a world of relaxation. The winery gift shop is within a 130-year-old bank barn where you're invited to sample the wine. If you wish, you can bring a picnic lunch, buy some wine to go with it, and enjoy your feast on the winery land. Free summer concerts are held every Saturday afternoon in July and August, and free tours of the winery are available. Adams County Winery is open daily, and it also has a small wine shop within Gettysburg, at 25 Chambersburg Street. The winery took part in the first annual Gettysburg Wine and Music Festival held in September 2005 at Gettysburg Recreation Park (see the Annual Events and Festivals chapter), and it's also represented at wine festivals throughout the region. Adams County Winery holds its own Art at the Winery Fest on its grounds in October, where it hosts several other wineries. This event lets you enjoy good wine, food, and music while admiring the work of local and regional artists.

ALLSTAR EVENTS COMPLEX $$
2638 Emmitsburg Road
(717) 334-6363, (888) 497-9386
www.allstarpa.com

Allstar is located 4 miles south of Gettysburg on Emmitsburg Road, and it functions as a 70,000-square-foot expo center (with parking for

2,000-plus cars) that's available for trade shows and group activities. Individuals can also enjoy the fun here, but to avoid long waits, it's best to call ahead to make sure a large group isn't already filling up the place. See the Kidstuff chapter for a full rundown of activities available here for kids of all ages, such as go-kart tracks and minigolf.

BOYDS BEAR COUNTRY
75 Cunningham Road
(717) 630-2600, (866) 367-8338
www.boydsbearcountry.com
Boyds Bear Country is open daily, and the 120,000-square-foot store is the home of 70,000 Boyds bears, hares, and other friends. The stuffed animals are grouped together and posed in adorable ways. Live entertainment goes on in the atrium on the first floor, and store displays change each season. The store has three display floors and a downstairs that's devoted to feeding hungry bears. See the Kidstuff chapter for information on making your own bear and the Shopping chapter for more information on the store.

HAUSER ESTATE WINERY
410 Cashtown Road, Biglerville
(717) 334-4888
www.hauserestate.com
This is the newest winery in the area, and it's locally owned and operated by the Hauser family. Since the family owns 500 acres of orchards, it probably was only a matter of time before they ventured into the wine-making business. The winery sits on a little more than 170 of those acres, and it overlooks miles of farmland, forest, and orchards as well as some of the roads the Confederates traveled on their way to Gettysburg back in July of 1863. You can admire the views as well as the wine produced here in their 360-degree glass-enclosed tasting room. Hauser Estate is located less than 10 miles from Lincoln Square. To reach it, head east on Chambersburg Road to Cashtown Road, and it will be on your left. There is also a satellite store at 17 Lincoln Square (see the Shopping chapter) for those who prefer not to drive to the winery. The winery, its in-town store, and the tasting room are open daily.

MR. ED'S ELEPHANT MUSEUM
6019 Chambersburg Road, Orrtanna
(717) 352-3792

17 on the Square (candy only)
(717) 339–0017
www.mistereds.com
Ed Gotwalt received his first elephant in 1967 as a good-luck gift on his wedding day. In 1975 his collection of all things elephant had grown so large that his wife made him open a museum so she could regain her house. His free museum contains more than 6,000 elephant collectibles from throughout the world, and they're made from just about every substance known to man. In addition to the selections of elephants, Ed has added a store that sells fresh-roasted peanuts and other nuts, fudge, classic candies from the 1950s through the 1970s (remember candy necklaces and penny candy?), sugar-free candy, and T-shirts and unusual gifts that relate to the museum collection. Mr. Ed's Elephant Museum appeared on *Good Morning America* on July 5, 2005, as part of a story on unusual attractions across America. The museum and candy shop are open daily; to get there, head west on US 30 (Chambersburg Road) for 12 miles. Between the many signs and the life-size elephant in front of the place, it's hard to miss.

NATIONAL APPLE MUSEUM $
154 West Hanover Street, Biglerville
(717) 677-4556
www.nationalapplemuseum.com
If you're out taking in the area orchards on a Saturday or Sunday, this is a great place to stop and learn more about the history of the fruit industry and how it contributed to the development and growth of Adams County. The National Apple Museum is owned and operated by the Biglerville Historical and Preservation Society. Opened in 1990, it's housed in a restored pre–Civil War bank barn, and exhibits include a re-created 1880s farm kitchen and General Store and collections of farming implements, apple peelers, and fruit labels. The museum is open weekends only May through October, and a tour is available. There's

also a museum gift shop, with most items having an agricultural or orchard-related theme. To reach the museum from Lincoln Square, take Route 34 (Carlisle Street) north from Gettysburg until you reach Route 394 (West Hanover Street) in Biglerville. Make a left, and the museum is about a quarter mile up the road.

PIONEER LINES SCENIC RAILWAY $$$$
106 North Washington Street
(717) 334-6932
www.gettysburgrail.com
Pioneer Lines offers a variety of train rides mostly on weekends from May through December, with the Scenic Train Ride being offered most frequently. This hour-and-15-minute afternoon ride covers 16 miles of the Adams County countryside and briefly passes by where fighting on the first day of the Battle of Gettysburg took place. The conductor provides narration on Civil War and local history during the ride, which can include a bagged lunch for an additional fee. If that ride just isn't long enough, there's also an Extended Scenic Train Ride that travels farther into the countryside and that lasts about three hours. This ride is an early evening tour, and it shares its schedule with the three-hour Murder Mystery and Evening Paradise Dinner Trains, both of which offer a catered meal. The Ghost Trains run almost as often as the Scenic Train, and they are also an hour and 15 minutes long. Guides from the Ghosts of Gettysburg Tours (see the write-up later in this chapter) relay their eerie tales as you venture into the haunted countryside around Gettysburg, including the Railroad Cut, Oak Ride, and Iverson's Pits, and then pull into the haunted Engine House, where you hear the voices of the dead captured on tape. No wonder the Engine House and the Ghost Trains have been featured on the Travel Channel's *Mysterious Journeys* series.

If you prefer a train ride that's just pure fun, with no chills except from the weather, try the Santa Train Ride. On this hour-and-15-minute excursion you have a chance to meet Santa's elves and to deliver your letter to Santa in person. There's also a train ride that includes lunch with Santa and his elves.

Reservations for the dinner trains are required, and they are strongly recommended for all other excursions. The trains have limited access for patrons with disabilities. Call the number above if you have questions about wheelchair accessibility. While waiting for your departure, be sure to check out the gift shop in the depot. You'll find plenty of railroad-related items, including hats, T-shirts, and Thomas the Tank Engine items.

SEGTOURS $$$$
380 Steinwehr Avenue
(rear parking lot of the Reliance Mine Saloon)
(717) 253-7987
www.segtours.com
A Segway personal transporter is a two-wheel self-balancing electric vehicle that is guided by your body movements. Its top speed is around 12 miles per hour, and this 30-minute excursion has no purpose other than the enjoyment of riding this new invention. After some training on this easy-to-use device, your group will be escorted by a staff member along some quiet residential streets on the outskirts of Gettysburg borough. Riders must be at least 16 years of age, and helmets are provided for rider safety. Reservations are recommended.

GENERAL TOURS

GETTYSBURG CARRIAGE CO. $$$$
(717) 337-3400
Gettysburg Carriage Co. offers two tours that take you along the battlefield and one town tour. The battlefield tours last about 90 minutes and go to either Culp's Hill or West Confederate Avenue, near where Pickett's Charge took place. These are scenic tours that relate stories of the battle as you enjoy the ride. The town tour runs about 35 minutes, and you get to see some of the older buildings in town and hear stories of what happened within the town during the Battle of Gettysburg. Reservations may be made if you like, but most people just show up where the carriage is parked along Baltimore Street by the Farnsworth House. Gettysburg Carriage Co. and Windmill Carriage (see entry within this section) alternate sides of

Baltimore Street daily, and each company has a sign out to let you know who's who.

GUIDED HISTORIC WALKING TOURS $$$
1 Lincoln Square
(717) 339-6161
www.gettysburgpa.org/guidedtour.htm
Begun in summer 2005, the guided historic walking tours bring to life what it was like for the civilians of Gettysburg during the Battle of Gettysburg. Much of the information given during the 90-minute tours is based on diary entries, personal accounts, and letters of the townspeople who were here during the battle, as well as drawings and photographs of the time. Tour guides must pass a test, and the tours are the creation of Main Street Gettysburg, a nonprofit organization dedicated to preserving and highlighting Gettysburg's rich history. (For more on Main Street Gettysburg, see The Arts chapter.) Tours depart from the Gettysburg Hotel, located on the town square, and run daily from 10:00 a.m. to 4:00 p.m. You can also arrange evening tours by reservation.

HISTORIC CHURCH WALKING TOURS $
(888) 882-1541
www.historicchurchwalkingtours.org
These 90-minute tours emphasize town churches that were turned into emergency hospitals during and after the Gettysburg battle. Eight churches host performances that portray the events of those days through narratives, plays, and music, with four churches featured each Wednesday evening during the summer starting in early June. Churches on the East Tour are St. James Lutheran, United Church of Christ, United Methodist, and Gettysburg Presbyterian, while on the West Tour are Christ Lutheran, St. Paul's AME Zion, Prince of Peace Episcopal, and St. Francis Xavier Roman Catholic. The East and West Tours alternate each Wednesday night, and all tours begin at 6:00 and 6:30 p.m. in front of the Gettysburg Presbyterian Church at Baltimore and High Streets. Tours are conducted by volunteer docents, and children age 12 and younger tour for free.

HISTORIC CONEWAGO VALLEY TOUR
Gettysburg Convention and Visitors Bureau
102 Carlisle Street
(717) 334-6274, (800) 337-5015
www.gettysburg.travel
Covering 40 miles east and northeast of Gettysburg, the Historic Conewago Valley Tour takes you by the East Cavalry battlefield, working farms, country churches, and the quaint towns of New Oxford and East Berlin. There's a lot of history along the way, especially in East Berlin, which was designated a Pennsylvania Historic Site in 1985. The town was laid out in 1764, and 52 structures that appear on an 1856 map of the town are still standing, including a house once owned by Thaddeus Stevens, a Pennsylvanian representative and famous abolitionist of the time. Many of the churches seen along the way date from the 1800s, and quite a few bank barns are also on the route. The tour is named for the Conewago Creek, which meanders through the eastern half of Adams County. Touring is done in the comfort of your car, and the approximate driving time is two hours. The route is clearly marked with signs, and the free brochure that's available from the Gettysburg Convention and Visitors Bureau explains what you're seeing and shows a good map of the tour. As the tour brochure emphasizes many times, this is a country tour, with steep hills and twisty roads. The tour route crosses busy roads, sometimes at places where visibility isn't always ideal, so careful driving is a must. Follow the brochure when it says to slow down, and pay attention if it says to proceed with caution at an intersection.

HISTORIC GETTYSBURG WALKING TOUR
Gettysburg Convention and Visitors Bureau
102 Carlisle Street
(717) 334-6274, (800) 337-5015
www.gettysburg.travel
You can view more than 100 restored buildings as this self-guided walking tour takes you through the downtown area. The free tour brochure, available at the Gettysburg Convention and Visitors Bureau, contains a brief description of the tour's 32 stops and a corresponding map.

Close-up

Covered Bridges of Adams County

Pennsylvania has the most covered bridges of any state (212), and Adams County has two covered bridges that are still open to the public. The Sachs Bridge crosses Marsh Creek on Water Works Road 3 miles southwest of town, and Jack's Mountain Bridge crosses Tom's Creek in Fairfield about 8 miles west of town. The Sachs Bridge, built by David Stoner in 1852, is 91 feet long and 15 feet wide and uses a truss system designed by Connecticut architect Ithiel Town. The bridge was used by both Union and Confederate troops during the Battle of Gettysburg and is listed in the National Register of Historic Places. Although you can't drive across it, walking across is allowed. To reach Sachs Bridge from Lincoln Square, travel Baltimore Street and turn right onto Steinwehr Avenue, which is called Emmitsburg Road once you leave town. Turn right onto Millerstown Road (there's a sign on the left for the Peach Orchard). Continue straight on Millerstown Road when it intersects with West Confederate Avenue, and in a bit the road name changes to Pumping Station Road. About a mile later you'll cross a bridge that spans Marsh Creek, where you can see Sachs Bridge about 200 yards downstream on the left. Immediately after the bridge, make a left onto Scott Road to explore the bridge.

The Jack's Mountain Bridge was constructed by Joseph Smith in 1894 and is still used for daily motor vehicle traffic. It's a Burr truss covered bridge that spans 75 feet with a width of 14 feet, 6 inches. To reach the bridge, travel south from the square and make a right onto West Middle Street (Route 116). Travel this road, which will change its name to Fairfield Road once you leave town, through the town of Fairfield. Follow Fairfield Road at the Y intersection with Iron Springs Road, and follow Jack's Mountain Road at the next Y intersection. You'll soon be crossing the covered bridge. Jack's Mountain Bridge carries a good deal of traffic, so be aware of other vehicles as you admire the bridge. There is a very limited area for parking if you want to get out and explore a bit.

Your adventure begins at the Gettysburg Lincoln Railroad Station off Carlisle Street, and you travel to Lincoln Square, up and down the first block of York Street, down Baltimore Street all the way to its intersection with Steinwehr Avenue, and back up to the square. Baltimore Street has the most stops along the way, and after returning to the square, you tour up and down the first block of Chambersburg Street, and the tour ends a block off the square, on Carlisle Street. Estimated to last about 90 minutes, the walking tour integrates the wayside markers located along the route, which relay in-depth information about the Battle of Gettysburg and its aftermath.

SCENIC VALLEY TOUR

Gettysburg Convention and Visitors Bureau
102 Carlisle Street
(717) 334-6274, (800) 337-5015
www.gettysburg.travel

Thirty-six miles of beautiful countryside can be seen on this self-guided drive through Adams County. The drive's accompanying free brochure, which has a map of the route, is available from the Gettysburg Convention and Visitors Bureau. Scenic Valley Tour signs mark the entire route, and the brochure gives you clear directions to the start of the tour from either the tourist bureau or Lincoln Square. Approximate driving time is two hours, and along the way you'll visit the Seminary

Ridge area of the Gettysburg National Military Park and take in some fabulous scenery. Easy detours from the route take you to a mid-19th-century covered bridge and a tavern where George Washington slept. (See the Close-up in this chapter for more on covered bridges in Adams County.)

TOWN TOUR GETTYSBURG $$$
Historic Tour Company
55 Steinwehr Avenue
(717) 334-8000
www.historictourcompany.com
The Historic Tour Company has been giving tours of the battlefield for years, and now they are branching out into town tours. (For more on their battlefield tours, see the Bus Tours section of the Gettysburg National Military Park chapter.) This hour-long tour promises to show you "all the great stuff you didn't see or hear about on your battlefield tour," and you do it in style by riding around town in a Yellowstone bus. The Yellowstone bus was developed specifically for sightseeing within the western national parks, and this smaller-size bus leads to a more intimate touring experience. You'll discover the true stories of how Gettysburg residents dealt with their town playing host to one of the most famous battles of the Civil War, such as the bravery of Catherine Foster, who hid a Union soldier in her basement while Confederate soldiers searched the house. When the Confederates asked her if there were any Yankees hiding in the house, she boldly replied, "Yes, of course. We're all Yankees here." If you'd like to hear more stories about how the battle affected those in the town of Gettysburg, and you'd rather ride rather than walk while doing it, this is the tour for you. Tours are tailored to customers' interests, and reservations are requested.

UNDERGROUND RAILROAD TOURS OF ADAMS COUNTY $$$
2699 Heidlersburg Road
(717) 528-8553
www.gettysburghistories.com,
www.freedomliesnorth.org
Begun in the summer of 2007, this new Gettysburg tour focuses on one of the causes of the Civil War—slavery. Local historian Debra McCauslin accompanies you in your car on a two-and-a-half to three-hour tour that explains how area African Americans and their Quaker neighbors worked together to help as many as 1,000 escaping slaves reach freedom by traveling the Underground Railroad. The beautiful fruit orchards of northern Adams County serve as the backdrop to the tour, which focuses on the African-American community of Yellow Hill and the neighboring Quaker Valley, located about 10 miles from Gettysburg. McCauslin reveals the area's history and you also meet people along the way who portray residents of Yellow Hill and the Quaker Valley, sharing their fascinating stories with you.

Stops on the tour include the Yellow Hill Cemetery and the Menallen Friends Meetinghouse, which are both listed on the National Park Service's National Network to Freedom, a program that tells the story of resistance against the institution of slavery in the United States through escape and flight. Tours cost $15 for adults and $5 for students, and a portion of the proceeds is donated to local preservation efforts, especially those concerning the Yellow Hill Cemetery.

WINDMILL CARRIAGE $$$$
(717) 677-6852, (717) 253-3732 (cell)
Windmill Carriage has two in-town locations; you can begin your horse-drawn carriage ride from the Dobbin House on Steinwehr Avenue or from Baltimore Street by the Farnsworth House. For a town tour that lasts half an hour, you can just walk up and make arrangements right when you want to leave. A battlefield ride is an hour long, and it's a scenic journey to Spangler's Spring and Culp's Hill, not a tour of the battlefield or the events of the battle. Although you can also walk up and request this tour, it's probably better to make reservations. Carriage rides are available daily, weather permitting. On Baltimore Street, Windmill Carriage and the Gettysburg Carriage Co. (see entry within this section) alternate sides of the street daily, and each company has a sign out so you know which company the beautiful horses and carriages belong to.

Besides the Gettysburg Convention and Visitors Bureau on Carlisle Street, brochures for the self-guided downtown walking tour can be found in the lobby of the James Gettys Hotel, just up the block from the square on Chambersburg Street.

GHOSTLY ATTRACTIONS

Tour companies operating walking ghost tours now need a license from the borough. No more than 26 people, including the guide, can be in one group, and the guide must wear an identifying badge.

BLUE MOON HAUNTINGS $$$$
341 Baltimore Street
(717) 334-0198
www.bluemoontours.com
This ghost tour hunts spirits over 6 miles of local roads in an open-air trolley. The adventure begins in the parlor on Baltimore Street, where you will learn the story of your ghostly guide's demise. Then you hop on the trolley and begin your hunt. Tales told along the route cover otherworldly occurrences from the days of the Battle of Gettysburg up to strange happenings from present day. Each person on the tour, which lasts about an hour and a half, gets a ghost hunters' map—and ghost repellent in case the hunt is successful! It's recommended that you leave children younger than age three at home, as the trolley cannot accommodate children's safety seats. Tours are given Thursday through Sunday nights. The headquarters on Baltimore Street also carries a variety of items for you to purchase if you want to try hunting on your own after the tour, such as dowsing rods, crystals, pendulums, smudge kits, and more.

CIVIL WAR HAUNTINGS $$
240 Steinwehr Avenue
(717) 752-5588 (cell)
Located next to Flex & Flannigan's store, you'll recognize Civil War Hauntings by the skeleton out front. The skeleton is where you buy your tickets and meet for candlelight ghost walks led by an experienced guide in Civil War–period dress. Tours are given seasonally Thursday through Sunday at 8:00 and 9:30 p.m. They last an hour and cover about half a mile, and the area toured is where some of the bloodiest fighting occurred during the Battle of Gettysburg. Civil War Hauntings includes the free use of an electronic ghost finder on its tours, and the EMF meter is just like the equipment professional ghost hunters use. Children age seven and younger may tour for free.

FARNSWORTH HOUSE CANDLELIGHT GHOST WALKS AND CIVIL WAR MOURNING THEATRE $$
401 Baltimore Street
(717) 334-8838
www.gettysburgshauntedaddress.com
The Farnsworth House gives you options on how you want to connect with the supernatural. You can go on one of their candlelight ghost walks or descend the house's staircase to the "viewing parlor," where you hear stories told by candlelight of ghosts still believed to haunt the town and battlefield. The theater presentation lasts an hour, and the Civil War Mourning Theatre has been featured on A&E's *Unexplained Sightings* and *Unsolved Mysteries* series. It's held nightly in season, as are the candlelight walking tours. Walking tours are led by guides dressed in period clothing, and many of the tales told are firsthand experiences of the guides. Candlelight walks are either 75 or 90 minutes long. The cost is the same to take a ghost walk or to attend the mourning theater, and children age seven and younger are admitted to both for free. Tickets can be bought at the bookstore on the premises until 5:00 p.m., or you can buy tickets at the end of the walk in front of the house up to 15 minutes prior to the beginning of the show or walking tour. You can't miss the people selling the tickets—they're in period dress.

GETTYSBURG GHOST TOURS $$
47 Steinwehr Avenue
(717) 338-1818 www.gettysburgghost tours.com

Gettysburg Ghost Tours offers a variety of ghost tours, with the Black Cat Tour being offered most frequently. It starts at the tour office and explores the first block of Steinwehr Avenue. Most stories on this tour focus on the first day of the Battle of Gettysburg. Tours are held rain or shine seven nights a week in season, and children age seven and younger tour for free.

GHOSTLY IMAGES OF
GETTYSBURG $$–$$$$
Gettysburg Tour Center
778 Baltimore Street
(717) 334-6296
www.gettysburgbattlefieldtours.com

A plethora of ghost tours are offered here in season, including walking tours, bus tours, and a tour that includes ghost stories told during dinner. Walking tours are led by guides in period dress, and they last 90 minutes. The Jennie Wade Fright Seeing Tour ends with a walk through the Jennie Wade House, which many believe to be haunted. The Soldiers Orphanage Tour covers Steinwehr Avenue and the National Cemetery Annex. This tour ends at the site of the Soldiers Orphanage, a place some psychics won't enter because of the ghosts they feel reside in the cellar.

The Mystical Mystery at the Hall Tour takes you along Steinwehr Avenue and ends in the cellar of the Hall of Presidents, where ghost stories are told.

A two-hour bus tour aboard an air-conditioned coach is also available. The tour ventures into the ghostly countryside and visits the area around the Lutheran Seminary and the Sachs Bridge.

Reservations are highly recommended for all tours, and tickets for any of the tours can be picked up at the Gettysburg Tour Center or the Jennie Wade Gift Shop.

i Before venturing out to hunt ghosts, you might want to pick up a bottle of "Ghost Away" at the Gettysburg Ghost Tours office at 47 Steinwehr Avenue. Kids like this sprayed on their hands to keep ghosts from getting too close.

GHOSTS OF GETTYSBURG
CANDLELIGHT WALKING TOURS $$
271 Baltimore Street
(717) 337-0445
www.ghostsofgettysburg.com

This is the original ghost tour in Gettysburg. You'll be treated to strange but true ghost tales from the best-selling *Ghosts of Gettysburg* book series by Mark Nesbitt, author, historian, former National Park Service ranger, and resident of Gettysburg. Mark collected his ghost stories while living in historic houses on the battlefield and in town, and they have been featured on *Unsolved Mysteries* and on A&E. The house that serves as tour headquarters dates from 1834; during the battle it was occupied by Confederate sharpshooters, and there were reports of paranormal events during the house's historical restoration. Ghosts of Gettysburg offers seasonal walking tours that cover different areas of town: the Carlisle Street/College Campus Tour, the Baltimore Street Tour, the Seminary Ridge Tour, and the Steinwehr Avenue Tour. There's also a bus tour that runs on Saturday evenings during the summer. Not all tours start from tour headquarters—ask where your tour begins. Tours are conducted rain or shine. The tour headquarters also houses a gift shop, a ghost bookstore, and a ghost photo gallery of spirits captured on the battlefield and in houses in town. Children age seven and younger are admitted for free on the walking tours, but children age five and younger are not permitted on the bus tour. Ghosts of Gettysburg has also partnered with Pioneer Lines to host a ghost train. See the entry for the railway in the General Attractions section of this chapter.

HAUNTED BATTLEFIELD AT
GETTYSBURG $$
531 Baltimore Street (in tent at rear)
(717) 337-9216, (877) 980-1313

This is the only attraction in town that guarantees you'll see a ghost during the show. That's because Haunted Battlefield puts its story about eerie sightings at the Gettysburg battlefield on a CD. An 1857 Civil War projector is used for the presentation, which also employs stereo music and sound effects. Haunted Battlefield is not a walking tour—it's held in a tent set up during the season behind the Blue and Grey Gift Shop. The CD features Joe Kerrigan, a local Civil War–era magician, actor, and storyteller, as the narrator. Joe also runs the Haunted Gettysburg ghost walks (see separate listing below) and performs at the dinner theater at the Fairfield Inn (see The Arts chapter). Haunted Battlefield at Gettysburg is presented nightly at 8:30 and 9:30 p.m.

HAUNTED GETTYSBURG GHOST TOURS $$
27 Steinwehr Avenue
(717) 334-1200
www.hauntedgettysburgtours.com
These seasonal walking tours are based on the books in the *Haunted Gettysburg* series, which feature eyewitness accounts of paranormal events that occurred in Gettysburg. On the tours you actually walk through the areas and see the locations where these events are reported to have happened. The tours last about an hour and are wheelchair accessible. You may also have a chance to meet Bob Wasel, author of the *Haunted Gettysburg* series, who owns the tour company with his wife, Bonnie. Candlelight tours led by experienced guides in period dress are offered daily at 7:30 and 9:00 p.m. Children age eight and younger tour for free.

SLEEPY HOLLOW CANDLELIGHT GHOST TOURS $$
89 Steinwehr Avenue
(717) 337-9322
www.sleepyhollowofgettysburg.com
Guides from Sleepy Hollow Candlelight Ghost Tours have been hunting ghosts in Gettysburg since 1997, making this the second-oldest ghost walk in Gettysburg. The operation is owned and operated by Cindy Codori Shultz, a sixth-generation granddaughter of Nicholas Codori of Historic Codori Farm (the site of Pickett's Charge).

Two tours are available, both with period-dressed guides who lead you on an adventure that encompasses a 3- to 5-block radius within the historic district. The Baltimore/High Street Tour departs from in front of the Dobbin House along Steinwehr Avenue while the Seminary Ridge Tour leaves from the steps of General Lee's Headquarters, on Buford Avenue. (See the write-up on the headquarters earlier in this chapter.) Tickets for both tours may be purchased at the Country Curiosity Store gift shop inside the Dobbin House. (See the Shopping chapter for more on the gift shop.) Tours are held rain or shine during the season, and children age seven and younger and people requiring the use of a wheelchair tour for free.

SHOPPING

Gettysburg is a shopper's haven, and browsing is almost an art form in this area. The main four streets in town (Baltimore, Chambersburg, York, and Carlisle Streets) have shop after shop along the way, and many people stroll along and browse in each shop. If you prefer a little structure to your shopping expeditions, this chapter is divided into different categories, such as Antiques, Gift Shops/Collectibles, and Specialty Shops. Shopping categories that have many listings (usually 10 or more) are arranged alphabetically according to the business's geographic location in relation to the square. If there aren't too many listings, shops will be listed only alphabetically. Many stores carry a range of different items, so I've done my best to list a place under the category that I feel represents the majority of its stock and the overall feel and appearance of the store. If you're looking for shops that carry mainly military memorabilia and Civil War clothing, these businesses are treated separately within the Gettysburg National Military Park chapter.

ANTIQUES

ABE'S ANTIQUES
22 Baltimore Street
(717) 337-2122

If you collect Lincoln memorabilia, you'll want to stop by this store. The owner even looks like Lincoln, and on some weekends he dresses the part. Abe's Antiques has been on Baltimore Street since 1994, and the antiques and collectibles offered here are reasonably priced, with many items less than $20. Lincoln-related items fill most of the back of the store, but take time to look at the stuff in the front, too. The Victrola phonograph and antique musical instruments right inside the door are worth a long look, and it's also fun to check out the tintype photos, antique kitchen gadgets, and other collectibles at the front of the store. Be sure to take notice of the turn-of-the-20th-century cash register, too. Abe's Antiques is open seven days a week.

ANTIQUE CENTER OF GETTYSBURG
30 Baltimore Street
(717) 337-3669
www.antiquecenter-getty.com

With 100 showcases of antiques and collectibles, the Antique Center of Gettysburg is bound to have something that will intrigue you. As you wander the aisles, you'll find military antiques from many different wars, toy soldiers, military-related books, antique tools, and Lincoln memorabilia. There's also jewelry, glass and pottery, and china. Upstairs you'll find more books, prints, and framed artwork. The Antique Center is closed on Tuesday.

RX ANTIQUES
28 Chambersburg Street
(717) 338-9092

If you're wondering about the unusual name, the owner used to be a podiatrist before he retired and opened this shop in 1998. This long, narrow shop has antique pottery and glassware, fabulous beer steins, and unusual and one-of-a-kind items. Rx Antiques is closed on Tuesday.

17 ON THE SQUARE
17 Lincoln Square
(717) 339-0017
www.17onthesquare.com

With a history that dates from 1785 when James Gettys laid out the town of Gettysburg, Lot #81 (as it was originally deeded) has operated as a private residence, as varied retail stores, and as office space over the decades. In 2001 the building was sold to three sisters, Melinda, Jane, and Hannah, who spent 14 months renovating the space, which had been vacant for many years. Their logo is "Antiques, Apples and Art"—antiques on two floors, specialty foods such as homemade jams and unusual candy and good old-fashioned apples (in season) for sale, and a stunning amount of art in many different forms. The building houses many tenants. Besides the antiques, art, and seasonal food items, you'll also discover the Civil War Center sutlery (see the GNMP chapter for more information), jewelry selections from Scott & Co. Jewelers (see the write-up later in this chapter), and Mr. Ed's candy offerings (see the Attractions chapter for more on Mr. Ed's Elephant Museum).

> **i** When shopping for antiques, be sure you and the seller are talking the same language. A true antique is at least 100 years old, a near antique is 75 to 99 years old, and anything called vintage is 25 to 74 years old.

WOGAN'S YORK STREET ANTIQUES & TREATS
26 York Street
(717) 337-3378

Wogan's York Street Antiques & Treats opened in 2004, and it holds a large portion of the items that used to be at Mel's Antiques Mall, which closed in 2005. It's a great area for browsing, with glassware, jewelry, china, Civil War–era memorabilia, furniture, and more among the offerings. The Treats part of the name comes from the delicious ice cream that's served here for a ridiculously low price ($1 for an ice-cream cone!). There are two booths at the front of the store where you can sit and watch the world go by on York Street as you savor your treat.

APPAREL

GETTYSBURG HOSPITAL AUXILIARY THRIFT SHOP
10 Lincoln Square
(717) 334-5264

This delightful shop is filled with clothing for everyone in the family, and the clothing is priced to sell. Used as well as new garments are intermingled, everything is nicely arranged on hangers, and there's plenty of room to look at what's on the racks. The thrift shop is open Monday through Saturday, and proceeds from sales at the store benefit Gettysburg Hospital.

> **i** Many shops in Gettysburg appear small from outside. Don't be deceived—there's often additional space either in back or upstairs. Sometimes it's fun just to explore how large that tiny-looking space really is!

T&S MENSWEAR, INC.
1 Chambersburg Street
(717) 334-7575

T&S has been around since the 1960s, and the owners have had their spot right off the square since 1991. The small shop is filled with men's fine clothing, casual clothing, and formal wear. Men can find dress shirts, sweaters, pants, and suits as well as plush robes and loungewear. The store is laid out nicely with room to browse, and it's always fun to see what's in the display window at this upscale shop. T&S Menswear is open every day of the week but Sunday.

BOOKS AND MUSIC

AMERICAN HISTORY STORE
461 Baltimore Street
(717) 338-0631
www.tbhabitat.com

The largest bookstore in Gettysburg is located within this beautiful 19th-century brick building that sits at the southern end of Baltimore Street. Its owners also own the next three shops around the corner on Steinwehr Avenue—Habitat, Battlefield Souvenirs, and Stoneham's Armory. (See this chapter for more on Habitat and Battlefield Souvenirs and the GNMP chapter for more on Stoneham's Armory.) As you might expect, books on history, especially Civil War history, fill many of the shelves at this shop, and it's a real joy to browse here. Among all this history you'll also find a nice selection of DVDs, artwork, chess sets, and fine collector-grade toy soldiers.

ARROW HORSE
49 Chambersburg Street
(717) 337–2899

This shop is all about bluegrass music. You'll find lots of banjos for sale, and a bluegrass jam that is free and open to the public is held here every Friday night (see the Nightlife chapter). There's also bluegrass sheet music for sale, bluegrass CDs, and bluegrass-related collectibles.

FARNSWORTH HOUSE MILITARY IMPRESSIONS
Farnsworth House
401 Baltimore Street
(717) 334-8838
www.farnsworthhouseinn.com

This place reminds me of a scholarly library. The rich wood of the shelves holding the rows of tomes and the art prints that are displayed set the mood in this orderly and well-laid-out bookshop. You'll find extensive collections of new and out-of-print books on the Civil War and WWII, as well as books on other military history. If you've enjoyed a dining adventure at the Farnsworth House (see the Restaurants chapter), you may want to pick up a copy of *The Farnsworth House Recipe Book;* it is carried here exclusively. The

i **If visiting Gettysburg gets you thinking about what you can do for the troops who are making sacrifices right now for the good of our country, visit www .adoptaplatoon.com for numerous ideas on ways you can support our troops.**

bookshop, which is open daily, also carries a line of Civil War bronze sculptures, Civil War music, and art prints by Don Troiani and other well-known Civil War artists.

GETTYSBURG BOOK CELLAR
22 Carlisle Street
(717) 337-0557

If you love losing yourself among books, this is the place for you. Bookshelf after bookshelf is filled to overflowing with used, out-of-print, and old and rare books. You enter by going down a few steps (hence the cellar in the name), and you're immediately surrounded by books. As you browse, each corner you turn offers the opportunity to find new treasure.

Bookcases are labeled by subject for easy hunting, and first editions are among the offerings. There are also comic books and more recent titles on display. The Gettysburg Book Cellar is closed on Wednesday and Thursday.

GETTYSBURG CHRISTIAN BOOKSTORE
24 Chambersburg Street
(717) 334-8634

Since 1972 Gettysburg Christian Bookstore has been offering a wide array of items with something to please just about everyone. Of course you'll find books, some on religious topics and some on the Civil War. But the bookstore also stocks plaques, cards, artwork, and knickknacks. The children's section carries a nice selection of books for various ages. (See the Kidstuff chapter for more details.) Gettysburg Christian Bookstore shares its address with Gettysburg Electronics, a small but fascinating shop at the back of the store where you can buy metal detectors. (See the Specialty Shops section of this chapter for more on Gettysburg Electronics.)

NOTEWORTHY MUSIC
52 York Street
(717) 334-3522

In business since 1978, Noteworthy Music is a bit of a Gettysburg institution. It's even one of the buildings portrayed in miniature for sale in the gift shops around town. Owner Bob Ranalli, who does repairs on instruments, can often be found tinkering with something or other at his table in the back of the store. Bob also sells and rents guitars, drums, amps, music, and accessories, as well as doing sound engineering and rentals.

SEMINARY BOOKSTORE
Lutheran Theological Seminary at Gettysburg
61 Seminary Ridge (Milton Valentine Hall)
(717) 338-3005
www.ltsg.edu
This is the bookstore for students of the seminary, but it also has much to offer the public. One aisle is devoted to textbooks while the rest of the space has religious books, devotional resources, greeting cards, gifts, jewelry, and more. Maybe you'd like a toe ring with an inspirational message on it, or a beautiful silver cross. Most of the books deal with the Lutheran faith, but other Christian denominations are also represented. The bookstore is open Monday through Friday; it's closed for lunchtime from noon to 1:00 p.m. Parking is available behind Valentine Hall, and the bookstore is on the right as you enter the building from the rear. Since there's very little if any signage on the seminary grounds, finding what you're looking for can be tricky. Valentine Hall is on Seminary Ridge (also called Confederate Avenue) beside the Adams County Historical Society, which is located in Schmucker Hall and which does have a sign out front. (For information on the historical society, which offers tours, see the Attractions chapter.)

FINE GIFTS AND HOME ACCENTS

South of Lincoln Square

BATTLEFIELD BASKETS & GIFTS
100 Baltimore Street
(717) 338-1565
www.acivilaffair.com
This charming shop that's open daily has a nice selection of Victorian gifts, including baskets, bells, teapots, tins, and porcelain dolls. The Victorian gifts occupy a small portion of the larger space that is filled with the Civil War clothing offered by A Civil Affair. (For more on A Civil Affair, see the Civil War Clothing and Accessories section of the GNMP chapter.) If you want to surround yourself with period knickknacks while being properly dressed, be sure to visit this charming shop. Battlefield Baskets & Gifts is closed on Monday and Tuesday.

HABITAT
1 Steinwehr Avenue
(717) 334-1218
www.tbhabitat.com
Tiffany lamps, pottery, candles, country dolls, bears, framed art, and gourmet foods and coffees are displayed in this charming clapboard Victorian house, circa 1860. Among the displays downstairs are miniature hand-painted historic houses of Gettysburg by artist L. A. Fox and lots of Christmas-related gifts. Upstairs you'll find a room filled with delightful dog- and cat-related knickknacks, two rooms filled with country dolls and wooden novelties, and another room with all kinds and shapes of candles.

Downstairs in the back of the store, you can pick out a sack of coffee and grind the beans right there. Habitat also has its own line of preserves, jams, jellies, and honey for you to take along home. The owners of Habitat also own the next two shops down Steinwehr Avenue, Battlefield Souvenirs (see the Gift Shops/Collectibles section of this chapter) and Stoneham's Armory (see the Military Memorabilia Shops section of the GNMP chapter), as well as the American History Store (see the Books and Music section of this chapter) next door on Baltimore Street.

East of Lincoln Square

CATHY'S COUNTRY HOME
2891 York Road
(717) 337–2883
www.cathyscountryhome.net
Cathy's Country Home is a country-style house 5 miles east of Lincoln Square in which fine home furnishings for every room of your house are

displayed on three floors. Each room setting is completely decorated with all the details that complete a room, not just the main furniture. Nooks and crannies can be found throughout the house, especially on the third floor, so be sure not to miss any rooms. Cathy's Country Home opened in 1991, and although it's a bit out of town, most tourists who visit the store end up returning on subsequent trips to Gettysburg. Closed Tuesday.

CODORI'S FINE ART AND GIFTS
2 York Street
(717) 334-6371

This charming shop located on the square beside the Gettysburg Hotel displays beautiful examples of European fine gifts every day of the week. Among the many choices are German nutcrackers, teddy bears, dolls, handcrafted Santas, glass ornaments, chess sets, jewelry, Swiss music boxes, Russian lacquer boxes, and numerous different styles and types of nesting dolls.

MCDANNELL UNIQUE GIFTS & CRAFTS
2031 York Road
(717) 334-9915

The name of this shop certainly is right on the money. Porcelain dolls and Native American art and crafts take up a good amount of the space, and you'll also find a large selection of Keystone candles, Americana crafts, display plates, garden knickknacks, gnomes, and a wealth of other unique goods. And that's just on the porch and in the first room you enter. In a second room is an area that contains living- and dining-room sets and the "Back Room," where you can pick up some great bargains. McDannell's, which is closed on Wednesday, is located just east of the U.S. Route 15 interchange with U.S. Route 30 (York Road).

West of Lincoln Square

ACCESSORIES: FASHION—HOME—KIDS
52 Chambersburg Street
(717) 338-9700

This small shop has an eclectic mix of just what its name implies. Fashion includes a fabulous selection of handbags, both designer and name brand and day and evening styles, as well as handmade jewelry and an assortment of lotions and soaps. Original artwork, handcrafted furniture, and various displays of home accents make up the accessories available for your home, and kid accessories include new and lightly used clothes for sizes infant to 2T, kid-size furniture pieces, and a nice array of gifts.

DESERT FLOWER
2747 Chambersburg Road
(717) 338-3456

If you're an aficionado of contemporary art, be sure to stop by this place, which is located about 5 miles west of the square. The outside of the property is decorated with traditional lawn and garden ornaments, and inside the store you'll find modern art and pottery, much of it in southwestern or Egyptian style. The pottery runs the gamut from large, tall vases that look like Egyptian water pitchers to smaller eclectic works. You'll also find statues of cacti, tin men, wooden Indians, and cowboys. Once you visit, you'll probably want to stop by frequently, since new stock is always arriving at this fun store that's open daily.

FIDDLE FADDLES AND CRYING NECESSITIES
54 Chambersburg Street
(717) 334-8270

Although not a large store, Fiddle Faddles has beautiful handcrafted folk art and primitives. Owners Dick and Carol Cole have run Fiddle Faddles since its opening in 1997, and many of the items in the store are handcrafted by one of them. Fiddle Faddles is closed on Tuesday.

JILL'S HOUSE INC.
53 Chambersburg Street
(717) 338-0200
www.jills-house.com

Jill's House has two sides to it, so be sure to see all the cool stuff here. There are primitive and Americana gifts, lots of examples of folk art on the walls and as knickknacks, Boyds Bears, Vanmark

Civil War figurines, Maple City Pottery stoneware adorned with Gettysburg farm scenes, Williraye collectibles, and Longaberger baskets and accessories, including those that are hard to find since they've been "retired." Take time to notice the thickness of the Civil War–era walls as you walk from one side of the house to the other. Owners Sandy and Irv Tarner opened Jill's House in November 2002, and the store is usually closed on either Monday or Tuesday.

POTTERY BOX & GIFT SHOP
23 Chambersburg Street
(717) 334-2459
www.thepotterybox.com

This charming store just steps off the square offers unique and affordable art and crafts. Selections include handcrafted pottery, handblown glass pieces and jewelry, fine wood items, original artwork, and more. If you love paintings of landscapes, you'll definitely want to stop by here to browse the work of area resident Patricia Cavenaugh. You'll also want to admire the pottery created by Nick Corso, who uses his own glazes and fires his work in a kiln he built himself. And the crystalline pottery is not to be missed. This type of pottery is made by growing crystals in the firing process. The glaze uses 25 percent zinc, which crystallizes in the cooling cycle. Quartz is then used to make it a glass and a third mineral, such as nickel, copper, or cobalt, is used to get its color. The Pottery Box is closed Monday and Tuesday and Sunday hours are by chance.

GIFT SHOPS/COLLECTIBLES

Lincoln Square

T&S GIFTS AND MEMENTOS
19 Lincoln Square
(717) 334-3929
www.gettysburgstuff.com

Here you'll find a cornucopia of Americana items. There are T-shirts, sweatshirts, collectibles, Civil War memorabilia, coffee mugs bearing Gettysburg sites, and knickknacks sure to appeal to everyone. T&S Gifts and Mementos is open daily,

and it's owned by Strickland Enterprises, a family-owned and -operated business that has served Gettysburg shoppers since 1970.

South of Lincoln Square

BATTLEFIELD SOUVENIRS
3 Steinwehr Avenue
(717) 338-9516
www.tbhabitat.com

Battlefield Souvenirs sits in a late 19th-century brick building between its two sister stores, Stoneham's Armory (see the Military Memorabilia Shops section of the GNMP chapter) and Habitat (see this chapter's Fine Gifts and Home Accents section). T-shirts, baseball caps, toy soldiers, and other Gettysburg memorabilia join educational games, puzzles, and cards to create a huge selection of souvenirs for kids and adults to enjoy poring over. I especially like to stop and read the many plaques that line both sides of the walls as I climb the stairs. Upstairs you'll find a variety of country crafts and dolls among the interesting items on display.

BLUE & GREY GIFT SHOP
531 Baltimore Street
(717) 334-2472
www.gettysburgstuff.com

The Blue & Grey is owned by Strickland Enterprises, a family-owned and -operated Gettysburg-based business that does the custom screen printing and embroidery found on many of the T-shirts sold here and in their other shops in town. Besides the huge assortment of T-shirts that covers the shelves along the entire perimeter of Blue & Grey, you'll also find hats, flags, and other Gettysburg memorabilia. There's even a room dedicated to children's clothes and appropriate memorabilia.

COUNTRY CURIOSITY STORE
89 Steinwehr Avenue
(717) 334-2100
www.dobbinhouse.com

This shop is located at the Dobbin House, the oldest house in Gettysburg, and it's set up to remind you of a general store. Here you'll discover souvenirs, tinware, jams, jellies, foodstuffs, dolls, and much more. It's easy to while away some time here before or after enjoying the great food served at the Dobbin House's tavern or fine-dining restaurant. (See the Restaurants chapter for more on the Dobbin House.)

FLEX & FLANNIGAN'S 1863 SUTLER SHOP
240 Steinwehr Avenue
(717) 338-0451

In business since 1999, Flex & Flannigan's has souvenirs in the front of the shop, and then it's all clothes, clothes, and more clothes in the next three rooms up the stairs. There are T-shirts with all kinds of messages on them and sweatshirts in all kinds of styles and sizes. Although packed with merchandise, the store has a tiered effect that makes the area seem large, with plenty of room to browse the racks. Open late into the evening in summer.

i Gettysburg stores that use *sutler* in their names do so to signal that they have the goods to fulfill the needs of Civil War reenactors. During the Civil War a regiment usually had one sutler—a civilian camp follower who traveled with the troops and sold them "luxury" items, which could range from food and liquors to pens and paper and military goods.

GETTYSBURG SOUVENIRS AND GIFTS
27 Steinwehr Avenue
(717) 334-1200

213 Steinwehr Avenue
(717) 337-0020

The partners who own these shops keep each location chock-full. The store at 213 Steinwehr used to house the Conflict Museum, and the store at 27 Steinwehr was formerly called Bases Loaded. The partners changed the name to reflect that there's lots more here than baseball-card collections. Most noticeable are the abundance of T-shirts for sale. More than 350 styles are available, and they are displayed everywhere,

even as you go up the staircase to the rooms above. The store at 213 Steinwehr has a more orderly layout, with a wide range of souvenirs on display as well as T-shirts and leather vests and jackets.

GRANNIE'S II
13 Steinwehr Avenue
(717) 334-8704, (800) 827-5127
www.grannies.com

Grannie's II offers apparel with custom screen printing and embroidery as well as Gettysburg-related souvenirs, flags, and books. Vanmark military figures and soy candles from Old Virginia are also featured in the shop. Most of the shirts sold here are made by the staff at Grannie's North Fifth Street manufacturing location. Grannie's II opened in Gettysburg in 1995; the original Grannie's has been around since 1987 and is located about 20 minutes away in Emmitsburg, Maryland. Grannie's is proud to have been the first company to offer the National Fire Academy, located in Emmitsburg, embroidered class shirts, an operation they continue to this day. If you're interested, Grannie's can also custom make apparel that features your company or organization.

GREAT T SHIRT COMPANY
65 Steinwehr Avenue
(717) 334-8611
www.greattshirtco.com

This spacious store features T-shirts and sweatshirts as well as other apparel and Gettysburg-related souvenirs on its first floor. When you climb the wide stairs to the second floor, you'll discover fine dolls and Civil War–period memorabilia.

HOUSE OF BENDER
1 Baltimore Street
(717) 334-4315

The building the House of Bender gift shop occupies has quite a history. Built in 1817, it was a general store and a professor's home at the time of the Battle of Gettysburg. During the battle it served as a Union hospital, and the third floor was used by Union sharpshooters. Today, the House of Bender resides in the building's first floor, offering Colonial and Old Virginia soy candles, pewter, picture frames, and jewelry. Civil War books, T-shirts and sweatshirts, Pennsylvania Dutch hex signs, Civil War art, Civil War chess sets, and a myriad of souvenirs are for sale as well. House of Bender has an engraving service for plaques and awards. The store is open daily.

REALMS OF ENCHANTMENT
12 Baltimore Street
(717) 334-6326, (717) 337-0903
This charming shop features a range of whimsical collectibles, with special attention lavished on fairies. There are also quite a few dragons in the store, as well as artwork, jewelry, parasols, and a wide array of other delightful creations. Within the section of the store called Mary's Hollow, you can find exquisitely made carpetbags, and the complete series of Flower Fairies and Faerie Glenn is available for purchase.

THE TURNING POINT
244 Steinwehr Avenue
(717) 334-5993
www.gettysburgstuff.com
The Turning Point is owned by Strickland Enterprises, a Gettysburg family-owned and -operated business that runs numerous shops in town. This shop has lots of Gettysburg-related souvenirs and apparel, and one section of the store is reserved for Christmas collectibles. You'll find Department 56, Dickens' Village, Snowbabies, and other series on display.

West of Lincoln Square
THE FRONT PORCH ON BUFORD
114 Buford Avenue
(717) 334-0808, (717) 495-4510
www.thefrontporchonbuford.com
One-of-a-kind items for the garden and home decorate this beautiful two-story Victorian house that sits across from the post office. The Front Porch on Buford fills its two floors with furniture, fine linens, designer jewelry, gourmet food, home

and garden accents, antiques and reproductions, prints and frames, and more. Goods are creatively grouped together in galleries throughout the house, and unique treasures await around each corner. Finding that perfect gift for someone special is easy here, and a gift registry is available for weddings and anniversaries. Baby gifts are also on display, and gift baskets can be custom made. The Victorian's front porch has comfy chairs where nonshoppers can rest a bit, and during nice weather they can treat themselves to cookies and lemonade and read a magazine (*Fortune, Field & Stream,* and *Popular Science* are usually available) while they wait for the shoppers of their group. Inside, there's a children's nook, a tiny portion of the store that has a table with chairs where kids can draw or play while you shop. The Front Porch on Buford is open Tuesday through Saturday and by appointment on Sunday and Monday.

JEWELRY
COFFMAN JEWELERS
28 Baltimore Street
(717) 334-1510
Talk about staying power—Coffman Jewelers was established in 1948. Today the third generation of this family of jewelers will serve you in this elegant shop. You'll find exquisite diamonds and gemstone jewelry within the glass cases on each side of the store. Prices are reasonable—and browsing is always free!

THE JEWELER'S DAUGHTER
49 Steinwehr Avenue
(717) 338-0770
www.jewelersdaughter.com
The Jeweler's Daughter is a line of jewelry that focuses on the period from 1840 to 1870. The jewelry fills two cases, and the reenactment clothes of the Regimental Quartermaster (see the Military Memorabilia Shops section of the GNMP chapter) surround the cases. The stones and styling of the jewelry have been researched to ensure that the pieces truly represent the era. The

Jeweler's Daughter also repairs antique jewelry and watches, many times right on the premises.

MINE RUN GEMS
53 Steinwehr Avenue
(717) 334-9398

Mine Run Gems owner C. S. Hammer announced in spring 2005 that he is retiring once he sells his merchandise. As of this writing, the shop is still around. If it's still there when you visit, this is an excellent opportunity to acquire fine jewelry at a good price. Be sure to look for the custom jewelry made by C.S. himself.

SCOTT & CO. FINE JEWELERS
17 Lincoln Square
(717) 338-3902
www.scottandcofinejewelers.com

This shop is tucked into a cozy corner of 17 on the Square, a group of businesses that share space in a historic building with a great location right on the square. Fine jewelry is exquisitely displayed in cases, with a nice selection of gemstones available. Watch repair is available also. You can find the shop by turning to the left as soon as you enter the 17 on the Square space.

MARKETS

If your kids like to eat fresh-from-the-field fruit, see the Kidstuff chapter for farms and orchards that allow you to pick your own vitamin-filled treat.

GETTYSBURG FARMERS' MARKET
Lincoln Square
(717) 334-8151 (chamber of commerce)

Since 1992 the Gettysburg Farmers' Market on Lincoln Square has been held on Saturday mornings beginning at 7:00 a.m. from spring to early fall. This is a "producer-only" market, meaning that vendors must grow, produce, bake, or otherwise create their wares. You'll find fresh produce, baked goods, herbal products, and more. Ask a vendor for tokens for on-street parking near the market or park in the Racehorse Alley parking garage behind the Gettysburg Hotel.

ROUND BARN AND FARM MARKET
298 Cashtown Road, Biglerville
(717) 334-1984
www.roundbarngettysburg.com

The historic Round Barn, located 8 miles west of Gettysburg, was built in 1914. It's one of only three round barns, also called barrel barns, left in Pennsylvania, and it's owned by Knouse Fruitlands, Inc., which is owned and operated by the Knouse family. The family bought the barn in 1985 and opened the market in 1993 for two weeks during the National Apple Harvest Festival (see the Annual Events and Festivals chapter). Those two weeks were so successful they decided to open the barn for the next year's season, and it's been operating every year since on a daily basis from May through October. The Round Barn offers one of the largest selections of apple varieties throughout the season, and whatever produce is in season is sure to be on sale here, as well as crafts, clothing with Red Barn logos, jams, jellies, preserves, candy, fudge, and more. The barn itself is an attraction; its circumference is 282 feet, with a diameter of more than 87 feet. It was constructed around a central silo measuring 60 feet high and 12 feet wide, with a storage capacity of 145 tons of silage. The silo is the hub, with 38 spokes that form the interior structure and support for the second floor. All but one of the spokes are single lengths of wood—each nearly 37 feet long. As originally constructed, the barn could house 50 head of cattle and about 16 horses or mules. After you check out the wide selection of goods on the first floor, climb the narrow steps to the second floor. When you enter, go ahead and look up, and up, in awe at the magnificent construction—everyone does. To reach the Round Barn, head out of town on Chambersburg Road (US 30 West), make a right onto Cashtown Road, and follow the signs for Round Barn. The barn is less than 0.5 mile from the turn onto Cashtown Road.

Apple Country

When in Gettysburg, you're never far from a fruit farm, and Adams County is especially known for its apples. There are even two festivals held in honor of apples—the Apple Blossom Festival in May and the National Apple Harvest Festival in October (see the Annual Events and Festivals chapter for more on these festivals). Apples are low in calories, fat-free, sodium-free, and cholesterol-free, while providing an excellent source of fiber. Here's a short list of the more than 100 varieties of apples that are grown in the United States.

Empire: Color is red or green; sweet, tart taste

Fuji: Color is a red blush with green and yellow stripes; sweet taste

Gala: Color is red orange with yellow stripes; sweet taste

Golden Delicious: Color is yellow green with a pink blush; sweet taste

Granny Smith: Color is green, sometimes with a pink blush; tart taste

Jonagold: Color is bright red and gold; sweet or slightly tart taste

Jonathan: Color is light red stripes over yellow or deep red; moderately tart taste

McIntosh: Color is red or green; sweet-tart taste

Newtown Pippin: Color is green; slightly tart taste

Red Delicious: Color is striped to solid red; sweet taste

Rome: Color is deep solid red; slightly sweet taste

MINIMALLS

The shops below offer you downtown shopping in quaint settings, but there are also a few shopping centers around town that offer more everyday shopping experiences. At the east end of town along York Street you'll find a Wal-Mart on one side of the road and the Peebles Shopping Center on the other. The main store in the shopping center is the Peebles department store. There's also a Giant food store along this stretch of road. At the western end of town, there's a Kennie's food market along West Street and the Gettysburg Shopping Center on Springs Avenue, which has eateries and a Dollar General store. The North Mall, north of town along U.S. Business Route 15, is the home of the Gettysburg campus of the Harrisburg Area Community College (see the Education and Child Care chapter). It also houses among its tenants a Weis grocery store as well as the area's Curves for Women (see the Recreation chapter).

OLD GETTYSBURG VILLAGE
777 Baltimore Street

This charming area has the ambience of a small village, with its shops connected by wooden walkways with an abundance of places to sit and relax. There's a separate parking lot for the village behind the Gettysburg Travelodge, which can be accessed from Baltimore or Steinwehr Street. The biggest store in the village is the Horse Soldier (see the Military Memorabilia Shops section of the GNMP chapter), which expanded as space became available. The Horse Soldier has a separate gift shop, called Hallowed Ground, which offers mainly T-shirts and a small selection of books, souvenirs, and gifts. Other shops within the village include the Mystical Marketplace, which sells incense, candles, and other items for the mind, body, and spirit, and the Moccasin Shop, where you can find Minnetonka moccasins in all styles and sizes.

OUTLET SHOPPING

THE OUTLET SHOPPES AT GETTYSBURG
Junction of U.S. Route 15 and Route 97
(Baltimore Street)
(717) 337-9705, (800) 868-7553
www.gettysburgvillage.com
The Outlet Shoppes at Gettysburg is reminiscent
of a quaint Main Street in 1860s America. Brand-
name outlets line each side of a wide boulevard,
and there's parking right in front of the stores.
Among the 70 stores at this 260,000-square-foot
shopping center are such brand-name factory
outlets as Old Navy, Liz Claiborne, Van Heu-
sen, Jones New York, Bass, Naturalizer, OshKosh
B'Gosh, Pfaltzgraff, Eddie Bauer, GAP, Dress Barn,
and Zales the Diamond Store. Specialty stores
include Kulpsville Antiques and the Civil War
Store, where you can find Gettysburg and Civil
War clothing and memorabilia. A food court
with casual food and an entertainment area are
located at the one end of the mall. And there
are plenty of places to find snacks along the
way, including Harry and David and Pepperidge
Farms outlets, an Auntie Anne's pretzel store, and
the Fuzziwigs Candy Factory. Fuzziwigs is a fun
store that stocks delicious candy and nostalgic
items such as an array of different Pez candy
and dispensers. Not attached to but on the mall
grounds in separate buildings are Country Inn &
Suites (see the Hotels, Motels, and Resorts chapter), a TGI Friday's restaurant, and the Gettysburg
Village Cinema Ten (see the Recreation chapter).
The Outlet Shoppes at Gettysburg is located just
a few miles south of town off Baltimore Street.

SPECIALTY SHOPS

Lincoln Square

HAUSER ESTATE WINE SHOP
17 Lincoln Square
(717) 334-4888
www.hauserestate.com
This shop may be tiny, but it's big enough to
showcase some of the delicious products of
the local Hauser Estate Winery (see the Attrac-

tions chapter for full details on the winery). You
can taste wines, get some cheese to go with
your libation, and watch the crowds stroll by on
Lincoln Square. Bottles of wine are available for
purchase, as are all kinds of wine accoutrements,
including wine purses, glasses, corkscrews and
stoppers, and more.

North of Lincoln Square

AN EARLY ELEGANCE
113 Carlisle Street
(717) 338-9311, (800) 750-6130
www.anearlyelegance.com
Owner Mary Myers established An Early Elegance
in 1988, and she's had a shop in Gettysburg since
1995. She started out on Steinwehr Avenue,
resided for a while in Old Gettysburg Village, and
moved in fall of 2005 to this location right up the
street from the Majestic Theater (see The Arts
chapter) and the Lincoln Diner (see the Restaurants chapter). Mary's new space is bright and
welcoming, and there's plenty of room for her to
display her goods, which include more than 300
loose or bagged teas, tea accessories, books, and
ladies' hats and accoutrements. An Early Elegance
is the largest tea merchant in the area. The store
is closed on Tuesday.

TOMMY GILBERT'S HOBBY SHOP
346 East Water Street
(717) 337-1992
www.gilbertshobbies.com
Although it's not in an area with a lot of other
businesses, this hobby shop is definitely worth a
separate stop. You'll find art supplies, kits to build
models from scratch, and a mountain of stuff
for the railroad builder. Tommy's main claim to
fame is his Gettysburg souvenir railcars, which he
designs himself and has produced by Co. K. The
two boxcars that are currently available come in
HO, O, and N gauge, and other cars are in development. There are also a variety of brass engines
and other cars to pick from here, as well as all the
accoutrements a great railroad layout needs.

Tommy's store is open daily year-round
except on New Year's, Easter Sunday, Thanksgiv-

ing, and Christmas. Tommy's uncle started the business, which was then located along Steinwehr Avenue, in 1944, and Tommy's been at this location since 1987. To get to the shop from Lincoln Square, travel 1 block up Carlisle Street and turn right onto East Water Street. After you cross North Stratton Street, the store is located near the end of the street on the left.

South of Lincoln Square

BOYDS BEAR COUNTRY
75 Cunningham Road
(717) 630-2600, (866) 367-8338
www.boydsbearcountry.com
This 120,000-square-foot store, which bills itself as the World's Most Humongous Teddy Bear Store, houses 70,000 Boyds bears, hares, and other friends about 5.5 miles south of Lincoln Square off Steinwehr Avenue. The stuffed animals come in all sizes, and the displays throughout the store are stunning. The animals are clothed in different costumes and placed in many, many creative settings such as a Civil War encampment, a farm, and Noah's Ark. Boyds Bears and collectibles have become collectors' items, and certain bears are retired each year, which increases the bears' worth. Benches are placed by the store's second- and third-floor windows so you can sit and enjoy fantastic views of the countryside. The store also has a beautiful two-story stone fireplace, and live entertainment is often featured in the first-floor atrium. The first floor also houses the Boyds History Hall Museum, which chronicles the inspirational story of Boyds Bear Country. You can make your own teddy bear at Boyds Super Duper Bear Factory™ or adopt a baby bear cub at Boyds Teddy Bear Nursery™ on the third floor. This floor also contains an unbelievable range of outfits for clothing the new member of your family. The downstairs is devoted to satisfying your hunger, offering dining areas that serve full meals and sandwiches, a bakery, and a candy store. Boyds Bear Country is open to 6:00 p.m. daily.

CAT'S MEOW OF GETTYSBURG
341 Baltimore Street
(717) 337-0016
www.thecatsmeowofgettysburg.com
Holistic health is the goal of this shop, which was opened by Cathi Hunt in June 2007. Cathi stocks her store with holistic products as well as literature on alternative cultures, healing, and spiritual choices. She loves discussing alternative choices and hopes her shop will encourage a better understanding and acceptance of those choices. The shop is an oasis of calm, and a wonderful place to begin reconnecting mind, body, and spirit. Cathi will also work with customers to create unique products just for them. Cat's Meow is closed on Monday.

GETTYSBURG CIGAR CO.
523 Baltimore Street
(717) 339-0400
Owner Gary Mohan first came to Gettysburg on a trip to research an ancestor who had been in the Battle of Gettysburg. Gary and his wife liked the town so much they decided to make it their own. Some of the fine cigars available here are Arturo Fuente (including opus x), Drew Estate, Cusano, and Padron (1964 series). Gary also has a beautiful selection of pipes, many in custom-designed cases. Be sure to check out his Church Warden pipes when you stop by. If you're not really a smoker but you'd love to walk the battlefield with a cigar, Gary can also steer you to a mild blend that won't have you regretting your indulgence. Also available are tobacco melds, snuff and chew, period-appropriate pipes, and logo shirts and hats. Gettysburg Cigar Co. is closed on Tuesday.

IRISH BRIGADE SHOP
504 Baltimore Street
(717) 337-2519
www.irishbrigadegiftshop.com
This elegant, air-conditioned shop celebrates the Fighting Irish brigade of the Union army and all things Irish on T-shirts, hats, and sweatshirts, through music and videos, and with beautiful

Irish fine gifts. Claddagh rings are among the jewelry offerings, and Irish cut glass and china are on display. Irish sayings adorn a good share of the merchandise, often making your visit quite amusing. Open daily, the Irish Brigade also has clothes for the little ones that are sure to make anyone say, "Ahh, isn't that cute." The Web site mainly concentrates on the Irish Brigade, while the store has a much broader selection of Irish goods.

KEYSTONE FIREWORKS
3640 Emmitsburg Road
(717) 334-0925
www.keystonefireworks.com
This 10,000-square-foot superstore of fireworks is located off US 15 at the Steinwehr exit. It and two other recently opened superstores have expanded Keystone Fireworks, the leader in Pennsylvania fireworks retailing, beyond the more than 200 temporary tent outlets it already runs across Pennsylvania, Maryland, Virginia, and West Virginia around the Fourth of July. The stores feature the company's Keystone Brand Fireworks as well as such other popular brands as Firehawk, Dragon Eggs, Mighty Max, and more.

Ironically, Pennsylvania residents are prohibited from purchasing many of the items in the store unless they possess a permit issued by an appropriate official of the municipality in which the fireworks will be used. (Permit applications can be downloaded from the Web site.) A small section at the front of the store is accessible to anyone, but the majority of the store is beyond a velvet rope, where shoppers must stop and show ID. Without the appropriate permit Pennsylvanians cannot even browse the rest of the store. Keystone Fireworks is open seven days a week.

SERVANT'S OLD TYME PHOTOS
237 Steinwehr Avenue
(717) 334-7256
You can dress in period clothing and have your picture taken in the building where General Reynolds was taken after he was shot and killed on the battlefield during the first day of the Battle of Gettysburg. Pictures are taken with a digital camera, and prices are based on the number of people in the photo. The cost for two people is $25, and the wardrobe and accessories are included in the price. After you've sat for your portrait, you choose which picture you want printed out. You receive either two 5-by-7-inch or one 8-by-10-inch portrait with one standard heirloom-look mat. Servant's Old Tyme Photos is open daily within the stone building known as the Historic General Reynolds House.

UNION CIGAR CLUB
5 Baltimore Street
(717) 339-0009
www.unioncigarclub.com
Located just steps from Lincoln Square, the Union Cigar Club offers a relaxing place where you can purchase and enjoy premium cigars. The front of the store is filled with a wall of humidifier-controlled cabinets with glass doors that hold seemingly endless brands of cigars, with something for the casual smoker as well as the aficionado. Fresh coffee is also available, and there are comfortable bistro table settings so you can sit and enjoy smoking your cigar while drinking a cup of coffee. Beyond the front area is a private lounge, with soft leather sofas and chairs, a warming fireplace, and a 52-inch high-definition plasma TV. Visitors are welcome everywhere, although the lounge is technically for members only. Membership costs range from $100 to $300 and include such perks as personal humidors, invitations to special events and promotions, and store discounts. Although almost everyone in the place is smoking, the club's state-of-the-art ventilation system keeps the place from being smoky.

WILDERNESS LODGE LEATHER & HAT SHOP
11 Steinwehr Avenue
(717) 334-8866
Here you'll find a fine selection of leather goods, including hats, handbags, wallets, belts, vests, chaps, gloves, and jackets. The case in the front of the store contains jewelry also. You're likely to find Jack the Black Cat among all the great-smelling leather, probably in the back of the shop sleeping. Give him a pet as you browse the shop, which also has jars of hot sauces for sale.

East of Lincoln Square

BATTLEFIELD HARLEY DAVIDSON/BUELL

21 Calvary Field Road

(717) 337-9005, (877) 595-9005

www.battlefieldharley-davidson.com

Open since July 2000, this large Harley Davidson store is located about a mile east of the US 30 and US 15 interchange. Open daily, you'll find everything here you need to ride your hog in style. You can also buy a bike here, rent a bike, or have your bike repaired. Battlefield also participates in many area events, such as History Meets the Arts in April (see the Annual Events and Festivals chapter), when they host artists who create hog art.

CHROME GARDENS

147 York Street

(717) 337-3725

www.chromegardens.com

This is Gettysburg's tattoo and body-piercing shop, open since 1994. Owner Stacy McCleaf has won numerous awards for her tattoo and flash designs and considers herself an artist, which is why you won't find any temporary tattoos in this shop. Most tattoos done here are custom designed, and strict sterilization techniques are employed. You must be 18 years old to enter the shop, and there is no smoking or alcohol allowed.

METAPHYSICAL CENTER OF GETTYSBURG

26 North Fourth Street

(717) 253-6634

www.francinemilano.com

The metaphysical center is where spiritualist medium and nationally renowned radio psychic Francine Milano conducts classes and workshops and gives private readings by appointment Friday through Sunday. Workshops include learning how to develop your own psychic abilities and participating in message circles, where Francine relays messages from spirit guides and loved ones who have passed over. Francine can be heard on radio station FM 97 the first Monday morning of each month or at www.fm97.com outside the local listening area.

West of Lincoln Square

ADAMS COUNTY WINERY WINE SHOP

25 Chambersburg Street

(717) 334-4631

www.adamscountywinery.com

Opened in summer 2006, this shop is a satellite store for Adams County Winery, which is located 9 miles outside of Gettysburg in Orrtanna. (For a full review of Adams County Winery, see the Attractions chapter.) The store showcases the winery's full range of wines, including the unique Gettysburg Winery label. Reserved for the winery's premium wines, this label features pictures of historic Gettysburg monuments and Civil War scenes and makes for a great souvenir. Tastings of the wines are offered at the shop, and you may also purchase wine by the glass and gourmet picnic foods and savor them at cafe tables. Just about any type of wine accoutrement is also available here, including wine purses, corkscrews, glasses, picnic baskets, and wine racks. The shop and the winery are open seven days a week for tastings and consultations.

A LIT'LE IRISH, TOO

62 Chambersburg Street

(717) 334-6609

www.alittleirishtoo.com

Gettysburg now has two shops in town dedicated to all things Irish—the Irish Brigade Shop in the southern end of town and this shop west of Lincoln Square that opened in the summer of 2006. The two complement each other, with the Irish Brigade offering mostly elegant gifts and this one offering mostly fun and whimsical items. The fun items include glittery tiaras, costume jewelry, toys, and plenty of items with Irish sayings on them, such as plaques, license plates, garden stones, and Irish Princess shirts for your little ones. You'll also find Irish foods, county crests, artwork, tapestries, books, and music. And elegant items include Irish jewelry and fine Belleek china. A Lit'le Irish, Too is closed on Tuesday.

SHOPPING

CARVER'S TOYLAND
305 Buford Avenue
(717) 334-6937

This place is easy to find—its sign is in the shape of a train engine. Carver's Toyland stocks trains—Lionel, American Flyer, Thomas the Tank Engine—and all the accessories to complete your railroad layout. The owner compares the place to Madison Hardware of New York City in the 1950s, where you could pick up any and all types of toy trains and accessories. Though it looks really small from the outside, the shop just keeps unfolding into additional rooms once you're inside, with each room holding more train-related treasure. One of the rooms even has a working train layout that you can run. You can bring your trains here for repair, and Mr. Carver also works on clocks. The store has cuckoo clocks, grandfather clocks, and unique clocks for sale. Christmas collectibles are Mrs. Carver's passion, and one room is filled with cases of whimsical offerings for sale. Although it's not for sale, be sure to check out Mrs. Carver's personal collection of Christmas memorabilia that's on display. The Carvers have been at this location since before 1975, and they buy and sell their trains and collectibles seven days a week.

GETTYSBURG ELECTRONICS
24 Chambersburg Street
(717) 334-8634, (717) 334-1282
www.gettysburgelectronics.com

Gettysburg Electronics has a wide range of metal detectors in a few aisles at the back of the Gettysburg Christian Bookstore, also at this address. (See the Books and Music section of this chapter for more on the Gettysburg Christian Bookstore.) An avid detectorist himself since the late 1960s, owner Don Hicks opened the place in 1972. Don supplies a wide assortment of accessories for treasure hunting, and he's also a wealth of knowledge on the subject. Don't be shy about bartering if you have some Civil War relics or other cool stuff you've found with your detector; Don will sometimes accept these as partial payment on your purchase. If you're considering hunting for

relics on the battlefield—don't. Metal detectors or any relic hunting is prohibited in the park (and all national parks), and heavy fines and confiscation of your equipment and even your car await you if you disobey the rules.

HACIENDA SHILOH—INTERNATIONAL GARLIC, TEAS & HERBS
327 Knox Road
(717) 642-9161
www.haciendashiloh.com

Hacienda Shiloh means House of Tranquillity, and this small organic herb farm tucked away in the back roads of Gettysburg certainly lives up to its name. You wind along country lanes to a home that sits on a hill about 8 miles west of town, surrounded by trees and nature. Follow the path to the garden and garlic shed, where more than 20 varieties of garlic from Russia, Italy, France, the Czech Republic, Germany, and Poland are hanging. After you admire the plants and garlic, head back to the small shop that's attached to the house to discover a grand selection of culinary and medicinal herbs; more than 200 custom-blended teas; handmade herbal soaps and lotions; dehydrated rice, soup, and stew blends that are ideal for camping meals; beeswax candles; herbal blends, rubs, flavored sea salts, and salt substitutes; and much more. Hacienda Shiloh has one of the largest collections of medicinal herbs in the mid-Atlantic region, and the owners supply herbs to the patients of the nearby Gettysburg Holistic Health Center (see the Health Care and Wellness chapter). Gift baskets are available, and one corner of the store has medicinal head wraps and a wealth of other eclectic items. To reach Hacienda Shiloh, head west from town on Route 116 (Middle Street), and turn right when you reach the Needle & Thread Fabrics shop (see the Civil War Clothing and Accessories section of the GNMP chapter). Follow the country road for about 3 miles and veer left onto Knox Road at the KOA Kampground (see the Campgrounds and RV Parks chapter). Hacienda Shiloh is about a mile farther on the right.

ROSE GARDEN NATURAL FOODS
39 West Street
(717) 338-0835
www.rosegardennatural.com
A large selection of natural and unprocessed food, organic produce, bulk products, and vitamin supplements can be found at this store located in the Gettysburg Shopping Center, which is next to the Dollar General that's along Chambersburg Street. Owners Jacky and Kitty Rose began the store in 1997, and it's open every day but Sunday. Three-quarters of the store is dedicated to natural-food selections, while the rest of the area holds health-related items. Also stocked are environmentally safe cleaning supplies and laundry detergent, organic personal-hygiene items, books on subjects from cooking to healthy healing, and natural pet foods. When buying bulk products, shoppers can bag just the amount they want.

SPIRITED LADIES SHOPPE
45 Chambersburg Stret
(717) 683-6797
www.uniquely-yours-creations.com
This eclectic shop features the works of a consortium of women artists known as the Spirited Ladies. The group was cofounded by local artists Sue Hudson and Martha Wolf, and its mission is to inspire, unite, and promote the artistic endeavors of women. Sue and Martha share a passion for beading, and the shop shows off the beautiful jewelry, clothing, embroidery, and other handcrafts they create and enhance with their beads of glass, gemstones, and crystal. Works on display by other artists might include stained glass, jewelry, photography, home accessories, gourmet cakes, and more. The Spirited Ladies Shoppe is closed on Monday.

SWEETS & TREATS

CANNONBALL OLDE TYME MALT SHOPPE
11 York Street
(717) 334-9695
This small shop has only five tables, but it carries 49 flavors of milk shakes and malts. Cones, sundaes, ice-cream sodas, and banana splits round out the ice-cream treats, while soups, sandwiches, salads, wraps, and quesadillas are available for those who like to eat before they snack.

Look up and a little to the left of the entrance to Cannonball Old Tyme Malt Shoppe and you'll see how the shop got its name. Yep, that's a projectile from the Battle of Gettysburg embedded in the wall.

Cannonball is a family-run business that's open seasonally; during the season it's closed on Tuesday. If you've never had a phosphate or a malt, this is a great place to treat your taste buds.

GARRAHY'S FUDGE KITCHEN
625 Baltimore Street
(717) 334-7342
This small shop is across from the Gettysburg Tour Center at the entrance to Old Gettysburg Village. All that's sold here is great-tasting fudge, and the no-frills store consists of a glass case where the fudge is displayed and an area where the fudge is made, which is in plain view. Since there's only one thing to buy here, and the fudge comes in only six flavors, you can get your fudge quickly and be on your way, happily satisfied and avoiding long lines elsewhere. Garrahy's Fudge Kitchen is open daily.

GETTYSBURG PRETZEL & SNACK COMPANY
1875 York Road
(717) 338-9081
www.gettysburgpretzel.com
The pretzels here are hand rolled and baked in a brick oven, giving them a just-baked taste. The store consists of a counter and some shelves that hold boxes of hard pretzels. Soft pretzels are sold out of a large cardboard box on the counter. The whole operation occurs at this building, from the making of the dough to the rolling and the baking of the pretzels. If you're curious how it's done, tours are cheerfully given. Pretzels can be shipped throughout the country, and once you taste these goodies, you'll be placing your order.

KILWIN'S OF GETTYSBURG
37 Steinwehr Avenue
(717) 337-2252
www.kilwins.com

The first Kilwin's was opened by Don and Katy Kilwin in 1947 in Petoskey, Michigan. Today there are franchises in 10 states. Sisters and co-owners Paige Levan and Polly Parone opened the Gettysburg Kilwin's, the only one in Pennsylvania, in 1993. Since then they have been treating the people in Gettysburg to homemade chocolates, fudge, and ice cream daily from the ground floor of a frame house built more than a century ago. If you're lucky, you can watch the chocolate being made in the shop; the heavenly smells alone make the trip worthwhile.

KOOL SCOOPS
531 Baltimore Street
(917) 613-8046

This seasonal shop is a walk-up window at a small building that looks like it used to be a garage.

Italian ice and ice cream are available in cones or dishes for walk-away orders; there are no seats here. Because you simply look over the ice-cream flavors and make your selection, the line here moves quickly—a welcome relief on a hot day.

SUNSET ICE CREAM PARLOR
33 Steinwehr Avenue
(717) 337-3125

With its bright orange, red, and yellow exterior, you can't miss the Sunset Ice Cream Parlor. This old-fashioned ice-cream shop sells Sunset brand ice cream, which is made in Williamsport, Pennsylvania. The bright colors outside are carried inside, where there are about five small tables that give you a place to enjoy your ice cream while cooling off in the store's air-conditioning. Outside there are picnic tables for those who prefer to people watch as they enjoy their treats. Sunset accepts cash only and is open daily.

THE ARTS

The arts are an integral part of the Gettysburg community, and many shops feature the works of local artists on their walls and shelves. You'll find galleries boasting the art of well-known Civil War artists alongside the works of regional artists, and this delightful mix guarantees a new experience on every visit. The biggest event for those who admire fine art is the annual History Meets the Arts, held every April, when the town galleries show off their collections and host artists and events throughout the weekend. (See the Annual Events and Festivals chapter for more on History Meets the Arts.) But you can be sure there are plenty of places in town to discover interesting art anytime you visit. Although a great many of the galleries offer art representing the Civil War genre, you'll also discover contemporary and unique shops along the way. Entries for Gettysburg galleries and studios are listed alphabetically within geographic direction from Lincoln Square.

The performing arts are also well represented here, as they have been for decades. The Totem Pole Playhouse has been entertaining theatergoers since the 1950s, and the Majestic Theater hosted the Eisenhowers during the '50s when Ike was president. Today both theaters are still integral parts of the local entertainment scene, which has grown to include dinner and regional theater. Of course, arts flourish best when they are locally supported, and Gettysburg has numerous organizations that promote art throughout the region.

ℹ Many galleries host artists on the first Friday of every month during the summer season, usually from 6:00 to 8:00 p.m. You can meet the artists and enjoy wine and cheese as you admire the art. It's part of the town's First Friday program, where some businesses hold special events or stay open longer. Look for colorful First Friday flags outside participating shops.

GALLERIES AND STUDIOS

North of Lincoln Square

SCHMUCKER ART GALLERY
Gettysburg College
North Washington and Water Streets
(717) 337-6080
www.gettysburg.edu
This 1,600-square-foot gallery space is located on the main floor of Schmucker Hall on the Gettysburg College campus. Seven to eight different exhibitions are displayed at the gallery each year, and everyone from the campus and the community is welcome to attend the opening receptions that are held for each event. Every year includes shows by local, national, and international contemporary artists, a faculty exhibition, a student exhibition, the annual senior art-major show, and traveling exhibits.

During the summer the gallery is open every day but Monday and is closed on college holidays. You can park for free in one of the visitor parking lots on campus, and some free two-hour parking can be found on North Washington and Water Streets. The main entrance is through the quadrangle side of the building.

South of Lincoln Square

ACES HIGH GALLERY
433 Baltimore Street
(717) 337-0779
www.aceshighgallery.com
Aces High is owned by Steve and Barbara Shultz,

who were raised in Gettysburg. Steve left his position as chef at the historic Farnsworth House and Barbara left a career in real estate in January 1992 to open an art- and picture-framing studio, which they named Lasting Impressions. Steve decided to sell some of his collection of WWII aviation art at the studio, and in 1995 the couple renamed the business to reflect this, giving it its current name. Aces High is open daily and offers die-casts, model kits, prints, posters, frames, and autographed books and photos. Many veteran gatherings, book signings, and symposiums are also held at the gallery. Aces High Gallery is located within A Sentimental Journey Bed & Breakfast, which the Shultzes also own and which consists of five rooms decorated in WWI- and WWII-era decor. (See the Bed-and-Breakfasts and Guesthouses chapter for more details.)

CIVIL WAR FINE ART
333 Baltimore Street
(717) 338-3463
www.civilwarfineart.com
Artist and owner A. V. Lindenberger's work is featured at Civil War Fine Art, a cozy space that opened in 2004. Amy works in colored pencil, and you can often watch her drawing as she sits by the window along Baltimore Street. Originals and prints are offered at the gallery, and there's something to fit everyone's price range. To date Amy has completed 19 images in her series "Beyond the Battlefield," which has two categories within it—"Sword across the Threshold" and "Women of Distinction." The first category depicts situations the average citizen-soldier of the Civil War and his family may have found themselves in while the second category depicts women who made notable contributions to the Civil War. Because Amy has another studio in Ohio, where she also teaches art, the studio in Gettysburg is

i The *Battle of Gettysburg* is one of only two cyclorama paintings on display within the United States. The circular oil painting is also the largest painting in the country.

open only for limited hours, usually Friday from 4:00 to 8:00 p.m., Saturday from 11:00 a.m. to 8:00 p.m., and Sunday from 11:00 a.m. to 2:00 p.m.

GALLON HISTORICAL ART, INC.
9 Steinwehr Avenue
(717) 334-8666
www.gallon.com
Here you can enjoy historical art created by Dale Gallon, a well-known artist in the Civil War market for more than 25 years. Dale has more than 100 images in his complete works, which include paintings and limited-edition prints. He has published four limited-edition prints each year since 1980, and his work is displayed in many prominent places, including the Pentagon and the U.S. Army War College. Known for his historical accuracy and attention to detail, Dale identifies important people and landmarks on the upper and lower borders of his prints. He also employs a staff historian, who is responsible for researching every detail of the scene depicted and writing a historical essay that accompanies each print.

i Although Civil War painter Dale Gallon is closely associated with Gettysburg, he is not a native of the area. Born in California, Dale moved to Gettysburg in 1988. He released his first limited-edition Civil War print in 1980 and has published a new image every three months since.

GETTYSBURG HISTORICAL PRINTS, INC.
219 Steinwehr Avenue
(717) 334-3800, (888) 447-2515
www.fhphistoricalprints.com
This spacious shop has the feel of an art museum with its open layout and recessed lighting above the artwork. The framed work of John Paul Strain, Tom Freeman, Keith Rocco, Mort Künstler, and other notable artists hangs throughout the gallery, and unframed prints are available as well. Framing services are also provided in the shop, which is open daily.

GIBSON'S PHOTOGRAPHIC STUDIO
65 Steinwehr Avenue
(717) 337-9393
www.civilwarphotography.com

Photographs are taken the way they were in 1860 at this studio. A camera from the time of the Civil War is used to take your picture, and the photograph is developed using the wet-plate process that was utilized in those days. This is a painstaking process requiring exactitude in which the photo is taken on glass. Owner Rob Gibson left his job as an engineer at General Motors to open a Civil War–era photo studio in Gettysburg in 1999, and today he is considered the world's foremost wet-plate photographer. His movie credits include *Gods and Generals* and *Cold Mountain,* and his latest work involves Steven Spielberg's miniseries *Into the West.* He has also given demonstrations and lectures at the Smithsonian Institute and has appeared on and done consulting work for PBS, the History Channel, and A&E.

At this shop you'll truly experience what having your picture taken was like in the 1860s, and you'll end up with a photograph that is authentic to the times. Development of your photograph is done using 1860s laboratory equipment and techniques, and either a military or civilian wardrobe is provided for you to wear. The studio is open seven days a week, and walk-ins are welcome. Most people choose to have a 5-by-7-inch plate taken, which costs around $95.

THE INKWELL AUTOGRAPH GALLERY
529 Baltimore Street
(717) 337-2220
www.inkwellgallery.com

Opened in 1995, this treasure is tucked away in a small space across from the Jennie Wade House. Although the gallery isn't huge, it holds the largest selection of authentic Civil War autographs to be found in one place in Gettysburg. The offerings are varied, running the gamut from lower-priced autographs for the beginning collector to utmost rarities worthy of the finest collections.

Autographs are guaranteed authentic, and many are museum-quality framed. For those who collect all things Lincoln, you will definitely want to visit here. The gallery also displays autographs of athletes, politicians, and celebrities; browsing at this place is a must. Many of the signed books for sale were obtained personally by the owner, who travels to meet the famous signatories and witness the signing. The gallery is closed on Wednesday.

VICTORIAN PHOTO STUDIO
76 Steinwehr Avenue
(717) 338-1515
www.victorianphotostudio.com

Open daily, this shop shares space with Somewear in Time, a historical clothing shop. (For more on Somewear in Time, see the Civil War Clothing and Accessories section of the GNMP chapter.) The photo studio gives you the choice of having your picture taken the old-fashioned way by using a wet-plate process, which captures your image on glass or tin, or the most up-to-date way, using a digital camera. If you want to dress up for your photo, you can choose from a variety of Victorian and Civil War military outfits, and children's clothing is also available. Victorian-style picture frames are just waiting for you to fill them with your remembrance of your visit to Gettysburg, and there are also plenty of books on historic photography for sale if you want to learn more about the wet process that was used in 19th-century photography.

East of Lincoln Square

ARTWORKS
42 York Street
(717) 334-4250

Opened in April 2005, Artworks features the work of local and regional artists. The front of the store contains paintings, pottery, and fine gifts. Handmade quilts are on display, and the lady who makes some of them is often sitting in the shop sewing as she minds the store on Wednesday. Owner Linda Atiyeh, who also owns Gallery 30 (see next write-up) is enthusiastic about the artists whose works she displays. A room in the back has a good selection of T-shirts bearing original designs. This fun and visually stimulating gallery is open daily.

GALLERY 30
30 York Street
(717) 334-0335
www.gallery30.com

Gallery 30 has been operating since 1978. Current owner Linda Atiyeh took over in August 2007, and previous owners Lois Starkey and William Gilmartin had run the place since 1993. The work of local and regional artists is displayed throughout the gallery in the varied forms of paintings, fiber art, pottery, blown glass, contemporary crafts, handmade jewelry, and other mediums of fine art. Be sure to check out the children's section in the back of the store, where you'll find toys, board and card games, and educational and fun games and puzzles. There's also a nice selection of currently released books along the left wall of Gallery 30, which is open daily.

JUST JENNIFER GALLERY AND FRAMERY
33 & 35 York Street
(717) 338-9099 (gallery),
(717) 338-9609 (framery)
www.JustJenniferGallery.com

Just Jennifer is actually two stores; each store has its own entrance. The gallery showcases Native American and silver jewelry, fine art from more than 40 artists, gifts, candles, housewares, pottery, glassware, spa and bath products, and gourmet foods. The walls of the staircase and the second floor of the gallery contain the fine art that's for sale, and no one younger than age 16 is allowed upstairs without adult supervision. The downstairs area of the gallery groups the rest of the offerings in eye-catching displays. The frame shop offers custom framing and has more than 2,000 frame samples in stock. The gallery is closed on Monday and Tuesday, and the frame shop is closed on Sunday and Monday.

M. KÜNSTLER GALLERY
10 York Street
(717) 334-0513, (877) 334-0513
www.mkunstlergallery.com

Known as America's artist, Mort Künstler is considered one of the greatest historical artists in the country. Once he decided in the 1980s to focus exclusively on Civil War art, he quickly became the most collected artist of the genre, and this is the only gallery that is dedicated solely to his works. It's also the only gallery in town where you can view some of his original pieces, which are kept in the back of the shop in the "vault." (The space was previously a bank, and the vault door was retained during the refurbishment.) Mr. Künstler painstakingly researches the historical events he describes on canvas so that his paintings are accurate down to the last meticulous detail. The gallery was opened not only to highlight Mr. Künstler's talent but also to make his art available at reasonable (for this caliber of art) prices. Personal appearances by Mr. Künstler occur at the gallery a few times each year.

WENTZ STAINED-GLASS STUDIO
48 York Street
(717) 334-0906
www.wentzstainedglass.com

Items made of stained glass in all shapes and sizes shimmer in Wentz's window display, beckoning you inside, and owner Bonnie Wentz is likely to be the one greeting you as you enter. Bonnie opened this working stained-glass studio in 1982, and custom work is de rigueur here. You'll be able to admire glass bead jewelry, stained-glass sun catchers, candle lamps, wind chimes, and many more unique gifts. Custom-designed windows, lamps, and cabinet doors show Bonnie's breadth of experience, knowledge Bonnie imparts to students through workshops held in the studio. Supplies and the tools needed to make your own stained-glass masterpiece are available, and Bonnie also sells patterns. The studio is open every day but Sunday, when all you can do is admire the cool stuff in the front window.

West of Lincoln Square

GETTYSBURG FRAME SHOP AND GALLERY

17 Chambersburg Street
(717) 337-2796
www.gettysburgframe.com

Here you'll find artwork concerning the American Civil War, with art available for all price ranges. You'll be able to choose from limited-edition prints, canvas-edition prints, giclees, original paintings, and shadow boxes. Art can be bought framed, or you can pick out a print and a frame that will be uniquely yours. Sculpture, books, music, and replicas of Civil War–era weaponry are also available. The gallery has been in business since 1989 and features the work of such highly respected military artists as Don Troiani, Keith Rocco, and John Paul Strain. Gettysburg Frame Shop and Gallery is open daily.

LORD NELSON'S GALLERY

27½ Chambersburg Street
(717) 334-7950, (800) 664-9797
www.lordnelsons.com

Located within the James Gettys Hotel (see the Bed-and-Breakfasts and Guesthouses chapter), this two-story gallery is the country's largest exhibitor of eastern American Indian/frontier art of the French and Indian War period. Lord Nelson's also features wildlife art, and the Native American/frontier and wildlife art comprises about half the gallery. The other half has nostalgic/Americana art, sculptures crafted from bronze, Native American pottery, handcrafted gifts, decorative decoys, art glass, soapstone, collectibles, and a large collection of books and fine accoutrements dealing with the French and Indian War period. The art prices range from prints for $40 to framed works by well-known artists selling for $20,000. The business began in 1990 as an import shop selling Guatemalan goods and Belgian lace and chocolates, among other things. The owners named the store for Nelson, their 14-year-old black lab. One of the co-owners of Lord Nelson's purchased the building that is now the James Gettys Hotel in 1995, and the space between the first floor of the hotel and gallery is fluid, with archways leading from one area to the other. Lord Nelson's Gallery is open daily.

SUPPORT ORGANIZATIONS

ADAMS COUNTY ARTS COUNCIL (ACAC)

18 Carlisle Street, Suite 201
(717) 334-5006
www.adamscountyartscouncil.org

Started by a small group in 1993, the Adams County Arts Council has evolved into a 500–member nonprofit agency supporting artistic efforts throughout the county's schools and communities. The council partners with organizations and businesses to promote art in many forms in Adams County, and they accomplish their goal in many ways. Every Saturday during July, member artists add their work to the wide array of goods available at the farmers' market in Lincoln Square, and the council's Arts in Education program has brought musical groups, theater companies, dance troupes, and other artists into every school district in Adams County. Financial support for many arts programs and projects throughout the country are provided by the Adams County Arts Council's STAR (Supporting the Arts Regionally) grant. Dancing the night away in the Gettysburg Hotel Grande Ballroom at the council's annual Masquerade Ball is one of many fun ways this organization raises money to support regional arts.

ADAMS COUNTY PUBLIC LIBRARY SYSTEM

140 Baltimore Street
(717) 334-5716
www.adamslibrary.org

The Adams County library system has seven branches and a bookmobile. The library in Gettysburg is the system's main branch, and programs for children and the community at large are offered. Children's programs include story times for preschoolers and a book club for middle-school students, and all levels of computer courses are offered free to members of the community. The Gettysburg branch is open seven days a week, and the library system's bookmobile runs five days a week and visits an average of eight locations a day. A bookmobile first started operating in the county in 1946, and the current bookmobile is the system's fifth. The 28-foot vehicle holds around 3,000 volumes of books, and it also brings videos, DVDs, and books on tape to county residents.

GETTYSBURG COMMUNITY CONCERT ASSOCIATION
(717) 334-3788
www.gettysburg.com/gca/gcca.htm
This member-supported nonprofit organization has been in existence since 1939, and its purpose is to cultivate an interest in good music and dance. The association provides opportunities for its members to attend performances by outstanding professional artists that are held in the Gettysburg Area Middle School and High School auditoriums. Members may also attend for free the concerts of associations in Chambersburg and Waynesboro in Pennsylvania and Hagerstown and Westminster in Maryland. The association also conducts community outreach programs, such as in-school visits by performers.

MAIN STREET GETTYSBURG
571 West Middle Street
(717) 337-3491
www.mainstreetgettysburg.org
Main Street Gettysburg is a nonprofit organization committed to the preservation and revitalization of historic Gettysburg for the benefit of its citizens, businesses, and visitors. The organization arranges incentives and zero-interest loans for businesses to aid in the revitalization of storefronts, façades, and residential buildings. This group often leads the effort to restore and preserve local landmarks, and its goal is to help guide Gettysburg's future and maintain its historic integrity by forging partnerships among key preservation, community, and government groups as well as interested citizens from all over the United States. Main Street Gettysburg was the driving force behind the restoration and preservation of the David Wills House on Lincoln Square and currently operates the facility. (See the Attractions chapter for more on the David Wills House.)

In the summer of 2005, Main Street Gettysburg introduced a 90-minute walking tour of the town. The tour is led by a licensed tour guide, and it highlights the civilian experience during the Battle of Gettysburg. (For more on this and other tours available, see the Attractions chapter.)

PERFORMING ARTS

GETTYSBURG CIVIL WAR ERA DINNER THEATRE
The Fairfield Inn 1757
15 Main Street, Fairfield
(717) 642-5410, (888) 246-4432
www.civilwartheater.com
The Fairfield Inn opened its dinner theater in August 2001, and entertainment is provided by Civil War illusionist and storyteller Joe Kerrigan. The one-man show lasts 2½ hours, and Joe comes to life as three different characters. He leads off as Professor Kerrigan, who performs Civil War–era magic, and then he changes to a gifted storyteller who talks about being a civilian at the time of the Battle of Gettysburg. This character also chills the audience with a few stories of ghosts haunting the area. Joe then stages a theatrical re-creation of a Civil War séance. A full-course meal accompanies all this fun, and you can catch a show Tuesday through Saturday at 7:00 p.m. and Sunday at 1:00 p.m. Reservations are required, and the dinner theater costs $39.95 for adults and $19.95 for children age 12 and younger.

GETTYSBURG STAGE
(866) 859-5192
www.gettysburgstage.org
With the support of the Adams County Arts Council (see the earlier listing within this chapter), Gettysburg Stage was founded in the summer of 2003. A nonprofit organization, it consists of professional and amateur artists from the region who stage six productions each year. Productions are meant to be thought-provoking, and some plays may contain themes or language suitable for mature audiences only. Open seating accommodates about 50 people in this no-frills space, and free refreshments are available. Tickets run

$12, and the price is reduced to $10 for seniors, students, groups of 10 or more, or anyone who donates an old cell phone. The cell phones are processed, with profits going to buy phone cards for our soldiers overseas.

For reservations, call the toll-free number above, which is a recording. You're given information on current and upcoming performances and asked to leave a message with your reservation request. The message is then forwarded to the volunteers at Gettysburg Stage, and someone gets in touch with you.

MAJESTIC THEATER PERFORMING ARTS & CULTURAL CENTER
25 Carlisle Street
(717) 337-8200
www.gettysburgmajestic.org
Since the Majestic Theater opened its doors in November 1925, it's not surprising to find that it's listed on the National Register of Historic Places. It was constructed as an annex to the Gettysburg Hotel, and when it opened, it was the largest vaudeville and silent-movie theater in southeastern Pennsylvania. The Eisenhowers also added to the theater's history—they attended performances held at the Majestic, and part of the theater was sometimes used for press conferences with President Eisenhower. Gettysburg College purchased the theater in the early 1990s and conducted a five-year study to determine the best use for the property. The college decided to restore the theater and operate it as a community center for the performing arts and movies. After closing in March 2004 to undergo a $16 million renovation, the theater's 80th anniversary was celebrated with its grand reopening on November 14, 2005, exactly 80 years from its original opening night. The Vienna Boys Choir was among the first performers to appear in the 850-seat theater beautifully restored to its 1925 Colonial Revival style. About 30 live performances are held here annually. You'll want to look up while attending a performance and admire the theater's original pressed-tin ceiling, which was

removed, renovated, and reinstalled. In addition to the theater, the center also has two movie theaters with stadium seating, and movies will be shown nightly. In Cinema 1, each row will have a "cuddle seat"—a seat for two that has no armrest in the middle. There's also an art gallery, well-appointed bathrooms, a cinema cafe, and a backstage production wing with a rehearsal studio. State-of-the-art theatrical systems for lighting, rigging, sound, and film projection round out the theater experience.

i Music, Gettysburg! offers more than a dozen concerts a year at the chapel of Gettysburg Lutheran Theological Seminary, which is noted for its superb acoustics. Begun in 1980, the concert series features international, regional, and local musical artists, and music presented ranges from popular to Civil War to the classics. Call (717) 338-3000, ext. 2197, or visit www .musicgettysburg.org for information.

TOTEM POLE PLAYHOUSE
Caledonia State Park
40 Rocky Mountain Road, Fayetteville
(717) 352-2164, (888) 805-7056
www.totempoleplayhouse.org
Opened in the early 1950s, Totem Pole Playhouse presents professional summer theater within Caledonia State Park. The late William H. Putch was the playhouse's second artistic director, and he guided the playhouse to national prominence during his tenure from 1954 to 1984. Working closely with his wife, actress Jean Stapleton, William Putch was responsible for 270 productions at Totem Pole, in addition to directing several national tours. Totem Pole Playhouse is one of the few remaining summer theaters that maintain a resident company of actors. Interspersed with the regular faces have been a series of well-known actors, including Keir Dullea, Sada Thompson, John Ritter, Sandy Dennis, Harry Groener, and Curtis Armstrong.

Six plays are staged per season in the air-conditioned playhouse, and a postshow discussion is scheduled for one night during each play's run. Here the audience can join the cast, staff, and directors for informal chats about the show and the playhouse. Plays are held in the evening on Tuesday through Sunday, and matinee shows are held on Tuesday, Wednesday, Saturday, and Sunday afternoons. Tickets run around $35, and three subscription plans are available. Students can attend any performance for just $13. Children younger than age five are not admitted to the theater.

Totem Pole Playhouse also hosts a popular summer theater camp for students age 8 to 16. Enrollment is on a first-come, first-serve basis, and no theater experience is necessary.

KIDSTUFF

Kids love stories, and Gettysburg has some of the best. Stories of honor and bravery in wartime, stories of ghosts and eerie happenings, stories of the Underground Railroad—you can find them all and many more as you explore Gettysburg and the battlefield. The area also allows kids to get physical, whether it be by hitting a golf ball, driving go-karts, or making a teddy bear. And the richness of the orchards that surround the area gives the kids an opportunity to commune with nature, and to eat some fruit that they pick themselves.

Gettysburg has something for every member of the family. Many of the other chapters of this book have activities kids would also enjoy; be sure to especially check out the Recreation and Attractions chapters for other kid-friendly fun. Most of the activities within this chapter are either free of charge or cost between $4 and $6 per child.

PRICE CODE

Prices represent the cost for one adult admission. Most places reduce the price for children and senior citizens, but each establishment sets its age ranges differently, so be sure to ask about prices for specific ages. Many attractions allow children younger than a certain age to be admitted for free, and I'll mention this in the write-ups where it applies.

$..................$2.00 to $5.50
$$ ....$5.51 to $7.50
$$$ ....$7.51 to $15.00
$$$$ .... More than $15

AMUSEMENT COMPLEXES

ALLSTAR EVENTS COMPLEX $$
2638 Emmitsburg Road
(717) 334-6363, (888) 497-9386
www.allstarpa.com
This place is a kid's dream—two go-kart tracks, two minigolf courses, batting cages, a virtual-reality ride, virtual-reality golf, billiards, video games, and more. But since Allstar is a 50,000-square-foot expo center (with parking for 2,000-plus cars), you need to call ahead to make sure it's not already booked with large parties. And unfortunately, the paddleboats that you see on the 14-acre lake

are available only to groups. Groups also rent the basketball court, volleyball court, and soccer fields (one of which is indoors). Each activity is individually priced, and activities are paid for with tickets, tokens, or cash based on half-hour or hourly rates. For instance, the minigolf and go-kart tracks are paid for with tickets, the batting cages take tokens, and billiards and virtual-reality golf are paid for in cash. Your child must be 58 inches tall to drive on the Family Track and 60 inches tall to drive on the oval track. There are also walking trails for those who want to connect with nature for free. A full-service snack bar is available when all the activity leads to hunger.

ATTRACTIONS

AMERICAN CIVIL WAR MUSEUM $
297 Steinwehr Avenue
(717) 334-6245
www.gettysburgmuseum.com
Kids will enjoy all this museum has to offer inside (see the Attractions chapter), and outside they will find reenactors in living-history encampments on weekends from April through November. A different unit camps in front of the museum each weekend, and some civilian reenactors are usually on hand. Reenactors have in-depth knowledge about the history they're representing, and they will answer all your questions gladly. The

encampments have been held for more than two decades, and you can wander around for free. Most Saturdays from June through August, the museum also runs a program where kids can make a craft representative of the Civil War era. The program lasts about 30 to 45 minutes. One week kids may make a drum, the next week it's a yarn doll, and another Saturday might find the kids making a haversack.

BOYDS BEAR COUNTRY
75 Cunningham Road
(717) 630-2600, (866) 367-8338
www.boydsbearcountry.com

Kids will love this 120,000-square-foot store where 70,000 Boyds bears, hares, and other friends hang out. Located about 5.5 miles south of Lincoln Square off Steinwehr Avenue, the store has displays that appeal to all ages. There are bears on Noah's Ark, bears in NASCAR regalia, bears in Civil War and military garb, and bears in college sweaters. Kids are especially interested in making their own bear at Boyds Super Duper Bear Factory™ on the third floor. As you enter the factory, you don a yellow construction hat and grab a time card. Then you pick out your future stuffed animal and assemble it at stations along the way. The last step is to choose the Magic Bean that makes your new friend come to life. Then you name your friend and clothe him with just the right outfit and accessories. The third floor also has a Boyds Teddy Bear Nursery™ for those who prefer to adopt a bear, who you then name and clothe as you would have if you'd made him yourself. When kids get rambunctious, there's a play area on the third floor where they can blow off steam. When they get hungry from all the fun, the downstairs level has dining areas that serve full meals and sandwiches, a bakery, and a candy store. All this fun is available daily to 6:00 p.m.

EAST COAST EXOTIC ANIMAL RESCUE $$
320 Zoo Road, Fairfield
(717) 642-5229
www.eastcoastrescue.org

Formerly known as the Gettysburg Game Park, in 2000 this area became a nonprofit wildlife sanctuary rather than a private zoo. Besides saving unwanted exotic animals, the sanctuary also strives to educate the public about these animals' special needs, so people realize what is involved before deciding to own a wild species. Animals you're likely to see include bear, alligator, deer, elk, goat, llama, parrot, macaw, cockatoo, emu, conure, ostrich, peacock, gibbon, rhesus monkey, ring-tailed lemur, tigers, lynxes, and a lion. The rescue is located 9 miles southwest of Gettysburg off Route 116 and is open only weekends. Children younger than age two are admitted free.

EISENHOWER NATIONAL HISTORIC SITE $
250 Eisenhower Farm Lane
(717) 338-9114
www.nps.gov/eise/

Eisenhower National Historic Site preserves the house and farm where the Eisenhowers lived in the 1950s and 1960s. While exploring the grounds, the farm, and the house, kids can become Junior Secret Service Agents. Kids age 7 through 12 who visit the site receive a *Secret Service Agent Training Manual,* which contains assignments that must be completed to earn a Secret Service badge and certificate. These interactive tasks are fun and informative, such as reporting to a senior agent using code names and correct procedures. For more on all the activities at the Eisenhower National Historic Site, see the Attractions chapter. The site is open daily except for New Year's Day, Thanksgiving, and Christmas, and you reach it by taking a shuttle bus from the visitor center at Gettysburg National Military Park. Although the Secret Service program is free, the Eisenhower Farm has an admission fee.

EXPLORE & MORE HANDS-ON
CHILDREN'S MUSEUM $
20 East High Street
(717) 337-9151
www.exploreandmore.com

Explore & More was created by preschool teachers, and this is a place where kids will learn as they play. Seven rooms hold activities that are specially geared toward kids age three through eight, but everyone will have fun as they participate. Popular activities include standing inside a bubble made by a giant bubble machine, learning about building and assembly lines in the construction zone, and playing in an 1860s-era house and general store in the room that's dedicated to the Battle of Gettysburg and life in the 1860s. The museum also has an educational toy store, where you can pick up something that will continue the fun of learning at home. To reach the museum, travel south 2 blocks from Lincoln Square and make a left onto High Street; the museum is on the left.

i Kids seem especially drawn to the area of the battlefield known as Devil's Den, where there are huge rocks that existed long before the Battle of Gettysburg took place. Climbing around Devil's Den is fun, but you need to warn your kids to watch for snakes sunning themselves on the rocks.

GETTYSBURG COUNTRY DAY CAMP $$$$
Granite Hill Camping Resort
3340 Fairfield Road
(717) 642-8749, (800) 642-TENT
www.granitehillcampingresort.com
This summer camp is held during June, July, and August, and it takes full advantage of all the recreational activities available at the Granite Hill Camping Resort. Swimming, golfing, fishing, cycling, and boating are among the offerings, as well as group games, arts and crafts projects, and visits from the Adams County Bookmobile (learn more about the bookmobile in the write-up on the Adams County library system in The Arts chapter).

The camp is for children age 7 to 12, and there are usually nine weekly sessions. Children are welcome to take part in one, some, or all the sessions, with discounted pricing applying when all sessions are chosen. Parents who enroll more than one child also receive a discount. An Extended Camp, which extends the regular hours of the camp to include early morning and late-afternoon time, is also available. Lunch is served for an additional fee.

GETTYSBURG NATIONAL MILITARY PARK
1195 Baltimore Pike
(717) 334-1124
www.nps.gov/gett
The park has many programs that are specifically geared toward kids. Probably the best known is the Junior Ranger Program, which is open to kids age 5 through 13. Children become junior rangers by completing an activity guide as they visit the battlefield. Details on this program and other kid-friendly programs can be obtained at the visitor center information desk, or you can check out the park's Web site. Perhaps your kids would like to join the army and see what being a soldier in the Civil War was like. If so, don't miss the program that ends with the kids reenacting Pickett's Charge. Or maybe the whole family would enjoy viewing some of the park's educational shows together.

The visitor center is open 8:00 a.m. to 6:00 (sometimes 7:00) p.m. daily. Call or stop by the visitor center or check the Web site for the full roster of programs offered at the park.

JUNIOR NATURALIST CAMP $
Strawberry Hill Nature Center
1537 Mount Hope Road, Fairfield
(717) 642-5840
www.strawberryhill.org
The Junior Naturalist Camp teaches kids about the natural world in a fun way through an assortment of hands-on activities, games, and crafts. It's one of the programs offered by Strawberry Hill Nature Center & Preserve, which has walking and hiking trails and offers nature programs within its 609 acres. (See the Recreation chapter for details on all there is to do at Strawberry Hill and directions to get you to the fun.) At the naturalist camp kids from age 4 to 10 explore ponds and streams and take hikes through forests to learn how various habitats support different animals and plants. Camps are held from the end of June to the beginning of August, rain or shine. The number of days of the camp varies, but all camps are daylight hours only; these are not overnight excursions. Different sessions are held for children age 4 and 5, age 6 and 7, and age 8 to 10, and some of the older age group's sessions

Close-up

Civil War Soldier Food

If your kids are attending one of the many programs at the military park or attending a Civil War camp, maybe you'd like to send them off on their day with some authentic Civil War food. Staples of the diets of soldiers from both sides were hardtack for the Union soldiers and johnnycake for the Confederates. Both are very easy to make. I found these recipes on the military park's Web site (www.nps.gov/gett), which has a wealth of interesting tidbits you and your kids can browse at your leisure.

HARDTACK

2 cups of flour

1/2 to 3/4 cup of water

1 tbsp of Crisco or vegetable fat

6 pinches of salt

Mix the ingredients together into a stiff batter, knead the dough several times, and spread it out flat to a thickness of 1/2 inch on a nongreased cookie sheet. Bake the dough for half an hour at 400 degrees. Remove the dough from the oven and cut it into 3-inch squares. Punch four rows of holes into each square, with four holes in each row. Turn the dough over, return it to the oven, and let it bake another half hour. Turn the oven off and leave the hardtack in the oven with the door closed until it's cool.

JOHNNYCAKE

2 cups cornmeal

2/3 cup milk

2 tbsp vegetable oil

2 tsp baking soda

1/2 tsp salt

Mix the ingredients into a stiff batter and form eight biscuits. Place the biscuits on a lightly greased cookie sheet and bake at 350 degrees for 20 to 25 minutes or until brown.

---

include a cookout on one of the days. The number of children involved is limited to 10 for the youngest age group and 12 for the older groups. Cost is based on the length of the program, with members of Strawberry Hill paying slightly less per hour than nonmembers. Two staff members work with each of the camps and cookouts, ensuring that each camper receives personal attention and the chance to be an active participant in all activities.

LAND OF LITTLE HORSES $$$

125 Glenwood Drive

(717) 334-7259

www.landoflittlehorses.com

This was always a must-see attraction for my nephews from Oregon when they visited during the summer. Kids (and adults) love the arena shows, in which miniature ponies perform routines and show off their smarts. The ponies are Falabella miniature horses, and you'll see horses that are only 26 inches tall! More than 100 creatures make their home within the animal park, including llamas, fallow deer, miniature donkeys, miniature cows, and sheep. Kids can participate in hands-on activities such as milking goats and grooming horses, or they can just take advantage of the opportunities to get close and pet some of the animals. The Hobby Horse Cafe is open for a snack or a complete meal when hunger strikes, and a visit to Gift Horse gift shop will surely uncover just the right memento of your trip. During June, July, and August, Land of Little Horses is open daily until 5:00 p.m., and arena shows are at 11:00 a.m. and 2:00 p.m. (Only the 2:00 p.m. show is offered on Sunday.) From the square head west on Chambersburg Street (U.S. Route 30) for about 3 miles, turn left onto Knoxlyn Road, and follow the signs for about another 3 miles. Admission doesn't include the available hayride or the pony ride.

Pick Your Own Fruit

Adams County leads the state in the amount of fruit that's produced and processed within a county, and there's no fresher fruit than the fruit you pick yourself. These three farms are all about 10 miles from town, and each is open daily. You should call ahead for specific picking hours and to find out what's being harvested at the time you want to visit.

Boyer Nurseries & Orchards, Inc.
  405 Boyer Nursery Road,
  Biglerville
  (717) 677-8558, (717) 677-9567
  www.boyernurseries.com

Brent's Berry Farm
  138 Brent Road, Fairfield
  (717) 642-8354, (717) 642-1555

Hollabaugh Bros. Inc. Fruit Farms &
  Market
  545 Carlisle Road, Biglerville
  (717) 677-9494, (717) 677-8412
  www.hollabaughbros.com

BOOKSTORES

GETTYSBURG CHRISTIAN BOOKSTORE
24 Chambersburg Street
(717) 334-8634
Although the children's section in Gettysburg Christian Bookstore isn't particularly large, it is very inviting. Colorful book covers draw the little ones in, and a nice selection of titles awaits the older siblings. The kids will also enjoy checking out the metal detectors that are sold at Gettysburg Electronics, which shares an address with the bookstore.

MINIATURE GOLF

Both of the amusement complexes in Gettysburg have miniature golf courses among their offerings. See the Amusement Complexes section within this chapter for full details.

GRANITE HILL ADVENTURE GOLF $
Granite Hill Camping Resort
3340 Fairfield Road
(717) 642-8749, (800) 642-TENT
www.granitehillcampingresort.com
Although Granite Hill Adventure Golf is within the Granite Hill Campground, you don't have to be staying at the campground to enjoy a round of minigolf. The 18-hole course is sculpted from a stone mountain overlooking the campground's Bass Lake, where boating and fishing are also available to the public. The golf is challenging, with realistic water hazards, sand traps, and roughs, and many players say it's the best course they've ever negotiated. Granite Hill Campground is located 6 miles west of town along Fairfield Road (Route 116), and the lake and golf course are to the left as you enter the campground. A snack bar is also nearby for when hunger hits. The entire facility is open April through October, with daily hours during June, July, and August. (See the Campgrounds and RV Parks chapter for more on Granite Hill Camping Resort.) Minigolf hours are from 10:00 a.m. to 10:00 p.m. daily.

MULLIGAN MACDUFFER ADVENTURE GOLF & ICE CREAM PARLOUR $$
1360 Baltimore Pike
(717) 337-1518
www.mulliganmacduffer.com
MacDuffer has been a favorite of locals since 1989, with its great combination of minigolf and ice-cream treats. Its two 18-hole minigolf courses sit on more than four acres, and the courses feature great landscaping, waterfalls, streams, and even caves. The "clubhouse" is an ice-cream parlor that's decorated with all kinds of golf memorabilia, and it has a video game room, too. Soft pretzels, hot dogs, and nachos are available in addition to the ice cream. You can enjoy your

food at tables inside or outside on the 35-foot deck, where you have a spectacular view of both golf courses and the pond. Located about a mile south of town off Baltimore Street, MacDuffer is open from April through October. April, May, and September it opens at 1:00 p.m.; closing time is 9:00 p.m. Sunday through Thursday and 10:00 p.m. on Friday and Saturday. June, July, and August it opens at 10:00 a.m.; closing time is 11:00 p.m. Sunday through Thursday and midnight on Friday and Saturday. MacDuffer also operates a frequent golfer club. Every day a member pays full price for a round of golf, it's recorded on his club card. Club cards never expire, and the number of visits recorded can span from season to season. Free games of golf are awarded after you reach 10 and 15 visits, and free ice cream is the prize for having played 20 rounds of golf. You can also print coupons off the Internet for savings, and if you print out, color, and bring in the picture of Mulligan MacDuffer's golf scene that's on the Web site, everyone in your group gets a dollar off the price of the golf round.

ANNUAL EVENTS AND FESTIVALS

There always seems to be something going on in Gettysburg lately. Businesses in town work hard to draw visitors throughout the year, and their efforts seem to be paying off. Summertime is still the most-visited time for Gettysburg, and there are many Civil War–related events held then, especially around the anniversary of the Battle of Gettysburg. But many popular annual events have nothing to do with Gettysburg's Civil War history; instead, they celebrate the beauty of Gettysburg's setting and the area's rich agricultural heritage. One of the largest festivals is the National Apple Harvest Festival, where everyone gathers at the fairgrounds to check out the arts and crafts and to enjoy all kinds of goodies made with apples. Most annual events here reflect the area's laid-back nature. Many involve nothing more than enjoying the day—listening to music, checking out some art or wine or apples or whatever, having something good to eat, and spending time with friends.

Most of the agriculture-related festivals are held within 15 miles or so of Gettysburg, in the middle of orchards and farms. The spring and fall bluegrass festivals, also very popular events, are held at a local campground, and some events are held at the Eisenhower National Historic Site. But also many events are held right in town. By traveling only to the streets of Gettysburg, you can find art festivals, tours of historic sites, antiques shows, and music festivals.

Annual events are listed by month in order of occurrence. Keep in mind that dates of festivals do sometimes change, so double-check the date(s) of any event that you're particularly interested in.

APRIL

HISTORY MEETS THE ARTS
Locations throughout town
(717) 334-7950
www.lordnelsons.com

The work of artists, sculptors, authors, and artisans is presented at this show, and all eras of American history are represented—the colonial era, the French and Indian War, the American Revolution, the Civil War, the American West, WWI, and WWII. You can also enjoy the art of other genres—aviation art, wildlife paintings and sculpture, Native American prints—as you stroll from gallery to gallery.

History Meets the Arts was first held in April 1998 when a group of galleries in town decided to put on a cooperative show with each gallery hosting its own artist(s) on the same weekend. The show was an instant success and has continued to be so year after year. Some of the partici-

pating artists come back annually and have quite a following, with the artists often creating special works just for the show. Although attendance figures aren't available since it's a free show where people stroll from venue to venue, the event does fill the hotel rooms in town, so be sure to call early for your accommodations.

The show draws visitors from all over as well as Gettysburg. Since each gallery decides for itself which artist(s) it will showcase, the type of art presented varies each year. One gallery may be presenting Native American art, another Civil War prints, another wildlife sculptures . . . the possibilities are endless, and this is what keeps the locals as well as visitors returning every year.

Past participating artisans include Tom Freeman, whose artwork hangs in the White House and the Vatican, John Barrett, weapons safety instructor for Mel Gibson's film *The Patriot,* and Joseph L. Galloway, coauthor of *We Were Soldiers*

Once . . . and Young, which was made into the movie *We Were Soldiers*, starring Mel Gibson. Dale Gallon, John Paul Strain, and Keith Rocco are other renowned artists who usually participate in the show.

MAY

GETTYSBURG BLUEGRASS FESTIVALS
Granite Hill Camping Resort
3340 Fairfield Road
(717) 642-8749, (800) 642–TENT
www.gettysburgbluegrass.com
Gettysburg has hosted bluegrass festivals in May and August since 1979, and both festivals attract some of the top groups in bluegrass and traditional country music. During the four-day events, musicians perform on the main stage, present informative workshops, and meet and greet their fans. The festivals showcase more than 50 hours of music. Past groups have included the Grascals, who were named Entertainer of the Year by the International Bluegrass Music Association (IBMA) in 2006 and 2007, Rhonda Vincent, who has been named Female Vocalist of the Year seven times by IBMA, and the Del McCoury Band, eight-time winners of the IBMA Entertainer of the Year Award.

The festivals are held at the Granite Hill Camping Resort on Route 116, 6 miles west of Gettysburg. Camping, including RV and tent sites, is available throughout the weekend, and a plain-cup rule for alcohol consumption is in effect. Tickets may be purchased for one, two, three, or four days, with fees at the gate in 2009 ranging from $25 to $125. You must pay with cash if you buy

i Seeing lots of greyhounds around town? It's probably Greyhounds in Gettysburg weekend. More than 1,000 greyhounds and their owners visit during this annual April event. Held to raise awareness of the greyhounds' need for adoption, there are always numerous planned activities for both dogs and owners, including a canine parade. Visit www.trianglegreyhound.org/gig to learn more.

your ticket at the gate. Call the number above for advance tickets, which are reduced in price. The festivals are held in what is basically a natural amphitheater in the middle of the campground. These are rain-or-shine events, so be sure to pack rain gear as well as lawn chairs. The campground also has a pool, which is right beside the stage, so you might want to pack a bathing suit. If you're coming for only one day, free parking is available at the campsite or in a nearby grass field.

i Each weekend from April through October reenactors camp at the American Civil War Museum on Steinwehr Avenue. The living-history units portray the life of soldiers and civilians of the Civil War time. For more information contact the American Civil War Museum at (717) 334-6245.

GETTYSBURG SPRING OUTDOOR ANTIQUE SHOW
Sidewalks around Lincoln Square
(717) 334-4510, (800) 337-5015
Antiques are a big draw in Gettysburg, and many people make this show and its sister show in September (see separate entry within this chapter) a must-attend event. More than 150 antiques dealers display their wares on tables set up on the sidewalks around Lincoln Square. With that many dealers attending, you're bound to find something that strikes your fancy. Dishes, dolls, glassware, quilts, and tinware are just a fraction of the many types of items you'll find here.

JUNE

GETTYSBURG FESTIVAL
Locations throughout town
(717) 334-0853
www.gettysburgfestival.org
This 10-day arts festival encompassing visual arts, dance, theater, culinary arts, children's events, and music debuted in 2008 and was immediately named by the prestigious American Bus Association as one of the Top 100 Events in North

America for 2009. Nearly 16,000 people attended the festival in 2008, which hosted a total of 85 arts-related events and more than 850 artists and performers. The annual Gettysburg Brass Band Festival, which has been held in town since 1997, is now part of this larger festival, where you can also enjoy cabaret, chamber, choral, jazz, and orchestral music.

All programming at the event is American-themed and celebrates America's contributions to the arts. Works by iconic American artists as well as innovative modern talents are highlighted in venues throughout town, including the Majestic Theater, the Historic Gettysburg Train Station, Lincoln Square, and Gettysburg College. The college is the site of the festival's main stage, and many festivalgoers bring picnics and lawn chairs or blankets so they can spread out on the shady lawn next to historic Pennsylvania Hall and enjoy the festivities all day long. Many events are free and open to the public; others require tickets, which are available through the Majestic Theater Box Office, 25 Carlisle Street, (717) 337-8200.

i Be sure to check yourself for ticks if you venture into fields or tall grass. Pennsylvania is one of the four top states for occurrences of Lyme disease, and Adams County is among the top five counties in Pennsylvania in number of Lyme disease cases. Become familiar with what a tick looks like and the symptoms of the disease before venturing out. If left untreated, Lyme disease can have serious consequences, including arthritis and cardiac and neurological disorders.

EISENHOWER '50s WEEKEND
Eisenhower National Historic Site
(717) 338-9114
www.nps.gov/eise/
This weekend program revisits the 1950s—the clothes, the fads, the cars, and more serious topics, such as the Cold War. This look into the past is included in the admission to the site, which includes a tour of the grounds, the farm, and the house. The site has been preserved as it was when the Eisenhowers lived here during Ike's presidency and his retirement. (For more on the Eisenhower National Historic Site, see the Attractions chapter.)

During the weekend, ranger programs revisit the issues of the 1950s and the President Eisenhower era. Topics might include the Civil Rights Movement, the protection of the president, the Nike missile program, which had missiles positioned to protect major U.S. cities from nuclear attack, and the relationship between President Eisenhower and Soviet leader Khrushchev.

CIVIL WAR INSTITUTE AT GETTYSBURG COLLEGE
300 North Washington Street
(717) 337-6590
www.gettysburg.edu/civilwar/institute
The Civil War Institute at Gettysburg College has been held every summer since 1983, and the program features lectures by prominent Civil War scholars. Attendees also take battlefield tours, view films, and partake in special activities, all to gain a better understanding of the intricacies of the Civil War. The program accepts 300 students each year, and a limited number of scholarships are available for students and for history teachers; check the Web site for scholarship qualifications and applications. Past Civil War scholars who have spoken during the weeklong study include James McPherson, Gary Gallagher, John Waugh, Stephen Wise, and Ed Bearss. Students may sign up for the tuition-only price or the price that includes tuition and room and board for the week.

GETTYSBURG HERITAGE DAYS
Locations throughout town
(866) 889-1243
www.gettysburgfoundation.org/visit/heritagedays.htm
Heritage Days honors the Civil War in general and the Battle of Gettysburg (July 1–3, 1863) in particular. Events start the weekend before the anniversary of the Battle of Gettysburg and end on July 4. There are activities daily, and the program features reenactments of some of

the battles that occurred during the Gettysburg battle of July 1, 2, and 3. (For more on the reenactments, see the Gettysburg National Military Park chapter.) In addition to the reenactments, you can attend a Civil War Collectors Show and a Civil War book show (see separate listings in this chapter) and also enjoy living-history soldier encampments, period music, a Civil War lecture series, and National Park Service anniversary walks. Additional events include the Fireman's Carnival (see listing within this chapter), author appearances, band concerts, and kids' programs. And each year brings new events. For instance, in a past year you could have watched a reenactment of Confederate troops taking control of the Shriver House on Baltimore Street during the day and participated in a haunted trolley tour to look for ghosts in the evening.

GETTYSBURG FIREMAN'S CARNIVAL
Gettysburg Recreational Park
545 Long Lane
(717) 334-7548
The Fireman's Carnival features rides, midway entertainment, and a fireworks display, and it's part of the Gettysburg Heritage Days (see earlier listing). This fun annual event has been eagerly anticipated by the people of Gettysburg since 1949, and it offers something for everyone. As with many events in this area, food is a main attraction, and the soup here is one of the key reasons people attend. The chicken corn soup (a Pennsylvania Dutch staple) is always popular, and there's also a soup of the day. If you want to feel like a true insider, bring your own container to carry out quarts and gallons of the soups. Food is served outside on the grounds as well as in the park's air-conditioned dining room. The carnival usually attracts 8,000 to 10,000 people on a weekend night.

GETTYSBURG CIVIL WAR COLLECTORS SHOW
Allstar Events Complex
2638 Emmitsburg Road
(717) 334-6363, (888) 497-9386
This show marks its 35th anniversary in 2009

and is considered one of the best of its kind in the United States, with hundreds of displays relating to American military history goods from 1865 and earlier. Weapons, uniforms, documents, books, photographs, accoutrements—they're all on display for both the serious collector and the interested browser. The show is held on the first weekend of the Gettysburg Heritage Days at the Allstar Complex, which is right beside the Eisenhower Inn & Conference Center, just 4.5 miles south of town. (See the Hotels, Motels, and Resorts chapter for more on this lodging.) For more information on future shows, contact Bill or Brendan Synnamon of the Union Drummer Boy store at (717) 334-2350. The show has an admission price of $5, with children age 12 and younger admitted free.

JULY

CIVIL WAR BOOK AND EPHEMERA SHOW
Best Western Historic Gettysburg Hotel
1 Lincoln Square
(717) 334-6274, (800) 337-5015
Let me save you a trip to the dictionary— *ephemera* is defined in *Merriam-Webster* as paper items that were originally meant to be discarded after use but have since become collectibles. This three-day event is held annually from July 1 through July 3 as part of Gettysburg Heritage Days (see entry above). The show, which was introduced in 1987, is held in the ballroom of the Best Western Gettysburg Hotel. This is the place to find just the Civil War book you've been hunting for, since the show features new, rare, used, out-of-print, and reprinted books on the subject. More than 40 Civil War book dealers also offer photographs, diaries, letters, documents, and autographs for your perusal. For information on upcoming shows, contact Bill or Brendan Synnamon of the Union Drummer Boy store at (717) 334-2350.

GETTYSBURG BIKE WEEK
P.O. Box 3333, Gettysburg, PA 17325
(800) 374-7540
www.gettysburgbikeweek.com

Area Events Worth the Drive

MAY

Apple Blossom Festival
South Mountain Fairgrounds
Arendtsville
(10 miles northwest of Gettysburg)
(717) 677-7444

The South Mountain Fairgrounds sit in the midst of Adams County's 20,000 acres of fruit orchards. The Apple Blossom Festival began in 1955, and today you'll find hundreds of crafters, live musical entertainment, all the food you'd want to eat, antique cars, and free guided orchard bus tours to see the blossoms on the trees. Admission is $5 for adults, with children age 12 and younger admitted for free.

JUNE

New Oxford Antique Market & Craft Show
Downtown New Oxford
(8 miles east of Gettysburg)
(717) 624-2800

New Oxford is known as the antiques capital of central Pennsylvania, and this show is one of the largest and oldest one-day antiques shows on the East Coast. All permanent antiques shops in town are open, and the area around the square hosts antiques dealers, craftspeople, and artists. Crowds usually number around 20,000.

AUGUST

Littlestown Good Ole Days Festival
Littlestown Town Park, Littlestown
(10 miles southeast of Gettysburg)
(717) 334-6274, (800) 337-5015

Started in 1971, this old-fashioned festival offers an antiques fair and flea market, craft displays, and hometown cooking, a 5K race, an antique car show, live musical entertainment, and a parade.

South Mountain Fair
South Mountain Fairgrounds
Arendtsville
(10 miles northwest of Gettysburg)
(717) 677-9663

This is a traditional country fair with agricultural displays, musical entertainment, carnival rides, food, and more. Admission is $4 for adults, and children age 12 and younger are admitted for free.

SEPTEMBER

East Berlin Colonial Day
King Street, East Berlin
(19 miles northeast of Gettysburg)
(717) 259-0822

This craft festival that began in 1976 has been estimated to attract 20,000 people. It features crafts, entertainment, demonstrations, and great food, especially the handmade funnel cake. King Street is closed to traffic as more than 100 craftspeople set up their booths selling all

You'll know if you're here during Gettysburg Bike Week—there's no missing the sight or the sounds of the many motorcycles that are ridden around town during this event, which was first held in 2001. Attendance often tops more than 15,000 bikers, who participate in games and contests. There are also bands playing music and vendors selling bike-related items. Bikers also take guided motorcycle tours of the battlefield and observation rides. The activities are held at the Allstar Events Complex (see the Attractions chapter) and at Gateway Gettysburg (see the Close-up in the Area Overview chapter). Many visitors avoid town during this event (and many residents wish they could), which is usually held the second Thursday through the second Sunday in July.

kinds of goods while dressed in traditional colonial wear. There are also demonstrations by colonial artisans.

Fairfield Pippinfest
Downtown Fairfield
(8 miles west of Gettysburg)
(717) 642-5640
This festival has grown since 1980 to a townwide event featuring apple products, music, crafts, and vintage cars in a street-fair setting.

Chili Cookoff
Forney Avenue ball field
(behind KClinger's Tavern)
304 Poplar Street, Hanover
(14 miles southeast of Gettysburg)
(717) 633-9197
Admission to this fun event is $5, and the proceeds go to different charities each year. You can partake in as much chili as you can eat, and additional food and refreshments are available, including beer for those of age. A variety of live musical entertainment is offered throughout the day. Anyone may compete in the chili cookoff; call Jeff Sherrod at the number above for details.

OCTOBER
National Apple Harvest Festival
South Mountain Fairgrounds
Arendtsville
(10 miles northwest of Gettysburg)
(717) 677-9413
www.appleharvest.com

Begun in 1964, this is one of the largest festivals in the area, attracting 18,000 to 25,000 visitors each day. Recent festivals have had more than 400 food vendors and crafts dealers and 35 to 40 groups of entertainers on six different stages. There's also plenty of delightful food, antique autos, steam engines, orchard tours, and pony rides.

Art at the Winery Fest
Adams County Winery
251 Peachtree Road, Orrtanna
(9 miles west of Gettysburg)
(717) 334-4631
www.adamscountywinery.com
Since 2000 Adams County Winery has hosted this free event that features local and regional artists, a glass-blowing and a pottery-making demonstration, live music, food, and—of course—wine.

NOVEMBER
Farm-City Day Festival
Location varies
(717) 337-5859
This free festival is held to show what it's like to live on a farm. You'll find good old-fashioned family fun, with hayrides, horsemanship shows, and lots of food, much of it free.

SPIRIT OF GETTYSBURG 5K RUN
(717) 334-9171
www.ywcagettysburg.org
Spirit of Gettysburg is one of the few races in America where participants actually traverse Civil War battlefields. Begun in 1990 and sponsored by the YWCA of Gettysburg and Adams County, this race begins along Seminary Ridge, where

the Battle of Gettysburg began on July 1, 1863, and 2 of its 5 miles cover the area where the first day's battle took place. This isn't a huge event (participants usually total fewer than 1,000), but it does draw runners from across Pennsylvania and other East Coast states. The 5K is the main race, but other competitions are also held for every age and level of ability. There's a wheelchair race, a 1-mile fun run/fitness walk, a 1-mile kids' sprint for ages 7 through 12, a ¼-mile kids' sprint, and a kids' minitrot. Entry fees range from $10 to $25 on the day of the race, with reduced rates available with advance registration. If you preregister, you can also arrange for babysitting services for children age 10 and younger.

ADAMS COUNTY IRISH FESTIVAL
Gettysburg Moose Park
100 Moose Road
(717) 337-3500
www.adamscountyirishfestival.com

This festival celebrates all things Irish by showcasing Irish bands and music, Irish dance, Irish food, Irish beer, and Irish crafts. Entertainment also includes Civil War reenactment groups and sword-fighting demonstrations, and Irish wolfhounds eager to be petted are usually on hand. Begun in 1999, it's held at Gettysburg Moose Park, which is off U.S. Route 30 about 1.5 miles east of its intersection with U.S. Route 15. Proceeds from the festival benefit Children's Friendship Project for Northern Ireland (www.cfpni.org), a program that promotes interaction between Catholic and Protestant teenagers of Northern Ireland. The committee also hopes to eventually open an Adams County Irish History Museum and Library to research family names and collect artifacts. Festivalgoers are encouraged to bring a blanket or chair and ample amounts of sunscreen so they can sit back and relax for the day. Cost is $10, and children younger than age 12 are admitted for free. There's no charge for parking. The festival is the oldest and largest Irish festival in south central Pennsylvania, and more than 3,000 people attended the event in 2007.

AUGUST

CIVIL WAR MUSIC MUSTER
Gettysburg National Military Park
(717) 334-1124, ext. 3251

The Gettysburg Music Muster features Civil War bands, fife and drum musicians, and parlor music, and you can listen to all this entertainment for free. Concerts begin at 10:00 a.m. at the Gettysburg National Military Park Visitor Center. Performances are held throughout the day at the military park and at the Dobbin House, on Steinwehr Avenue. The final performance, which runs from 5:30 p.m. to sundown, is held at the Pennsylvania Memorial. Attendees should bring lawn chairs and blankets to spread on the ground. The year 2009 will mark the music muster's 15th anniversary and the Victorian Dance Ensemble's 9th year performing at the muster. The 50-plus-member ensemble, which was formed in 1995, demonstrates dances of the mid-19th century. Be warned—audience participation is a highlight of every presentation.

SEPTEMBER

GETTYSBURG WINE AND MUSIC FESTIVAL
Gateway Gettysburg
95 Presidential Circle
(717) 334-8151
www.gettysburgwine.com

The first annual wine and music festival was held in 2005, and it just keeps getting bigger and better every year. Besides sampling wines from Pennsylvania and across the country, participants can enjoy gourmet food, arts and crafts, cooking demonstrations, and live entertainment. The admission price ($18 for advance ticket or $22 at the door) includes all performances, cooking demonstrations, a souvenir wineglass, and wine tastings. Admission for designated drivers is $12, and children age 12 and younger pay no admittance fee.

EISENHOWER WORLD WAR II WEEKEND
Eisenhower National Historic Site
(717) 338-9114
www.nps.gov/eise

Here you'll experience what Allied and German camps were like in World War II, complete with original WWII vehicles and more than 100 participants portraying military personnel from the European theater of the war. During this living-history weekend, programs are presented on medical services, weapons and equipment, communications, transportation, and the every-day life of the soldier. World War II veterans from both sides of the conflict share their battle stories as the featured speakers. Visitors can complete their experience by having lunch in a re-created mess tent and attending the "USO" dance held Saturday night at the U.S. Army Reserve Center, which features live 1940s Big Band music.

The weekend is held at the Eisenhower National Historic Site, which preserves the grounds, the farm, and the house where the Eisenhowers lived after Ike retired from the military, during his presidency, and after his retirement. Admission to the site is by shuttle buses that depart regularly from the GNMP visitor center. On-site parking for cars only may also be available on this weekend only, weather permitting, in a nearby farm field. For more on the activities available at the Eisenhower National Historic Site and for admission information, see the Attractions chapter.

ADAMS COUNTY HERITAGE FESTIVAL
Gettysburg Recreational Park
545 Long Lane
(717) 334-0752
Begun in 1991, this one-day event's mission is to share and appreciate the cultures of Adams County through music, food, and art. In 2008 you could be entertained by Mexican dancers, bagpipers, folk music, an Irish band, a trio of three women playing 12 instruments, and more. All this music and dance is the perfect backdrop for enjoying the ethnic foods available and for attending the craft demonstrations. Admission is free.

GETTYSBURG FALL OUTDOOR ANTIQUE SHOW
Sidewalks around Lincoln Square
(717) 334-6274, (800) 337-5015
Antiques and Gettysburg go hand in hand, and this show lets you enjoy America of old and crisp

fall weather at the same time. More than 150 antiques dealers set up tables around Lincoln Square to display their wares, which include china, games, tinware, and myriad other items. There's also a spring antiques show held in May (see separate entry within this chapter), so you can admire antiques and enjoy the spring weather.

i Gettysburg hosts Memorial Day, Halloween, Remembrance Day (anniversary of Lincoln's Gettysburg Address), and Christmas parades. The Memorial Day and Remembrance Day parades are especially meaningful, with wreaths laid at the National Cemetery at their conclusions, while the Halloween and Christmas parades are just fun events.

OCTOBER

AUTUMN GETTYSBURG CIVIL WAR SHOW
Location varies
(717) 642-6600 (Thomas Publications, which sponsors the show)
This show features more than 300 tables containing accoutrements, guns, swords, uniforms, documents, books, photographs, personal effects, and relics of American military history from 1865 and earlier. Serious collectors attend to buy, sell, and trade their treasures, while others come to admire the military memorabilia that's on display. Admission was $6 in 2008.

DECEMBER

NEW YEAR'S EVE
Lincoln Square
(717) 334-5006
The end of one year and the beginning of the next is celebrated in style with entertainment, food, and fireworks.

STATE PARKS AND PUBLIC LANDS

Five state parks, Michaux State Forest, and the Appalachian Trail are within 30 miles of Gettysburg, offering ample opportunities to enjoy the outdoors. You'll find camping, boating, fishing, ice-skating, ice fishing, horseback riding, swimming, hiking, and more.

If a park offers camping, a site can be reserved from 11 months in advance up to noon of the day of your arrival. Cabins and picnic pavilions, if offered, may be reserved from 11 months up to 2 days in advance of your arrival. Call (888) PA-PARKS between 7:00 a.m. and 5:00 p.m. Monday through Saturday to reserve your spot.

Lands that allow fishing, hunting, and/or boating have strict guidelines about these activities. For complete information on fishing and boating rules and regulations in Pennsylvania, visit the Pennsylvania Fish and Boat Commission Web site at www.fish.state.pa.us or call (717) 705-7800. Hunting rules and regulations in Pennsylvania can be found at the Pennsylvania Game Commission Web site at www.pgc.state.pa.us or by calling (717) 787-2084.

Appalachian Trail

The Appalachian Trail is a continuous, marked footpath that extends along the crest of the Appalachian Mountain range for more than 2,100 miles from Maine to Georgia, crossing 14 states along the way. It runs diagonally across eastern Pennsylvania for almost 229 miles. Forty-nine of those miles are on state forestlands, and 39 of those miles are within Michaux State Forest. The Appalachian Trail traverses Caledonia State Park, and the halfway point on the trail is located within Pine Grove Furnace State Park. Both state parks are within the boundaries of the Michaux State Forest, which also is the site of Mont Alto State Park. The Appalachian Trail is marked by two different signs. One is a white rectangular paint blaze 2 inches wide by 6 inches high, which is usually found on trees. The other is a diamond-shaped metal marker with the trail monogram on it. About 200 people a year hike the entire length of the trail in one trip, an endeavor that usually takes four to six months to complete.

CALEDONIA STATE PARK

40 Rocky Mountain Road, Fayetteville
(717) 352-2161
www.dcnr.state.pa.us

Located 15 miles west of Gettysburg, Caledonia is the closest state park to Gettysburg. It sits in Adams and Franklin Counties, 1,125 acres within Michaux State Forest in the northernmost section of the Blue Ridge Mountains known locally as South Mountain. South Mountain is mostly composed of a hard rock called quartzite, and the valleys on either side of the mountain are underlain with limestone and shale. This makes the soil ideal for fruit production, which is evidenced by the number of fruit farms in the area.

Park visitors can enjoy a range of activities, including camping, fishing, hiking, swimming, hunting, and picnicking. The park is also home to Caledonia Golf Club, an 18-hole, par 68 public course, and the Totem Pole Playhouse, a summer-stock theater that's operated here since the 1950s. (To learn more, see the Golf and The Arts chapters.)

The park is named for Thaddeus Stevens's charcoal iron furnace, which was named Caledonia (see the Close-up in this chapter for information on the charcoal industry in Pennsylvania). Thaddeus Stevens, originally from Caledonia County in Vermont, was a famous statesman and abolitionist who practiced law at Gettysburg. The furnace began operating in 1837, and the watercourse along Route 233 was once the millrace that operated the furnace waterwheel. In June 1863 Confederate cavalry under the command of General Early destroyed the furnace, and the pastures you see now were used as field hospitals for the wounded of the Battle of Gettysburg. After Stevens's death the iron furnace changed hands many times, and in 1902 the land was sold to the Commonwealth of Pennsylvania. In 1927 the Pennsylvania Alpine Club rebuilt the stack of the old furnace as a reduced-scale monument, and this stack and a blacksmith shop that serves as a historical center are the only visible reminders of the early ironworks.

Caledonia has 10 miles of hiking trails, and the Appalachian Trail crosses the central portion of the park. A brochure on the hiking trails is available at the park office. Anglers can enjoy fishing at the East Branch Conococheague and Rocky Mountain Creeks and at Carbaugh Run, which flow through the park and the surrounding Michaux State Forest. Brown trout, rainbow trout, native brook trout, and some warm-water game fish are found here. About 740 acres of the park are open to hunting, trapping, and the training of hunting dogs during established seasons. Deer, rabbit, squirrel, and turkey are common game hunted, but the hunting of woodchucks, also known as groundhogs, is prohibited. The park has a swimming pool that can be enjoyed from Memorial Day weekend to Labor Day for an additional fee, and more than 450 picnic tables are located throughout the park. During the summer, campfire programs, guided hikes, and environmental education programs are offered by a naturalist. An arts and crafts fair is held in the park annually on the second Saturday of July. Admission is free, and about 200 artisans display their handcrafted items, including wood carvings, folk art, pottery, stained glass, and more. The first fair was held in 1981, and today around 10,000 people usually attend this fun event.

If you decide to spend the night, there are two campgrounds within the park, with a total of 170 tent and trailer sites available from the day before trout season in March until after the end of deer season in December. Amenities include hot showers, flush toilets, and a sanitary dump station, and electricity is available at some sites. Two modern cabins are also available for rent year-round. One is a 1½-story frame house, and the other is a two-story frame house, and both houses come with a modern kitchen, bathroom, dining room, living room, central heat, and three bedrooms that can sleep 10 people.

To get to the park from Gettysburg, take U.S. Route 30 west to the intersection with Route 233.

Just outside the park is **Bobby A's Grill and Bar** (6880 Chambersburg Road, Fayetteville; 717-352-2252). About 12 miles west of Gettysburg on US 30, this is a popular restaurant. Open seven days a week for lunch and dinner, Bobby A's offers prime rib, steaks, seafood, pasta, broasted chicken, and a wide variety of appetizers. Owner Bob Arahovas knows the restaurant business—his family has owned the Lincoln Diner in Gettysburg since the 1980s. (See the Restaurants chapter for more on the Lincoln Diner.)

i Caledonia State Park hosts a Sunday church service during the summer in its Cathedral of the Pines, an open area surrounded by pine trees just inside the entrance to the park. The nondenominational service is held at 10:30 a.m., and all are welcome to attend.

CODORUS STATE PARK
1066 Blooming Grove Road, Hanover
(717) 637-2816
www.dcnr.state.pa.us
The 3,452 acres of Codorus State Park sit 20 miles southeast of Gettysburg in York County, about 3 miles southeast of Hanover. The park's main claim to fame is Lake Marburg, which totals 1,275 acres and has 26 miles of shoreline. But there's more than just boating and fishing on the lake to enjoy: You can also mountain bike, hike, camp,

hunt, picnic, swim, ride horses, and play disc golf. In winter you can snowmobile, cross-country ski, sled, and ice-skate.

Parkland here was bought by the commonwealth between 1965 and 1966 under Project 70, a land-acquisition program that resulted in the purchase of many state parks. The design and construction of the park facilities were funded by Project 500, which raised money to improve the lands purchased by Project 70. The main boat-launching area, off Sinsheim Road, was the first project in Pennsylvania completed for public use under the Project 500 Program. The impoundment of Codorus Creek is the result of a cooperative project between the commonwealth and the P. H. Glatfelter Paper Company, a private company located in Spring Grove, Pennsylvania. The project is the first of its kind in the state, and it's designed not only to provide a public recreation area but also to satisfy the water supply needs of the company as well as the town of Spring Grove.

Lake Marburg has seven boat-launch ramps around the lake, and all but the campground launch are open to the public; the campground launch is for the use of registered campers only. Motorboats up to 20 horsepower are allowed, and they must display a current boat registration. Nonpowered boats must have either a launching or mooring permit from Pennsylvania State Parks (available at most park offices) or a boat registration or launching permit from the Pennsylvania Fish and Boat Commission. Mooring spaces for canoes, sailboats, and boats up to 24 feet long are available for rent if you want to bring your own boat, or you can rent pontoon boats, rowboats, canoes, paddleboats, and motorboats at the marina.

The lake is also a warm-water fishery, and popular species are yellow perch, bluegill, northern pike, crappie, largemouth bass, catfish, and muskellunge. Bow fishing is permitted in the lake's shallow cove areas. Codorus Creek is in the Selective Harvest Program, and East Branch Codorus Creek is an approved trout stream.

For visitors who prefer to recreate on ground rather than water, a wide selection of activities is available. Two hiking trails are within the park.

Mary Ann Furnace Trail is three interconnected loops totaling 4.5 miles, winding through hardwood forests, pine plantations, and wetlands. The 1.5-mile LaHo Trail follows the lakeshore through hardwoods and wetlands. A 6.5-mile network of bridle trails winds through the west side of the park, and the northern shore is the site of the 195-acre Cross-country Skiing and Snowmobile Area. This northern area also contains 6.5 miles of trails for mountain biking. Hunting, trapping, and the training of hunting dogs take place on about 2,800 acres during established seasons. Hunting is limited to the use of shotguns, muzzleloaders, and bows during the appropriate seasons. Deer, pheasant, rabbit, squirrel, and waterfowl are available, but the hunting of woodchucks, also known as groundhogs, is prohibited. Waterfowl hunting is especially popular, and the park's 25 duck blinds are awarded by lottery each year. The park has a swimming pool that can be enjoyed from Memorial Day weekend to Labor Day for an additional fee, and picnic tables are scattered throughout the park. There's also a 54-hole disc-golf course along Marina Road that is open year-round. Scorecards are at the first hole, which is by the first parking lot on the right side of Marina Road. The park also provides programs on environmental education from May to October, and birders will enjoy the park's bird-viewing station.

Winter activities also abound in this park. Registered snowmobiles are allowed on 6.5 miles of the designated Cross-country Skiing and Snowmobile Area after the end of deer season in late December. Cross-country skiing is also allowed on these trails; skiers should wear fluorescent orange during hunting season. Sledding takes place on a 2.5-acre slope near the Cross-country Skiing and Snowmobile Area, at the west end of Chapel Cove. There's another sledding area with gentle slopes in the marina area. When Lake Marburg freezes over sufficiently, you can ice-skate on a 25-acre section of the lake in Chapel Cove, and ice fishing and iceboating are permitted on the rest of the lake. (A state park launch permit is required for iceboats.)

Codorus State Park has a 190-site campground that's suitable for tents or RVs up to 50 feet long. Sites are available from the second Friday in April to the third Sunday in October. Hot showers, flush toilets, and a sanitary dump station are available, and many sites have electric hookups. From Memorial Day to Labor Day, you cannot stay longer than 14 consecutive nights. Pets are allowed in some designated campsites.

To reach the park from Gettysburg, take Route 116 east through Hanover, turn right onto Route 216 East, and travel 3 miles to the park.

i It's not uncommon to see copperheads and rattlesnakes hunting rodents around the mansion in the Mansion Day Use Area of Kings Gap. These snakes are venomous and should be left alone, although they usually will retreat if approached in their natural habitat.

KINGS GAP ENVIRONMENTAL EDUCATION AND TRAINING CENTER

500 Kings Gap Road, Carlisle
(717) 486-5031
www.dcnr.state.pa.us

Sitting about 30 miles north of Gettysburg in Cumberland County, Kings Gap is not a traditional state park. It's operated by the Pennsylvania Department of Conservation and National Resources of the Bureau of State Parks, and its 1,454 acres of forest function as an education and training center on the environment. Sixteen miles of hiking trails interconnect three main day-use areas and wind through different habitats the hiker can explore. The grounds are open to the public year-round from 8:00 a.m. to sunset. Kings Gap is on South Mountain, and its vistas offer a panoramic view of the Cumberland Valley. A 32-room mansion on the mountaintop at the Mansion Day Use Area offers the best views, as well as functioning as the center's office and a training center for state government agencies. The center also offers interpretive environmental programs to teachers, students, and the general public. A complete schedule of the programs offered is available from the center office or at the three day-use areas. The Bureau of State Parks'

Youth Environmental Learning Series for ages 4 to 17 is held here during the summer; the four programs of the series allow kids to explore and learn about the environment with other kids the same age.

Hunting, orienteering, hiking, and learning about the environment are the principal activities at Kings Gap. Several hundred acres are open to hunting, trapping, and the training of dogs during established seasons, and the entire property is open to hunting during antlerless deer season. Hunters will find deer, turkey, and squirrel to hunt, but the hunting of woodchucks, also known as groundhogs, is prohibited. The sport of orienteering involves negotiating a designated course through the use of only a map and compass. A permanent orienteering course is located here, and copies of the course map are available at the center office. Thirteen hiking trails traverse 16 miles, and each has trailheads at the three day-use areas. (See the box on hiking within this chapter for a description of the trails.)

Each of the day-use areas of the center represents a different habitat. The Pine Plantation Day Use Area is located near the entrance of Kings Gap, and here you experience a coniferous forest of white pine, Douglas fir, and larch trees. Several vernal ponds are found here.

Vernal ponds are temporary ponds that retain water as a result of snowmelt, spring rains, and/or elevated groundwater tables. Many amphibians, including spotted salamanders, spring peepers, and wood frogs, use the ponds as breeding areas. A reconstructed log house from the 1850s sits in a small clearing within the area, and this is where a lot of the center's educational programming takes place.

The Pond Day Use Area is about 2 miles from Kings Gap's entrance, and it features a scenic pond and the mountain stream Kings Gap Hollow Run. The pond gives you a chance to observe aquatic animals adapted to slower water, such as frogs, salamanders, turtles, and water snakes. Kings Gap Hollow Run periodically dries up and reveals a stony bottom, which is home to many aquatic species when the water flow is at its peak. A deciduous forest surrounds the stream, resulting in wetland areas where you can observe sphagnum moss, cinnamon ferns, skunk cabbage, and tulip trees.

On the mountaintop 4 miles from Kings Gap's entrance is the Mansion Day Use Area. Here you can enjoy a stunning view of the Cumberland Valley from the mansion's patio. This area contains an oak forest habitat, which supports a variety of reptiles, including the box turtle, the northern copperhead, the timber rattlesnake, and the five-lined skink, one of the few lizards found in Pennsylvania. There's also a garden that is divided into three educational areas—an herb garden, a wildlife-habitat garden, and a compost-demonstration garden.

To reach the park from Gettysburg, drive north on Carlisle Street (Route 34) through Biglerville and make a left onto West Pine Street. Travel on West Pine Street for almost 1.5 miles, and then turn right onto Mountainview Road. At about half a mile, bear left onto Pine Road and follow it for almost 4 miles, and then turn left onto Kings Gap Road. The park is about 4 miles down the road. By the way you won't find any trash containers at Kings Gap. A carry-in, carry-out policy directs visitors to take their trash home.

MICHAUX STATE FOREST

10099 Lincoln Way East, Fayetteville
(717) 352-2211
www.dcnr.state.pa.us

Michaux State Forest spans three counties, Adams, Cumberland, and Franklin, and contains three state parks within its boundaries, Caledonia, Mont Alto, and Pine Grove Furnace. It stretches from just southwest of Harrisburg, the state capital, to the Maryland border. This forest of 85,000-plus acres is in the South Mountain range, which is 6 to 7 miles wide and bordered on both sides by agricultural valleys. Within the forest are 130 miles of state forest roads and 39 miles of the Appalachian Trail. Hunting, fishing, camping, hiking, horseback riding, rock climbing, bicycling, and snowmobiling are among the many outdoor pursuits available on the grounds. Picnics and day-use activities go on at the Old Forge State Forest Picnic Area.

Hiking at Kings Gap Environmental Education and Training Center

Kings Gap has 13 trails that offer 16 miles of hiking, with trailheads located at the center's three day-use areas. Here's a brief rundown of the trails, their lengths, and the difficulty rating state park authorities have assigned to them.

Boundary Trail: 1.5 miles, easy to moderate
Forest Heritage Trail: 1.6 miles, easy to moderate
Kings Gap Hollow Trail: 1.7 miles, easy
Locust Point Trail: 1 mile, easy to moderate
Maple Hollow Trail: 1.3 miles, easy to moderate
Pine Plantation Trail: 0.6 mile, easy
Ridge Overlook: 0.8 mile, moderate to difficult
Rock Scree Trail: 1.9 miles, easy to moderate
Scenic Vista Trail: 2.5 miles, easy to moderate
Watershed Trail: 1.8 miles, easy to moderate
Whispering Pines Trail: 0.3 mile, paved
White Oaks Trail: 0.3 mile, paved
Woodland Ecology Trail: 0.6 mile, easy

The state bought its first parcel of land here in 1901, and most of what is today Michaux State Forest was purchased by the early 1930s. The area was originally two separate forests, the Michaux and the Mont Alto, but the forests were consolidated in 1942. The first forest tree nursery in any Pennsylvania state forest was created in

Close-up

Visit Where Cannonballs Were Made for the Revolutionary War

Much of the South Mountain land in the area is dotted with iron furnaces, which were used in Pennsylvania from the 1700s through the late 1800s. Before the discovery of coal, charcoal was used to fuel the nearby iron furnaces that processed iron ore into "pig iron," which was then forged into iron tools, stoves, kettles, and other implements. The largest iron furnaces in the area were located at Caledonia, Mont Alto, and Pine Grove Furnace, and cannonballs made at these furnaces were used during the Revolutionary War.

Huge amounts of charcoal were needed to fire the furnaces; in 1786 an acre of forest would be consumed by an average furnace in one day of operation. The forests of South Mountain were clear-cut on a 20- to 25-year cycle to feed the demand, and today a relatively young forest grows on the mountain. The making of charcoal was an involved process. Wood was cut and stored during the winter, and the collier would select a site for the hearth once milder weather arrived. Here the wood would be stacked into a conical shape by standing it on end around a central chimney. Firing and tending the hearth was done by the collier and one or two helpers, and the men usually managed eight or nine hearths at a time. Sleeping quarters were huts near the group of hearths, and fires burned 24 hours a day for 10 to 14 days, the time needed to produce the charred wood, or charcoal. After the wood was ready, the collier would put the fire out, rake the charcoal into piles, load the charcoal onto wagons, and deliver the charcoal to the furnaces.

The demand for charcoal died once hotter-burning coal was discovered, and the charcoal industry was gone by the end of the 19th century. But remnants of the industry still dot the area. Caledonia State Park is named for the furnace that operated there, and the stack of the old furnace was rebuilt as a reduced-scale monument in 1927. Remains of hearth sites can be seen throughout Kings Gap—look for flat, dry spots about 30 to 50 feet in diameter that are fairly free of vegetation. The furnace in Pine Grove Furnace State Park, which is listed on the National Register of Historic Places, is still visible, as are remnants of charcoal hearths. Pieces of charcoal are still sometimes found by hikers.

1902 at Mont Alto, and a year later the Pennsylvania State Forest Academy was opened near the nursery. When it opened, the academy was one of only two schools in the country that was dedicated to training professional foresters. Mont Alto also erected the first wooden fire tower in the state parks in 1905, and in 1914 it erected the state park system's first steel structure.

Today state-forest timber is harvested to create many wood products, but potable water is Michaux's most valuable resource. The municipal water supplies of many local communities depend on the pure water found in the forest.

MONT ALTO STATE PARK

c/o Caledonia State Park

(717) 352-2161

www.dcnr.state.pa.us

With 23 acres Mont Alto is the smallest of the state parks in the area. Located within the Michaux Forest in Franklin County, it sits about 20 miles west of Gettysburg. The Mont Alto Iron Furnace, which was built in 1807, used to operate at a site adjacent to the park. At its peak it produced two to three tons of iron per day. In 1875 the area was turned into a summer resort by private enterprise. The commonwealth bought the area in 1902, and Mont Alto became Pennsylvania's first "state forest park."

Excellent trout fishing can be found at the West Branch of Antietam Creek, which flows through the park. Hiking, picnicking, and riding snowmobiles can also be enjoyed, but no hunting is allowed within the park. Trash containers are not available at the park. Visitors are asked to carry only what they need into the park and to take their trash home with them. The Mont Alto Campus of Pennsylvania State University (see the Education and Child Care chapter) is adjacent to the west boundary of the park.

To reach the park from Gettysburg, take US 30 west to the intersection with Route 233, where you'll arrive at Caledonia State Park. Then travel 7 miles south on Route 233 to the entrance for Mont Alto State Park.

PINE GROVE FURNACE STATE PARK
1100 Pine Grove Road, Gardners
(717) 486-7174
www.dcnr.state.pa.us

About 25 miles north of Gettysburg in Cumberland County, Pine Grove Furnace State Park occupies 696 acres within the Michaux State Forest. The park is known for its historic sites and buildings, which transport the visitor to the days when cast-iron products were made here. (See this chapter's Close-up for more on how iron furnaces in the area operated.) The first iron furnace was built at Pine Grove in 1764. Today's park office was once an inn, and the A.Y.H. Hostel was originally a mansion built by one of the ironmasters. The final blast from a furnace here occurred in 1895, 131 years after it all began. In 1913 the company that owned the ironworks sold 17,000 acres to the commonwealth. Much of the land became Michaux State Forest, but a portion became Pine Grove Furnace State Park.

The park hosts a range of activities on its lands. There are two lakes within the park, 25-acre Laurel Lake and 1.7-acre Fuller Lake, and they offer many recreational opportunities. (Fuller Lake was created by filling the major ore quarry on the site with groundwater when mining ceased.) Swimming is allowed at both lakes. Laurel Lake also has boating, with a boat launch, 85 mooring spaces, and a boat rental. Fishing for pickerel, perch, and stocked trout goes on at both lakes, and anglers try to hook brown, brook, and rainbow trout along Mountain Creek, which flows through the park. Ice fishing is allowed at Laurel Lake, and a small area by the lake's boat launch is reserved for ice-skating.

Biking is allowed on all park roads, and 4 miles of trails and access to the Appalachian Trail are available to hikers. The Buck Ridge Trail travels through Michaux State Forest and connects Kings Gap Environmental Education and Training Center with the park. The trail is marked with orange paint blazes, and a trailhead is located across from the park office. Picnic sites are available throughout the park. Hunting, trapping, and the training of dogs are allowed on 75-plus acres during established seasons. Hunters usually find deer, turkey, rabbit, pheasant, and squirrel to hunt, but the hunting of woodchucks, also known as groundhogs, is prohibited. During the winter, cross-country skiing and snowmobiling are allowed in the park and surrounding forestlands. Spring and fall in the park are excellent times for bird-watching, since the park is a rest stop for many migrating forest birds. The park is home to at least six species of woodpeckers, and waterfowl abound at Laurel Lake.

Overnight accommodations are available, with the option of staying at a primitive tent site or staying in a modern cabin. Seventy tent and trailer sites are available year-round, but accessibility cannot be guaranteed during severe winter weather. Drinking water, nonflush toilets, and a sanitary dump station are available at the campground, and some sites have electricity. Free primitive camping is available if you agree to act as a campground host, which requires you to work with park personnel for 40 hours a week for a two-week minimum stay. Two two-story cabins are available, both with a modern kitchen, bathroom, dining room, living room, and central heat. One cabin can sleep six persons, and the other can sleep eight.

To reach the park, drive north from Gettysburg on Carlisle Street (Route 34) through Biglerville. After leaving Biglerville, bear left onto Main Street. The name of the road will change to Bendersville-Wenksville Road. Turn right onto Pine Grove Furnace Road in about 2.5 miles. This road will change its name to Bendersville Road and end at the junction of Route 233 (Pine Grove Road). Turn right onto Route 233, and the park entrance will be a short distance up the road.

i A through-hiker (someone hiking the Appalachian Trail in one trip) will reach the trail's halfway point at Pine Grove Furnace State Park. Many hikers celebrate the milestone with the "half-gallon challenge" at the Pine Grove General Store—eating half a gallon of ice cream.

GOLF

Golf courses abound within a short drive of Gettysburg, and many of them emphasize the rural beauty of the area. If you prefer to walk the course rather than drive a cart, all area golf clubs allow you to walk during some part of the day. All costs quoted are for the weekend rate, which is the highest rate you can expect to pay. Besides the golf courses the Gettysburg Golf Driving Range (717-334-4308) is located east of town at Smith Road along U.S. Route 30 (York Road).

THE BRIDGES GOLF CLUB
6729 York Road, Abbottstown
(717) 624-9551
www.bridgesgc.com

Getting its name from the 10 bridges that are along many of the paved cart paths that meander over this 6,713-yard, par 72, 18-hole course, the Bridges is located less than 15 miles east of Gettysburg. The golf club is a member of the Audubon Cooperative Sanctuary, and the course is designed to allow woodlands and wetlands to remain undisturbed, so you have an excellent chance of seeing plenty of wildlife as you golf here. The clubhouse, which is actually a refurbished furniture factory from the 1800s, has 12 rooms for overnight stays, and golf packages are available. Meals are served at the charming Bridges Grill and Deck, which overlooks the course. A pro shop is located within the clubhouse, and a driving range, a putting green, lessons, and club rentals are available.

The course has received a four-star rating in *Golf Digest* and a top-100 rating in *Golf for Women* magazine. The lengthy 558-yard par 5 No. 8 hole is probably the trickiest, and the 534-yard par 5 No. 15 hole is probably the most scenic, with a hill that overlooks the entire back nine holes. Tee times are required, and you're not allowed to wear metal-spike shoes on the course. The Bridges requires proper golf attire, specifically a collared shirt and midlength hemmed shorts. The cost to ride the course is $59 from 7:00 to 11:00 a.m., $49 before 7:00 a.m., $50 from 11:00 a.m. to

1:00 p.m., and $45 from 1:00 to 4:00 p.m. A greens fee of $21 is charged after 6:00 p.m. every day.

CALEDONIA GOLF CLUB
9515 Golf Course Road, Fayetteville
(717) 352-7271

The first nine holes of this golf course were built in 1922 and the second nine were added in 1926, and this oldie is still a goody. It's designed and constructed to put a premium on accuracy instead of distance, with plenty of trees and streams and narrow fairways to navigate over the par 68, 5,154-yard course. Located 12 miles west of Gettysburg behind the Totem Pole Playhouse in Caledonia State Park, club amenities include a clubhouse with a pro shop and snack bar, a putting green, and club rentals. (See the State Parks and Public Lands chapter for more activities offered in Caledonia State Park and The Arts chapter for more information on the Totem Pole Playhouse.) Although the Caledonia Golf Club is open to the public, memberships are also available.

Caledonia is usually one of the last courses in the area to open in the spring because it has small streams that crisscross the fairways, and it takes awhile for the course to dry out from the winter snows. Many golfers consider the No. 9 hole to be the prettiest on the course, especially in the fall. It has about a 60-foot drop from the tee to the green and a stand of trees to the right and left of the green. The hole is a par 3 with a length of 169 yards. The club requests (but doesn't require) that you make tee times daily up to 3:00

p.m., and they can be made up to six months in advance if you wish. Fees run $19 to walk and $34 to ride the course.

CARROLL VALLEY GOLF RESORT
Carroll Valley Resort 121 Sanders Road, Fairfield
(717) 642-8211, (800) 548-8504
www.carrollvalley.com

Carroll Valley Resort offers two golf courses, this one located at the site of the resort and the Mountain View Golf Course, located 3 miles away on Bullfrog Road (see listing later in this chapter). Carroll Valley Resort sits at the foothills of the Catoctin Mountains, and skiing is available during the winter. There are two restaurants at the resort, which is often used for conferences, meetings, and wedding receptions; its ballroom can accommodate 350 people. (For complete information on all that's offered at Carroll Valley Resort, see the Hotels, Motels, and Resorts chapter.)

The Carroll Valley Golf Resort is located about 10 miles west of Gettysburg off Route 116 (Middle Street). The hotel at Carroll Valley overlooks the course, and golf packages combining golfing, accommodations, and meals are available, as well as a clubhouse with a pro shop, a driving range, and a putting green. Golfers are not allowed to wear metal-spike shoes, and proper golf attire is required, specifically a collared shirt and no jeans or cutoffs. You'll find a kid-friendly golfing environment at Carroll Valley Resort. Family golf packages and new Kids on Course programs are offered, and the course has kid-friendly tees.

This 18-hole, 6,345-yard, and par 71 championship course designed by Ault & Clark has received a four-and-a-half-star rating by *Golf Digest* and has been named one of the 100 Must-Play Courses of the Middle Atlantic by *GolfStyles Magazine*. The course winds through the valley floor, and hills surround you as you golf. A mountain stream also cuts through the layout, making water a major factor on seven holes. One of the more challenging holes is No. 9, a 477-yard dogleg right par 4 that has water running along the right side for about 300 yards, creating a split

fairway. Cost is $45 to walk and $59 to ride the Carroll Valley course, and after 1:00 p.m. the price drops to $39 to walk and $49 to ride. Carts are mandatory before 2:00 p.m. on weekends and holidays. Tee times are required, and they may be scheduled up to one month in advance.

CEDAR RIDGE GOLF COURSE
1225 Barlow-Two Taverns Road
(717) 359-4480

This 18-hole course opened in the late 1980s, and it was designed by Roger Weaver, who also later designed the Meadowbrook Golf course (see listing in this chapter). Amenities include a clubhouse with a pro shop, a restaurant, a lounge, and a putting green. No metal-spike shoes are allowed, and proper golf attire is required. Cedar Ridge Golf Course is located less than 10 miles from Gettysburg. To reach the course, travel south on Baltimore Pike for about 5 miles and turn right onto Two Taverns Road. The course is on the right in about 2 miles.

At 5,938 yards and a par 72, the course's first nine holes are relatively straightforward while the back nine are more challenging. A good round here requires accuracy—large cedar trees line many of the fairways, and about a third of the holes feature water hazards. The No. 11 hole is deceivingly difficult—although only 93 yards, this par 3 combines water and cedar trees. Tee times are recommended but not required, and it costs $23 to walk and $38 to ride the course. Seniors can ride the course for $28 on weekdays.

FLATBUSH GOLF COURSE
940 Littlestown Road, Littlestown
(717) 359-7125, (877) 359-7125
www.flatbushgolfcourse.com

Don't let the windmill and gazebos that decorate the course deceive you; this is a challenging course that features open fairways, many in a dogleg configuration, water hazards, and well-placed trees. (Course rules allow the windmill and gazebos to be taken out of the line of flight without penalty.) The 6,205-yard, par 71 layout was designed by Ault, Clark and Assoc. and opened in July 1989. One of the more interesting holes is the 510-yard, par 5 No. 15, which has a double dogleg. Tee times are recommended and may be scheduled up to 10 days in advance on the Web site or 6 days in advance by phone. The fee is $26 to walk and $38 to ride the course, which is located about 10 miles southeast of Gettysburg. The best way to get there is to take Hanover Street (Route 116) east for 7 miles, turn right onto Littlestown Road, and travel for about 2 more miles. You'll also find a log-cabin-style clubhouse with a pro shop and locker rooms with showers; a driving range, putting green, and practice bunker; and a lounge and snack bar. Lessons are available, and proper golf attire is required.

THE LINKS AT GETTYSBURG
601 Mason Dixon Road
(717) 359-8000
www.thelinksatgettysburg.com
This Links was built in 1999, but it's more than just a golf course. The first homes of the Links Community Development were built in 2004, and the Links at Gettysburg course is part of the community. Its clubhouse can accommodate 260 people for weddings, receptions, and other special occasions. George T. Keeney, the chef of the place, even has a food column in the local newspaper. If you're interested in joining the community, memberships and homesites are available, but you don't have to be a member to enjoy the golf here. Among the many amenities offered are a clubhouse with a pro shop, locker rooms with showers, a driving range and putting green, a restaurant, and a lounge and snack bar. Golf lessons are offered, and proper golf attire is required; specifically, jeans are not allowed. Golfers must also wear shoes without metal spikes. Civil War cannons serve as tee markers at the Links, which specializes in golf outings, corporate retreats, and fund-raising tournaments.

The 18-hole, 6,184-yard, par 72 layout features red-rock cliffs that come into play on 6 holes, dense forests, and 10 lakes. Precise play is necessitated by every hole's being lined with one or two lakes and thick forest. The course has rated four stars in *Golf Digest*, and it's been rated the No. 6 public course in Pennsylvania by *Golfweek*. The Links is also a member course of the exclusive National Golf Club. Its driving range and practice facility were redesigned in 2004, and tee times are required and may be made seven days in advance. This is the most expensive course in the area, with a weekend rate of $86.38 that drops to $45.04 after 2:00 p.m. To reach the Links, take Taneytown Road (Route 134) south about 4.5 miles, almost to the Maryland border. Turn right onto Mason-Dixon Road, and the course is a mile farther on the right.

MEADOWBROOK GOLF CLUB
835 Goulden Road
(717) 334-0569
This course began in 2000, and the final holes of this 18-hole course were completed in 2003. During the Battle of Gettysburg, Union troops occupied the land where the course sits. To reach Meadowbrook, travel Baltimore Pike south and at 0.5 mile past the intersection with U.S. Route 15, turn right onto White Church Road. Travel another 0.5 mile and turn right onto Goulden Road to the course. The clubhouse here has a pro shop and snack bar, and a putting green is available.

Meadowbrook was designed by Roger Weaver, who also designed the Cedar Ridge Golf Course (see previous listing). At 6,029 yards, it's a par 72 course, and the No. 7 hole is the most visually appealing. It has a view of the small valley that faces Big Round Top Mountain. The No. 6 hole is one of the most demanding of the course, requiring accuracy to place the ball in the sloping fairway from the tees. Tee-time reservations are preferred but not required, and the course costs $48 to play a round with a cart.

MOUNTAIN VIEW GOLF COURSE
Bullfrog Road and Route 116, Fairfield
(717) 642-5848, (800) 548-8504
www.carrollvalley.com
The Mountain View Golf Course is part of the Carroll Valley Resort, which offers this course and a sister course located at the main resort area. Golf pack-

ages that include golfing and accommodations and meals at the main lodge are available. (See the Hotels, Motels, and Resorts chapter for more on the Carroll Valley Resort; for more on the Carroll Valley Golf Resort, see the previous listing in this chapter.) Both of the resort courses are dedicated to creating a kid-friendly golfing environment by offering kid-friendly tees, family golf packages, and Kids on Course programs. Golfers are not allowed to wear metal-spike shoes on either course, and proper golf attire is required, specifically a collared shirt and no jeans or cutoffs.

The Mountain View Golf Course sits about 3 miles from the main resort area, and it's considered by many to be the easier of the two courses. Golfers here enjoy a natural grass driving range and a bit of history. The pro shop is within a pre–Civil War clubhouse that was built around 1800, and the brick farmhouse was used by the Confederates during their retreat from Gettysburg in July 1863. Slightly shorter than its sister course at 6,092 yards, this is also an 18-hole, par 71 championship course designed by Ault & Clark that's received a four-and-a-half-star rating by *Golf Digest*. Mountain View gets its name from the mountains that you can admire as you golf, and one of the best views of the mountains and the valley can be had on the No. 15 hole, a 415-yard downhill par 4. It costs nonresidents $35 to walk and $49 to ride the course, while residents pay $34 to walk and $44 to ride. Tee times are not required, but they are preferred one to two days in advance, and seniors (age 50 and older) get a reduced rate on riding the course on weekdays.

PENN NATIONAL GOLF CLUB & INN
3720 Clubhouse Drive, Fayetteville
(717) 352-3000, (800) 221-7366
www.penngolf.com
Penn National is considered by many area golfers to be the top golf facility in the area, but it is a bit of a drive (20 miles) from Gettysburg. It features two championship courses that are drastically different, each of which has earned a four-and-a-half-star rating by *Golf Digest*. *Golfweek* rated it the 10th best public course in Pennsylvania. This

is also a golf-course community, with residential housing blending with the golf courses. The Penn National Inn, with 52 hotel rooms, is on the grounds, and it offers stay-and-play packages that include golf, lodging, and meals on-site. Amenities include a pro shop in the clubhouse, locker rooms with showers, a restaurant and snack bar, a lighted driving range, and a putting green. Clubs may be rented here, and lessons are available at Bumble Bee Hollow Golf Academy, which offers one-, two-, and three-day programs for new as well as advanced players. To get to Penn National, take Chambersburg Street west for about 18 miles to Route 997 South. Turn left onto Route 997 and follow it for 3.5 miles to the golf club, which is about 1 mile north of Mont Alto. Both courses require proper golf attire and are non-metal-spike facilities. Tee times are required and may be made up to 30 days in advance. The cost at either course is $79, with reduced afternoon rates and special weekday pricing for seniors.

The **Founders Course** is a traditional 18-hole course with a classic blend of tree-lined bluegrass fairways, a seven-acre lake, and large, sculpted greens. Many of the fairways are lined with mature trees, so accuracy off the tee is a must, and the lake comes into play on four of the holes. This 6,492-yard, par 72 course was built in 1968 and designed by Edmund Ault. It has a $1.3 million double-row irrigation system that was completed in 2003, and its greenside bunkers were completely renovated in 2006.

The **Iron Forge Course** is a modern course with an open-style layout with bent-grass fairways, fast bent-grass greens, and rolling elevation changes. Since it is so open, wind can dramatically factor into your game here. The par 72, 6,300-yard, 18-hole course was built in 1996 and designed by Bill Love. The signature hole is No. 15, a par 4 with yardage of 347. It's a tough hole that involves steep hills, bunkers, and water, and it plays shorter than its yardage because the tee shot is downhill. A 40-foot drop from the tee to the green makes the vista from the tee just beautiful.

PINEY APPLE GOLF COURSE
165 Slatersville Road, Biglerville
(717) 677-9264
www.pineyapplegolf.com

This course's location a little more than 15 miles north of Gettysburg puts it in the middle of what's known as apple country around here. Many points along the 18-hole, 5,635-yard, par 71 course are scenic overlooks of orchards in the valley below and mountains ringing the skyline. Amenities include a clubhouse with a limited pro shop, a driving range and a putting green, and a practice chipping area with sand traps and a green. Lessons and club rentals are available. Tee times are recommended for weekends and accepted up to two days in advance. The cost of a round is $18 to walk ($15 after 2:00 p.m.) and $32 to ride ($23 after 2:00 p.m.), and senior specials are offered during the week. To find the course, head north on Carlisle Street and continue on Route 34 (Biglerville Road) through the town of Biglerville. After you pass Rampike Hill Road, you'll want to bear left, and the name of the road will change to Bendersville-Wilkesville Road. The name of the road changes once again, this time to Wenksville Road, and you turn right onto Slatersville Road to the course.

QUAIL VALLEY GOLF COURSE
901 Teeter Road, Littlestown
(717) 359-8453
www.quailvalleygc.com

This course in Littlestown was purchased in March 2004 by Scott and Colyn Keller, and the brothers have made many changes. They didn't alter the course's great layout, but they have improved the conditions of the tees, greens, and fairways. The clubhouse pro shop and the restaurant have also been remodeled, and amenities include a lounge and snack bar, a driving range, and a putting green. Lessons are also available. This 18-hole, 6,567-yard, par 72 course is about 10 miles southeast of Gettysburg; take Baltimore Pike southeast for about 7 miles and turn right onto Gettysburg Road. Travel 2 more miles and turn right onto Teeter Road, and the course is just another ¾ mile down the road. Tee times are required and may be made up to eight days in advance at this non-metal-spike facility, where proper golf attire is also required. Cost is $49 to ride the course.

RECREATION

Recreational choices abound in the Gettysburg area. Active folks will find plenty of ways to release their pent-up energy, with options ranging from the tame pastime of bowling to the thrill of skiing. People who prefer to watch rather than participate can enjoy cheering at a car race or at one of the horse shows hosted by the Gettysburg Riding Club. To make finding your choice easy, entries within this chapter are listed alphabetically by type of activity.

Golf is a popular leisure pursuit, and an entire chapter of this book has been dedicated to the sport. The numerous state parks in the area offer many forms of recreation, and they are also covered in their own chapter. Many carnivals and bingo nights are sponsored by area fire companies, and they are usually advertised in the *Gettysburg Times* newspaper. Also be sure to check out the Annual Events and Festivals chapter to find other fun ways to spend your time in Gettysburg.

BOATING

CODORUS STATE PARK
1066 Blooming Grove Road, Hanover
(717) 637-2816
www.dcnr.state.pa.us
Most area boaters travel the 20 miles to Codorus State Park to run their boats on Lake Marburg, which covers 1,275 acres and has 26 miles of shoreline. Motorboats up to 20 horsepower and nonpowered boats are both welcome, and there are six public boat-launch ramps around the lake and one ramp at the campground reserved for registered campers. If you don't have your own boat, there's a boat rental at the marina run by Appalachian Outdoor School and Adventure Sports (717-632-7484). You can rent pontoon boats, canoes, kayaks, double kayaks, paddleboats, and V-bottom motorboats. The boating season at the lake runs daily from Memorial Day to Labor Day and weekends only during April, May, September, and October. Reservations are recommended, and taxes and gas are extra.

GRANITE HILL CAMPING RESORT
3340 Fairfield Road
(717) 642-8749, (800) 642-TENT
www.granitehillcampingresort.com

The 150 acres that comprise Granite Hill Campground are an outdoor enthusiast's dream come true. (To get a full rundown of all this campground has to offer, see the Campgrounds and RV Parks chapter.) Even if you're not staying at Granite Hill, you can enter the property and enjoy its lake. (The campground's minigolf course and snack bar are also open to the public; see the Kidstuff chapter for information on the minigolf.) Kayaks and paddleboats are available for rent at Bass Lake, which is just inside and to the left of the campground entrance.

PINE GROVE FURNACE STATE PARK
1100 Pine Grove Road, Gardners
(717) 486-7174
www.dcnr.state.pa.us
Laurel Lake, one of the two lakes found within this park, offers boating, but it doesn't allow any gas-powered motors, only small electric boats. You'll find a boat launch, 85 mooring spaces, and a boat rental at the shore of this 25-acre lake. Rowboats, electric-powered rowboats, canoes, and paddleboats can be rented daily from Memorial Day to Labor Day and usually on weekends only during April, May, September, and October.

i If you enjoy dancing, check out the ballroom dance held at the American Legion, 528 East Middle Street, on the fourth Sunday of each month. Admission is $5, a very reasonably priced buffet is offered before the dancing begins, and refreshments are available. Reservations are suggested, and dress is casual. Call (717) 677-7198 or visit www.gettysburg bigband.com for more information.

BOWLING

EDGEWOOD LANES
1880 Emmitsburg Road
(717) 337-1818

This is one of the few businesses in town that has shorter hours during the tourist season than during the rest of the year. Open daily in the off-season, during the season Edgewood Lanes is open from 6:00 to 10:00 p.m. on Monday, Wednesday, Thursday, Friday, and Saturday nights and from 10:00 a.m. to 2:00 p.m. on Monday. The bowling alley sits at the edge of town, and it offers 16 bowling lanes and a video room with a pool table and video games. Leagues bowl every evening, and there's a kids' league on Saturday. Bumper guards are also available for those learning the sport. Edgewood Lanes has been a place to relax, bowl a few games, and have fun since 1978. It will cost you $3.75 to bowl a game, and shoe rental is $2.25.

CAR RACING

LINCOLN SPEEDWAY
800 Racetrack Road, Abbottstown
(717) 624-2755
www.lincolnspeedway.com

Abbottstown hosts summer dirt-track racing at the Lincoln Speedway on Saturday nights. Races are held for 410 Sprints, Thunder Cars, and 358 Sprints, and drivers compete for points, money, and bragging rights. All this racing excitement is less than 15 miles east of Gettysburg. To get to the track, take U.S. Route 30 (York Street) east

for about 13 miles and turn right onto Kinneman Road. Follow Kinneman Road for almost a mile to Racetrack Road. Admission varies based on which divisions are racing and if there are extra events such as fireworks going on, but expect to pay a minimum of $13 for adults, $8 for students age 12 to 17, and $2 for children age 6 to 11. Admission for the pit area (adults only) is at least $20. The speedway also offers season passes and bulk ticket rates. Gates open around 5:30 p.m., and the races usually begin at 7:30 p.m.

TRAIL-WAY SPEEDWAY
100 Speedway Lane, Hanover
(717) 359-4310
www.trail-wayspeedway.com

Friday and Saturday nights during summer in Hanover are for dirt-track racing. At Trail-way Speedway, you can see 358 Super Sprints, Thunder Cars, Street Stocks, 270cc and 600cc Micro Sprints, Scramble Cars, and Figure 8s in action. Drivers compete for points, money, and fame within local racing circles. Friday-night races feature the 358 Super Sprints, Thunder Cars, and Street Stocks, while the Micro Sprints, Scramble Cars, and Figure 8s race on Saturday nights.

To reach the track from Gettysburg, take Route 116 (Hanover Road) east about 10 miles, turn right onto Littlestown Road and then left onto Hostetter Road, and follow the arrow signs to the speedway. Admission is $12 on Friday night and $10 on Saturday night. Children younger than age 12 are admitted for free. Admission to the pit area is $20 on either night, and anyone younger than age 18 must have a parent or guardian sign a release to enter the pits. If there's a special show going on, $2 is added to the general and pit admission prices. On Friday nights, gates open at 5:30 p.m. and race time is 7:30. Saturdays start earlier—gates open at 4:00 p.m. and race time is 6:30.

FISHING

Adams County doesn't have the limestone substratum that makes the creeks in adjoining

Cumberland and Franklin Counties so good for fly-fishing, but there are still some nice fishing creeks around Gettysburg. The best-known destination in Adams County is the Conewago Creek, which has a section where only fly-fishing is allowed. The stream is stocked with several hundred trout in mid-March and in October, so success comes easily here. To get to the fly-fishing section of Conewago Creek, head north from Gettysburg on Route 34 for about 5 miles and park where the bridge crosses the creek. Fly-fishing is allowed upstream from the bridge; bait fishing and fly-fishing are allowed downstream.

Many anglers also venture to the state parks for fishing. Codorus State Park, Mont Alto State Park, and Pine Grove Furnace State Park all offer fishing. See the State Parks and Public Lands chapter for full details.

A fishing license is required for anyone age 16 or older to fish Pennsylvania waterways. Applications are available at the Treasurer's Office, which is in the Adams County Courthouse (111 Baltimore Street; 717-337-9833). Tourist licenses may be purchased for three or seven days of fishing if you don't need a license for the entire year. Senior citizens who are residents of Adams County can purchase a lifetime license. An additional fee is charged if you wish to fish for trout or salmon.

GYMS

CLUB 50 FITNESS OF GETTYSBURG
1400 Proline Place (Commerce Park)
(717) 339-0050
www.club50fitness.com
Husband-and-wife team Larry and Darla Conover run this franchise fitness center aimed at keeping the older generation active and fit. Open to persons age 40 and older, the club features a 30-minute circuit. Members alternate between using adjustable hydraulic-resistance machines for strength training and exercising aerobically at interval stations for a cardio workout. Club 50 considers nutrition to be the first step in any fitness program, so it offers many nutritional products

and supplements, including multivitamins, protein beverages and snacks, and sports drinks. The Conovers received comprehensive training at Club 50 University on the fitness and nutrition programs offered at their gym so they are equipped to give members personal training and attention.

Open since late 2007, the fitness center has expanded to include night group classes in yoga and total body toning. Club 50 Fitness is located outside of Gettysburg at Commerce Park, near the U.S. Route 15 and U.S. Route 30 interchange east of town, and it's open every day except Sunday.

CURVES FOR WOMEN
1707B Old Harrisburg Road
(717) 337-9886
www.curves.com
If you don't have a Curves near you, it's pretty likely you will have one soon. Curves for Women is the largest chain of franchised fitness centers in the world, with more than 10,000 locations and four million members as of December 2008. As with all Curves, this facility is equipped with hydraulic-resistance machines that are arrayed in a circuit where you move from machine to machine on a time interval. The pieces of equipment in the circuit target specific body parts, and you exercise aerobically at stations between the machines to keep your heart rate up. The circuit moves you from station to station and is directed by music and taped instruction. Curves is located within the North Gettysburg Shopping Mall, and it's open Monday through Saturday. If you belong to a different Curves franchise, your membership there allows you to use these facilities while you're visiting Gettysburg.

i There's probably a game of bingo going on somewhere in town during your stay. Check the numerous ads for bingo in the *Gettysburg Times* newspaper. The American Legion, at 123 Baltimore Street (717-334-4513), is one of many places that host bingo, with games on Wednesday evenings.

GETTYSBURG HEALTH & FITNESS
1080 Chambersburg Road
(717) 334-4777
www.gettysburgfitness.com

This coed gym is 1.5 miles west of Lincoln Square, and members range from 13 through 95 years old. When you join the club, you receive two free personal training sessions, where you'll be shown how to use the club's wide variety of equipment, including Star Trac and Life Fitness treadmills, Precor elliptical machines, Star Trac exercise bikes and steppers, and Schwinn Airdynes and Concept2 rowing machines. For strength training there's a full set of Paramount and Cybex machines and a large free-weight area. Exercise classes are held in the aerobics room, which has a state-of-the-art floating floor. Traditional fitness classes include step, cycling, dancing, senior fitness, low-impact, weight lifting, and kickboxing. Mind-body-spirit classes such as yoga and Pilates are also offered. Certified personal trainers are available, as are certified massage therapists, and the club also has tanning beds. Gettysburg Health & Fitness has a staffed KinderCare room that's open Monday through Friday mornings. Children age seven and younger are permitted, but only one child younger than one year old will be taken at any one time. Advance reservations are required, and you should let the staff know 24 hours in advance that you want their services. Club memberships may be for lengths of 1, 3, 6, or 12 months, and visitors to Gettysburg may purchase day passes.

YWCA
909 Fairfield Road
(717) 334-9171
www.ywcagettysburg.org

This member association offers fitness opportunities and is home to dozens of community programs. Guest passes are available for a daily fee, and membership is open to all. A basic membership gives you access to support programs and services held at the Y, while a Recreation Pass allows you the use of the fitness facilities, which include a 25-meter indoor pool, a whirlpool, two racquetball courts, and fitness and training equipment. Members must be 16 years old to use the fitness center. A variety of groups meet at the facilities, including a book group, a single-mom support group, and a group that meets to talk about how to have the -isms of our society unite us as a culture rather than divide us. On-site babysitting services are available to members or holders of a Recreation Pass.

HORSEBACK RIDING

GETTYSBURG RIDING CLUB
102 Hounds Run
(717) 334-4396
www.geocities.com/gettysburgridingclub

Located on 10 acres east of Gettysburg off York Street and Hunterstown Road, the Gettysburg Riding Club first organized in 1952 to have trail rides and hold horse shows, and both traditions carry on today. The club grounds hold a vinyl-covered fenced riding ring, a storage shed, a secretary stand attached to a judges' stand, and a parking area. Well water and electricity are available, and a second area is graded off for use by the trail classes. Club members have trail rides about once a month, and they also have a monthly meeting at an area restaurant. A Christmas party and end-of-show-season dinner is held annually. The club is a member of two show circuits, the Maryland-Pennsylvania Horse Show Circuit (MPHSC) and the Blue and Gray Hunter Circuit, and it also holds a show that benefits the Pennsylvania Sudden Infant Death Syndrome Alliance. Club grounds are rented to other horse organizations for shows and to the local 4-H club. Membership is open to anyone with an interest in horses, and you don't have to be a rider to enjoy being part of the club.

HICKORY HOLLOW FARMS
219 Crooked Creek Road
(717) 334-0349
www.hickoryhollowfarm.com

You can board your horse at Hickory Hollow Farms, which offers private stalls, feeding, and turning out of the horses daily. Boarders can exercise their mounts in the 100-foot-by-200-foot lighted outdoor ring with all-weather footing or the 70-foot-by-120-foot indoor arena. There's also an outdoor round training ring, and the horse trails on the farm are waiting to be explored. Hickory Hollow Farms, which encompasses 70 acres of fields and woodlands, served as a Confederate field hospital during the Battle of Gettysburg. Horseback tours of the battlefield are available through the farm, with both scenic rides and historic rides offered (see the Gettysburg National Military Park chapter).

NATIONAL RIDING STABLES
Artillery Ridge Campground
610 Taneytown Road
(717) 334-1288, (877) 335-5596
www.artilleryridge.com
The National Riding Stables, located at Artillery Ridge Campground, is best known for its two-hour battlefield ride where riders listen on headsets to a CD prepared by a licensed battlefield guide (see the Gettysburg National Military Park chapter). The stable also boards horses, and box stalls and corrals are available. Artillery Ridge sits about a mile south of town on Route 134 (Taneytown Road), and it's also where you can find the Gettysburg Miniature Battlefield Diorama (see the Attractions chapter). If you have little ones, the campground offers pony rides on Sunday as one of its scheduled activities. (See the Campgrounds and RV Parks to find out about all the activities available at Artillery Ridge Campground.)

MARTIAL ARTS

DUBBS KARATE ACADEMY
165 York Street
(717) 337-0315, (800) 788-5623
Dubbs Karate Academy has been teaching area residents the martial arts since 1989, and you can sometimes see people practicing their moves through the floor-to-ceiling windows that front York Street. Children and adults can earn their black belt here, and children as young as age three can start off with kinderkarate. Classes are held for beginners, and children and adults are taught in separate classes. Self-defense and self-confidence training are also offered, and the academy sells martial-arts supplies and has a pro shop. Dubbs is open every day but Sunday.

MOVIES

GATEWAY THEATERS
Gateway Gettysburg
(717) 334-5576 (customer service),
(717) 334-5577 (movie times)
www.gatewaygettysburg.com
These are the newest theaters in town, built as part of the new Gateway Gettysburg complex (see the Close-up on the complex in the Area Overview chapter). Eight theaters are available, and two have large-format, high-definition giant screens with digital projectors. And I do mean giant—they're three stories high! These two theaters also offer giant amounts of seating, with the ability to accommodate 300 to 400 people. All eight theaters boast state-of-the-art amenities you would expect, such as stadium seating in comfy chairs with cup holders.

The film *Fields of Freedom* runs on the giant screen every half hour, and many visitors have added to their Gettysburg itinerary a viewing of this riveting film that displays how the Battle of Gettysburg affected two young soldiers on opposing sides. (For more details on the film, see the Attractions chapter.)

i Movie buffs may want to drive about 15 miles southeast to the Hanover Movies at 380 Eisenhower Drive in Hanover (717-646-1111; www.rctheatres.com). The movie theater features a digital light processor projection system. The movie comes off a computer hard drive instead of film, which improves clarity significantly.

GETTYSBURG VILLAGE CINEMA TEN

The Outlet Shoppes at Gettysburg
Junction of U.S. Route 15 and Route 97
(Baltimore Street)
(717) 338-0101
www.village10cinema.com

These state-of-the-art theaters opened in early 2006, and they're located at the Gettysburg Village, which consists of an outlet mall, a TGI Friday's restaurant, and lodging at the Country Inn & Suites. Gettysburg Village is located just off the Baltimore Street exit of US 15, and from town you follow Baltimore Street for a few miles to reach it. Village Ten theaters feature full stadium seating, wall-to-wall wide screens in every room, Dolby digital sound, high-back rockers, and flip-up cup holders. Armrests flip up so two theatergoers can turn their seats into a loveseat. The cinemas also have party rooms and offer VIP ticketing.

HAAR'S DRIVE-IN

U.S. Route 15, Dillsburg
(717) 432-3011
www.haars.com

If you love drive-in movies and don't mind driving a half an hour or so, you might want to check what's playing at Haar's. This is an authentic 1950s drive-in, and it's been family owned since 1953. It's open only on Friday, Saturday, and Sunday nights from April through September, and two current movies are shown each night. The box office opens at 6:30 p.m., and the first show begins at dusk. To hear the movie, you tune your radio to station 101.1 FM. (The first five rows have speakers if your car doesn't have a radio.) Vans, trucks, or other high-profile vehicles are to park in the first two and last six rows, and the theater has room for about 500 cars total. Nostalgia abounds at Haar's, from the layout to the traditional snack bar, but the days of pricing by the carload are long gone. Moviegoers age 12 and older are charged $7 each, and children age 3 through 11 are charged $2. Pets are not allowed, and the theater accepts cash only at the ticket office. Be aware that the bathroom situations are not the best here—the ladies' room has only two stalls, and keeping them clean does not always appear to be a high priority. To reach Haar's, drive north on US 15, and the theater will be on your right after the third traffic light in the town of Dillsburg.

Famed pitcher Eddie Plank, who's in the Baseball Hall of Fame, was a Gettysburg native. Nicknamed Gettysburg Eddie, he joined the Philadelphia Athletics after graduating from Gettysburg College in 1901, and he pitched in the majors for 17 seasons. But Eddie was a hometown boy—he spent his off-seasons working at Gettysburg National Military Park as a battlefield tour guide.

OUTDOOR ACTIVITIES

GETTYSBURG RECREATION PARK

545 Long Lane

The Gettysburg Recreation Park consists of 52 acres situated within the borough. The park has a 20-station outdoor fitness trail, 7 baseball diamonds, 2 basketball courts, tennis courts, and a football field. There are also three playgrounds within the park, with one specifically designed for children age four and younger. The park entrance is across from Gettysburg Hospital, and it can be reached from Baltimore Street by turning westward onto Breckenridge Street and then turning onto Long Lane.

STRAWBERRY HILL NATURE CENTER & PRESERVE

1537 Mount Hope Road, Fairfield
(717) 642-5840
www.strawberryhill.org

Exploring the habitats of wet and dry woodlands, three ponds, two pristine mountain streams, and more is possible within the 609 acres of Strawberry Hill Nature Center & Preserve. This private nonprofit education and conservation institution opens its land to the public for free. More than 10 miles of blazed trails meander through the property, with trails to please both the strolling family and the more serious hiker. White-tailed deer, bobcats, coyotes, and many other animals live here, and birders will be thrilled by all the species of birds to be discovered.

The Nature Center hosts a variety of programs that explore nature. In 2008 the programs taught participants how to read animal markings in a forest, how animals and plants adapt to the changing seasons, and how our actions affect the environment. A junior naturalist camp is also held here during the summer; see the Kidstuff chapter for full details on the camp. Strawberry Hill holds an annual pancake breakfast and maple-sugaring event, where participants actually see a maple tree being tapped and the syrup being cooked down over an open fire. Most programs are free to members of Strawberry Hill, and nonmembers pay a nominal fee, usually $2 to $3.

To reach Strawberry Hill, take Route 116 (Middle Street) west for 8.5 miles and turn right onto Carroll's Tract Road. Head north toward Cashtown to the first intersection and turn left onto Mt. Hope Road. Proceed another 3.5 miles to a parking area; the nature center is on the left. Hiking trails in the preserve are open daily dawn to dusk, and the nature center is open when staff is on-site or by prearrangement.

SKATING AND SKATEBOARDING

GETTYSBURG ALTERNATIVE SKATE PARK (GASP)
Gettysburg Recreation Park
545 Long Lane
(717) 334-1160

BMXers, in-line skaters, and skateboarders have a home in Gettysburg. The fenced-in park is operated by members of the Gettysburg Alternative Sports Association (GASA), and it has metal ramps and obstacles to challenge riders with varying levels of ability. All participants are required to wear helmets, and children younger than age 10 must also wear wrist guards. Children younger than age 10 must be accompanied by an active

supervisor who is at least 16 years old. The park is generally open from afternoon to dusk, and spectators are always welcome. Cost per usage is $5 for Pennsylvania residents and $10 for out-of-state visitors; day passes are available for $10 for Pennsylvania residents and $20 for out-of-state visitors. Yearly membership is available to Adams County residents for $50 per individual or $100 per family.

SKIING

SKI LIBERTY
78 Country Club Trail, Carroll Valley
(717) 642-8282
www.skiliberty.com

When you're approaching Gettysburg by heading west on US 30, Ski Liberty is visible in the distance, and swishing down the mountainside can be done after only a short drive from town. You'll find 16 slopes here, with 35 percent of the slopes geared toward beginner skiers, 40 percent toward intermediate skiers, and 25 percent toward expert skiers. The elevation of the front base is 570 feet, and elevation of the back base is 650 feet; the vertical drop on the front side is 620 feet, and on the back side it's 550 feet. You reach the mountain summit at 1,190 feet, and the longest run on the mountain is 5,200 feet. During the season, which usually runs from Thanksgiving to March, the mountain is open seven days a week for day and night skiing. Long lines are not usually a problem here—ski lifts can carry 13,400 skiers per hour. Ski Liberty has snowmaking capabilities, and you can rent all the equipment for a day on the slopes at the lodge. The Liberty Mountain Sports Shop is located on the deck level in the main lodge and is open any time the mountain is open. As at most ski slopes, snowboarding and snow tubing have become quite popular, and the ski resort offers a half-pipe and a snow-tubing area that has 15 lanes and a kiddie tubing area. Ten acres are set aside for three terrain parks that are broken into beginner, intermediate, and advanced areas. Skiing and snowboarding lessons are available for all ages, and many programs specifically designed for children are available.

Ski Liberty can be experienced as a day at the slopes, or you can stay overnight and make a vacation out of your adventure. The Liberty Mountain Hotel is slopeside, and the hotel at the Carroll Valley Resort is just steps away. (See the Hotels, Motels, and Resorts chapter for details on both resorts.) The ski lodge sits at the base of the mountain, and this is where you'll find McKee's Tavern, a great place to relax after skiing and enjoy a meal or snack, drinks, and often live entertainment. The resort also operates a full-service day care for nonskiing children age 6 months to 10 years, where your child can enjoy story time, movie time, games, songs, crafts, walks, free play, and snacks while you enjoy the slopes. Reservations are requested, and the fee is based on an hourly rate.

i **Ski Liberty offers advantage cards, which are a combination between a discount and a frequent-skier card. With an advantage card, you get 40 percent off your lift ticket each time you visit, and after you ski five times, your sixth lift ticket is free.**

NIGHTLIFE

G ettysburg certainly is not known for its nightlife, and most of the entertainment you'll find around town is pretty low key. Many visitors and residents spend their evenings on the battlefield, which is open to 10:00 p.m. April through October and to 7:00 p.m. November through March. Watching the sun set while on the soil where so many gave their lives for their cause is akin to a religious experience for many. Ghost walks also fill up many visitors' evenings, and you'll see troupes of ghost hunters wandering through town on candlelight tours. (See the Attractions chapter for a complete review of all the ghost tours available.)

For those who are looking to relax with some music and/or a few drinks, there are places in town that fit the bill, and dancing happens at Mamma Ventura's, the Pike, and the Flying Bull Saloon. If you want to keep your Gettysburg trip as Civil War–oriented as possible, try the Farnsworth's Killer Angel Tavern, which has waitstaff dressed in period clothing and Civil War–era music performed live on Friday and Saturday nights. Or stop by O'Rorke's, where you'll probably run into some reenactors. And although it's not technically a nightspot, many night owls spend time at the Lincoln Diner, on Carlisle Street beside the Flying Bull. The diner is open 24 hours daily, and many residents, college students, and visitors congregate here to enjoy good yet inexpensive fare in an environment that invites you to linger. If you decide to hit the Lincoln, bring cash—that's all that's accepted as payment.

ARROW HORSE
49 Chambersburg Street
(717) 337-2899

The Arrow Horse is a shop that sells banjos and bluegrass music, and bluegrass jam sessions are held here from 7:00 to 10:00 p.m. every Friday night. There's no formal schedule of performers; whoever shows up jams together. This laissez-faire attitude keeps each session fresh, and every Friday-night experience at Arrow Horse is a new adventure to look forward to.

BLUE PARROT BISTRO
35 Chambersburg Street
(717) 337-3739

Outside tables along the side of the Blue Parrot allow patrons to have a quiet drink or dinner while watching the people strolling by on Chambersburg Street, contributing to the "bistro" feel of the place. The lounge inside has a few small, intimate tables as well as seats at the large bar. Although the Blue Parrot doesn't offer regularly

scheduled entertainment, many patrons play pool on the table that separates the lounge and dining areas. Dinner is served until 9:30 p.m., and last call is usually around 1:00 a.m. (See the Restaurants chapter for more on the delicious offerings at Blue Parrot.)

EASTSIDE LOUNGE AND RESTAURANT
1063 York Road
(717) 337-0118

You won't find musical entertainment at the Eastside, but there are three pool tables and a game room in addition to the long bar that's the main seating area. The lounge has a separate entrance, or you can enter through the restaurant area. Be sure to check out the Eastside's large and varied menu while you're enjoying a libation. (See the Restaurants chapter for a full rundown of their offerings.) The Eastside is open seven days a week from 10:00 a.m. to 2:00 a.m., and there's also a carryout six-pack store in front of the restaurant.

FLYING BULL SALOON
28 Carlisle Street
(717) 334-6202

It might look small and dark from the sidewalk, but the Flying Bull is anything but. As you enter, the first thing you see is the long, long bar, which occupies the entire right side of the area, with just enough room behind the bar stools to move through the crowd that usually gathers here. About halfway down this aisle on the left is another room with plenty of space for people to dance to the music that fills the place most nights. While you're dancing, take time to read the messages written in chalk on the wall that runs along this area. The wall is reserved for military personnel, who are invited to sign it. At the end of the bar, there's another room that has some pool tables for those who prefer to cue up rather than dance. The Flying Bull usually hosts live bands on Tuesday, Wednesday is open-mike night, and DJs provide the entertainment Thursday through Saturday nights. Many local residents frequent the Flying Bull, and students from Gettysburg College also make up a good portion of the crowd while school is in session. The place is always closed on Sunday, and it's also closed on Monday when the college kids are on break.

GARRYOWEN IRISH PUB
126 Chambersburg Street
(717) 337-2719

This wonderful new addition to Gettysburg's nightlife opened during the summer of 2007 and took over the location formerly occupied by Hamilton's Tavern. Owner Kevin McCready is a native of Ireland, and he brings a bit of his homeland to Gettysburg through "cool, cainte, and craic." For those of you not up on your Irish, that's music (cool), talk (cainte), and fun (craic), and all are available in abundance. Celtic bands are often booked here, and unlike many bars the music is not at the noise level where you have to shout to carry on a conversation. Musicians are welcome to bring their own gear or they can use the two guitars, bass, drum kit, and microphones that are always on hand in case the mood to jam strikes any of the patrons. The pub offers a full bar with a good

selection of draft beer and a varied menu (see the Restaurants chapter) that includes some traditional Irish fare. It's open till 11:30 p.m. on Monday through Wednesday, till 2:00 a.m. on Thursday through Saturday, and till 10:30 p.m. on Sunday.

KILLER ANGEL TAVERN
Farnsworth House Inn
401 Baltimore Street
(717) 334-8838
www.farnsworthhouseinn.com

The Killer Angel Tavern is located on the grounds of the Farnsworth House Inn, a sprawling complex that includes a bed-and-breakfast, indoor and outdoor dining areas open to the public, a bookshop, and a sutlery. Sitting at the rear of the complex, the tavern has its own entrance, and light fare is served. South Street Pizza (717-334-4419) also operates a thriving pizza and hoagie business within the tavern. An interesting collection of uniforms and props from the movie *Gettysburg* is housed at the tavern, and the Civil War is always an avid topic of conversation, especially among the reenactors who gather here. Entertainment offered keeps with the Civil War theme of the complex, with live Civil War music every Friday and Saturday night from 9:00 to 11:00 p.m. The tavern closes after the group is done on those nights, while its regular hours are from 11:30 a.m. to 10:30 p.m.

THE LIVERY
Herr Tavern & Publick House
900 Chambersburg Road
(717) 334-4332, (800) 362-9849
www.herrtavern.com

A casual atmosphere rules at the Livery, which sits in its own building across the parking lot from Herr Tavern & Publick House, an elegant bed-and-breakfast steeped in Civil War history. (See the Bed-and-Breakfasts and Guesthouses chapter for more on the bed-and-breakfast.) The Livery runs different food and beer specials each night, and it has a large outside deck on one side of the building. Entertainment available inside consists of black-light pool, darts, foosball, and touch-screen video games. You'll also find big-screen TVs, and light fare is available if hunger hits. The Livery is open Monday through Thursday 3:30 p.m. to 2:00 a.m., Friday and Saturday noon to 2:00 a.m., and Sunday noon to midnight.

MAMMA VENTURA'S LOUNGE
13 Chambersburg Street
(717) 334-5548

Mamma Ventura's Lounge is a favorite haunt of Gettysburg College students, who gather here to dance and to sing karaoke. The lounge is actually beneath Mamma Ventura's Restaurant, and it has its own entrance. To reach the lounge, you need to walk between the buildings on Chambersburg Street to the back of the street; the entrance for the lounge is to your left as you leave the small walkway. A sign at the restaurant points you in the right direction, and you need to be careful while walking between the buildings so you don't knock into any of the stairs that are within the walkway. Once you enter the lounge, you're greeted by a large open space with tables, two bar areas on the left, and an area in the back that has pool tables. DJs spin tunes on Wednesday and Friday nights, and karaoke rules on Thursday and Saturday nights.

OLIVIA'S MEDITERRANEAN GRILLE
3015 Baltimore Street
(717) 359-9357
www.olivias.biz

Although known more as a restaurant than a nightspot, Olivia's does have Kenny Gibson playing love ballads on the keyboards on Friday and Saturday nights, so this is the perfect place for a quiet drink with your significant other. If you're in the mood for something a bit more lively, there are always specials being featured on the deck, which is called Paradise Island. There's the weekly Jimmy Buffet night, martini specials, and more, and on Fridays in July a DJ plays the latest hits.

O'RORKE'S FAMILY EATERY AND SPIRITS
44 Steinwehr Avenue
(717) 334-2333

Reenactors tend to congregate at O'Rorke's, which is named for Patrick O'Rorke, an Irish-born American soldier who was killed on Little Round Top during the Battle of Gettysburg. O'Rorke's has a large deck that overlooks the activity along Steinwehr Avenue, which makes it perfect for people watching. Inside you'll find good food and a nice selection of beer, wine, and specialty drinks. Six beers are on tap, including Guinness and Harp, and wine is available by the glass. Live entertainment takes place on Friday and Saturday from 8:00 to 11:00 p.m., with all types of music represented throughout the season. O'Rorke's opens daily at 11:00 a.m., and food is available until 10:00 p.m. Drinks are served until midnight except on Sunday, when the place closes an hour earlier.

THE PIKE RESTAURANT & LOUNGE
985 Baltimore Pike
(717) 334-9227
www.thepikerestaurant.com

Something always seems to be going on at the lounge at the Pike on weekends. DJs and live bands provide dance music on Friday and Saturday nights, and on Sunday you can find karaoke going on. A mechanical bull is also a big draw. The Pike boasts that it has Gettysburg's largest dance floor, and although it's not really very big, you usually will find it jam-packed on weekend nights. This nightspot sits at the edge of town, and plenty of parking is available in front of and across the street from the place.

Besides the lounge the Pike also has a large deck out front and a separate bar off the deck, and live bands also play on the deck.

i The State of Pennsylvania allows the sale of liquor and wine through state-run stores only. Gettysburg's state store is within the Peebles Shopping Center east of town along York Road. The store is open seven days a week; call (717) 334-3814.

THE PUB & RESTAURANT
20–22 Lincoln Square
(717) 334-7100
www.the-pub.com

The Pub doesn't have any entertainment, unless you count the people watching that goes on here. This fun place offers its patrons a bird's-eye view of all the activity that flows through Lincoln Square. There are even tables outside for those who like to be a part of the goings-on. Separate entrances for the pub and the restaurant are available, but you can reach both through either door. The pub side's rich wood lends an old-world ambience to the place, which is outfitted with a nice-size bar and a few tables. You can choose from a wide range of cocktails, wines, and beers here. In fact, there are 12 drafts on tap, one of which is always Guinness. The Pub serves until 1:00 a.m. Monday through Saturday and until 11:00 p.m. on Sunday.

RAGGED EDGE COFFEEHOUSE
110 Chambersburg Street
(717) 334-4464
www.raggededgecoffeehs.com

Ragged Edge has plenty of room for you to spread out as you sip a relaxing beverage. You'll find people hanging out on the front porch, in the rooms downstairs, out on the patio in back, and in the rooms upstairs. Sandwiches, salads, and baked goods are available, as well as juices, smoothies, supplement drinks, and hot and cold specialty (nonalcoholic) drinks. The second floor is where you'll find live entertainment provided by local musicians on Saturday nights, and you can enjoy the unpredictability of open-mike nights during the week. Ragged Edge opens daily at 6:00 a.m. and is usually open until around 10:00 p.m.

RELIANCE MINE SALOON
380 Steinwehr Avenue
(717) 334-9870

This unique cocktail lounge is part of the Quality Inn Gettysburg Motor Lodge, and it's within an underground coal mine. The lodge is completely nonsmoking and so is the saloon, which serves only drinks and snacks and seats about 50. Unfortunately, nonsmokers have to make it through the long hallway that leads to the lounge, where all the smokers congregate, to reach a smoke-free environment. Once you're inside the saloon, there's a small bar and plenty tables available, and the saloon's lack of windows makes you feel isolated from the outside world. The saloon is open daily from 6:00 p.m. to 1:00 a.m.

SQUIRE MILLER TAVERN
The Fairfield Inn
15 West Main Street, Fairfield
(717) 334-8868, (717) 642-5410
www.thefairfieldinn.com

If you like to drink in history, stop at the Squire Miller Tavern, about 8 miles west of town off Route 116. In November 2004 a colonial-era tavern license dating from 1786 was discovered by the local historical society, making the Squire Miller Tavern one of the oldest taverns in the United States still operating. The inn itself dates from 1757, and the house now serves as a bed-and-breakfast (see the Bed-and-Breakfasts and Guesthouses chapter). The tavern has its own entrance on the side of the inn, or you can reach it by turning left after entering through the front door, which has the original pulley-type lock. A key feature of the tavern is its huge fireplace, which is complete with the original kettle arm and kettle. The bar itself is magnificent. Gleaming mahogany woodwork has large archways cut into it, and this is where the liquor is displayed. The tavern has enough tables to seat about 25 people in addition to the seats at the bar.

DAY TRIPS

Gettysburg is within easy driving distance to major East Coast cities. Washington, D.C., is only 79 miles away, Philadelphia is 125 miles, and New York City is 224 miles from town. The cities I've chosen for day trips are a bit closer to home. Both Baltimore and Hershey are less than 60 miles from Gettysburg, and Harrisburg is just a bit more than 30 miles up U.S. Route 15 North. So why not take a little road trip while you're in the area? Each destination has unique charms that are just waiting to be discovered by you.

BALTIMORE'S INNER HARBOR

Located less than 60 miles by car from Gettysburg, Baltimore's Inner Harbor makes an easy and relaxing day trip. To reach it, travel out of town on Baltimore Street, which will become Route 97 South. At Westminster, Maryland, pick up Maryland Route 140 South and follow it to Reisterstown, where you connect with Interstate 795 South. Take I-795 South to its merger with Interstate 695. From I-695 pick up Interstate 95 East. From I-95 take exit 53 (Interstate 395 North, Downtown), and turn right at the third light onto Pratt Street. The Inner Harbor is 4 blocks up Pratt Street on your right. Once you park the car in one of the many lots near the harbor, you can walk or take a water taxi to all the area attractions, which include historic ships, shopping and dining areas, museums, and the National Aquarium.

Although Inner Harbor was created during the 1960s, it really took off as a destination spot in the 1980s when **Harborplace** opened as two glass-enclosed pavilions (Light Street Pavilion and Pratt Street Pavilion) where visitors could find small shops, abundant restaurants, and often live entertainment. In 1987 Harborplace added **The Gallery** across from Pratt Street Pavilion, with more shops and a parking garage beneath the shops. Harborplace is where most visitors begin their exploration of Inner Harbor, and for some, it's the sole reason they come to Baltimore.

Call Harborplace and the Gallery at Harborplace at (800) HARBOR-1 or visit www.harbor place.com for details on the restaurants and shops within the three locations that make up Harborplace.

Civil War buffs will not want to miss touring the **USS *Constellation,*** the only surviving Civil War–era naval vessel and all-sail warship built by the navy. Events, reenactments, and tours are always going on aboard this 1,400-ton, 179-foot sailing sloop that was built in 1854 and now serves as a museum. Once a year, the USS *Constellation* departs its berth at Pier 1 for a journey to Fort McHenry and back, with cannon firing along the way. The cost to tour the Constellation is $10 for adults, $8 for seniors age 60 and older, and $5 for kids age 6 through 14. Military personnel and children age five and younger get to tour for free. Call (410) 539-1797 or visit www.constellation.org for more information.

No tour to Baltimore would be complete without visiting the **National Aquarium** (410-576-3800; www.aqua.org), which is located on Pier 3. This is Maryland's top tourist destination, with about 1.6 million visitors per year, and it's strongly recommended that you buy your tickets in advance of your visit. The aquarium includes an Atlantic coral reef tank that is home to more than 600 fish, a 225,000-gallon shark tank, an area filled with bottlenose dolphins, and a replica of an Amazon River rain forest. Tickets cost $21.95 for adults, $20.95 for seniors age 60 and older, and $12.95 for children age 3 to 11; children younger than age three are admitted for free.

A brick-lined promenade is perfect for walking around Inner Harbor, or you can hop aboard one of the blue and white water shuttles that transport travelers around the harbor as well as to nearby Little Italy, Fell's Point, Canton, and Fort McHenry. This is the oldest water-taxi service in the country, and you pay one price to ride the shuttles all day. Visit www.thewatertaxi.com or call (800) 658-8947 for details. If you'd like to take a cruise, **Spirit Cruises** (866–312–2469; www .spiritcruisesbaltimore.com) has a range of choices, including dinner, lunch, sunset, and moonlight options. A 75-minute narrated sightseeing tour and specialty tours are also available. They're located at 561 Light Street, adjacent to the **Maryland Science Center** (410-685-5225; www.mdsci .org), which has three floors of hands-on exhibits, a planetarium, and a five-story IMAX theater. Or you can play pirate aboard the Fearless, an interactive cruise that departs from Fells Point. Call (410) 800-4998 or visit www.clippercity.com for details.

A visitor's packet, maps, and useful information on other attractions at Inner Harbor and Baltimore can be obtained by contacting the Baltimore Visitor Center at (877) BALTIMORE or by visiting www.baltimore.org. Seeing the Orioles play baseball at Camden Yards or the Ravens play football at M&T Bank Stadium, visiting Fort McHenry or the Baltimore Civil War Museum, touring the distinct neighborhoods that make up Baltimore, and a plethora of other enjoyable excursions await you.

i One convenient place to park is the Gallery garage, which is under the Gallery and across from Harborplace. To get to the garage from Pratt Street, turn left onto Calvert Street and make an immediate right into the garage.

CITY ISLAND AND DOWNTOWN HARRISBURG

Harrisburg is the capital of Pennsylvania, and locals describe the city and its environs as the East Shore and the West Shore, which are divided by the Susquehanna River. Between the two shores sits **City Island**, which has been transformed from what used to be just a large parking area into an entertainment complex with food kiosks, picnic grounds, water golf, minor-league baseball, water sports, and more. The Island is located about 35 miles north of Gettysburg, and it's a snap to reach. Just travel US 15 north from Gettysburg and turn right at the light at the intersection of US 15 and Market Street in Camp Hill. (This is the second light after you pass the Camp Hill Shopping Mall on your left.) Follow Market Street through Camp Hill and Lemoyne, and stay in the right lane as you go through some S curves. At the next light take a right to head toward Harrisburg by crossing the Market Street Bridge; the entrance for City Island is about halfway across the bridge. At the stop sign at the end of the off-ramp, make a left to park closest to the activities. (Handicap parking is also to the left; follow the signs.)

Once you park the car, you can either climb the steps or walk along the ramp to the right of the steps under the overpass to begin your day of fun. Horse-drawn carriage rides are available at the stables straight ahead. Batting cages are available, and a train takes the little ones on a ride around the island. An oval paved walking track circles the Island, and you'll discover all the different activities available by following the path. The Harrisburg Senators play minor-league baseball at the Commerce Park field, and soccer and football games are held in the stadium behind the ballpark. An area to the right fronts the Susquehanna River, and you can enjoy a picnic along the banks of the river with food you bring or food you buy at the many kiosks that dot the area. This area also often features live entertainment, and there are a few shops to browse. The *Pride of the Susquehanna* paddle wheeler is located along the bank, and public cruises that last about 45 minutes depart throughout the day From Tuesday through Sunday. Dinner and special cruises are also available. Call (717) 234-6500 or visit www .harrisburgriverboat.com for more information.

Farther up the Island is an area especially for kids, with tot-size playground equipment, and you can rent Jet Skis at the marina that's also along this stretch of the island (there is another marina off the parking lots that are to the right when you enter City Island). Swimming and sunbathing are allowed at the far end of the island, and a water golf course is along the oval path as it starts to turn back toward your starting point. The minigolf course incorporates water on almost every hole, and this challenging course is a great way to see the river. Beyond the minigolf some hiking paths are available if you'd like to travel off the oval track into nature.

Once you fully explore the island, you may want to stroll across the walking bridge and discover some of the fun things to do in the city. Riverfront Park is along the Susquehanna on the city side, and there's a walking path and steps that you can take down to the riverfront. If you walk straight when you leave the walking bridge and turn left when you reach Second Street, you can discover a renovated area that is called **Restaurant Row** because of all the eating establishments and nightclubs that run north for blocks. If you continue on Walnut Street to Third Street and turn left, you will reach the **Capitol Complex,** where the Pennsylvania State Legislature resides. After admiring the architecture of the capitol and the surrounding buildings and maybe observing a session of the legislature, you can continue up Third Street to the **State Museum of Pennsylvania** (717-787-4980; www.statemuseumpa .org). This always-interesting museum covers all aspects of Pennsylvania history, and it's visited by 315,000 schoolchildren and adults annually. Among its many significant collections is the permanent exhibit "The Keystone of the Union," which interprets Gettysburg's role in the Civil War. Admission to the museum is free.

After you explore downtown, you can head back to your car by either going back the way you came or heading over to the river and walking the paved path that parallels the river all the way to the walking bridge.

For more information on City Island and other activities available in the capital city, call (717) 255-3004 or visit www.harrisburgpa.gov.

i The East Shore consists of the city of Harrisburg and communities to the east as far as Hershey, while the West Shore includes the communities west of the river to Carlisle. Although separated by only a river, some residents feel the shores are two different worlds, and many longtime residents don't even think to venture across the river to the other shore.

HERSHEYPARK

Milton S. Hershey, founder of the town of Hershey and Hershey Chocolate, opened Hersheypark in 1907, and this amusement park is still a major attraction of the area today. The park opens at 10:00 a.m., is open most nights during the summer till 10:00 or 11:00 p.m., and is located a little more than 50 miles north of Gettysburg. From Gettysburg travel north on US 15 to Route 581 East (the sign will say to 83 North). Route 581 becomes Interstate 83 as you cross the Susquehanna River, and the road eventually splits into I-83, U.S. Route 322, and Route 283. Follow the signs for US 322, which will take you to Hershey, where you pick up Route 39, also called Hersheypark Drive. The park is a few miles up Route 39, and there are plenty of signs to guide you.

The park has 65 rides, including 11 roller coasters, 5 water rides, and more than 20 kiddie rides. Games, live entertainment, paddleboats, a zoo, food, and shops round out the experience. Hersheypark is divided into the major theme areas of Comet Hollow, Founder's Circle, Midway America, Minetown, Music Box Way, Pioneer Frontier, and the Boardwalk at Hersheypark. The Boardwalk is the park's latest addition, and it features water attractions. Its latest roller coaster, Storm Runner, was added in 2004, and this

i You can pay a lot less for your fun day at Hersheypark by buying your tickets at a Giant Food Store, where tickets are deeply discounted. The nearest Giant is east of Lincoln Square off York Street. Call (717) 337-0017.

coaster goes from 0 to 72 mph in two seconds and intertwines with the park's monorail at two spots. Many of the coasters weave in and out of other rides. The Great Bear coaster intertwines with the Sooperdooperlooper roller coaster and the Coal Cracker water ride. Although you may love the wild rides, take time to ride the monorail and to visit the Kissing Tower, both of which give you a great view of the entire park. (The Kissing Tower is shaped like a giant Hershey's Kiss!) And check as you enter the park to see when the dolphin shows are—you definitely don't want to miss these entertaining creatures showing off their tricks.

A one-day admission in 2008 was $49.95 for those age 9 to 54, $30.95 for those age 3 to 8 and seniors age 55 to 69, and $19.95 for seniors age 70 or older; children age three and younger are admitted for free. Prices are reduced when buying tickets for multiple days or when entering the park later in the day. Admission includes a visit to **Zoo America,** an 11-acre walkthrough zoo with more than 200 animals representing five regions of North America. Visitors to Hersheypark almost always take a tour through **Chocolate World,** which is separate from Hersheypark but located right beside it. Entrance to Chocolate World is free, and you take a ride that explains how chocolate is made. Everyone receives a free sample of a Hershey's Chocolate product at the end of the tour, which lets you off at a huge shopping and dining area dedicated to all things chocolate.

A daily parking fee of $10 per vehicle is charged at Hersheypark. A tram service runs from the parking area to the park entrance approximately every 15 minutes during park hours. Before you get on the tram in the parking lot, look on a nearby light post to see in which section of the lot you're parked so you know where to get off the tram when leaving the park. If you have limited mobility but want to enjoy the park, the park rents wheelchairs and electric convenience vehicles (ECVs) on a first-come, first-serve basis. (We rented the electric scooters for my parents so they could enjoy the park with their grandkids, and it was the most enjoyable day the entire family ever had at the park—well worth the extra money.) The rental area is located behind the Tram Circle Group Sales Building. Families with children may bring in their own stroller or rent one inside the main entrance on a first-come, first-serve basis.

For more information call (800) HERSHEY or visit www.hersheypa.com. The Web site is extremely comprehensive, with details on rides, entertainment, shopping, and more within the park. You can even take some virtual rides! The site also covers area lodging, restaurants, entertainment, and other attractions.

ℹ **If you're leaving the park and plan to reenter later, be sure to have your hand stamped at the exit gate. Ticket stubs are not valid for reentry. Your parking ticket will allow you to reenter the parking lot upon your return.**

RELOCATION

People move to Gettysburg for all kinds of reasons, and two popular ones have perpetually been to enjoy the beauty of the area and to study the battlefield and the Civil War at leisure. Today there's a third reason that's becoming more and more prevalent—to get more house for the money while commuting to Baltimore or Washington for work. Gettysburg has become a bedroom community for those two metropolitan areas, and because of this, real estate is usually more expensive in the southern part of Adams County.

This bedroom-community effect has contributed to Adams County's being one of the fastest growing counties in the commonwealth. The 2007 Census estimate places the population at 100,779 while the 2000 census had the number at 91,292—a more than 10 percent increase. Housing developments are still springing up despite current difficult financial times for the real estate market, and most residents drive about 25 minutes to get to work. Unemployment statistics from the Pennsylvania Department of Labor and Industry for the year 2006 show that Adams County enjoys a low unemployment rate of 3.4 percent, much less than the Pennsylvania rate of 5.1 percent and the national rate of 4.6 percent. Of course, with the current financial crisis hitting all parts of America, those numbers are rising and they will probably continue to do so.

Gettysburg has always been a town of the "haves" and the "have-nots," and nowhere is this more discernible than when you look at the area real estate market. The average price for a home here is around $200,000, but executive homes can sell for $500,000, and many homes in planned housing developments range from $285,000 to $450,000. The average rent for a one-bedroom apartment is $450 to $600 per month, while a two- to three-bedroom apartment will cost you $600 to $950 a month. Renting a house that has three or more bedrooms averages $900 to $1500 per month. Although these costs may seem reasonable to some readers, many Gettysburg residents earn $7 per hour, and many jobs are seasonal. Affordable housing has become a major concern, and county officials have formed a task force to confront the issue. Still, Adams County as a whole continues to outpace the state in number of residents who own their own home, with 76.8 percent of county residents enjoying home ownership versus the state average of 71.3 percent.

Where you live has a profound effect on your day-to-day existence, and this chapter will cover neighborhoods in the surrounding area. Some basic community information is included, as are places to contact early in your relocation process. Information is also provided on the humdrum but necessary chores that accompany a move, including getting a new driver's license, registering your car, and registering to vote.

REAL ESTATE

When relocating to a new area, your best bet is to contact a real estate agent, and this is especially true in Gettysburg. Many developments have no identifying signage, so finding a particular neighborhood can be confusing for newcomers. Many of the homes are in rural settings and not part of any development, so you'll need an agent to coordinate your house hunting. (See the listings of real estate companies later in this chapter.) Renting before you buy so you get to know your new hometown is usually advised, but Gettysburg doesn't have an abundance of apartment complexes. Two complexes are the Devonshire Village Apartments south of town off Emmitsburg Road (717-334-8181) and the Gettysburg West Apartments west of town off Chambersburg Road (717-334-1600). Many people also rent downtown in houses that have been converted into apartments and on the floors above stores.

The neighborhoods around Gettysburg run the gamut from streets filled with mansions to modest homes on small streets. New developments meld with older communities, with most new housing starting around $300,000. Housing developments in the area have homes in the $200,000 to $300,000 range on average, but exceptions do exist. You'll pay considerably more if you look in two of the most desirable locations in town—the 3 blocks along Seminary Ridge across from the seminary and West and East Broadway Avenue by Gettysburg College, where prices reach into the millions. Also very desirable for those who can afford it is the development of Ridgewood, located north of town off Mummasburg Road, which is filled with an eclectic assortment of homes surrounded by acres of woods. At the other end of the spectrum are homes within the mobile home parks, which may sell for as low as $6,000 to $20,000. Prices for homes in rural settings vary widely, with location and the amount of acreage included affecting the asking price. Expect any home with a connection to the Civil War to automatically demand a higher price. Homes close to the Maryland line are currently in demand by commuters and are therefore also higher priced.

Within the borough of Gettysburg, you'll find a high proportion of attached homes, and in many parts of town, the downstairs are storefronts and the upstairs are apartments for rent. There's not an abundance of crime in the area,

i **The Adams County Newcomers Club meets on the fourth Monday of each month at 9:30 a.m. in the Eisenhower Room of the Adams County Library. Call (717) 337-2725 for more information.**

but like most places today, crime is increasing. One area that's considered a bit questionable is South Washington Street below Breckenridge Avenue, where drug activity and crime seem to go hand in hand.

But also at the southern end of town is the beautiful neighborhood of Colt Park, where there's a nice mix of old and new homes. Residents like that they can walk to the battlefield and many restaurants and attractions, and that Recreation Park and Gettysburg Hospital are nearby. Off Emmitsburg Road beside the Eisenhower Inn & Conference Center is Devonshire Village, with condos for rent and for sale. Farther away from town to the south is the gated community of Lake Heritage, which was established in the 1960s as a vacation-home community. Today it's a thriving residential area that has a nice range of homes usually priced according to how close they are to Lake Heritage, where residents can enjoy boating and other water activities.

Just outside of town to the east off Hunterstown Road is the residential community of Hunter's Crossing, where you'll discover newer homes that are nicely spaced out within the development. Off Hanover Street just east of its interchange with U.S. Route 15 is the neighborhood of Hazelbrook Hills, which has a good selection of homes in different price ranges.

Many developments are to the west of town. Along Chambersburg Road are the mobile home park of Lincoln Estates and the upscale townhome community of Foxridge. Housing developments off Herr's Ridge Road include the older community of Ridgeview, the homes of Canon Ridge, and the zero-lot homes within the community of Camelot Square. A zero-lot home is one where you own only the footprint of land your house occupies. Although these are single-family detached homes, the community works much as a condo or townhome development, with an association collecting fees for maintenance and upkeep of the common grounds. Also to the west of town but along Route 116 (Fairfield Road) are the developments of Woodcrest and Twin Lakes, both older communities with a good mix of homes. Woodcrest is across from the YWCA, and Twin Lakes is just a bit farther west. Twin Lakes has expanded over the years, and today there is Twin Lakes II and Twin Lakes West in addition to the original development.

At the northern end of town along Route 34, zero-lot homes can be found within the community of Roselawn, and the Meadows community has added condominiums to its development, which began in the 1990s. The Patriot's Choice development is filled with new homes, while the older community of Longview is filled with sprawling homes that command a great view. Off U.S. Business Route 15 just outside of town is

i Dave Ruff, one of the agents at Century 21, created and developed the Internet site www.gettysburgmarketplace. com, which lists Gettysburg-based businesses for free. The site holds a gold mine of information for visitors and residents alike, with links to many of the listed businesses.

Handy Numbers and Addresses

Gettysburg Hospital—147 Gettys Street; (717) 334-2121

Borough Police—59 East High Street; (717) 334-1168

Adams County Courthouse—111 Baltimore Street; (717) 334-6781

Borough Office—59 East High Street; (717) 334-1160

Post Office—115 Buford Avenue; (717) 337-3325

Adams County Public Library—140 Baltimore Street; (717) 334-5716

Adams County SPCA—11 Goldenville Road; (717) 334-8876

the Twin Oaks development, which was started in the 1960s and completed in the 1980s. Here you'll find a sprawling community with homes in an assortment of price ranges.

Real Estate Offices

CENTURY 21 NEIGHBORHOOD REALTY, INC.
344 Baltimore Street
(717) 334-9131, (800) 347-6834
www.century21neighborhood.com

This Century 21 office, like all Century 21 offices, is locally owned and operated. In September 2002 Roger Sprague purchased the firm and renewed a 10-year franchise agreement. Roger brought nine years of real estate experience to the franchise, including managing two other Gettysburg real estate offices, and he certainly knows the area—he was a dairy farmer in Adams County for 20 years. This Century 21 office has six agents in addition to Roger, and they deal in residential, commercial, and investment properties. One agent is dedicated full-time to finding tenants for investment properties and apartments and homes for renters. Century 21 Neighborhood Realty is a member of the Multiple Listing Services computer network and the National Association of Realtors.

COLDWELL BANKER BIGHAM, REALTORS®
121 Buford Avenue
(717) 334-7666
www.cbbigham.com
www.coldwellbanker.com

In business since 1955, this locally owned and independently operated company is the oldest continuously operating real estate firm in the area. The president and broker/owner of the company is Adams County native Barbara M. Hartman, who is the daughter of the company's deceased founder, William A. Bigham. In 1982 the company became a member of Coldwell Banker Residential Affiliates and changed its trade name to Coldwell Banker Bigham, REALTORS®. The company is licensed in both Pennsylvania and Maryland, and it provides a full range of real estate services, including residential and commercial/investment brokerage services, property management, appraisal services, and real estate consulting services.

Bigham's employs five agents besides the owner, and its philosophy is "Expect the Best." The company goal is not to necessarily be the largest in the area but to provide the highest possible level of service to clients and customers.

LONG & FOSTER REAL ESTATE, INC.
430 Baltimore Street
(717) 338-3406, (800) 667-2027
www.longandfoster.com

Sixteen agents are ready to assist you at this office of Long & Foster Real Estate, Inc., whose parent company, the Long & Foster® Companies, is the largest privately owned residential real estate and related financial services company in America. The states of Pennsylvania, Virginia, West Virginia, New Jersey, Maryland, Delaware, and North Carolina as well as the District of Columbia are serviced by Long & Foster offices, and the Gettysburg office handles the counties of York and Adams in Pennsylvania. The company works with residential, commercial, and rental properties, and relocation services and mortgage services are available.

i If you have a computer, ask your agent to implement the system that sends you daily e-mails that show houses for sale. The information comes from the Multiples Listings book, and this is an easy way to become familiar with the local real estate market.

PRUDENTIAL BOB YOST–SITES HOMESALE
1270 Fairfield Road
(717) 334-7636, (800) 383-3535
www.pruhomesaleservices.com

This is the largest realtor in the area, with more than 20 associates available to serve you. But this locally owned office hasn't lost its connection to the community because of its size. In 2008 agents distributed 2,000 American flags throughout the

county in celebration of July Fourth. Prudential Bob Yost–Sites Homesale handles residential, commercial, and rental properties, and this one-stop realtor also offers mortgage and title insurance services.

i *Homes & Land* is a free publication that is chock-full of local real estate companies showing you properties they have for sale. Pick up your copy at shops around town, on the Internet at www.homesand land.com, or by calling (800) 277-7800.

RE/MAX OF GETTYSBURG
18 Carlisle Street, Suite 300
(717) 338-0881, (800) 765-3280
www.gettysburgrealestate.com

Re/Max is a global real estate system of franchisee-owned and -operated offices, and throughout the network more than 100,000 agents do business in more than 50 countries in more than 50 languages. This Gettysburg franchise was established in 1995. The office offers residential, commercial, and rental services, and there are more than 20 agents available to help you find your new home. If possible, check out the main Re/Max Web site of www.remax.com. It offers great information, including the basics of buying or selling property, a glossary of real estate jargon, and mortgage tools that help you calculate how much house you can afford.

SOCIAL SERVICES

SOUTH CENTRAL COMMUNITY ACTION PROGRAMS, INC. (SCCAP)
153 North Stratton Street
(717) 334-7634, (800) 232-6562
www.sccap.org

Acting as an umbrella agency, SCCAP coordinates charitable programs in Adams County (and neighboring Franklin County) that help low-income individuals help themselves. At one place those in need can find access to a variety of programs that want to lend a hand. SCCAP is a private, nonprofit corporation that was established in April

1965, and its funding comes from federal, state, and local government, foundations, businesses, and individual donations. Programs that help you find day-care services and help you pay for them, that help you get a job, that help you keep your house up to code, and that help you with emergency assistance are just a few of the many programs SCCAP offers. The federal program Women, Infants, and Children (WIC), which helps families feed their children, is also run by SCCAP, as are the local food pantry and homeless shelter. The food pantry is open seven days a week at the same address as SCCAP, and the homeless shelter is located at 102 North Stratton Street.

UNITED WAY OF ADAMS COUNTY
123 Buford Avenue
(717) 334-5809
www.national.unitedway.org

This nonprofit organization delivers services to those in need and also provides links to local volunteers and businesses. Across America, there are approximately 1,300 community-based United Way organizations, and each is independent, separately incorporated, and governed by local volunteers.

VETERANS AFFAIRS OF ADAMS COUNTY
Union Square Building
23 Baltimore Street
(717) 337-9835, (888) 337-9835
www.va.gov

This local office of the Veterans Affairs can give you contact information and help you apply for veterans' benefits. It's staffed by one person and open on weekdays (closed for lunch from noon to 1:00 p.m.). Although its address is on Baltimore Street, its entrance is easily accessible from Middle Street.

COMMUNITY INFORMATION

GETTYSBURG ADAMS CHAMBER OF COMMERCE
18 Carlisle Street
(717) 334-8151
www.gettysburg-chamber.org

The Gettysburg Adams Chamber of Commerce began way back in 1919, and this is where new residents head to get vital information about the area. A relocation packet distributed by the chamber gives new or potential residents a good overview of Gettysburg and Adams County, and it's bursting with information on everything from top area employers to the median cost of a house in the area. Maps of Adams County, including an excellent map of Gettysburg, are available from the chamber, and telephone books are given to anyone who stops by the office for them. You can also pick up a community calendar of events open to the public in the upcoming year (the calendar is really comprehensive); school, church, and real estate information; lists of member clubs, organizations, banks, contractors, attorneys, and major employers; census information; and much, much more. The chamber is open Monday through Friday, and it's located within the first block off the square.

GETTYSBURG CONVENTION AND VISITORS BUREAU (CVB)
Wills House—first floor
8 Lincoln Square
(717) 334-6274, (800) 337-5015
www.gettysburg.travel

The Gettysburg CVB provides Gettysburg visitors and residents comprehensive information about area events. The official visitors guide distributed here is a compact booklet chock-full of information. You'll find listings for accommodations, restaurants, tours, attractions, shops, golf courses, and more along with excellent maps and a calendar of special events planned for the area. Brochures from area businesses are displayed at the office, and a very knowledgeable and pleasant staff is available to help with any questions you might have. The Gettysburg CVB also distributes an annual calendar of events at their office or by mail, as well as a quarterly newsletter titled *Destination Gettysburg,* which features events, packages, and activities in the area. The Gettysburg CVB should definitely be one of your first stops in town. The office is open daily.

Grocery Stores

Giant Food Stores
44 Natural Springs Road;
(717) 337-0017

Kennie's Market
217 West Middle Street;
(717) 334-2179

Weis Markets
735 Old Harrisburg Road;
(717) 337-1753

LICENSES AND REGISTRATIONS

Drivers' Licenses

IF THIS IS YOUR FIRST LICENSE

The State of Pennsylvania issues a learner's permit to residents at least 16 years old who have returned a completed physical form and paid the permit fee. The fee must be paid by check; no cash is accepted. You can pick up your permit and a booklet that gives you all the information you'll need to pass the license test at 59 North Fifth Street. This is also where you will take the tests for your license. The written exam is given from 8:30 a.m. to 4:15 p.m. on Wednesday and Friday, and the driving exam is given by appointment only on Wednesday and Friday.

IF YOU MOVED HERE FROM ANOTHER STATE

You are required to replace your out-of-state license with a Pennsylvania license within 60 days of moving to the state. To do so, head to 59 North Fifth Street on either a Wednesday or Friday with your current driver's license; your social security card, birth certificate, passport, or military ID; and a check for the fee (no cash is accepted). You must also present two forms of ID that provide your current Pennsylvania address (an electric bill, a telephone bill, etc.). If your out-of-state license has expired, you'll be required to take both the written and driving test.

IF YOU NEED TO GET YOUR LICENSE RENEWED

Every four years, you'll receive a camera card for a new photo license in the mail. For renewal of the license, you take the card to the License Photo Area at 59 North Fifth Street (717-334-0308). Hours are Tuesday, Wednesday, Friday, and Saturday from 8:30 a.m. to 4:15 p.m. and Thursday from 8:30 a.m. to 8:00 p.m.

Automobile Registration

Technically, you're required to register your car with the state within 30 days of moving to Pennsylvania, but most people begin this process once they acquire their Pennsylvania driver's license. To register your car, you'll need to fill out a Pennsylvania Auto Registration Form, which can be picked up at any notary public or at the AAA office at 1275 York Road (717-334-1155). You will need the car's out-of-state title, the vehicle mileage, proof of Pennsylvania insurance, and a legible pencil tracing of the Vehicle Identification Number (VIN). If you don't want to do a tracing, pick up an MV-1 form from the notary or AAA and take it to a state inspection mechanic to verify the VIN. The title fee is $22.50 for all vehicles, and the registration fee for passenger cars is $36.00. A new license plate is $10.

Voter Registration

You can vote in Pennsylvania public elections at age 18 if you have been a citizen of the United States for at least a month, you have resided in the state for at least 30 days before the election, and you are registered to vote.

Voter registration forms are available at all public libraries, municipal offices, and post offices throughout the state. The forms are also available at the Voter Registration Office at the Adams County Courthouse, 111 Baltimore Street (717-337-9832). The completed form can be mailed to or dropped off at the registration office. To vote in the state's primary elections, you must declare a party affiliation when registering. Registration closes 30 days before a primary or general election and opens 1 day after the election.

The League of Women Voters of Pennsylvania is a nonpartisan organization that disseminates information on voter registration, elections, national and state legislators, government agencies and services, and many more topics. Call (800) 692-7281 or visit their Web site at www.pa.lwv.org. The league has a branch in Adams County, which can be reached at (717) 334-7607.

WORSHIP

More than 100 houses of worship of all different Christian denominations can be found within Adams County. The Gettysburg area chamber of commerce's countywide roster of churches lists more than 35 churches with a Gettysburg address. Jewish synagogues, Muslim mosques, and Buddhist temples are not located within the county, but they can be found in Cumberland and Dauphin Counties to the north.

The area was settled by pioneers of German, Scotch, and Irish descent in the mid-1700s, and religion has always been an important part of the community. Reverend Alexander Dobbin, a leading early settler, headed a Presbyterian congregation, and the Gettysburg Lutheran Theological Seminary was established in 1826 by Samuel Simon Schmucker, a prominent American Lutheran. Schmucker also founded Pennsylvania College, now called Gettysburg College, in 1832. Christ Evangelical Lutheran Church (30 Chambersburg Street) was deeded in 1835, and its congregation formed in November 1836. Although it wasn't the first Lutheran congregation in Gettysburg, it was the first to use English rather than German as its exclusive language, and it is the oldest church in Gettysburg used continuously for worship. St. Paul AME Zion Church, at 269 South Washington Street, dates from 1835, and it's the oldest African-American congregation in the area.

When the Battle of Gettysburg began, churches in the area opened their doors to the wounded and became makeshift hospitals. The Historic Church Walking Tours feature eight town churches used in this way, and performances portray the events of those days through narratives, plays, and music. (For details on the Historic Church Walking Tours, see the Attractions chapter.) If you see a wayside marker outside a church, it's likely to describe the church's use during the battle. When President Lincoln visited Gettysburg to say a few words at the dedication of the National Cemetery, he attended services at the Presbyterian Church of Gettysburg, located at 208 Baltimore Street, and you can see the pew where he sat.

Religion is interwoven into many aspects of the local community. Many retirement and continuing-care centers are religiously affiliated, and there are many religiously affiliated schools throughout the area. Every Saturday about two pages of the *Gettysburg Times* newspaper are devoted to listing area churches and their services.

If you'd like to attend services on the battlefield, the Gettysburg Battlefield Summer Amphitheater services are held on Sunday at 8:00 a.m. rain or shine from the beginning of July to the end of the summer. The services are both interdenominational and ecumenical, and they're provided by the Gettysburg Ministerium. Offerings given during the service go to the Ministerium Transient Fund to help those in need. Outside services are also held at Caledonia State Park (see the State Parks and Public Lands chapter) and the National Shrine Grotto of Lourdes at Emmitsburg, Maryland (see the Attractions chapter).

EDUCATION AND CHILD CARE

A lmost from its very existence, Gettysburg has been a place of higher learning. Less than 45 years after the first settlers came to the area in 1734, the first classical school west of the Susquehanna River opened at the home of Alexander Dobbin, an Irish minister and community leader who had come to the area in 1773. He built his home in 1776, and today the Dobbin House serves up delicious food in an authentically restored building brimming with 18th-century atmosphere. (See the Close-up in the Restaurants chapter for more on the history of the Dobbin House.) Within 100 years from its beginnings, Gettysburg was also home to the Gettysburg Lutheran Theological Seminary (1826) and the Pennsylvania College, which is now known as Gettysburg College (1832).

Both the seminary and the college still exist today, and Gettysburg itself is a place where the history of the Civil War is studied in depth by tourists, scholars, lovers of history, and students of all ages. This history is an integral part of the area, and most public schools teach an entire course during sixth grade on the Civil War battle fought here and its aftermath. Students are required to learn the entire Gettysburg Address, not just the first few lines that most people are familiar with. This knowledge of Gettysburg and its historical significance is inspiring, and it infuses the area with a sense of pride.

The educational opportunities here are as varied as the area. A rural public school system shines with state-of-the-art technology, and arts and music are an integral part of a student's academic experience. An extension of the Harrisburg Area Community College has joined Gettysburg College and the Lutheran Theological Seminary as institutions of higher education located within Gettysburg. About 20 miles west of Gettysburg is the university of Mont Alto, an undergraduate extension campus of Penn State University. And less than 15 miles to the south is Mount St. Mary's College, located in Emmitsburg, Maryland. Back in Gettysburg, the YWCA runs an elderhostel for older adults that centers on the Battle of Gettysburg and the Civil War.

Families will also find many child-care options in the area. Some are franchises of national chains, others are private day cares, and still others are affiliated with church organizations. Both Gettysburg College and Gettysburg High School have centers at their facilities, and other centers are located throughout Gettysburg and the outlying areas.

PUBLIC SCHOOLS

In Pennsylvania, geographic areas are divided into boroughs and townships, and school districts draw their students from these areas. Adams County has a total of six public school districts, with an aggregate student population of almost 15,000 in the 2007–2008 school year.

The Gettysburg School District encompasses 185 square miles and includes students in the borough of Gettysburg and six surrounding townships. Total enrollment is around 3,500 students, and pupils are divided among four elementary schools, one middle school, and one high school. Each school has a library, and all classrooms are equipped with computers. Two of the elementary schools enroll students from kindergarten through third grade, one enrolls students in second and third grade, and the fourth elementary school enrolls students in fourth and fifth grades. Student-teacher ratios average 20:1 in the elementary schools, 13:1 in the middle school, and 14:1 in the high school. Among the many programs offered is the America Reads program, in which students from nearby Gettysburg College tutor students who need extra help. Extracurricular activities include music, art, and numerous clubs and organizations.

Students in the sixth through eighth grades attend Gettysburg Area Middle School. Activities available include Band-front, Intramurals, Knowledge Matters, and MATHCOUNTS programs, and there are clubs involving agriculture, art, mountain biking, skiing, writing, and other areas of interest. Sports include basketball, field hockey, football, track, wrestling, volleyball, and cheerleading. There is also a Bully Prevention Program, which has resulted in dramatically fewer bullying incidents since its implementation in 2001.

Gettysburg High School provides vocational/ technological education as well as traditional academic education. The school focuses on creating teams of teachers and students, developing

alternative education, integrating the curriculum, and restructuring the use of time. As of the 2003–2004 school year, Gettysburg High School is a Project 720 Implementation high school. Project 720 is a statewide initiative named for the number of days in a high school student's career, and it is designed to increase academic rigor for all students, provide educational opportunities, and create connections with postsecondary educational venues. It is working: More than 70 percent of graduates advance to higher educational opportunities.

See above for a listing of contact information for the Gettysburg School District and the other public school districts in Adams County.

PRIVATE SCHOOLS

Many Gettysburg-area private schools are quite small and religiously based. The schools included here enroll more than 100 pupils.

Adams County School Districts

Bermudian Springs School District
7335 Carlisle Pike, York Springs
(717) 528-4113
www.bermudian.org
Conewago Valley School District
130 Berlin Road, New Oxford
(717) 624-2157
www.conewago.k12.pa.us
Fairfield Area School District
4840 Fairfield Road, Fairfield
(717) 642-8228
www.fairfieldpaschools.org
Gettysburg School District
900 Biglerville Road
(717) 334-6254
www.gettysburg.k12.pa.us
Littlestown Area School District
162 Newark Street, Littlestown
(717) 359-4146
www.lasd.k12.pa.us
Upper Adams School District
161 North Main Street, Biglerville
(717) 677-7191
www.uasd.k12.pa.us

ADAMS COUNTY CHRISTIAN ACADEMY
1865 Biglerville Road
(717) 334-9177
www.adamscountychristian.org
The Adams County Christian Academy has about 120 students enrolled in prekindergarten through 12th grade. The school is coed and affiliated with the Baptist religion. The teacher-to-student ratio is 1:8.

DELONE CATHOLIC HIGH SCHOOL
140 South Oxford Street McSherrystown
(717) 637-5969
www.delonecatholic.org
This is the only Catholic high school within Adams County, and its student population comes from numerous local Catholic elementary schools. It enrolls more than 500 students and has a teacher-to-student ratio of 1:14.

ST. FRANCIS XAVIER SCHOOL
45 West High Street
(717) 334-4221
www.sfxs.org
This Catholic elementary school was established

in 1877, and about 280 students attend kindergarten through eighth grade here. Its staff consists of the Sisters of Mercy and Christian lay teachers, and enrollment is not limited to those of the Catholic faith. The teacher-to-student ratio is 1:21.

i Since 2002 Go-Sport Physical Therapy (16C Deatrick Drive; 717-337-3300) has held a speed and agility camp annually. The camp is for middle school and high school athletes who want to increase their speed and quickness. Students meet twice a week during the monthlong camp, which is usually held during July and August.

HIGHER EDUCATION

GETTYSBURG COLLEGE
300 North Washington Street
(717) 337-6000
www.gettysburg.edu

Samuel Simon Schmucker, a prominent American Lutheran who had founded the Lutheran Theological Seminary at Gettysburg in 1826, also founded Gettysburg College in 1832; today it covers 200 acres in the north end of town. Its beautiful campus is filled with stately buildings that fit perfectly with the town's Civil War history, even though the college predates the Civil War by about 30 years. It is situated less than a mile from the battlefield, and Pennsylvania Hall, the college's first building, served as a hospital for the wounded during the battle. More than 700 Union and Confederate soldiers were treated at Pennsylvania Hall, and in November 1863 Gettysburg College students were among the crowd that attended President Lincoln's short speech that would forever after be known as the Gettysburg Address. Another president, Dwight D. Eisenhower, spent a good deal of time at the college. He retired to Gettysburg after his presidency and wrote his memoirs in what is today the college's admissions office, now known as Eisenhower House. Gettysburg College is still a place where presidents like to visit; in 2000 President George

W. Bush delivered a speech to the Republican National Convention from Eisenhower House.

Today nearly 2,600 students attend this four-year liberal arts and science college, and the student population is pretty evenly split between men and women. About 90 percent of students live on campus, in more than 43 residence halls. The students come from 40 states and 35 countries, with the majority of students hailing from Pennsylvania, New Jersey, Maryland, Connecticut, and New York. About 75 percent of the student body receives some type of financial assistance, and need-based and merit-based aid is available. Students may choose from 41 majors, pursue interdisciplinary and self-designed majors, or complete one of several cooperative and dual-degree programs. Majors include those in the social sciences, the natural sciences, and the humanities, and study-abroad programs are also available. Faculty is composed of more than 190 full-time members, 95 percent of whom have a doctorate or the highest earned degree in their fields. Individualized teaching reigns at this small private school, with the student-to-faculty ratio at 11:1 and the average class size at 18 students. Gettysburg College is home to one of only 19 Phi Beta Kappa chapters in Pennsylvania, as well as honorary or professional societies in 16 academic areas. About a quarter of the students participates in 24 intercollegiate sports programs, and there are varied intramural and club activities available. There are also fraternities and sororities to join.

The college is an integral part of the town, and free community events are often held here, such as art exhibitions and artist receptions, musical performances, lectures, film showings, and planetarium shows. In addition, more than 1,400 students participate annually in community-service programs at the national, international, and regional level. Local and regional community-partnership projects include Big Brothers Big Sisters, after-school tutoring and mentoring of grade school students, volunteering at the community soup kitchen, working with the homeless, and working with children in inner-city Baltimore schools.

Programs that bond the students as a community are also available. First-year students can

Close-up

Famous Gettysburg College Alumni

Carson Kressley, one of the hosts of the Emmy-award-winning fashion makeover show *Queer Eye for the Straight Guy* and currently host of the makeover show *How to Look Good Naked,* received his bachelor's degree from Gettysburg College in 1991. He majored in management, was elected to Phi Beta Kappa, and was a member of the management club, the equestrian team, and Alpha Phi Omega. An accomplished horseman, Carson was a member of the U.S. team for the 1999 World Cup Equestrian Games in Capetown, South Africa, and the team took home a silver medal. Before *Queer Eye* Carson worked as division director of the U.S. Equestrian Federation. He then went on to work as associate director of retail advertising and then director of creative development for Polo Ralph Lauren. In addition to his TV show, Carson has written a book titled *Off the Cuff: The Essential Style Guide for Men and the Women Who Love Them*, and his movie credits include *The Perfect Man* and *The Year without a Santa Claus*.

Other Gettysburg alumni who have made a name for themselves are

Fred Fielding, who served on the 9/11 Commission and who, at one time, was thought to be "Deep Throat." He served as deputy to former White House counsel John Dean during the Nixon administration.

Ron Paul, a Republican congressman from Texas who was the 2008 Libertarian Party presidential nominee.

Eddie Plank, a native of Gettysburg who was inducted into the Baseball Hall of Fame for his pitching record.

Bruce S. Gordon, who sits on the board of directors of numerous companies, including CBS Corporation and Tyco International, who was the first business executive to head the NAACP.

Carol Bellamy, who served as a New York state senator and who was executive director of UNICEF from 1995 to 2005.

---

select a seminar that appeals to their interests, and students who choose the same seminar are housed together in theme residence halls, where they share living space and classroom experiences with others who have similar interests. There's the Culture House, the Civil War House, the Green House, the Sports History House, the Writing House, and many more theme houses. The Gettysburg Recreational Adventure Board (GRAB) is a popular program in which students enjoy weekend climbing, caving, kayaking, or backpacking excursions.

The academic achievements that can be attained here as well as the emphasis placed on developing each person as an individual have earned Gettysburg a reputation as a fine institu-

tion of higher learning. It is consistently ranked among the top 50 liberal arts colleges in *U.S. News & World Report*, ranking 49th in the 2008 report.

HARRISBURG AREA COMMUNITY COLLEGE–GETTYSBURG CAMPUS
731 Old Harrisburg Road
(717) 337-3855
www.hacc.edu/gettysburg
This branch campus of the Harrisburg Area Community College (HACC) was opened in September 1999. The school is located within the North Gettysburg Shopping Center, and 100 parking spaces in a designated area are reserved for students. The facility features a library, classrooms, three state-of-the-art computer laboratories, a hard-

ware repair lab to facilitate hands-on training in PC repair and testing, an Allied Health–equipped training classroom, a student multipurpose room, and offices for faculty and staff. A new expansion began in summer 2008 with plans to add a bookstore, a coffee shop, and more comfy space where students can gather. It will also expand the existing wireless Internet network and enhance classroom technology and lab equipment.

HACC employs an open-door admission policy, which allows high school graduates, GED recipients, and individuals 18 years or older to attend regardless of their educational background. The Gettysburg branch offers 23 associate degree, certificate, and diploma programs; credit and non-credit courses; and customized employee training programs for business, industry, and other organizations. Some of the associate degree programs are defined as transfer programs, geared toward students who plan to complete their education at a four-year college. Other associate degree programs are designated as career programs, and these are for students wishing to complete school with a two-year associate degree. About a third of the programs require taking some classes at the main campus in Harrisburg. A full range of student services are available at the Gettysburg campus, including placement testing, advising and counseling, financial aid, career planning, and student activities.

HACC–Gettysburg Campus has formed a partnership with the Adams County Tech Prep Consortium to develop industry-driven curriculums to guarantee local high school students a seamless secondary and postsecondary and technical education that can be completed in Gettysburg. Current programs include Allied Health technology, computer repair technology, and the culinary arts.

LUTHERAN THEOLOGICAL SEMINARY AT GETTYSBURG

61 Seminary Ridge
(717) 334-6286
www.ltsg.edu
Founded in 1826 by Samuel Simon Schmucker, a leading churchman in American Lutheran circles

(and founder of Gettysburg College in 1832), the Lutheran Theological Seminary at Gettysburg is the oldest continuing Lutheran seminary in the Americas. It was created to fill the specific need at the time for American-trained clergy. In 1832 the seminary moved from modest quarters in the center of town to its current 52-acre location on a ridge overlooking the borough of Gettysburg from the west. On July 1, 1863, the first day of the Battle of Gettysburg, the campus became a battleground and then the center of the Confederate line for two days. The cupola of the Old Dorm served as an observation tower first for Union and then for the Confederate officers. From that day and for two additional months, the rest of the building served as a hospital for the wounded from both sides. Three original buildings still stand at the seminary: Krauth House, Schmucker House, and Schmucker Hall.

The primary mission of the Lutheran Theological Seminary at Gettysburg (LTSG) is to prepare leaders for service in the Evangelical Lutheran Church in America as pastors, deaconesses, associates in ministry, and diaconal ministers. Two degree programs, the Master of Divinity and the Master of Arts in Ministerial Studies, serve as the academic foundation for that preparation. The seminary's Master of Arts in Religion program offers an opportunity for broad study in theological disciplines, while at the same time permitting specialization in one particular area of interest. The Master of Sacred Theology (STM) degree provides an opportunity for concentrated study in a given area of theological inquiry for persons who have completed a first theological degree or its equivalent. The Doctor of Ministry degree is received through the Eastern Cluster of Lutheran Seminaries, of which Gettysburg is a part. The seminary also offers a long list of one-day events and public lectures intended for broad audiences of both clergy and laypersons, and the Lay School of Theology has been held on campus each summer since 1963.

The student body numbers around 270 full- and part-time students, and there's a faculty of 18, plus another 10 part-time, adjunct, and distinguished visiting teachers. Students travel from 30 states and another half dozen countries to study theology here. Even though most students are members of the Evangelical Lutheran Church in America (ELCA), a growing number of students have religious backgrounds from other Christian traditions.

The Seminary Ridge Historic Preservation Foundation is in the process of creating an interpretive walking tour on Seminary Ridge. The 1-mile path will be for pedestrians and bicyclists, and there will be three primary entry points to the path and more than 10 wayside stops along the way. The walkway will focus on the importance of the battle on Seminary Ridge on the first day of the Battle of Gettysburg and the religious history of the seminary. The foundation raised money for the pathway by selling bricks engraved with the names of alumni, friends, and notable former residents of the ridge. Archaeological studies of the proposed pathway area have been completed, and the money has been raised. The foundation is now securing final approvals on the loop and hopes to have the path operational by 2010. For information on the foundation or its projects, call the seminary at (717) 334-6286.

MOUNT ST. MARY'S UNIVERSITY
16300 Old Emmitsburg Road
Emmitsburg, MD
(301) 447-6122
www.msmary.edu

Mount St. Mary's University was founded in 1808 by Fr. John Dubois, and its 1,400-acre campus is located less than 15 miles south of Gettysburg off U.S. Route 15. This Catholic liberal arts university shares its space with Mount St. Mary's Seminary, the second-largest seminary in the country, and the National Shrine Grotto of Lourdes, America's oldest replica of the Lourdes shrine in France. (For more on the National Shrine Grotto of Lourdes, see the Attractions chapter.) The Mount is home to about 1,700 undergraduate and 500 graduate students. The student body men-to-women ratio is approximately 6:4, and about 60 percent of undergraduate students come from the state of Maryland. The rest of the student population hails from 28 states and approximately 10 foreign

countries. The undergraduate student-to-faculty ratio is 14:1, and the average class size is 20. More than 95 percent of students receive financial aid.

The university offers 40 undergraduate majors, 5 postgraduate degrees, and the chance to study abroad in England, Italy, France, Costa Rica, Ireland, and Spain. In 2008 it made *U.S. News & World Report*'s top college list for the 13th consecutive year. Mount St. Mary's is one of the few universities where undergraduate students are guaranteed four entire years of on-campus housing. Eighty-five percent of undergraduates take advantage of this and live on campus in traditional or apartment-style residence halls or theme homes. Theme homes include Wellness Housing, the Women in Science floor, and Special Interest Housing. Wellness Housing is for students who wish to live in a substance-free (alcohol, drugs, tobacco) residence, and the Women in Science floor is for female residents majoring in or considering a major in science, math, or computer science. Special Interest Housing is for students who share a common interest. All undergraduate students may apply to live in Wellness Housing or on the Women in Science floor, and sophomores, juniors, and seniors who maintain a minimum grade point average of 2.5 may apply to live in a "Make Your Own" house or floor.

Students at the Mount have lots of activities to pick from, and 80 percent of students stay on campus on the weekends. There are 19 varsity sports to participate in as well as club sports, a full intramural program, and more than 70 clubs. The campus schedule is also full with dances, concerts, and guest lecturers.

PENN STATE MONT ALTO
1 Campus Drive, Mont Alto
(717) 749-6000, (800) 392-6173
www.ma.psu.edu

Both the Civil War and the area's iron furnaces played a role in the creation of a school at Mont Alto. Col. George Wiestling came to Mont Alto in 1864 after his medical discharge from the Union army. As a shareholder in the Mont Alto Iron Company and its last ironmaster, Wiestling lived here during the waning years of the iron furnaces, which converted local iron ore into pig iron. During peak production the fires of an iron furnace would use up to an acre of forest in a day, and the forests of South Mountain were clear-cut on a 20- to 25-year cycle to feed the demand. (For more on the many iron furnaces that were in the area, see the Close-up in the State Parks and Public Lands chapter.) All the clear-cutting eventually took its toll on the forest around the Mont Alto Furnace, as it did on the forests throughout Pennsylvania. After Wiestling's death the state purchased his estate as part of public use lands for reforestation.

Wiestling's abode became the site of the Pennsylvania State Forest Academy, a school devoted to the study of forestry and the reforestation of the state of Pennsylvania. The school opened in 1903 with an enrollment of 13 at the site of the present-day Mont Alto campus, becoming the only state-established and -operated forestry school in the nation. The Pennsylvania State Forest Academy merged with Penn State (then the Pennsylvania State College) in 1929; academy students protested, feeling Penn State's forestry curriculum was inferior to theirs. Mont Alto served as Penn State's forestry campus, and students completed the first year of their four-year degree here until 1942. The campus was closed due to World War II and reopened in 1946. Penn State Mont Alto became a Commonwealth Campus in 1963, offering the first one or two years of many Penn State degrees, as well as some associate degrees (including forest technology). In 1997 Mont Alto joined Penn State's Commonwealth College and began offering bachelor's degrees.

Today Penn State Mont Alto offers the first two years of study for more than 160 Penn State bachelor-degree programs, and 5 bachelor's degrees or 8 associate degrees may be attained while taking all classes at the Mont Alto campus. Bachelor's degree programs are in business, nursing, human development and family studies, and English. Two-year associate degree programs are in forest technology, business administration, nursing, physical therapy, occupational therapy,

human development and family studies, and letters, arts, and sciences. Enrollment numbers around 1,100 students, with a student-to-faculty ratio of 17:1 and an average class size of 24 students. Mont Alto is one of only 10 Penn State campuses to offer on-campus housing, with three residence halls that can accommodate 440 students on the campus's 91 wooded acres. Varsity sports include basketball, tennis, golf, soccer, volleyball, softball, cheerleading, and cross-country. Club sports and intramural sports are also offered.

CONTINUING EDUCATION

ELDERHOSTEL
YWCA of Gettysburg & Adams County
909 Fairfield Road
(717) 334-9171
www.ywcagettysburg.org

The first elderhostels in the United States began in 1975 on a few college and university campuses in New England. Then, as now, they were dedicated to providing high-quality and affordable educational opportunities to older adults. At Gettysburg the elderhostel program is put on with the association of the YWCA of Gettysburg, and the Gettysburg battlefield serves as the campus. Rather than staying at a college dormitory, accommodations are at the Historic Gettysburg Hotel, a premier hotel located on Lincoln Square (see the Hotels, Motels, and Resorts chapter).

Elderhostel offers a wide array of programs throughout the United States. Some are held entirely at Gettysburg while others include Gettysburg as part of a longer itinerary. The Gettysburg elderhostel programs focus on the battlefield, the surrounding area, and Civil War–related subjects. Stays usually are for three or five days. Grandparents may want to check out the program that allows them to bring grandchildren along on their learning experience. There's also a service program where participants work on the preservation of the Eisenhower National Historic Site.

CHILD CARE

CHILD CARE INFORMATION SERVICES (CCIS)
153 North Stratton Street
(717) 334-7634, (800) 232-6562
www.sccap.org
This service will supply you with listings of available child-care providers in the area. It also provides subsidies for day-care services for lower-income caretakers. The listing of day-care providers is available to anyone, regardless of income level, and it contains a wealth of useful information, including names, addresses, hours, curriculums, fees, and more. Child Care Information Services (CCIS) is one of the programs of the South Central Community Action Programs, Inc. (SCCAP), which coordinates charitable programs in Adams County that help low-income individuals help themselves. (For more on SCCAP, see the Relocation chapter.)

Day Cares and Preschools

Following are just a few of the many day cares and preschools that operate in the area. The list you receive from CCIS will also include names of caregivers who operate within their homes, but those included here are centers that operate at a place of business. Many of the centers participate in subsidy programs, so be sure to ask about available financial assistance.

CHRIST LUTHERAN NURSERY SCHOOL
44 Chambersburg Street
(717) 334-6532
Preschool education is offered here for children age three through five from September through May. The preschool program for children age three or four meets on Tuesday and Thursday mornings from 9:00 a.m. to noon. Children age four and five attend a prekindergarten program held on Monday, Wednesday, and Friday from 9:00 a.m. to noon. Both programs are sponsored by the Christ Evangelical Lutheran Church, and scholarships are available.

GETTYSBURG HIGH SCHOOL PRESCHOOL
1130 Old Harrisburg Road
(717) 334-6254, ext. 6149
This preschool is part of the school district's vocational child-care education program, and it has its own private entrance at the high school. It operates two sessions, a fall session that runs 9:00 to 10:10 a.m. from mid-October to early January and a spring session that runs 8:00 to 10:10 a.m. from late January to mid-May. Monday and Wednesday are reserved for children age three and four, while children age four and five are welcomed on Tuesday and Thursday.

GETTYSBURG'S GROWING PLACE
142 Constitution Avenue
(717) 337-8211
www.gettysburg.edu
Gettysburg's Growing Place is managed by Hildebrandt Learning Centers (HLC), which operates numerous child-care centers in Pennsylvania. Located at Gettysburg College, the day care is open Monday through Friday 6:30 a.m. to 6:00 p.m., and after-school, early-dismissal school-day, and full-year day care are available. The program enrolls newborns to children age nine, and it offers a multichild discount.

HEAD START
705 Old Harrisburg Road
(717) 337-1337
Head Start is a preschool program that offers a wide range of services to both children and their families, including educational, health, nutritional, and social services. The program is open to three-, four-, and five-year-olds who come from income-eligible families or who have a disability or special need. Services are offered during the regular school year on a part-day or full-day basis, with part-day classes running from 9:00 a.m. to 1:00 p.m. and full-day classes operating from 8:30 a.m. to 3:00 p.m.

LEARNING TREE CHILD CARE
Gettysburg Lutheran Retirement Village
1075 Old Harrisburg Road
(717) 334-6204
www.lutheranscp.org
This day care is affiliated with Lutheran Social Services, and it's located in the nursing-center building of Gettysburg Lutheran Retirement Village. Activities often include visits with the residents who live at the retirement village. Learning Tree is open Monday through Friday 6:00 a.m. to 5:30 p.m. and offers full-year day care. Newborns to children age five are eligible for the program.

ST. JAMES LUTHERAN CHURCH
109 York Street
(717) 334-7171
Open Monday through Friday 6:30 a.m. to 5:30 p.m., the program at St. James offers after-school, before-school, early-dismissal school-day, school-holiday, snow-day, and full-year day care. Applications are accepted for newborns to children age 12, and a multichild discount is available.

WEE CARE LEARNING CENTER
75 Springs Avenue
(717) 334-7634
Wee Care is open Monday through Friday 6:30 a.m. to 6:00 p.m. and offers after-school, before-school,

early-dismissal school-day, school-holiday, snow-day, and full-year day care. Enrollment is open to preshool children 18 months old to students in the fifth grade, and employee and early-payment discounts are available.

YWCA OF GETTYSBURG & ADAMS COUNTY
909 Fairfield Road
(717) 334-9171
www.ywcagettysburg.org
The day-care center is one of many programs held at the YWCA. (See the Recreation chapter for more on the YWCA.) It's open Monday through Friday 6:30 a.m. to 6:00 p.m. and offers after-school, before-school, early-dismissal school-day, some school-holiday, snow-day, and full-year day care. The program accepts infants from 6 weeks old to children age 12.

YWCA OF GETTYSBURG & ADAMS COUNTY
Commerce Park Child Care Center
1400 Proline Place
(717) 334-7150
Now the YWCA has a day care on the eastern as well as the western end of Gettysburg. Located in Commerce Park, this center is also open Monday through Friday 6:30 a.m. to 6:00 p.m., and it offers the same services as listed for the YWCA above.

HEALTH CARE AND WELLNESS

Although it's a rural community, Gettysburg has a complete system of health-care services. It has one of the two hospitals located within Adams County (the other is Hanover Hospital) within its borough, and WellSpan, the hospital's parent company, offers integrated health services throughout south central Pennsylvania and northern Maryland. Home-care services are available to give people a bit of help so they can stay in their homes, and health-care centers offer medical and rehabilitation services.

HOSPITALS AND HEALTH CENTERS

BREAKTIME MASSAGE
153 Carlisle Street
(717) 253-0836
www.breaktime-massage.com

This spa's slogan is "Take a Break and De-stress," and owner Steve Ayton helps you do just that through massage, which has proven effective in relieving muscle spasms, pain, and discomfort as well as everyday stress. Steve offers a variety of massages that range from a chair massage that involves no oils or creams to a full-body massage using smooth heated stones. There are specific massages tailor-made for pregnant women and sport enthusiasts, and face toning is also offered. Couples may have their massages in the same room if they wish. Steve graduated from the Pennsylvania Myotherapy Institute in November 2006 after completing a 700-hour massage-therapy program, and he is a member of the Associated Bodywork and Massage Professionals.

GETTYSBURG HOLISTIC HEALTH CENTER
2311 Fairfield Road
www.GettysburgHolisticHealthCenter.net

Located about 3 miles west of town, practitioners at this health center provide services related to natural health care and natural healing. The mantra here is that the client's emotional, physical, and spiritual health is always of the utmost importance. The center offers yoga, integrative medicine, acupuncture, therapeutic massage, and counseling services in a serene, rural setting. Although they share a building and a common outlook on holistic healing, each practitioner runs an independent operation. The Sacred Lotus Yoga Studio located within the center is run by Lynn Roby, who follows the Kripalu methodology of yoga. Lynn is director and owner of the center as well as one of the center's two counselors. The other counselor is Stacy Sechrist, and together Lynn and Stacy have 30 years of experience helping others. You can call Lynn at (717) 338-9777, and Stacy at (717) 752-5524.

Dr. Christine Sheridan practices integrative medicine at the center. She is board certified in both family practice and integrative holistic medicine and focuses on providing preventive care to her patients. Therapeutic massages are given at the center by Nancy Hill. Nancy specializes in deep-tissue massage, Swedish massage, stone therapy, craniosacral therapy, lomi lomi massage, and Reiki I and II. She may be contacted at (717) 334-5140. Ted O'Brien is a Pennsylvania-licensed acupuncturist, and he also writes the "Holistic Living" column for the Gettysburg Times newspaper. Ted has worked with hundreds of patients using acupuncture and Chinese herbs and treating mostly pain-related disorders, and he can be reached at (717) 586-7044. Dr. Len Maza, a chiropractic doctor, joined the staff in January 2006.

President Lincoln was suffering from a mild case of smallpox when he delivered the Gettysburg Address.

GETTYSBURG HOSPITAL
147 Gettys Street
(717) 334-2121
www.wellspan.org

Gettysburg Hospital has been serving the community for more than 80 years. Today it is a 99-bed acute- and emergency-care facility run by WellSpan Health, a community-based, not-for-profit organization that has more than 40 locations providing health and wellness services in south central Pennsylvania and northern Maryland. The hospital is located southwest of the square, surrounded by neighborhoods and the Recreational Park on Long Lane. The grounds include a medical building and the Gettysburg Hospital Heart Center, which offers patients cutting-edge diagnostics, access to state-of-the-art treatment, and comprehensive cardiac rehabilitation. The heart center also has a program that's especially designed to address the unique needs of women with heart-related health issues. Besides acute care and heart care, Gettysburg Hospital also provides the area's only Transitional Care Center, a Medicare-certified skilled nursing facility for patients who have been discharged from the hospital but are not quite well enough to go home on their own. Residents in the 19-bed center receive a number of medical and rehabilitative services to help them return to an independent lifestyle as quickly as possible. The Transitional Care Center also provides adult respite care on a short-term (3 to 13 days) basis.

Gettysburg Hospital Rehab offers comprehensive inpatient and outpatient rehabilitation services that provide treatment, exercise, and education for injuries and functional impairment. Physical, occupational, and speech therapy are offered. Inpatient and outpatient care is given within the hospital, while the WellSpan Health Center on Chambersburg Road offers only out-patient care. This center at Herr's Ridge features a warm-water aquatic therapy pool and certified aquatic therapist.

A sleep disorders lab is also housed at Gettysburg Hospital. It consists of two patient-friendly sleep rooms with bathroom and shower and a dedicated control room. More information on the sleep lab is available at (717) 337-4482. The hospital is justly proud of its maternity center, where you can choose to have a physician or a midwife deliver your baby. Childbirth classes and sibling-preparation programs are also offered, and family members can view a picture of your new baby at the hospital Web site's online nursery.

| i | The first hospital within Adams County opened in March 1921 and was called the Anne W. Warner Hospital. Total cost to equip the hospital, now known as Gettysburg Hospital, was $30,000. |

Gettysburg Pharmacies

CVS Drug Store—1275 York Road; (717) 337-2812; open Monday through Saturday 8:00 a.m. to 9:00 p.m. and Sunday 9:00 a.m. to 5:00 p.m.

Laslow's Pharmacy—6 Springs Avenue; (717) 337-0881; open Monday through Friday 9:00 a.m. to 6:00 p.m. and Saturday 9:00 a.m. to noon (closed on Sunday)

Giant Food Stores Pharmacy—44 Natural Springs Road; (717) 337-0585; open Monday through Friday 9:00 a.m. to 9:00 p.m., Saturday 9:00 a.m. to 6:00 p.m., and Sunday 10:00 a.m. to 4:00 p.m.

Rite Aid Discount Pharmacies—236 West Street; (717) 334-6447; open Monday through Saturday 9:00 a.m. to 6:00 p.m. and Sunday 10:00 a.m. to 6:00 p.m.

Wal-Mart Pharmacy—1270 York Road; (717) 334-1313; open Monday through Friday 9:00 a.m. to 9:00 p.m., Saturday 9:00 a.m. to 7:00 p.m., and Sunday 10:00 a.m. to 6:00 p.m.

The hospital is well equipped for visitors also, with a cafeteria on the ground floor that's open till 6:15 p.m. and a snack bar and gift shop located just off the main lobby that's open till 7:00 p.m. With the exception of Pediatrics and Maternity, children younger than 12 years of age are not permitted to visit unless special permission is given from the patient's physician.

STATE HEALTH CENTER
424 East Middle Street
(717) 334-2112

This is one of 68 health centers throughout the state run by the Pennsylvania Department of Health. The department implements its public health programs through the center, with the goal of protecting and improving the health of Pennsylvanians and visitors to the state. The clinic part of the center conducts childhood and adult immunizations, HIV testing and counseling, and tuberculosis treatment and management. Programs on health education and the prevention of injuries and disease are also available, and the center also handles communicable disease reporting and investigation. The center is open weekdays, and you should call for an appointment if you need the services of the clinic.

WELLSPAN HEALTH CENTERS
820 Chambersburg Street
450 South Washington Street
www.wellspan.org

The center on Washington Street is across from the hospital, and many women-focused health services are available here. A variety of doctor's groups dedicated to women's issues have their offices in the building, as does Gettysburg Hospital Women's Imaging Services. Women in need of a mammogram, a breast biopsy, or a bone density test can have their tests done here. The other center is out by Herr's Ridge and houses an internal medicine practice (717-338-3285) and the Gettysburg Hospital Rehab/Aquatic Center (717-337-4206), which offers massages as well as outpatient rehabilitation services.

REFERRAL SERVICES
WELLSPAN HEALTH SOURCE
(717) 851-3500, (800) 840-5905

This service imparts information on the services provided by all of WellSpan Health's various organizations. WellSpan Health can register you for a variety of health and wellness classes and provide referrals to physicians on staff at Gettysburg Hospital who are accepting new patients.

HOME CARE
COMFORT KEEPERS
2819 York Road
(717) 337-1409, (800) 207-4693
www.comfortkeepers.com

Comfort Keepers is a national network that has franchises in 47 states. The Gettysburg location is a satellite office of the franchise that's located in Fayetteville, about 20 miles west of Gettysburg. More than 80 caregivers are employed by the franchise, which has been in business since 2000. Nonmedical in-home care is provided, and services include companionship, light housekeeping, transportation, meal preparation, grocery shopping and errand running, personal-care assistance, bathing assistance, walking assistance, medication reminders, and help for clients needing to get to appointments. Most clients are fairly mobile, and Comfort Keepers rarely assists individuals who are bed bound. Caregivers are employed by the company, not independent contractors, so clients do not have to deal with paying one fee to the agency and one fee to the actual caregiver. Comfort Keepers also screens all caregivers, and the franchise and the caregivers are fully insured. All care is provided either at the client's home or assisted-living facility at times requested by the client, and the client determines how much care he or she needs. A minimum of 3 hours up to the day's entire 24 hours may be scheduled, and schedules are made up weekly to allow flexibility.

LUTHERAN HOME CARE SERVICES INC.
1075 Old Harrisburg Road
(717) 334-6208
www.lutheranscp.org

Lutheran Home Care Services provides a wide range of medical and nonmedical services delivered in the comfort of your home, whether "home" is a private residence or an assisted-living facility. Home-support services range from a few hours of help to 24-hour care, on a short- or long-term basis. Help is given with dressing and bathing, preparing meals, housekeeping and laundry, grocery shopping and errands, transportation, companionship, lab services, medication box fills, and a variety of other services, including respite care. For complete peace of mind, a home telemonitoring service is also available. By teaming with HomMed, the nation's leading provider of home telemonitoring equipment, Lutheran Home Care Services can collect vital signs and monitor clients every day—from the comfort of the client's home. The telemonitoring system is about the size of a clock radio, and each day a gentle, friendly voice guides the client through the simple procedure to collect the vital signs (weight, temperature, and blood sugar). The client is then asked up to 10 questions about his or her condition that can be answered by pressing a yes or no button on the monitor. The monitor automatically transmits the data via telephone connection to the offices of Lutheran Home Care Services, where it is reviewed daily by a nurse. For clients with other monitoring needs, medical devices and attachments such as a spirometer, glucose meter device, and more are available.

VISITING ANGELS
18 Carlisle Street, Suite 105
(717) 337-0620
www.visitingangels.com

Visiting Angels is a national network of franchised nonmedical senior home-care agencies whose goal is to help elderly and older adults continue to live in their homes rather than move to nursing homes or assisted-living facilities. They will also tend to your nonmedical needs if you're in an assisted-living facility and realize you need some help with daily-living activities. This local Visiting Angels franchise is owned by John Palone, who also runs an office in Carlisle, and it's one of 250 franchises of Visiting Angels operating across America. Living-assistance services provided include hygiene assistance, meal preparation, light housework, companionship, errand running and shopping, and respite care. Caregivers are employed by the franchise, and they are licensed and bonded. A unique feature of Visiting Angels is that the client gets to select his or her caregiver. The agency matches your needs to the best possible caregiver, and the caregiver is not assigned until you meet and approve the person. Caregivers are given temporary or long-term assignments, and they're available on weekends and holidays. You can schedule care in your home for just a few hours up to 24 hours per day, and the schedule is flexible to allow for clients' changing needs.

VISITING NURSES ASSOCIATION (VNA) HOME HEALTH
39 Fifth Street
(717) 334-1490
www.wellspan.org

VNA Home Health is part of the WellSpan Health system, and it offers medical services in the comfort and privacy of a patient's home. Services are available for patients of all ages, including postpartum mothers and children, and include skilled nursing care, home health aides, physical therapy, speech therapy, respiratory therapy, IV therapy, patient education, and more. Medicare, Medicaid, and most private insurances are accepted as payment.

RETIREMENT

Seniors have a wealth of programs and activities available to them in the Gettysburg area. Most area attractions offer special admission pricing, and many local restaurants also discount meals for seniors. In this area age is something to be respected, and elderly wisdom is passed along and cherished. A good number of resident seniors were not born in the area. They decided to relocate here for sundry reasons, with the area's beauty, relaxed pace, and wealth of history being three main incentives. Many seniors spend the majority of their time studying the battlefield and the Civil War at their leisure. Recreational opportunities are plentiful around Gettysburg, and active seniors can spend their days golfing, horseback riding, and fishing (see the Recreation chapter). Activity for the mind can be found at the area colleges and the elderhostel program held here that studies the Battle of Gettysburg (see the Education and Child Care chapter).

If you're in the area long enough, you're bound to see the buses of the Adams County Transit Authority on the roads, dropping off and picking up seniors as they go about their daily lives. This is just one of the many low- or no-cost programs available to seniors, and the Adams County Office for Aging runs a dynamic agency that can give you all kinds of information on senior programs and senior-related issues. This agency also runs the area senior centers, where seniors can always find companionship and activities.

The Gettysburg area also boasts numerous retirement communities and nursing homes, and many have a range of options to suit each person's independence level. In short, there's plenty here to occupy your time and keep you engaged in the community, and support systems are in place to help you deal with the health issues that come along with age.

SENIOR AGENCIES AND SERVICES

ADAMS COUNTY OFFICE FOR AGING (ACOFA)
318 West Middle Street
(717) 334-4715, (800) 548-3240
www.acofa.org
ACOFA, one of 52 agencies on aging located throughout Pennsylvania, is a private, not-for-profit operation dedicated to providing assistance to and advocacy for older people. They offer a wide range of services to seniors age 60 and older. Some of the services are free while others are billed on a sliding-fee scale, where seniors pay a portion of the fee for the services based on monthly income. And donations are always welcome!

Services available range from helping seniors fill out health insurance and government forms to providing help with everyday activities, such as meal preparation, bathing, dressing, and light housekeeping. ACOFA also runs the senior centers, delivers hot meals to homebound seniors through the Meals on Wheels program, and provides domiciliary care for adults who can't live independently. Seniors can also borrow limited medical equipment for a short time, such as canes, walkers, and shower benches, from the agency. In short, if you're a senior and you have a question about a service or a problem you need help with, ACOFA is the place to call. The staff is extremely knowledgeable about senior issues and who provides what services to seniors throughout the county.

Adams County Senior Centers

ACOFA runs seven senior centers in Adams County. Open to anyone age 60 or older, each operates on a part-time basis, either four or five days per week. Each center serves a hot meal, and games, conversation, exercise programs, health screenings and programs, educational and volunteer opportunities, trips, and much more are available. Senior-center staff will work with the Adams County Transit Authority (ACTA) to get seniors to and from the center. There's no charge to participate in center activities, but donations are gladly accepted.

East Berlin Senior Center
East Berlin Community Center
Fourth Street and North Avenue, East Berlin
(717) 259-9630
Open Monday through Thursday 9:00 a.m. to 1:00 p.m.

Fairfield Area Senior Center
St. John Lutheran Church
13 East Main Street, Fairfield
(717) 642-6523
Open Monday through Friday 10:00 a.m. to 2:00 p.m.

Gettysburg Senior Center
Harold Court
142 North Stratton Street
(717) 334-5012
Open Monday through Friday 9:00 a.m. to 1:00 p.m.

Littlestown Senior Center
10 Locust Street, Littlestown
(717) 359-7743
Open Monday through Friday 8:30 a.m. to 2:00 p.m.

McSherrystown Senior Center
201 South Third Street, McSherrystown
(717) 632-7998
Open Monday through Friday 9:00 a.m. to 1:00 p.m.

Upper Adams Senior Center
2950 Table Rock Road, Biglerville
(717) 677-6370
Open Monday through Friday 9:00 a.m. to 2:00 p.m.

York Springs Senior Center
Lion's Club Building
Main Street, York Springs
(717) 528-8921
Open Monday through Thursday 9:00 a.m. to 1:00 p.m.

ADAMS COUNTY TRANSIT AUTHORITY (ACTA)
Rear 257 North Fourth Street
(717) 337-1345, (800) 830-6473
www.adamstransit.org

The ACTA provides transportation throughout the county for seniors, and the fare depends on the age of the rider, the rider's income level, and the purpose and distance of the trip. Trips to medical appointments, senior centers, grocery stores, and banks are usually free for seniors age 60 or older. All subsidized transportation requires you to verify your qualifications for a particular program, so you need to call ACTA or the Adams County Office for Aging (see the listing within this chapter) for information before you begin to use the transportation. Reservations for your trip must be made by 11:00 a.m. the day before transportation is needed. Service for ambulatory seniors is available 24 hours a day, 7 days a week in the Gettysburg area. Residents who live in the Gettysburg area who require the use of a wheelchair can have transportation provided at various times Monday through Friday. Rides in other parts of the county are usually available from 6:00 a.m. to 6:00 p.m. on weekdays only, but times are limited in some outlying areas. If you use a wheelchair or live outside the Gettysburg area, ACTA suggests you call them to check on transportation availability before you schedule an appointment. The ACTA is closed and does not provide transportation on New Year's Day, Good Friday, Memorial Day, Independence Day, Labor Day, Thanksgiving and the day after Thanksgiving, and Christmas.

NURSING HOMES AND RETIREMENT COMMUNITIES

BRETHREN HOME COMMUNITY
2990 Carlisle Pike, New Oxford
(717) 624-2161, (888) 624-8242
www.brethrenhome.org

This nonprofit, faith-based continuing-care retirement community that sprawls across a 251-acre campus situated less than 15 miles east of Gettysburg has more than 900 residents who call the place home. The Brethren Home Community began in 1908, and today it includes apartments, cottages, and single homes in addition to its assisted-living center and health-care center. Individual retirement homes come in three different floor plans ranging from 1,782 to 2,041 square feet with 9-foot ceilings, two bedrooms, two baths, a two-car garage, and walk-in closets. Cross Keys Village features more than 320 cottages in 21 different models, from roomy one-bedroom to large two-bedroom models with a garage. One- and two-bedroom apartments are found at Harmony Ridge, and most feature a private patio or balcony in addition to modern conveniences.

i **The Web site for Comfort Keepers, a nonmedical in-home care company, has a section called Senior Care that has links to more than 50 senior-related Internet sites. Visit www.comfortkeepers.com to check it out. More information on services offered by Comfort Keepers can be found in the Health Care and Wellness chapter.**

If you prefer not to cook your own meals, you can dine at the Campus Inn Restaurant, which is open seven days a week. The campus also boasts a fitness center, a church, a community center, banking services, a gift shop, scheduled campus transportation, and walkways that let you take in the rural setting at a leisurely pace.

The assisted-living center of the Brethren Home Community is a licensed personal-care facility that allows you to continue your independent lifestyle while knowing personal assistance is available from the staff 24 hours a day. Meals are served restaurant style in the dining room three times a day, and a kitchenette is located on each floor of the center. Each floor also has a spacious living room where you can relax, and activities that provide social interaction with other residents take place every day.

Medical care is offered at the health care center, which offers long-term and short-term nursing care as well as respite care. Short-term medical treatment or rehabilitation that's needed after a hospital stay is given at the Cross Keys Subacute Center, and the health-care center also offers special-care nursing for clients with Alzheimer's and other dementia-related disorders. Adult daycare services are part of the Brethren Home Community, and day care is provided to those in the surrounding community as well as to campus residents. The day care is designed for adults who need some degree of daily supervision, and it's open to persons at least 18 years old who are physically challenged and/or cognitively impaired. Services at the day care include a hot meal and a wide range of activities, such as cooking, field trips, arts and crafts, music, gardening, and pet visits. Personal-care services, such as bathing and hair care, are also provided. A noon meal is served as well as morning and afternoon snacks. The cost for the adult day care is $42.00 for a full day and $32.50 for a half day. The noon meal costs $4.00. More information on the adult day care may be obtained by calling (717) 624-5955.

GETTYSBURG LUTHERAN RETIREMENT VILLAGE

1075 Old Harrisburg Road
(717) 334-6204
www.lutheranscp.org

Gettysburg Lutheran Retirement Village is a continuing-care retirement community (CCRC) that is part of Lutheran Social Services, an agency of the Evangelical Lutheran Church in America. Its attractive campus less than 2 miles north of Lincoln Square features residential-living townhomes and apartments, assisted-living/personal-care rooms, and a skilled-care center.

As a resident of Gettysburg Lutheran Retirement Village, your abode is a maintenance-free home, and you choose your level of activity and independence. The village has 57 one-, two-, and three-bedroom units, as well as 21 one- and two-bedroom apartments. Transportation is provided for local medical needs and grocery shopping as well as for cultural and pleasure trips. If you prefer not to cook, you can take advantage of the meal service that's available. While you're enjoying your carefree lifestyle, you are also ensuring that if you need more help, you have admission, as space allows, to any other level of care you may need in the future. A call system is provided in the apartments to obtain medical assistance in an emergency situation, and townhome residents are provided with a telephone number to gain access to medical assistance for medical emergencies.

If daily assistance is needed but daily medical care is not, the assisted-living/personal-care facility may be the ideal solution. Here you have a private or semiprivate room in a building that also has a communal dining room, a lounge area, and an outdoor walking trail. You choose your activities and daily routine with the security of knowing that support is available when you need it. The village bus is available to take you to local medical appointments and scheduled shopping and pleasure outings. A beauty shop and laundry service are available on a fee-for-service basis.

Physical or mental limitations may necessitate your living in a skilled-care center for either a limited or an extended period of time.

The 100-bed skilled-care center here provides skilled nursing care and full rehabilitation services including physical therapy, occupational therapy, and speech therapy. Programs focusing on social, creative, and intellectual interests are available, and there are plenty of group activities to participate in, including cooking, sports, crafts, parties, bus rides, and discussion groups. Beautician and barber services are provided on campus, and residents can also enjoy activities and visits with the young children from Learning Tree Child Care, the Lutheran Social Services child-care center that's located right in the nursing-center building. (See the Education and Child Care chapter for information on Learning Tree Child Care.)

Hospice services are offered by Lutheran Social Services through the Hospice of the Good Shepherd (717-334-6208), which employs a team of skilled professionals, paraprofessionals, and volunteers dedicated to caring for the dying patient and the patient's family. The team works with the family and caregivers to help them understand what to expect, to teach them special caregiving techniques, and to help them with emotional difficulties. Hospice care can be provided in the home, in a skilled nursing facility, in a personal-care setting, or in a hospital. Hospice of the Good Shepherd has a bereavement program designed to help families address issues that may arise after a loved one's death, and the program provides resources and support to aid in the family's grief recovery process.

For information on the varied home health-care services provided by Lutheran Social Services, see the Health Care and Wellness chapter.

GOLDEN LIVINGCENTER–GETTYSBURG

741 Chambersburg Road
(717) 334-6764, (866) 333-9416
www.goldenlivingcenters.com

The goal of this skilled nursing home located on the western outskirts of town is to provide personalized quality health care in a homelike environment. Short- or long-term care is available at the 102-bed facility, and patients may be admitted on weekends. Rehabilitative services include physical therapy, occupational therapy, and speech therapy. Though most residents require only general nursing services, complex medical services such as wound care and IV therapy are available. Golden LivingCenter also has an entire wing designed especially to address the needs of Alzheimer's patients. The nursing staff working on this unit must undergo continuing education specifically for Alzheimer's disease care. Recreational activities are available to residents, and respite care can be arranged. Golden LivingCenter–Gettysburg accepts payment for its services from Medicare, Medicaid, private insurance, and private pay.

i Seniors (age 60 or older) who meet income restrictions can get $20 worth of vouchers that can be used to purchase Pennsylvania fruits and vegetables at farmers' markets throughout the county. Vouchers are distributed on a first-come, first-serve basis. Contact the Adams County Office for Aging or any Adams County senior center.

GREEN ACRES
Adams County Nursing & Rehabilitation Center
595 Biglerville Road
(717) 334-6249
Green Acres is a not-for-profit skilled nursing facility with 154 beds that sits amid a rural setting of peach and apple orchards less than a mile north of Lincoln Square. The center is state licensed and Medicare and Medicaid approved, and it accepts payment for its services from Medicare, Medicaid, private insurance, and private pay. Green Acres has been providing care to area residents since it was established in 1891 as an alms house. Today state-of-the-art medical treatment is offered here, including dementia treatment and physical, speech, and occupational therapy. Residents have their choice of a wide range of activities; some activities are held at the center and some involve the community. Popular programs

include interacting with pet-therapy animals, baking, caroling, gardening, and trick-or-treating. The center also coordinates with hospice workers when clients need those services, respite care is available, and the Share and Care Adult Day Care (717-334-5970) is on the premises.

The goal of the Share and Care Adult Day Care is to improve or maintain an impaired adult's physical and mental functioning so he or she can remain living within the community. The day care is open Monday through Friday from 7:00 a.m. to 4:30 p.m., and adults may attend for either a half or a full day. Full-day participants receive lunch and two snacks, while those who attend for half a day receive one snack. Activities include music, bingo, painting, exercising, cooking, movies, and more. For an additional fee clients may have personal bathing assistance and podiatry services, and the services of the beauty/barber shop at Green Acres are available to them. Physical, occupational, and speech therapy, all of which must be ordered by the client's doctor, are offered here, and these services may be billed to the client's insurance. Applicants must have their doctor complete a patient history and physical, a tuberculosis test must be taken, and admission interviews are conducted before the adult is admitted to the program. The cost of the day care is $50 for a full day and $25 for a half day.

SHEPHERD'S CHOICE NURSING AND REHABILITATION CENTER
867 York Road
(717) 337-3238
This center's name is an acronym for its mission statement. It provides a Christian community extending God's love and compassion; Home environment for changing needs; Overall commitment to residents, families, employees, and the larger community; Individualized, professional services; Complete care for the body, mind, and spirit; and Empowerment to achieve the highest potential and victory in all areas of daily living. This 118-bed facility that opened in 1987 embraces the concept of resident-centered care, where nurses and assistants provide 24-hour hands-on individu-

alized care with a team approach. Services include physical, speech, and occupational therapy, and hospice and respite care are available. Shepherd's Choice is also a secured facility that uses a watch-mate system to protect residents who suffer from Alzheimer's or dementia-related diseases. At-risk patients wear a bracelet that triggers the outside doors to lock or alarms to sound if the patient begins to wander away. Residents' rooms feature floor-to-ceiling windows, providing an opportunity to watch deer and other wild animals, and clients are encouraged to personalize their rooms. The center provides dental and optometry services on-site, and it has a beauty/barber shop. Planned group and individualized activities are also available. This nonprofit skilled nursing facility accepts payment for its services from Medicare, Medicaid, private insurance, and private pay.

MEDIA

Local and national information can easily be obtained in Gettysburg, via print, radio, or television. Many places of business have an area by the door where you can find brochures for local attractions and events, and Lincoln Square and many street corners have coin-operated newspaper boxes. Gettysburg has its own newspaper, as well as publications that focus on what to do around the area. It also has an AM and an FM radio station, and cable TV is available throughout the area.

PRINT MEDIA

CELEBRATE GETTYSBURG

P.O. Box 3653, Gettysburg 17325
(717) 338-0457, (888) 521-6810
www.celebrategettysburg.com
Dedicated to commemorating modern life in the historic town of Gettysburg, this lifestyle magazine debuted in January 2007 and is published every two months. Each issue of the four-color magazine has a central theme, several departments, and three feature stories accompanied by outstanding photographs. One of the features is more news oriented and the other two relate to the theme of that issue. *Celebrate Gettysburg* also runs a number of ballots in the magazine to encourage community interaction.

Celebrate Gettysburg has a circulation of 10,000 magazines each issue, and a readership of 20,000. Although the magazine is geared primarily toward residents, there are a few departments that are dedicated to the tourists that visit town as well. Recurring features include listings of and in-depth articles about upcoming events, articles on local artisans, articles about the Civil War, and in-depth reviews of area restaurants. There is also a handy dining directory at the back of the magazine and plenty of advertisements from local businesses throughout the magazine's pages.

You can find the magazine in many area businesses for free, or you can visit the Web site and purchase a subscription for delivery. Subscription rates are $14.95 for one year, $24.95 for two years, and $30.95 for three years.

GETTYSBURG COMPANION

Times & News Publishing Company
1570 Fairfield Road
(717) 334-1131
www.gettysburgcompanion.com
The *Gettysburg Companion* is a glossy magazine that began publication in April 2004, and it's put out by the same company that publishes the *Gettysburg Times* newspaper. Issues come out five times a year on a bimonthly basis (there isn't a December/January issue). Each issue spotlights an area business in addition to having articles and pictures relating to Gettysburg people, places, and events. One article always features the Readers' Choice Award, which highlights an area overnight accommodation or restaurant that was nominated by readers of the magazine. In addition to the article, the winner also receives a wood plaque featuring the cover of the issue that their business was named in. You can pick up the *Gettysburg Companion* for free at area businesses or have it mailed to you for a fee.

GETTYSBURG EXPERIENCE

P.O. Box 4271, Gettysburg 17325
(717) 359-0776
www.thegettysburgexperience.com
Community events are highlighted in this free publication that's put out monthly by Leonard and Diana Loski. Its 6½-inch-by-10½-inch black-and-white format is designed like a small book, and its 100 or so pages are chock-full of interesting articles on Gettysburg and the Civil

War and pages and pages of ads for area businesses. Articles also feature area businesses. If you're wondering what to do or where to go while in town, the *Gettysburg Experience* will give you ample of choices. The center of the booklet also features a fantastic map of downtown Gettysburg, making finding where you want to go a breeze. Trivia questions are at the bottom of every other page, and the answers are contained within the articles, and there's also an answer key at the end of the booklet. The *Gettysburg Experience* is in just about every store you walk into, so finding a copy is never a problem, and most locals consider this the best reference when planning their leisure activities.

GETTYSBURG TIMES

1570 Fairfield Road
(717) 334-1131
www.gettysburgtimes.com

The *Gettysburg Times* newspaper is published daily Monday through Saturday (except Christmas and New Year's Day) by the Times & News Publishing Company. It has a circulation of about 9,000 subscribers, and it covers all the news of Gettysburg and the surrounding townships as well as national news. The *Times* isn't a thick paper, but it packs a lot of local news into its pages. The "Good Old Days" series runs once a week, and it gives locals a chance to write in and reminisce about how things used to be and what was where back in the day. Sides of national issues are represented with pieces by Molly Ivins, Cal Thomas, and other notable editorialists. Local issues take up a good amount of the space, with weekly columns devoted to pet issues, tourism, senior news, and other local interests. The *Gettysburg Times* is essentially a small-town newspaper, with birthday greetings that include pictures, announcements of divorces, engagements, and marriages, and pictures of reporters who cover the local scene. The paper also has weekly listings of events going on and an indepth religion section, which lists all the activities the local churches are sponsoring. In 2008 the *Times* received the Keystone Press Award and the Pennsylvania Associated Press Managing Editors Award. The paper's banner is ADAMS COUNTY NEWS FIRST and their slogan is MORNING'S GREAT, EVENING'S TOO LATE.

RADIO STATIONS

Gettysburg has two radio stations, both of which have been locally owned by the Jones family for many years. Both stations are part of the Times & News Publishing Company, which also publishes the *Gettysburg Times* newspaper and the *Gettysburg Companion* magazine.

WGET-AM (1320 AM)

1560 Fairfield Road
(717) 334-3101
www.wget.com

WGET is a CNNRadio News affiliate, and local topics are covered each weekday morning during the popular Breakfast Nook program that begins at 8:30 a.m. The segment features on-air personality Fred Snyder, who's been at the station for 10 years, interviewing prominent local, national, and international figures on a variety of topics. Sports are also big at this station, which is an affiliate of SportingNews Radio. Local residents tune in to hear coverage of the Phillies, the Redskins, Penn State University athletics, NFL games, and NASCAR races.

WGTY-FM (107.7 FM)

1560 Fairfield Road
(717) 334-3101
www.wgty.com

This is a country station, and its signal serves Adams and York Counties and nearby Maryland. You can hear the latest country hits as well as perennial favorites and bluegrass sounds. The station also broadcasts Nextel Cup Racing, making it York and Adams Counties' country home for NASCAR.

TV STATIONS

ADAMS COMMUNITY TELEVISION

44C South Franklin Street

(717) 334-3000

www.actv.org

Adams Community Television, or ACTV, as it's known, was founded in 1988 by Raymond Gouker, a teacher of visual communications at Gettysburg High School. He created the station as a way to showcase the history, people, and culture of the local communities, as well as to provide educational programming of interest to area residents. ACTV started out with 10 hours of airtime per week telecast to 6,000 households. Today it telecasts 77 hours per week to more than 32,000 households.

COMCAST CORPORATION

(800) 266-2278

www.comcast.net

Cable television is brought to the area by Comcast Corporation, the nation's leading provider of cable, entertainment, and communications products and services. As of September 30, 2008, Comcast served customers in 39 states and the District of Columbia, with 24.4 million cable customers, 14.7 million high-speed Internet customers, and 6.1 million Comcast Digital Voice customers. Comcast's main office is in Philadelphia, Pennsylvania, and it employs 100,000 people nationwide. Weekly TV listings can be found in the Wednesday edition of the *Gettysburg Times* newspaper.

INDEX

ABOUT THE AUTHOR

Kate Hertzog resides in Mechanicsburg, Pennsylvania, where she works as a freelance editor and proofreader. She shares her life with her husband, Tim, and their Maine coon cats, Dexter and Dillon. All three deserve kudos for giving up a normal routine in order to ensure this update stayed on schedule. Tim deserves extra kudos for being a loving and supportive husband, a role he has played to perfection for almost 30 years.

Kate began her career as an analyst who helped coordinate the systematic updating of the supplies for the Trident submarines, and she was bitten by the publishing bug when she went to work as an inventory analyst for Book-of-the-Month Club. From there Kate moved on to become a book club manager for the McGraw-Hill professional book clubs. When she left McGraw-Hill in 1996, she decided to establish her own business and perform freelance editorial work from home. Kate is also the author of *More than Petticoats: Remarkable Pennsylvania Women*, which profiles the lives of 15 women born before 1907 who broke through social, cultural, or political barriers to make contributions to society that still have an impact today.

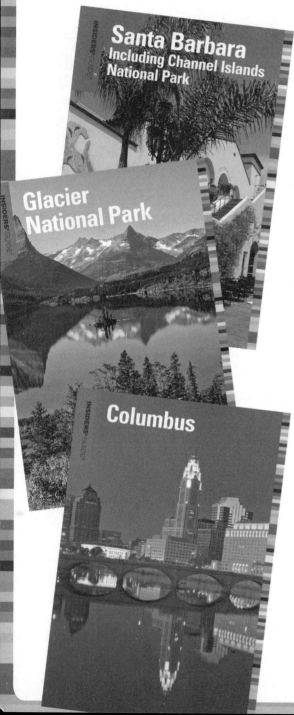